Dedicated to

Our teacher Prof. (Capt.) L. Sanjeev Kumar
and
Aspiring Engineers of Our Nation .... Mother India

Contents

Foreword............ *ix*
Preface............ *xi*
Acknowledgements............ *xiii*
About Autodesk............ *xv*

Chapter 1 Introduction to Electrical Drawing and CAD............ **1–10**

1.1 Introduction............ 1
1.2 Basic Tools Used in CAD with its Description............ 2
1.3 Use of Various Commands in CAD............ 5
1.3.1 Line............ 5
1.3.2 Circle............ 5
1.3.3 Arc............ 5
1.3.4 Ellipse............ 6
1.3.5 Poly Line............ 6
1.3.6 Polygon............ 6
1.3.7 Rectangle............ 6
1.3.8 Mirror............ 7
1.3.9 Array............ 7
1.3.10 Move............ 7
1.3.11 Trim............ 7
1.3.12 Dimension............ 8
1.3.13 Distance between Two Points and Angle between Two Lines............ 8
1.3.14 Radius and Diameter............ 8
1.3.15 Arc............ 8
1.3.16 Coordinates............ 9
Exercises............ 10

Chapter 2 DC Lap Winding 11–54

2.1 Introduction 11
2.2 Classification of Windings in DC Machine 14
  2.2.1 Single Layer Winding 14
  2.2.2 Two Layer Winding 15
  2.2.3 Multiplex Winding 15
2.3 Lap Winding 16
2.4 Solved Problems 17
Summary 53
Exercises 54

Chapter 3 DC Wave Winding 55–77

3.1 Introduction 55
3.2 Simplex and Duplex Wave Winding 57
3.3 Dummy Coil in Wave Winding 57
3.4 Solved Problems 58
Summary 76
Exercises 77

Chapter 4 AC Winding 78–101

4.1 Introduction 78
4.2 Windings in AC Machine 79
4.3 Some General Terms Related to AC Winding 81
4.4 Phase Spread 82
4.5 Terminals and Connections in AC Machines 82
4.6 Solved Problems 83
Exercises 100

Chapter 5 Single Line Diagrams and Sub-Stations 102–115

5.1 Introduction 102
5.2 Generating Station 103
5.3 Substation 103
  5.3.1 Pole Mounted Substation 103
  5.3.2 Plinth Mounted Substation 104
5.4 Receiving Station 105
5.5 Representation of Various Electrical Apparatus 105
5.6 List of Generating Stations in Karnataka 107
  5.6.1 Nonrenewable 107
  5.6.2 Renewable 107
5.7 Solved Problems 109
Exercises 113

Chapter 6 DC Machine Assembly 116–154

6.1 Introduction 116
6.2 Construction of a DC Machine 117
  6.2.1 Slots 119
  6.2.2 Commutator 120
  6.2.3 Brush 120
  6.2.4 Pole 122
6.3 Assembly Drawing of a Machine 124
6.4 Solved Problems 125
Exercises 151

Chapter 7 AC Machine Assembly 155–168

7.1 Introduction 155
7.2 Synchronous Machines 156
  7.2.1 Salient Pole Machines 156
  7.2.2 Non-salient Pole Machines 156
7.3 Asynchronous Machines/Induction Machines 157
  7.3.1 Squirrel Cage Rotor 157
  7.3.2 Slip Ring Induction Machine 158
7.4 Solved Problems 160
7.5 Photographs of Machines 165
Exercises 166

Chapter 8 Transformer Assembly 169–213

8.1 Introduction 169
8.2 Classification of Transformers 170
  8.2.1 Core of a Transformer 170
  8.2.2 Windings 172
8.3 Sectional Views and Elevations of Transformers 172
  8.3.1 Sectional View 172
  8.3.2 Elevation 173
8.4 Core Sectional Details of Transformers 175
8.5 Solved Problems 179
8.6 Photographs 208
Exercises 210

Appendix Print Procedure 215–218

Index 219–221

Foreword

Ever since the industrial revolution, electrical machines are the backbone for all industries. Till the advent of AC machines, DC machines were being extensively used for all the industrial applications. It is always essential for an Electrical Engineer to know the complete design aspect and assembly of machines. As the world is moving ahead towards digital era, it is necessary to use Computer Aided Software for design and development of all electrical apparatus.

This book entitled "Computer Aided Electrical Drawing" authored by Mr. Yogesh, M., Mr. Nagaraja, B.S. and Mr. Nandan, N. has many outstanding features. First and foremost the book discusses the merits of using computer aided software to draw electrical apparatus and the need of it to stay at par with the present day technology.

This book helps students to develop the fundamental drafting skills and expertise to draw various electrical drawings using computer aided software, both quantitatively and qualitatively. This book has been prepared to meet the needs of the students in a simpler manner, also emphasising the importance of the subject so that the students get a wide knowledge about the Electrical Engineering drawing. In this book, every topic has been dealt carefully with necessary explanation and presentation of the material is lucid.

This book has number of solved problems to help the readers to understand the theoretical aspects. I would like to congratulate the authors for their pains taking efforts, and I am confident that the Electrical Engineering fraternity will be benefited immensely by using this book.

Dr. B. Ramachandra
Professor and Head
Department of Electrical Engineering
P.E.S. College of Engineering
Mandya, Karnataka

Preface

The course on 'Computer Aided Electrical Drawing' is an applied engineering subject taught to engineering and polytechnic students. In some states, it is taught as an integrated subject along with electrical machines.

The material contained in this book has been tested for their validity by the second author, as a part of a research project undertaken by him.

The salient features of this book are its simple language, use of plenty of illustrations for explaining the concepts or the principles, inclusion of practical problems and their solutions, graded exercises, and model questions at the end of each chapter. The topics covered in this book is of direct relevance to the needs of aspiring engineers in electrical industries where manufacturing of a machine or winding is done in practise and finds its place in the curriculum of some of the state boards of technical education who have revised their curriculum in consultation with and involvement of professional engineers. This book mainly aims the Electrical Engineering students to give quite a good knowledge in design and drawing of electrical machines in a simplified approach using the modern day technology. Utmost care has been taken in authoring this book to cater to the needs of the students in the best possible manner.

This book covers topics like winding diagrams of different machines, its types along with the assembling technique of various electrical machine and also the single line representations of the power system with various standard symbols using computer aided software to stay in par with the digital era.

This book differs from the other existing books in the market from the point of view of its content coverage including those topics which are required by students in practical situations along with the present industrial requirements and standards. Through the use of the exercises included in each chapter of this book, students will develop open-ended problem solving abilities which are an important requirement of education and training.

For the illustration of the problems in this book, AutoCAD® software 2014 version is used. It holds good even for the earlier versions of AutoCAD® software.

Suggestions, remarks, compliments and comments to improve the book are always welcome and can be dropped at: caddrawingelectrical@gmail.com

M. Yogesh
B.S. Nagaraja
N. Nandan

Acknowledgements

We, the authors of this book, would like to thank Sri Devalapur, Sri Dargan and Sri Narang for imparting their knowledge to us through their books on Electrical Drawing. We would also like to thank the Autodesk, Inc, for providing a wonderful tool AutoCAD through which the design and drawing has been simplified to a greater extent.

We would like to express our deep sense of gratitude and indebtedness to Prof. (Capt.) L. Sanjeev Kumar and Dr. T.P. Bharateesh who have been our true inspiration to be in this field of teaching.

We would also like to express our deep sense of gratitude to Dr. K. Shanmukha Sundar, (Head, Department of E&EE, DSCE) and Prof. A.M. Nagaraj for their valuable guidance and support to carry out this work. We would also like to thank all the staff and students of Dayananda Sagar College of Engineering, Bangalore for their best wishes and support.

We are grateful to our parents and family members for their continuous support and best wishes. We would also like to thank our friend Mr. Sandeep Jayasheelan for his timely suggestions and support.

We would like to thank PHI Learning for accepting our work and publishing it to meet the needs of the students. We would like to thank Mr. Arun of PHI Learning for his continuous support and wishes.

M. Yogesh
B.S. Nagaraja
N. Nandan

About Autodesk

Autodesk is guiding educators to move beyond traditional academic constructs and to the use of advanced technology that helps to solve problems through inspiring design. Today's students can sharpen their vision with every new project, gain greater insight with every new challenge, and prepare for a 21st century workplace that will require all of their skills. Autodesk provides technology and resources that help educators to engage, prepare and inspire students for academic success and future careers as architects, construction managers, engineers, designers, animators, film producers and digital artists.

Autodesk Suites for Education

Autodesk® suites offer comprehensive software and services that introduce students to tools supporting industry practises such as digital prototyping, building information modelling (BIM), digital entertainment creation, sustainable design and interdisciplinary collaboration. Autodesk suites:

- Help to enable the students to move more easily between 2D and 3D design environments to design, visualise and simulate their ideas.
- Support curriculum resources through interactive exercises, modular projects, video tutorials and instructor lesson slides that focus on design concepts instead of software functionality.
- Offer access to resources including Autodesk® Education Community, the AREA site, Autodesk Certification, cloud services, free apps, Autodesk workshops and curriculum to optimise learning.

Autodesk Education Community

The Autodesk Education Community is an online resource that enables educators and students to download for free*, the same software used by professionals worldwide. It is also used where additional tools and materials can be accessed to design, visualise and simulate ideas.

- Connect with other learners to stay current with the latest trends.
- Access industry-relevant curricula to engage classroom learning.
- Use self-learning resources for additional knowledge and training.
- Download Autodesk® apps to design beyond the desktop.
- Join other learners by earning industry recognised credentials and certification.

The software used for illustrations in this book is AutoCAD® 2014.
AutoCAD® software can be obtained by registering at: www.autodesk.com/education

* Free Autodesk software and/or cloud-based services are subject to acceptance and compliance with the terms and conditions of the software licence agreement or terms of service that accompany such software or cloud-based services. Software and cloud-based services provided without charge to Education Community members and may be used solely for purposes directly related to learning, teaching, training, research or development and shall not be used for commercial, professional or any other for profit purposes.

1 Introduction to Electrical Drawing and CAD

Learning Objectives

This chapter illustrates the various advantages of drawing, the necessity for a computer aided design software along with its advantages, the basic tools, available and used in the AutoCAD software to design and draw various drawings.

1.1 INTRODUCTION

Using computer software for designing is widely in practise. With the arrival of multipurpose software like AutoCAD, the *computer aided designing* or CAD services have been put to use at a much wider scale. This software package offers a greater freedom of control over every aspect of the designing and planning. One of the main advantages of the CAD design software is the ability to manipulate and modify the design or drawing with ease. These design or drawing files can be stored in a computer in a digital format.

Unlike the conventional method in paper format, the design or drawing performed using CAD design software can be easily changed and edited as and when required and also protection can be given to the document to restrict access.

Another advantage of using CAD design software is the ability to store and save the files in a centralised database for the purpose of future calibration and record keeping. This is mainly useful for large scale projects like a designing master unit sub-station (MUSS), industrial layouts, electrical layouts, etc.

The use of CAD design software also helps to create modern and complex design and drawing with much better design and functionality. CAD design software provides multi-layered digital files. Each layer may represent only one aspect of the overall design. For example, one layer may be used to show electricity connection plans while the other may show emergency exit routes of a certain building. When the time comes to change one thing in the design, only the relevant layer can be changed. CAD design software provides all the necessary basic drawings which is readily available in the tool bar and the same can be used as many times as required by just the method of drag and drop which saves time, energy and money. The conventional method of paper based drawings or designs, lack the ability to save much information except text, images and charts. Saving the cost and having the digital files ready anytime are other advantages of CAD software package. These designs are created with 1:1 ratio and exactly like the original in scale and the scale also can be edited as and when required. Snapshot of AutoCAD is shown in Figure 1.1.

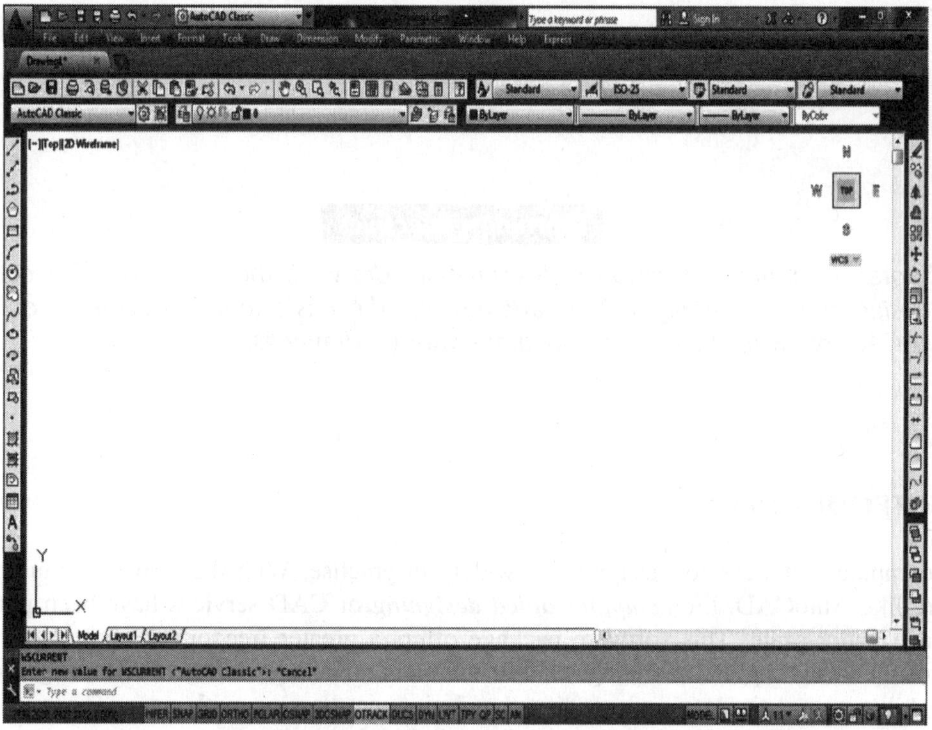

Figure 1.1 Snapshot of AutoCAD window, courtesy: AutoCAD®.

1.2 BASIC TOOLS USED IN CAD WITH ITS DESCRIPTION

TABLE 1.1 Various commands used in CAD

S.No.	*Icon*	*Description*	*Command*	*Use*
1		Line	LINE or L	To draw a line
2		Line with centre	XLINE or XL	Creates a line of infinite length

S.No.	Icon	Description	Command	Use
3	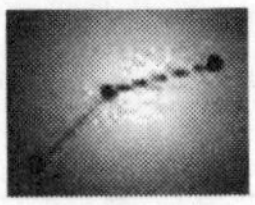	Poly line	PLINE or PL	Creates a multiple line depending on the points selected
4		Polygon	POLYGON	Creates a polygon. Number of sides to be specified
5		Array	ARRAY	Creates a multiple objects. Either linear or circular
6	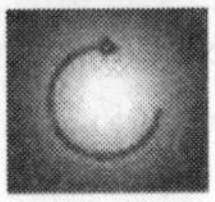	Rotate	ROTATE or R	Rotates an object
7	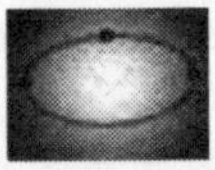	Ellipse	ELLIPSE	To draw an ellipse
8		Arc	ARC	To draw an arc
9		Circle	CIRCLE	To draw a circle of definite radius
10		Revision cloud	REVCLOUD	Highlights the part of drawing
11		Copy	COPY	Copies the selected object
12	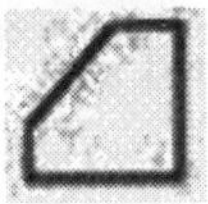	Chamfer	CHAMFER	Bevels the edges of objects
13	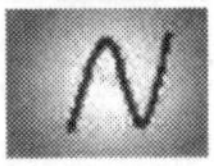	Spline	SPLINE	Creates smooth curve
14	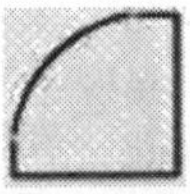	Fillet	FILLET	Rounds and fillets the edges of objects
15		Mirror	MIRROR	Creates a mirrored object of selected the object

S.No.	*Icon*	*Description*	*Command*	*Use*
16		Square	SQUARE	To draw a square
17		Gradient	GRADIENT or H	Fills the object with selected colour
18		Stretch	STRETCH or S	Stretches the selected object
19		Scale	SCALE	Increases the size of the object
20		Erase	ERASE or E	To delete the selected object
21		Explode	EXPLODE	To break the single object to a multiple points
22		Extend	EXTEND	Extends the line/arc/object to reach the end point
23		Trim	TRIM	To trim the edges of an object
24		Move	MOVE or M	To move an object to definite place/ point
25		Hatch	HATCH or H	Hatches the selected area
26		Rectangle	RECTANGLE	To draw a rectangle

ORTHO: It is used to obtain straight lines. If ORTHO is kept on, only straight lines can be drawn. The angle of projection is only in the angles 0°, 90°, 180° and 270°.

OSNAP: It refers to object snap. If OSNAP is kept on, it helps to identify the end points of lines and objects.

LWT: It refers to line weight. It shows the thickness of the line when it is kept on.

OTRACK: It refers to object snap tracking.

1.3 USE OF VARIOUS COMMANDS IN CAD

1.3.1 Line

1. From menu, select line icon or type L/LINE in command window.
2. Specify the start point.
3. Complete the first line segment by specifying on the endpoint.
4. Specify the endpoints of any additional line segments.
5. Press ENTER to end or C to close a series of line segments.

TABLE 1.2 Different types of lines

S. No.	*Types of line*	*Representation*
1	Thin line	————————————
2	Thick line	━━━━━━━━━━━━
3	Dotted line	. . . .
4	Long dash-small dash	——— —— —— —— ——— ——

1.3.2 Circle

1. From menu, select circle icon or type CIRCLE in command window.
2. Choose by what method you will draw the circle, i.e., centre with radius or centre with diameter.
3. Specify the centre point.
4. Now, drag the circle outwards and specify the radius or diameter.

1.3.3 Arc

There are many methods to draw an arc. One of the most convenient methods is specifying the centre, start point and end point. Also we can draw the arc by specifying the radius, angle and chord length.

1. From menu, select arc icon or type ARC in command window.
2. Specify starting point of the arc.
3. Specify the centre point.
4. Specify ending point of the arc. Then press ENTER or ESC to accept the value.

1.3.4 Ellipse

1. From menu, select ellipse icon or type ELLIPSE in command window.
2. Specify starting point of the ellipse.
3. Specify the centre point.
4. Specify ending point of the ellipse.
5. Move the cursor outside the ellipse, so that the distance can be seen from the centre of the axis line. Then press ENTER or ESC to accept the value.

1.3.5 Poly Line

In this type of command, we can draw multiple lines. The procedure is same as that of drawing a line.

1.3.6 Polygon

Polygon can be created as the number of sides specified by the designer. The minimum number of sides to be mentioned is 3 and of maximum is 1024.

1. From menu, select polygon icon or type POLYGON in command window.
2. Specify the number of sides to be created.
3. Specify the edge point of the polygon.
4. Specify the type of polygon to be created.
5. Now, mention the radius from the centre of the polygon and press ENTER button or ESC button.

Again the polygon can be created by two methods. Upon mentioning the radius the polygon will be created as shown in Figure 1.2.

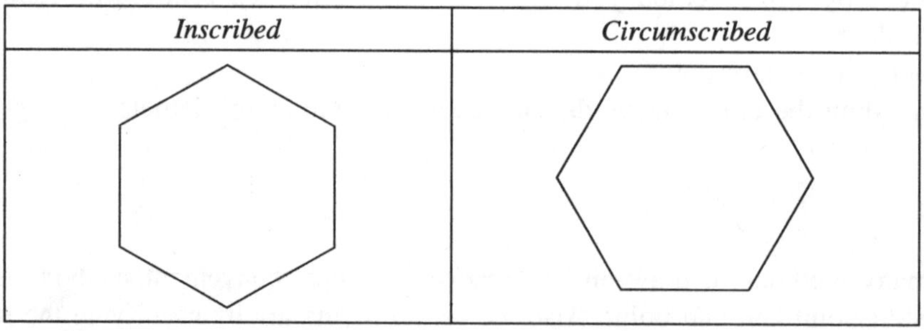

Figure 1.2 Methods to draw polygon.

1.3.7 Rectangle

1. From menu, select rectangle icon or type RECTANGLE in command window.
2. Specify the first point.
3. Specify the opposite corner point with the dimension required.

1.3.8 Mirror

1. From menu, select mirror icon or type MIRROR in command window.
2. Select the object which is to be mirrored.
3. Specify the distance where the object is to be placed. After placing the mirrored object, the command will ask whether the original object to be retained or erased.
4. Select NO and press ENTER button or ESC button to accept the object.

1.3.9 Array

From menu, select array icon or type ARRAY in command window.

Rectangle array:

1. The array window will pop-up after executing the command. In that select the rectangle array if you are placing the object along the straight line.
2. Now, select the object.
3. Enter the number of objects to be placed along the row as well as column, along with the distance between them.
4. Select OK to preview the objects which are generated.
5. If the objects are placed properly then press ENTER to accept if not ESC button.

Polar array:

1. The array window will pop-up after executing the command. In that select the polar array if you are placing the object keeping the centre as a reference.
2. Now, select the object.
3. Enter the number of objects to be placed and the angle from which the object should be placed. Even the angle between the objects can be mentioned.
4. Select OK to preview the objects which are generated.
5. If the objects are placed properly then press ENTER to accept if not ESC button.

1.3.10 Move

1. From menu, select move icon or type MOVE in command window.
2. Select the object which has to be moved to a new position.
3. Specify the displacement, i.e., the distance which has to be moved from the original point.
4. Place the object to your convenient position and press ENTER to accept the moved object.

1.3.11 Trim

1. From menu, select trim icon or type TRIM in command window.
2. Select the object that has to trim, and then press ENTER.
3. Now, click on the object that has to be trimmed.

1.3.12 Dimension

1. From menu, select dimension icon or type DIMENSION in command window.
2. There are many ways to mention the dimension of an object, depending on the type of the object either it is linear, angular, angle, arc or coordinates.

1.3.13 Distance between Two Points and Angle between Two Lines

For example, let us take the triangle ABC as shown in Figure 1.3. Here, the line joining the points AB is linear we should use the LINEAR type dimension.

The line joining the points BC is also straight line, but it is inclined at some angle. In this case we can't use LINEAR type, even if we use it will show the perpendicular distance between the points BC. Hence, we should use the ALIGNED type dimension to know the distance between those two points.

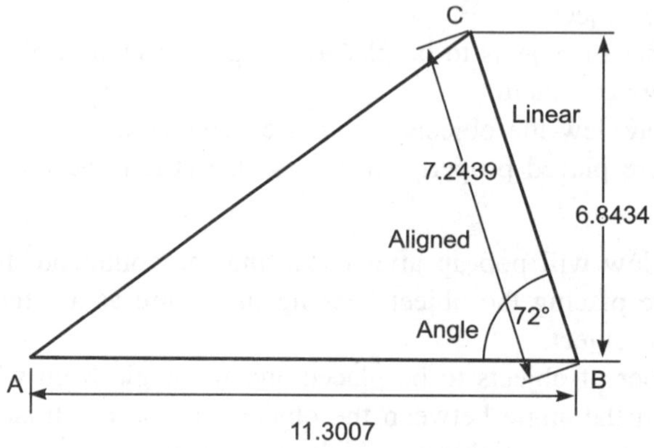

Figure 1.3 Measuring distance and angle between two lines.

1.3.14 Radius and Diameter

The radius and diameter of a circle as shown in Figure 1.4 will be mentioned by selecting the corresponding dimension type. The distance between two circles can be measured by selection the ALIGNED type dimension.

1.3.15 Arc

LINEAR or ALIGNED type dimension cannot be used for measuring an arc length, even if we use any one of the dimension type, it will show the distance of starting and ending of an arc.

In this case we should use the ARC type dimension to measure the length of the arc. The length of the arc shown in Figure 1.5 is 10.1645.

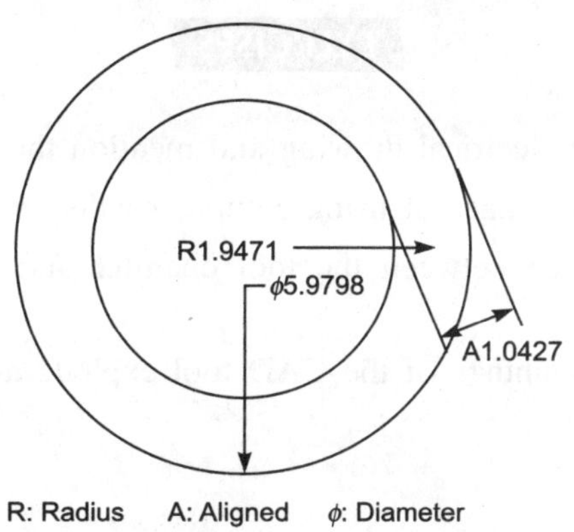

Figure 1.4 Method to measure radius and diameter of a circle.

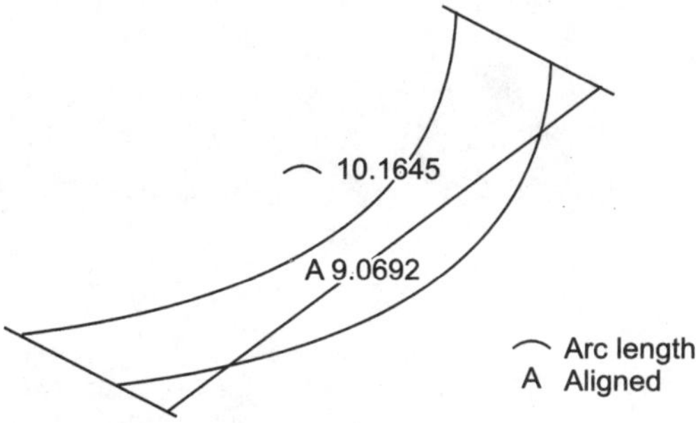

Figure 1.5 Method to measure aligned dimensions of an object.

1.3.16 Coordinates

The values of any point in two dimension coordinate system can be measured on both the X and Y axis. To know the values of any point in the 2-D plan, we need to select the ORDIANTE type dimension and by clicking on the point, it will show the values of X and Y axis. The method to measure coordinate dimensions is shown in Figure 1.6.

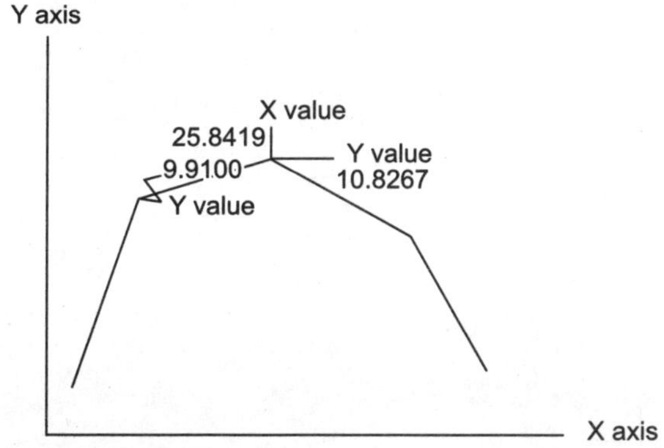

Figure 1.6 Method to measure coordinate dimensions.

EXERCISES

1. Explain the need for electrical drawing and mention the methods of drafting.
2. State the various advantages of using computer aided design software for drawing.
3. What is the difference between the tool chamfer and fillet available in AutoCAD software?
4. State the use and advantage of the CAD tool explode and mention any one instance where it can be used.

2 DC Lap Winding

Learning Objectives

This chapter illustrates the various types of windings employed in electrical machines, its design and applications. It mainly illustrates the lap winding employed in DC machines and using the AutoCAD software to develop the winding diagrams in a step by step manner.

2.1 INTRODUCTION

Machines are the devices which make human work much simpler. Machines are of various kinds and of different rating; size is available depending on our requirement. Every aspect of human need requires a machine in one or the other form. Machines always provide rotational motion and are cylindrical in structure.

Winding forms the most integral part of an electrical machine. A machine is simply a dead object without winding. Electrical machines operate with the interaction of currents that flow through the windings and the magnetic field established within it. The type of the electrical machine is determined by currents and voltages fed into the windings.

In simple terms *winding* can be defined as a precise pattern of placing conductors or coils in a group so that it carries current and produces the desired power. Hence, winding performed to these machines which are cylindrical in nature is also called as *drum windings*. Based on their functionality, windings in DC machines can be termed as follows:

- ***Armature windings:*** The specific pattern of arrangement of conductors in the slots of the rotating member, i.e., the armature of the machine so as to carry the current and contribute to the generation of required torque is termed as *armature windings*. These windings are rotating-field windings, in which the rotating-field induced voltage required in energy conversion is induced. Figure 2.1(a) and 2.1(b) show a typical drum-type armature and Figure 2.1(c) shows a typical drum-type armature with windings.

Figure 2.1(a) A typical drum-type armature.

Figure 2.1(b) A typical drum-type armature.

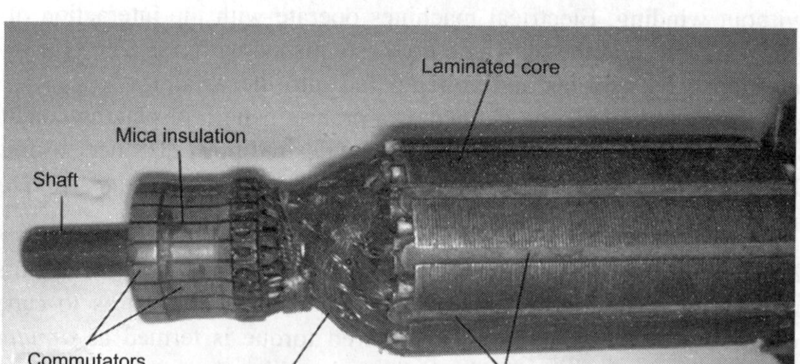

Figure 2.1(c) A typical drum-type armature with windings.

The armature windings are placed inside the slots cut in an iron core drum-shaped armature. The iron core is completely surrounded by each winding throughout the length of the conductor that cuts the magnetic field.

- ***Field windings:*** Winding done in the precise format on the poles (stationary part) of the machine, which is responsible to create magnetic field required for energy conversion. Figure 2.2 shows a typical laminated pole core.

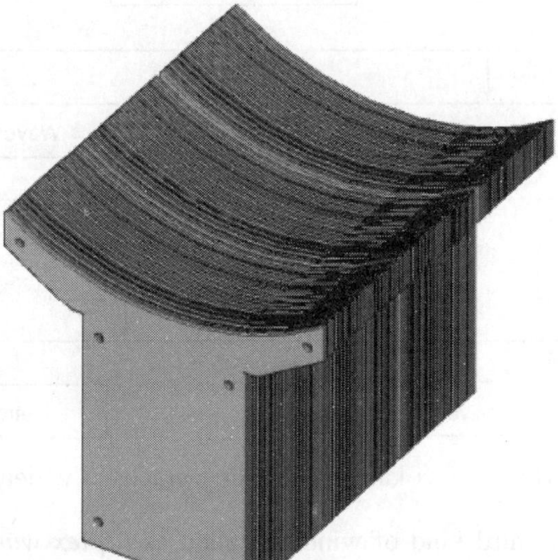

Figure 2.2(a) A typical laminated pole core.

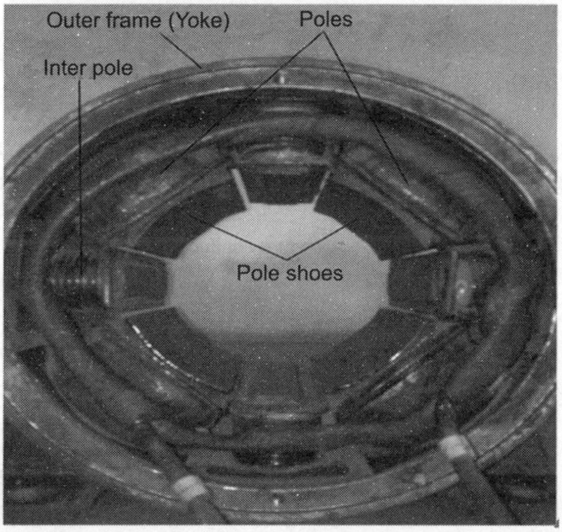

Figure 2.2(b) A typical cross section of a DC machine.

2.2 CLASSIFICATION OF WINDINGS IN DC MACHINE

There are variety of windings that are practised in present days which depends on the requirement and specifications of the machine. The Figure 2.3 gives the different types of windings employed in DC machines which are widely in practise.

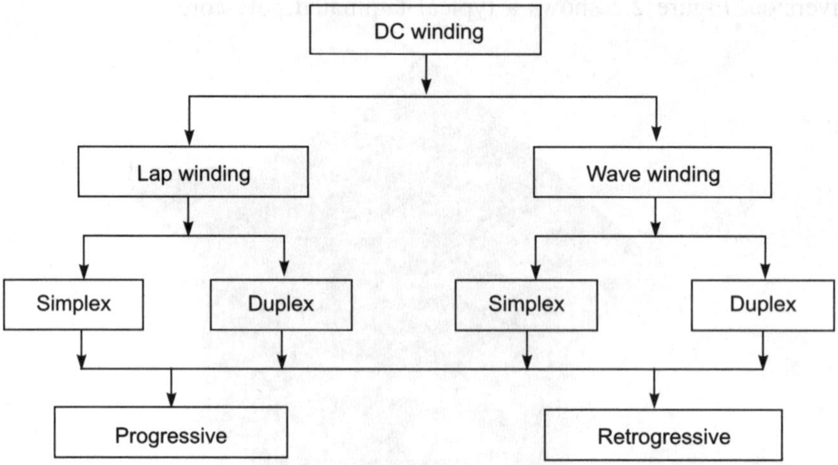

Figure 2.3 The various kinds of winding practised widely in DC machines.

Note: There is also a third kind of winding called as *triplex winding* but is rarely used.

Drum-type armatures are wound with either of two types of windings i.e., the *lap winding* or the *wave winding*. The difference between these two types of windings is mainly with respect to the difference in arrangement of the end connections at the front (commutator) end of armature.

2.2.1 Single Layer Winding

In this kind of winding only one conductor is placed in each armature slot as shown in Figure 2.4. This winding is not widely in practise as it contributes to very low rating machines.

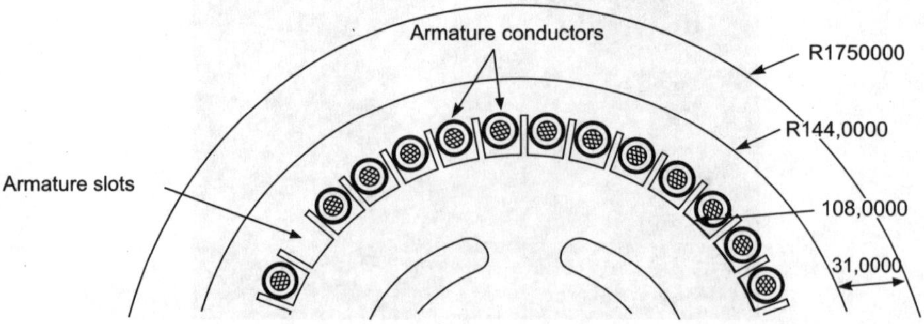

Figure 2.4 The cross sectional view of armature of a DC machine with armature slots and conductors employing single layer or simplex form of winding.

2.2.2 Two Layer Winding

In this winding, there are two conductors placed in each slot in two layers as shown in Figure 2.5. Usually, one side of every coil lies in the upper half of one slot and other side lies in the lower half of some other slot at a distance of approximately one pitch away. This is used for all medium-sized machines.

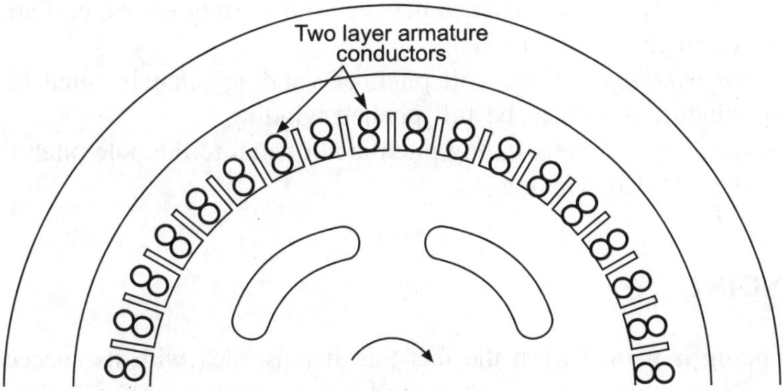

Figure 2.5 The cross sectional view of armature of a DC machine with armature slots and conductors employing two layer form of winding.

2.2.3 Multiplex Winding

In this form of winding, there are several conductors or coil sides are placed in each slot of the armature. The multiplicity depends directly on the number of parallel paths in the armature. For an armature with the specified number of slots and coils, the multiplicity increases if the number of parallel paths in the armature increases. Thereby this contributes to the increase in the current rating of the machine but decreases the voltage rating.

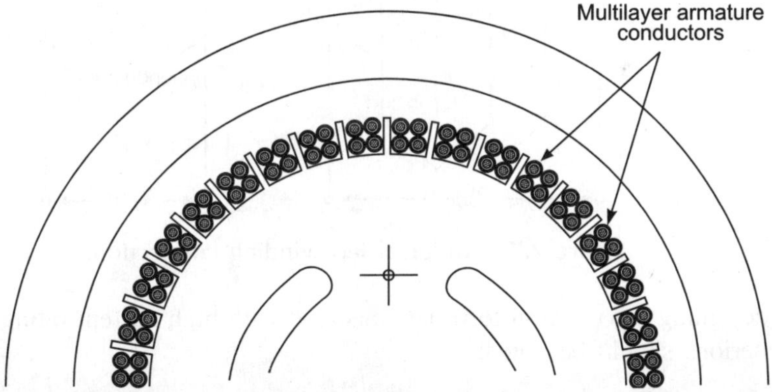

Figure 2.6 The cross sectional view of armature of a DC machine with armature slots and conductors employing multiple layer form of winding.

Some important definitions with respect to windings:

- *Pole pitch* (Y_p): Number of conductors per pole is known as pole pitch.
- *Front pitch* (Y_f): It is the distance in terms of number of conductors between any two coils connected to the same commutator segment.
- *Back pitch* (Y_b): It is the distance in terms of number of conductors between the two sides of the coil.
- *Resultant pitch* (Y_r): It is distance between the starting of one coil and starting of the next coil to which it is connected.
- *Full pitched winding:* If the coil pitch or winding pitch is equal to the pole pitch. Then the winding is said to be full pitched winding.
- *Chorded winding:* If the winding pitch is not equal to the pole pitch then the winding is said to be chorded winding.

2.3 LAP WINDING

This type of winding is named from the fact that it laps back with its succeeding coils. It is most suitable for DC machines with high current rating and low voltage. This winding is also known as parallel winding. The windings are connected to provide several parallel paths for current in the armature. In this method the windings are connected in parallel, hence this permits the current capacity of each winding to be added and provides a higher operating current.

In lap winding, the finishing end of one coil is connected to a commutator segment and to the starting end of the adjacent coil situated under the same pole and so on, till all the coils have been connected. Figure 2.7 shows a typical lap winding connection. A connection of two conductors form one turn and a number of turns connected in series forms a coil.

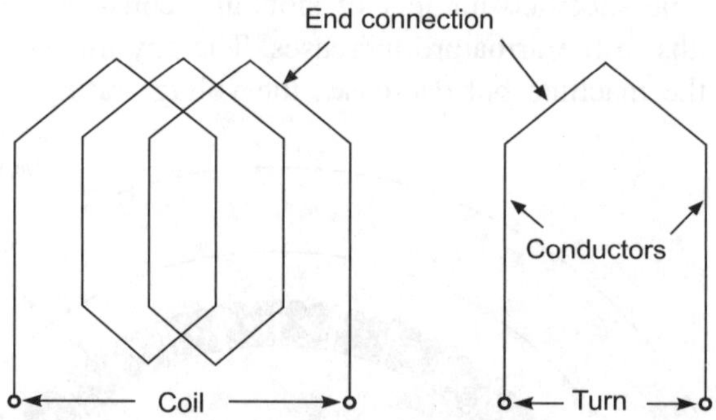

Figure 2.7 A typical lap winding connection.

While designing lap winding for a DC machine with high current rating and low voltage, following criterions should be noted:

1. The front pitch Y_f and back pitch Y_b are always odd numbers. They differ by 2 or it's multiple and is never equal. For example if Y_b and Y_f were both even, then all the coil sides and conductors would lie either in the upper half of slots or in the lower half.

Hence, it would become impossible for one side of the coil to lie in the upper half of one slot and the other side of the same coil to lie in the lower half of some other slot.

2. Front pitch Y_f and back pitch Y_b should be nearly equal to a pole pitch.
3. The pole pitch = Z/P = $(Y_b + Y_f)/2$.
4. Y_b = (Z/P) ± 1 [+ for progressive] [– for retrogressive]
   - If $Y_b > Y_f$ hence, $Y_b = Y_f + 2$, then we get a right-handed winding which means that it progresses in the clockwise direction as seen from the commutator end and is known as *progressive lap winding*.
   - If $Y_b < Y_f$ hence, $Y_b = Y_f - 2$, then we get a left-handed winding which means that it advances in the anti-clockwise direction as seen from the commutator side and is known as *retrogressive lap winding*.
5. The number of slots for a 2-layer winding is equal to the number of coils.
6. The number of parallel paths in the armature = mP, where 'm' is the multiplicity of the winding and 'P' is the number of poles. Taking the first condition, we have $Y_b = Y_f \pm 2\,m$, where m = 1 for simplex lap and m = 2 for duplex winding and so on.

Note: Winding in DC Machine is always seen from the commutator side. The windings are represented in rectangular format because of the reason that when the machine is cut and spread it appears in the form of a rectangle.

2.4 SOLVED PROBLEMS

PROBLEM 2.1: Develop a single layer lap winding diagram for a DC machine having 32 armature conductors and 4 poles. Mark the poles, draw the sequence diagram, indicate the position of the brushes and show the direction of induced emf.

Solution:

Analyse the problem: This particular problem states us to develop a single layer lap winding diagram for a DC machine having 32 armature conductors and 4 poles. Drawing sequence diagram helps us to analyse the flow of current and also helps to locate the brushes.

Given data:

Number of poles $(P) = 4$

In single layer, number of conductors (Z) = slots = 32

Step 1: First calculate the pole pitch, front pitch Y_f and back pitch Y_b.

Hence, pole pitch = $Z/P = 32/4 = 8$

But pole pitch = $(Y_b + Y_f)/2$

Hence,
$$(Y_b + Y_f)/2 = 8$$
$$(Y_b + Y_f) = 16 \quad \text{(i)}$$

But,
$$Y_b = Y_f \pm 2m$$

(where, m = 1 for simplex, 2 for duplex and 3 for triplex)

$$(Y_b - Y_f) = 2 \quad \text{(ii)}$$

Solving Eqs. (i) and (ii), we get

$$\boxed{Y_b = 9} \quad \text{and} \quad \boxed{Y_f = 7}$$

Step 2: Now, develop the winding table so as to establish the coil connection in various slots as shown in Table 2.1.

TABLE 2.1 Winding Table

At the back $Y_b = 9$	*At the front* $Y_f = 7$	*At the back* $Y_b = 9$	*At the front* $Y_f = 7$
1 + 9 = 10	10 – 7 = 3	17 + 9 = 26	26 – 7 = 19
3 + 9 = 12	12 – 7 = 5	19 + 9 = 28	28 – 7 = 21
5 + 9 = 14	14 – 7 = 7	21 + 9 = 30	30 – 7 = 23
7 + 9 = 16	16 – 7 = 9	23 + 9 = 32	32 – 7 = 25
9 + 9 = 18	18 – 7 = 11	25 + 9 = 34(2)	34 – 7 = 27
11 + 9 = 20	20 – 7 = 13	27 + 9 = 36(4)	36 – 7 = 29
13 + 9 = 22	22 – 7 = 15	29 + 9 = 38(6)	38 – 7 = 31
15 + 9 = 24	24 – 7 = 17	31 + 9 = 40(8)	40 – 7 = 33(1)

Note: Winding table is read horizontally for one set of Y_b and Y_f. For example, on the back 1st conductor is connected to 10th conductor and again on the front, the 10th conductor is connected to 3rd conductor and it repeats as shown in the Table 2.1.

Now, this winding table shows the connection of coils on both front and back pitches.

Steps to develop the winding diagram using CAD:

Step 1: Click on the AutoCAD 2014 icon appearing on the computer screen. A new window of AutoCAD will open.

Step 2: Select FILE in the AutoCAD window and open a new drawing (.dwg) file.

Step 3: In the command window type as UNITS ↵, a new dialog box will pop-up as shown in Figure 2.8(a). In this dialog box select the precision type, lighting and units as required. Generally, the precision set is 0.00, units to scale inserted are millimetre and lighting selected is International as shown in Figure 2.8(b).

Step 4: Now, select the sheet size required for the drawing by typing as LIMITS↵ in the command window, here itself it specifies as:

Specify lower left corner or (ON/OFF) <0.0000, 0.0000>: ↵
Specify upper right corner or (ON/OFF) <300, 300>: 1500, 1500 ↵

The lower left corner should always start from <0.0000, 0.0000> whereas for the upper right corner will have a default value. It can be set to any value depending on our requirement. The setting of page limits in CAD window is shown in Figure 2.9.

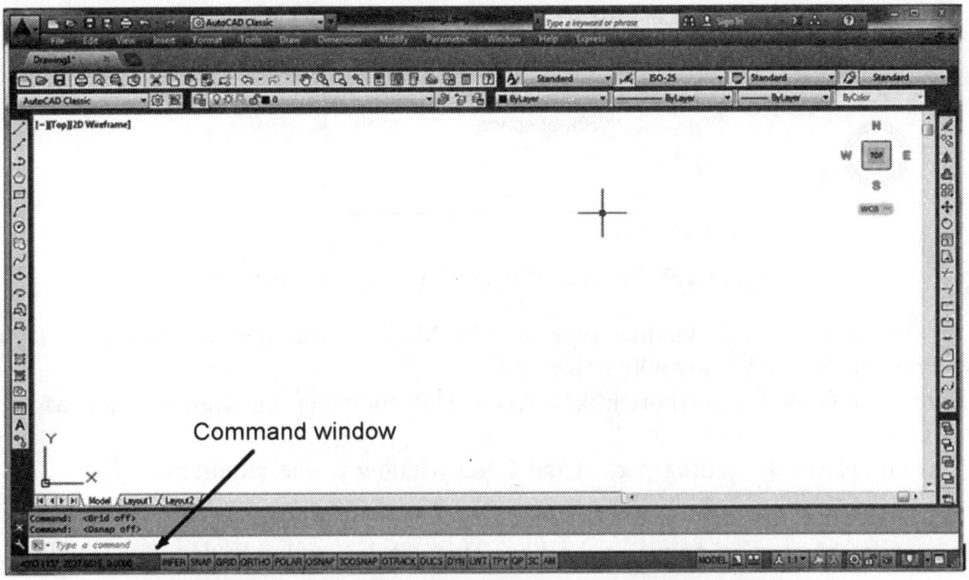

Figure 2.8(a) Command window, *courtesy:* AutoCAD®.

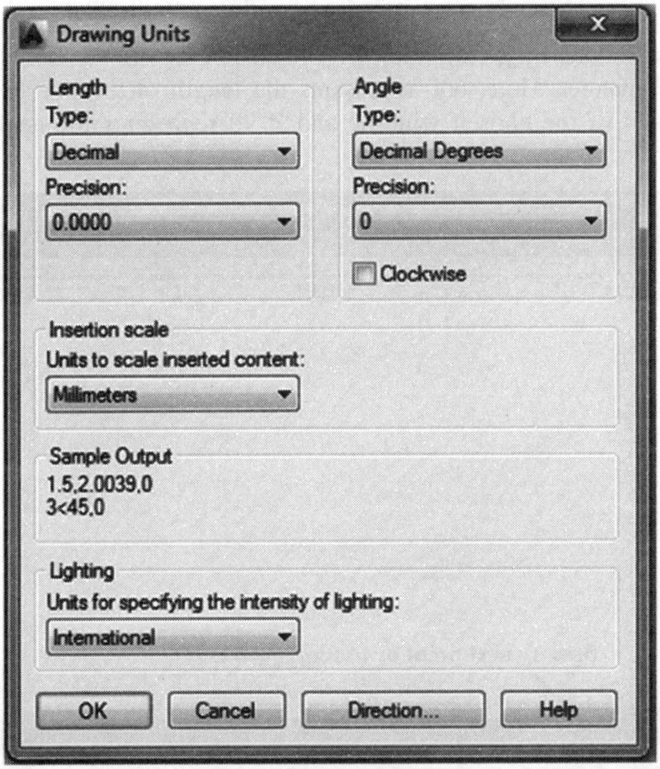

Figure 2.8(b) Drawing units' window, *courtesy:* AutoCAD®.

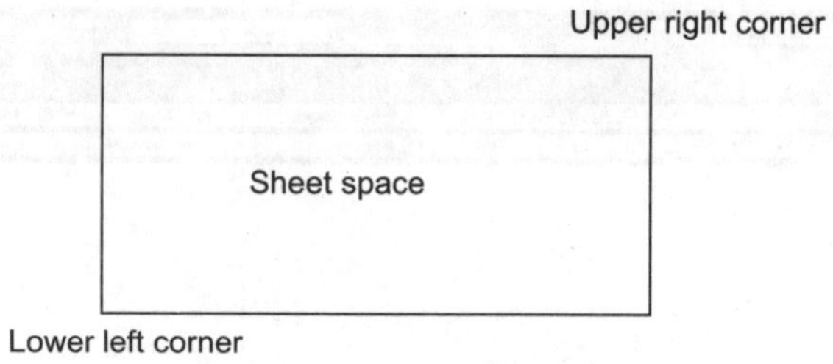

Figure 2.9 Setting of page limits in CAD window.

Step 5: In the command window type as ZOOM↵, it specifies as [All/Centre/Dynamic/Extents/Previous/Scale/Window/Object]<real time>:

Here, specify as All (or shortcut key A)↵. This zooms up the drawing sheet as specified in the limits.

This completes the setting part of the CAD window to the requirement.

Step 6: Select the line icon on the left tool bar of the CAD window. The command window asks to specify the starting point for the line. This can be randomly done by clicking on the CAD window.

Now, command window asks to specify the next point for the line, in the form:

Specify next point or [undo]: @600<90

This should always be done by giving a known dimension for the line and specifying the angle in the above stated manner. Here, 600 represents the length of the line to be drawn and this depends on the limits of the chosen window and < 90 represents the angle at which it is to be drawn as shown in Figure 2.10.

Figure 2.10 Line specifications in command window, *courtesy:* AutoCAD®.

Note: All dimensions are in millimetre (mm). Always ensure that ORTHO is kept on, in order to obtain straight line.

Step 7: Now, click on the icon 'A' available on the toolbar which represents multiline text. Now, select a size and style for the text as shown in Figure 2.11 and then enter the number for the conductor. Then place this number (text) next to the conductor (the line drawn).

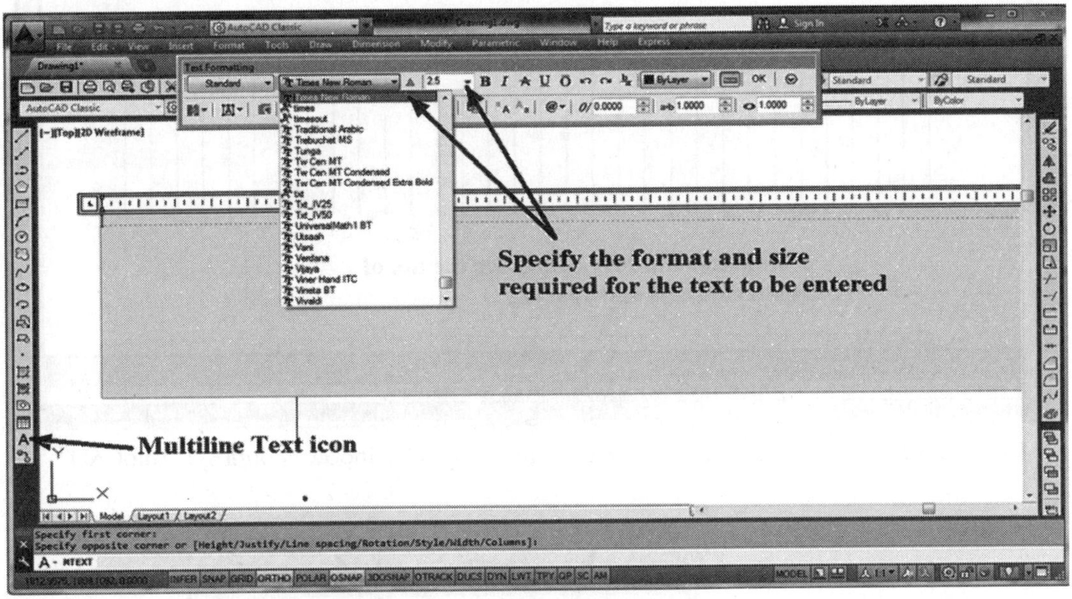

Figure 2.11 Text format to enter a text in CAD window, *courtesy:* AutoCAD®.

Step 8: Now, select the conductor (the line drawn) and the text together and then click on the array icon available on the right hand side of the toolbar of the CAD window. Now in the command window, it asks to specify the base point/ angle/ count. We are interested in rectangular array, hence first select the number of rows, i.e., type as '*r*' which indicates the rows and enter as 1, then select or type COL which indicates the number of columns and type the required value which is 32 in this case and enter. Then specify the distance between each column that is 100 as shown in Figure 2.12.

******Note:*** If a lower version of AutoCAD like AutoCAD 2009 or below version is used, then a dialog box will pop-up when array command is selected as shown in Figure 2.12(b). In that dialog box select rectangular array and then specify the number of rows (which is obviously 1 in case of winding diagrams) then specify the number of columns, which represents the number of conductors. In this case it is 32 hence enter 32 and then specify the distance between the conductors in column offset. Here, it is entered as 100 and then click preview in order to verify and then click OK. This creates the 32 number of conductors as required.

Step 9: Now, select all the conductors and text and explode it in order to make them individual entity and then click on the text available next to each conductor and edit it in the form of 1, 2, 3, ..., 32.

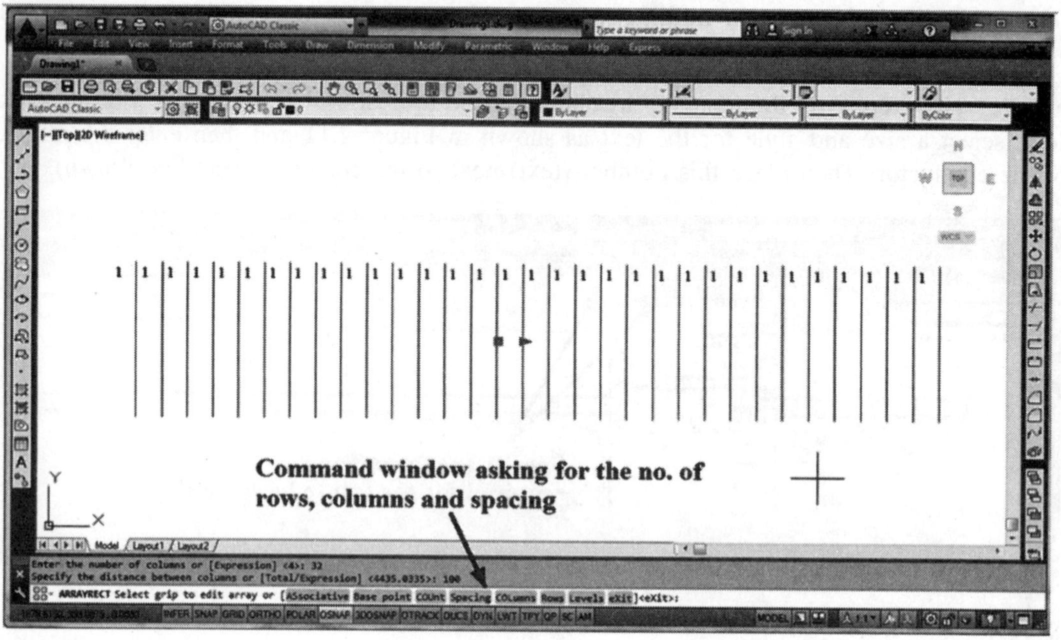

Figure 2.12(a) Array format to enter an array in CAD window, *courtesy:* AutoCAD®.

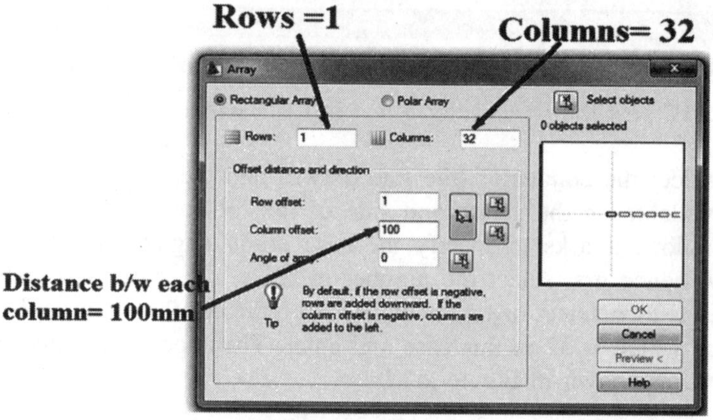

Figure 2.12(b) Array format to enter an array in CAD window, *courtesy:* AutoCAD®.

Step 10: Now, referring to the winding table developed the back pitch (that appears on the top) of the 1st conductor is connected to the 10th conductor. Hence, select the line icon and switch off ORTHO (as it does not support drawing lines in an inclined position). Now, select the first point for the line, i.e., the top end of the 1st conductor. The command window asks to specify the next point. Now, in the command window type the dimension of the line and its angle of inclination. **For example: @500 < 45,** here 500 represents the length of the line and < 45 refers to the angle of inclination as shown in Figure 2.14. After this, in the back pitch, the 10th conductor is connected to 1st conductor, again select the line icon and specify

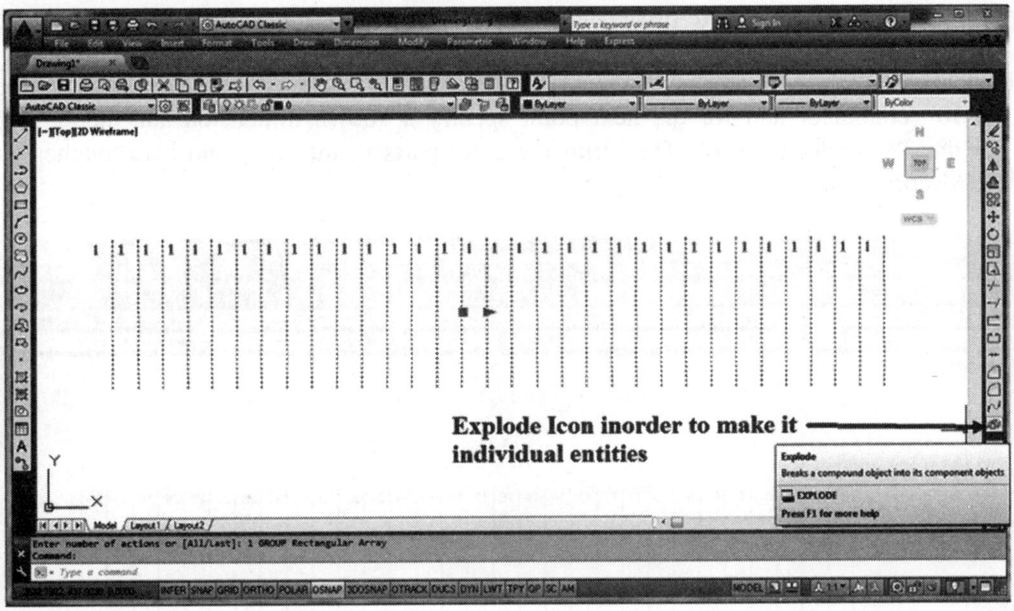

Figure 2.13 Exploding to obtain individual entities from a block in CAD window, *courtesy:* AutoCAD®.

the starting point on the top of the 10th conductor. The command window asks to specify the next point. Now, in the command window type the dimension of the line and its angle of inclination. **For example: @500<135.** The <135 is given as it is to be inclined in the reverse direction to connect to the 1st conductor. Both the lines meet each other if not extend them, if both meet and if there is excess of line then trim it using TRIM command. Similarly, connect the conductors on the front pitch also.

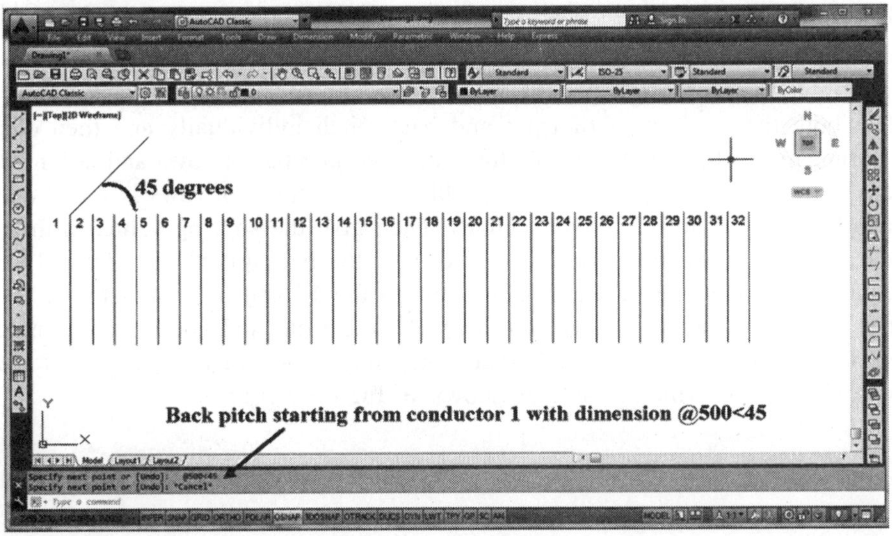

Figure 2.14 Back pitch line dimension with angle in CAD window, *courtesy:* AutoCAD®.

Step 11: Repeat the procedure of step 10 and form the connection of the front pitch as shown in Figure 2.15. (For example: referring to the winding table in the front pitch (bottom of the conductor), the 10th conductor is connected to 3rd conductor. Hence, select line first point on bottom 10th conductor and for the next point specify a known dimension and angle. Repeat this for the 3rd conductor also). Then trim the extra parts in the front and back pitches using the TRIM command.

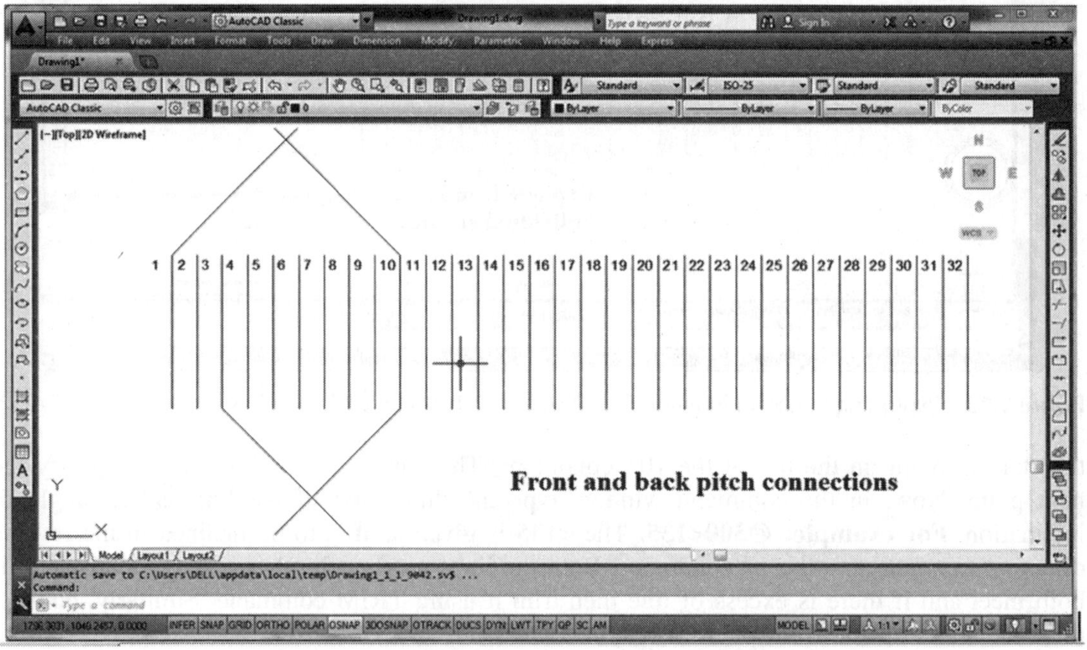

Figure 2.15 Back and front pitch connections CAD window, *courtesy:* AutoCAD®.

Step 12: Now, the winding connection for one set of front and back pitch is done. Now, select both the connection of front and back pitch individually and then click on the ARRAY command. In the command window enter the number of rows and columns required as illustrated earlier in step 8. Here in this problem, the number of rows is 1 and columns are 16 (this can be analysed in the winding table). Then give the spacing value, in this case it is 200 (as the distance between each conductor is 100, the back pitch starts from 1st conductor its successor is 3rd conductor. The distance between the 1st and 3rd conductor is 200. Hence, the spacing between columns is given as 200). All the front and back pitch connections are completed as shown in Figure 2.16(a). Place the end connections properly and number the conductors referring the winding table as shown in Figure 2.16(b).

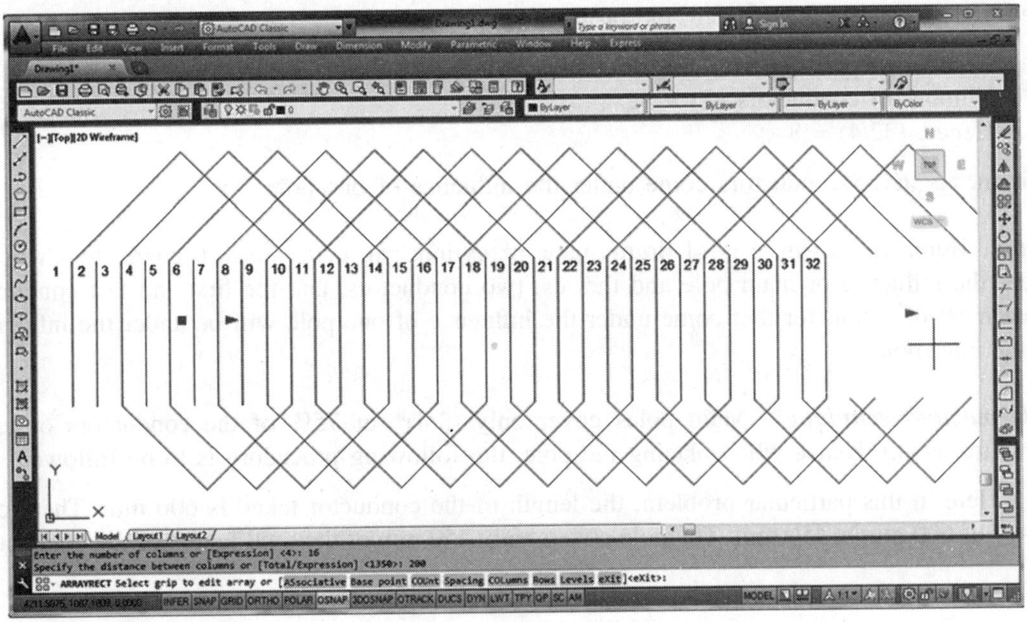

Figure 2.16(a) Creating front and back pitch using array command in CAD window, *courtesy:* AutoCAD®.

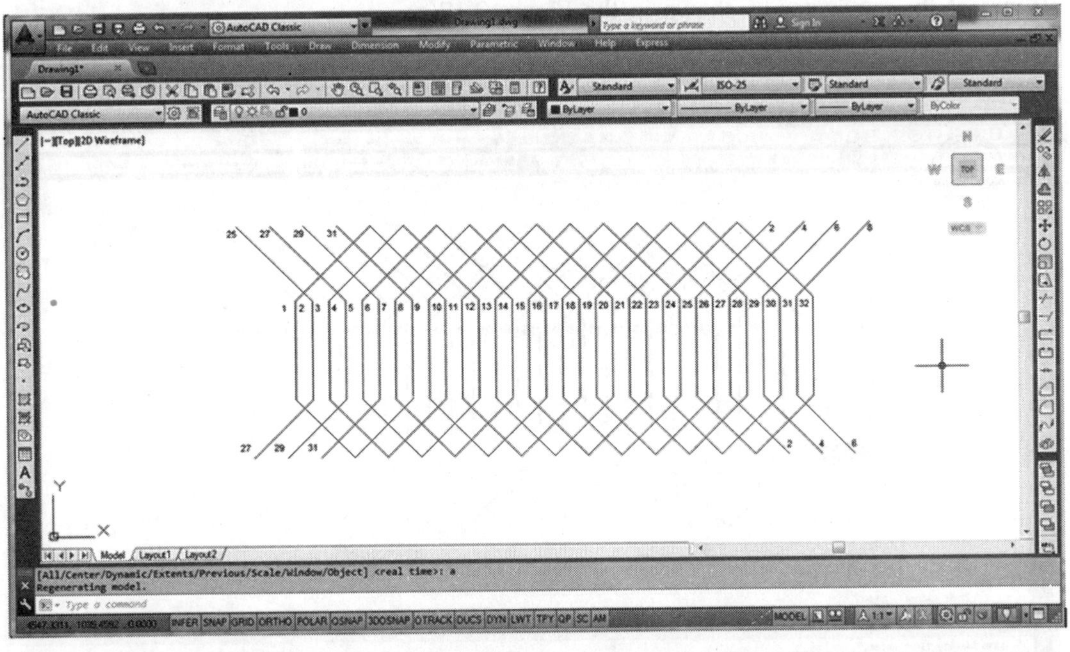

Figure 2.16(b) Winding format with back and front pitch connections in CAD window, *courtesy:* AutoCAD®.

Step 13: ***Pole placing:*** Here, the problem states that:

Number of poles (P) = 4
Number of conductors (Z) = 32
Hence, (32/4) = 8

This means that 8 conductors come under the influence of one pole.

Note: Here, the armature is of drum shape or cylindrical, hence only 6 conductors will be under the influence of main pole and the rest two conductors, i.e., the first and last conductor in each set of conductor that come under the influence of one pole will be under the influence of the inter-pole.

Pole placing technique: Main poles cover only $(3/4)^{\text{th}}$ or 75% of the conductors or total armature length. Hence when placing the pole, the following procedure is to be followed:

Here in this particular problem, the length of the conductor taken is 600 mm. Therefore, $(3/4)^{\text{th}}$ of 600 mm is 450 mm. The pole covers only 450 mm of the total length of the conductor.

$$600 - 450 = 150 \text{ mm}$$

$$150/2 = 75 \text{ mm}$$

Now, leave a gap of 75 mm on both upper and lower part of the conductor and then draw a line by selecting the midpoint in between the conductors 1 and 2 in such a way that it covers 450 mm of the conductor as shown in the Figure 2.17(a).

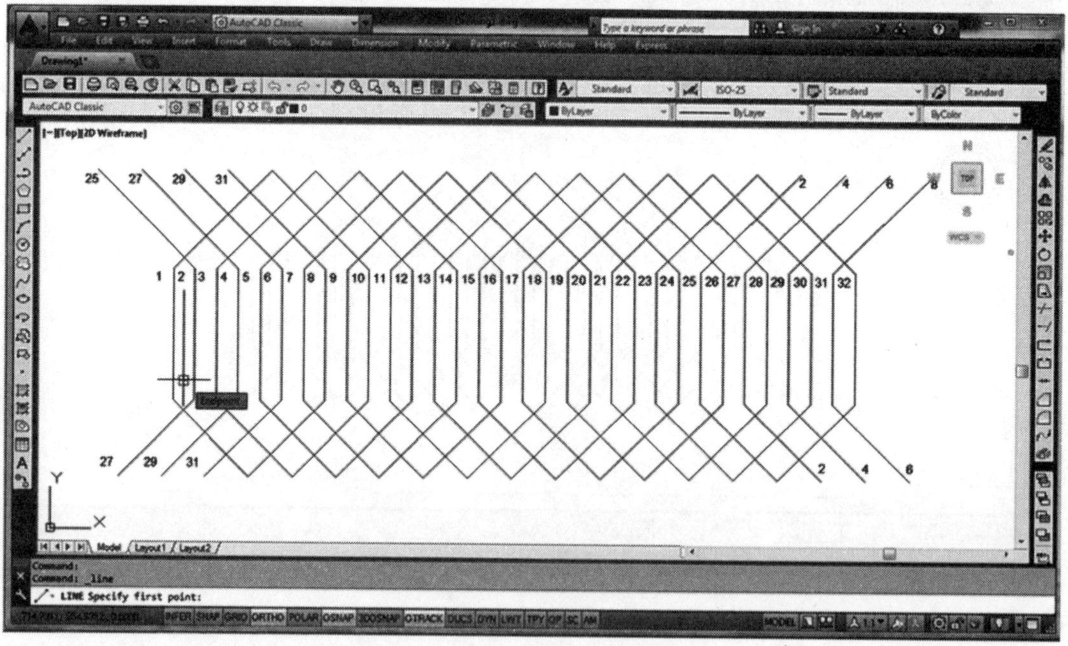

Figure 2.17(a) Pole placing drawing in CAD window, *courtesy:* AutoCAD®.

Now, complete the drawing of all the 4 sides of the pole as shown in Figure 2.17(b).

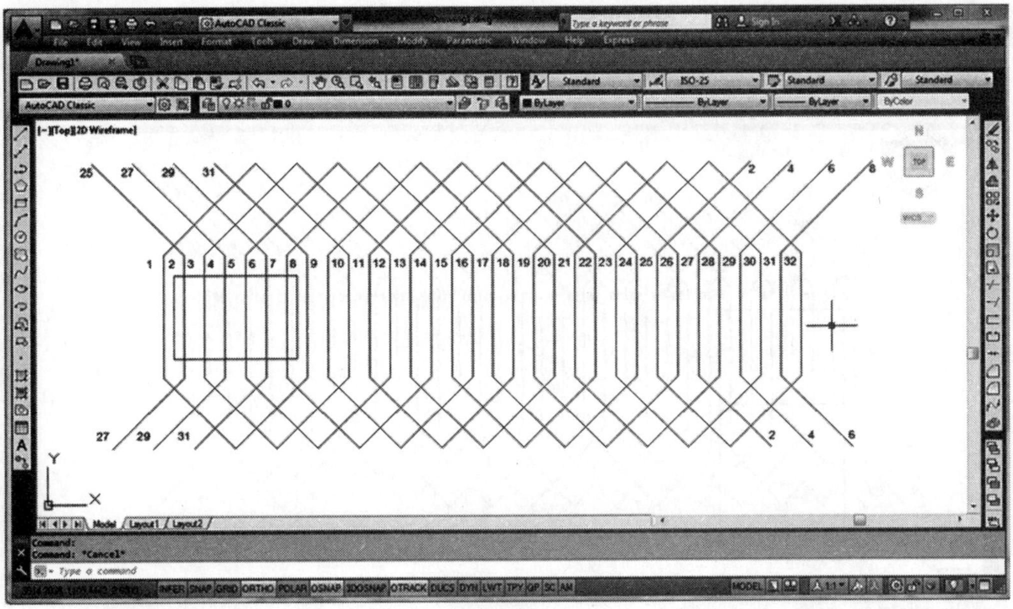

Figure 2.17(b) One pole drawn in CAD window, *courtesy:* AutoCAD®.

Step 14: Now, check the dimension of the pole, i.e., its length and breadth by using the tool dimension in the toolbar and select linear dimension in it as shown in Figure 2.18.

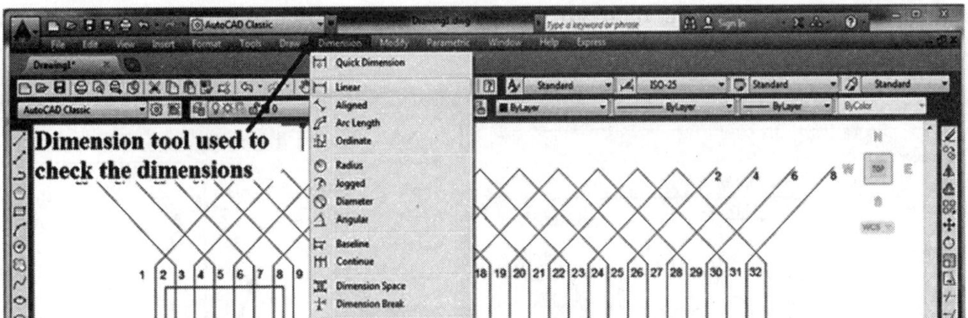

Figure 2.18 Dimension tool to check the dimension of pole in CAD window, *courtesy:* AutoCAD®.

Now, check the dimension of the pole drawn in the Figure 2.19.

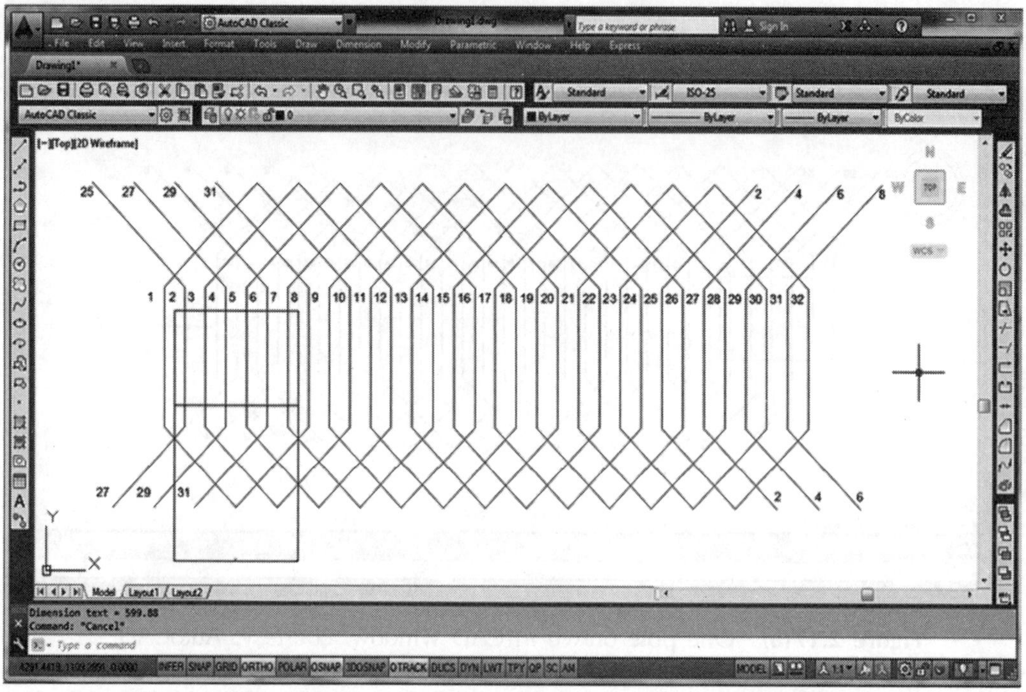

Figure 2.19 Dimension of pole in CAD window, *courtesy:* AutoCAD®.

If the dimension is not visible then go to dimension style manager and set the height and format for the text as shown in Figure 2.20.

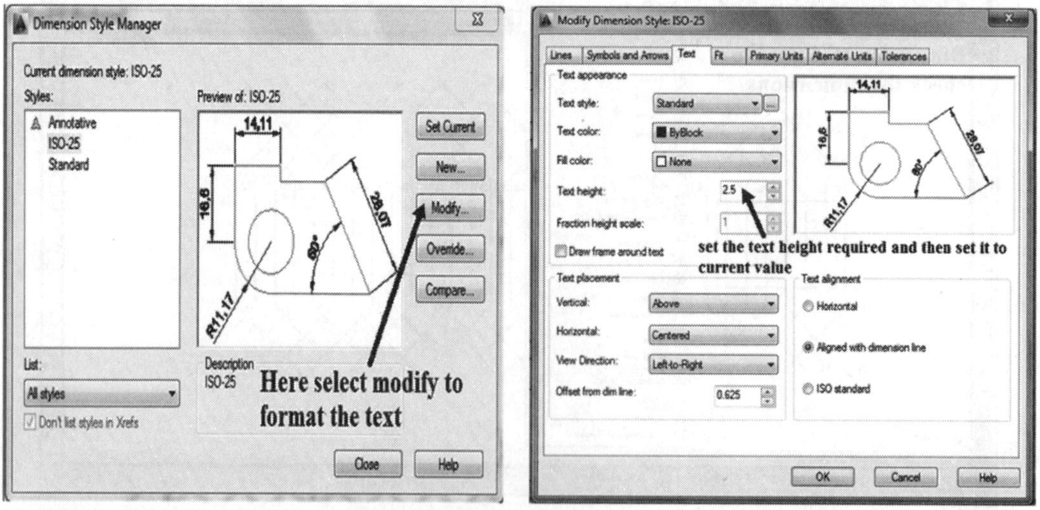

Figure 2.20 Dimension style manager to edit dimension text in CAD window, *courtesy:* AutoCAD®.

Step 15: After measuring the dimension of the pole, use this dimension to obtain the distance of the other poles from each other and then with the help of rectangular array, create the other poles as shown in Figure 2.21.

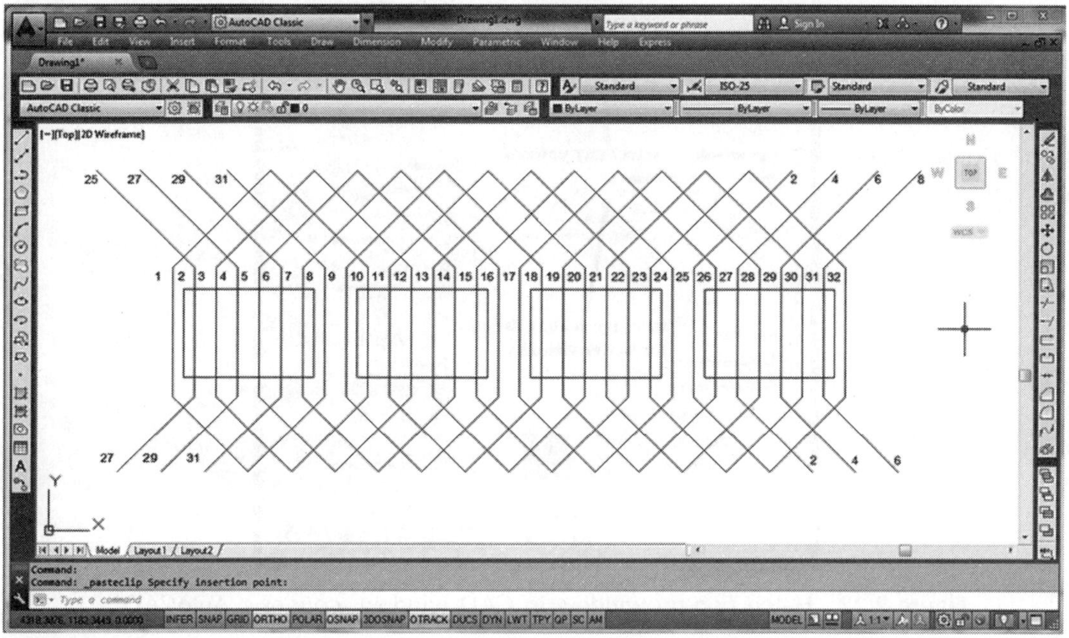

Figure 2.21 Winding diagram with poles in CAD window, *courtesy:* AutoCAD®.

Step 16: Now, mark the poles with the help of multiline text command and then hatch it in order to identify using hatch command. If the hatching is not visible then increase the scaling factor as shown in Figure 2.22.

Step 17: Now, the direction of current is to be assigned. The direction of current in the conductors coming under the influence of North Pole is always towards the downwards whereas in the South Pole it is in upward direction.

Arrow marks to show the direction of current flow can be drawn in the following manner:

Select the icon polyline in the command window, it asks to specify the starting point. Now, select any point on the screen by just a random click. In the command window it displays as specify next point or [arc/ half width/ undo/width]: w↵.

Command window now asks to specify starting width<0.0000>: 50↵

Specify ending width <0.0000>: 0↵

This creates an arrow which can be used as required. The Figure 2.24(a) shows the arrow creating and Figure 2.24(b) shows the direction of current in the winding.

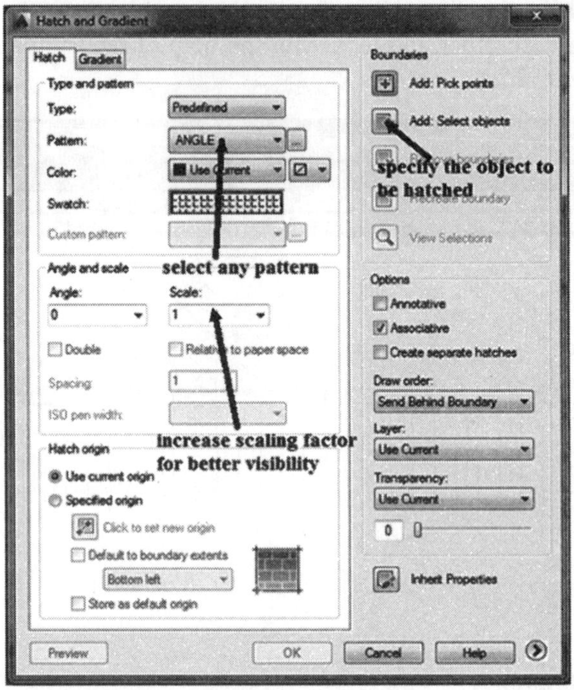

Figure 2.22 Hatch pop-up window in CAD window, *courtesy:* AutoCAD®.

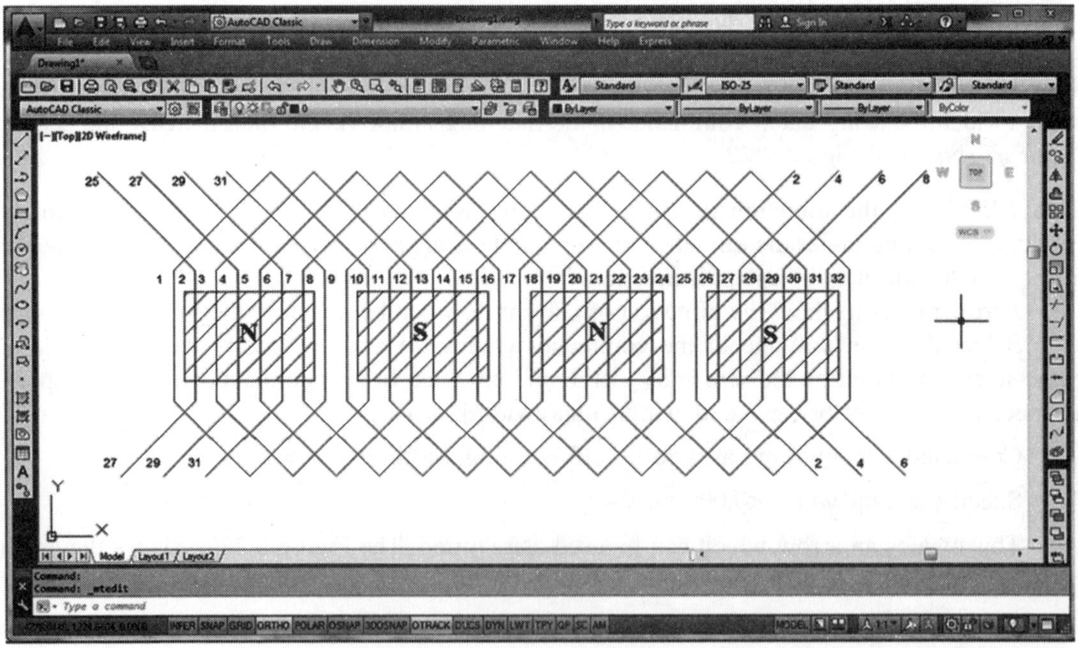

Figure 2.23 Winding diagram with poles in CAD window, *courtesy:* AutoCAD®.

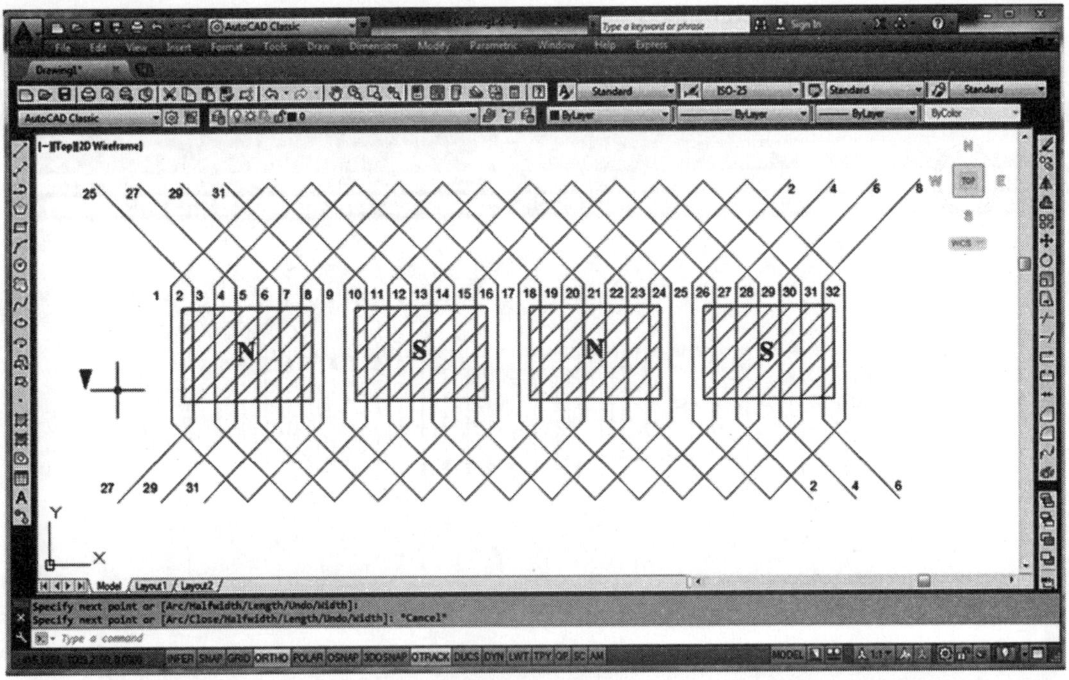

Figure 2.24(a) Arrow created in CAD window, *courtesy:* AutoCAD®.

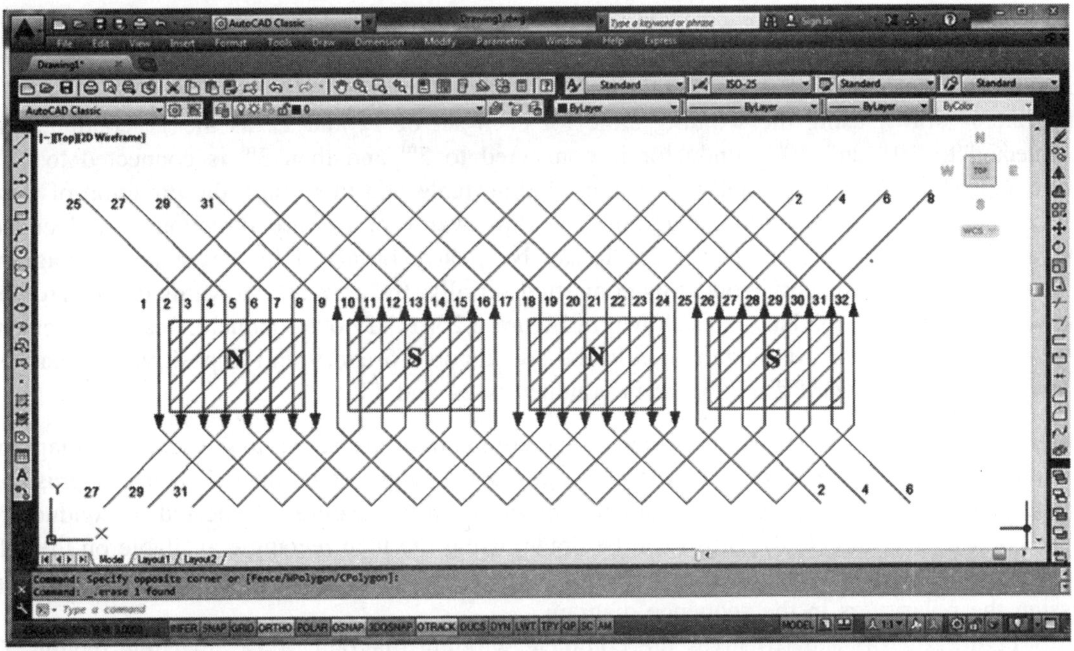

Figure 2.24(b) Direction of current flows in windings in CAD window, *courtesy:* AutoCAD®.

Step 18: Now, from each coil take a tapping and connect it to the commutator and number of the commutator segments is half the total number of conductors as shown in Figure 2.25.

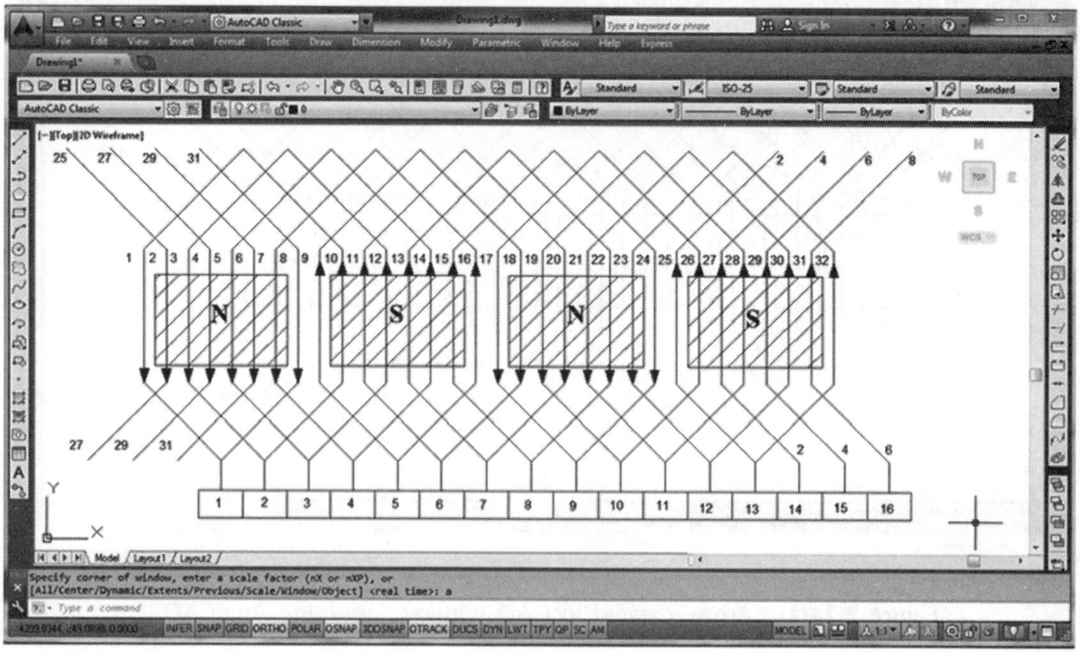

Figure 2.25 Commutator with winding diagram in CAD window, *courtesy:* AutoCAD®.

Step 19: Draw the sequence diagram to obtain the current and place the brushes. Sequence diagram is drawn using the winding table for each set of Y_b and Y_f, as the 1st conductor is connected to 10th and 10th conductor is connected to 3rd and then 3rd is connected to 12th conductor and repeat this serially as in the winding table and then mark the direction of flow current as done in the winding diagram, i.e., downwards or upward direction as influenced by the pole as shown in Figure 2.25. It can be clearly observed in the sequence diagram Figure 2.26(b) that for few conductors connected serially; the current is towards downwards or upwards in both the conductors as shown in Figure 2.26(b). If both conductors carry current in upward direction then it is negative as in the conductors 16 and 9 and is positive if it carries current in the downward direction as in conductors 24 and 17.

Step 20: Now, brushes are to be placed on the commutator. Referring to the sequence diagram conductors 16 and 9 are connected to the commutator segment number 5, hence a brush is to be placed on this commutator segment. Similarly, the procedure is repeated to conductors (24, 17), (32, 25) and (1, 8). Brush can be drawn using the icon rectangle available on the left tool bar of CAD software and then placed on the segment as shown in Figure 2.27 and then assign the polarity as in the sequence diagram.

Figure 2.27(a) and (b) gives the complete winding diagram of DC machine having 32 armature conductors and 4 poles with the direction of induced emf.

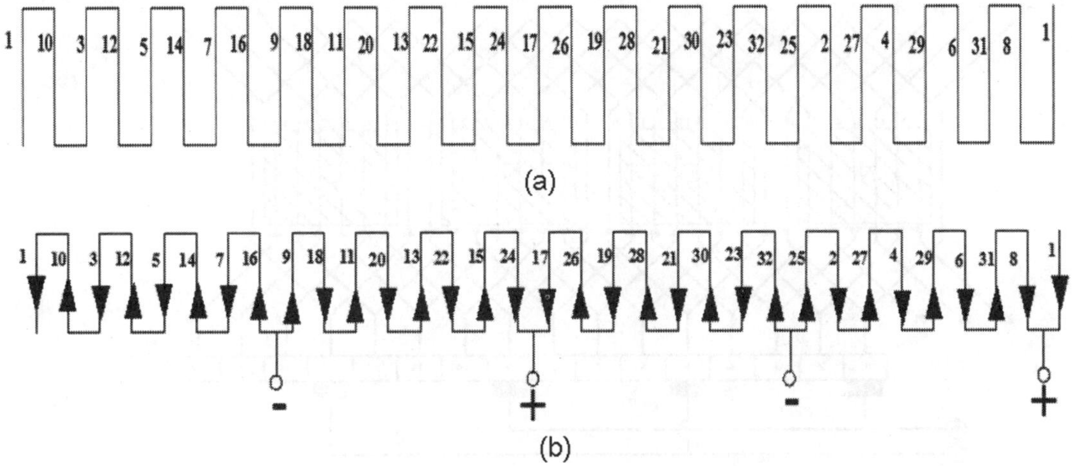

Figure 2.26 (a) Sequence diagram drawn on the basis of winding Table. (b) Complete sequence diagram showing the induced emf and positions of brushes.

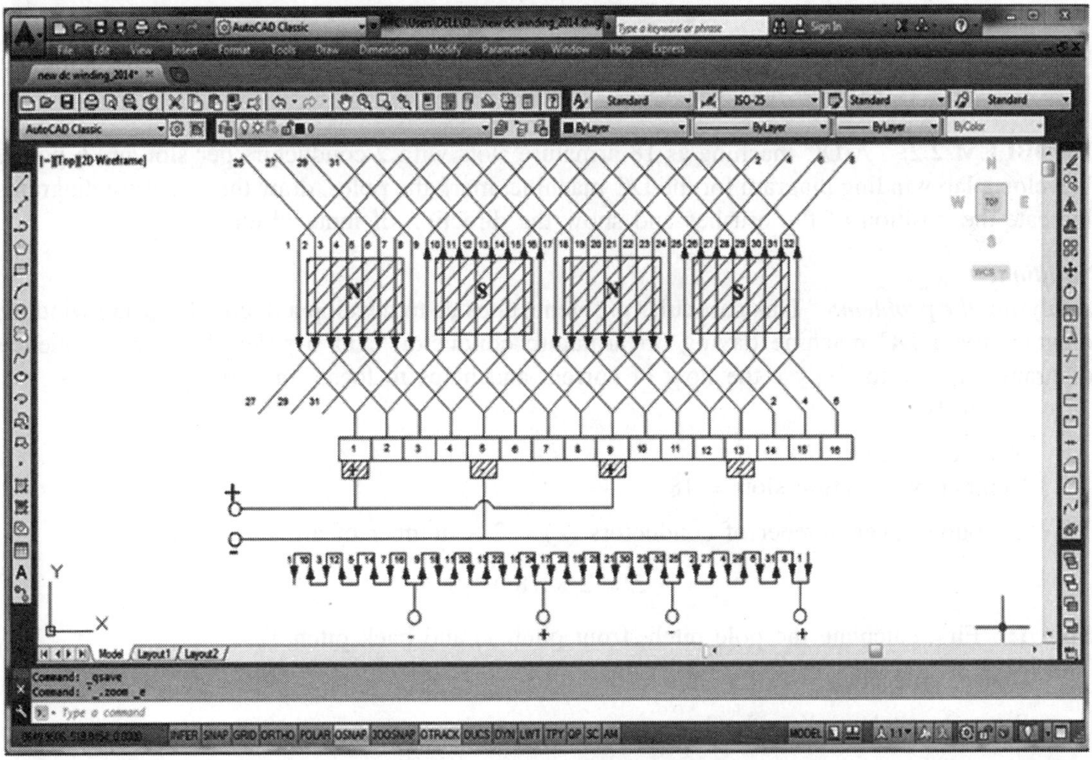

Figure 2.27(a) Complete winding and sequence diagram of DC machine with 32 armature conductor and 4 poles, *courtesy:* AutoCAD®.

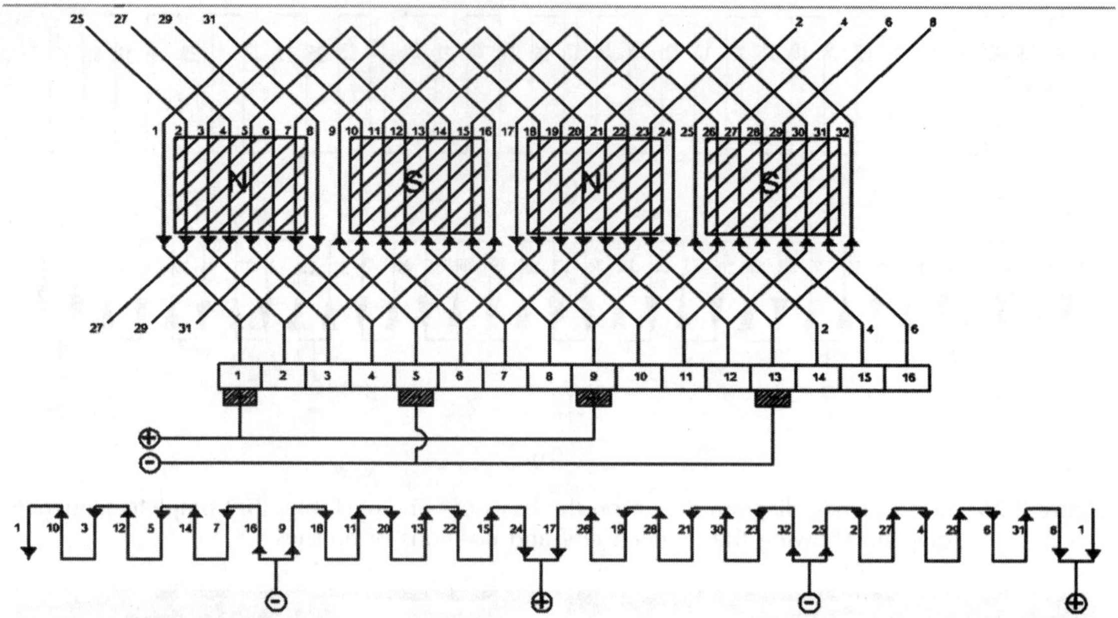

Figure 2.27(b) Complete winding and sequence diagram of DC machine with 32 armature conductor and 4 poles.

PROBLEM 2.2: A DC machine as 18 armature slots with 2 conductors per slot and 6 poles. Develop a lap winding diagram for the DC machine, mark the poles, draw the sequence diagram, indicate the position of the brushes and show the direction of induced emf.

Solution:

Analysing the problem: This particular problem states us to develop a double layer lap winding diagram for a DC machine having 36 armature conductors and 6 poles. Drawing sequence diagram helps us to analyse the flow of current and helps to locate the brushes.

Given data:

Number of poles (P) = 6

Number of armature slots = 18

In double layer number of conductors (Z) = 2 × number of armature slots

$$Z = 2 \times 18 = 36$$

Step 1: First calculate the pole pitch, front pitch Y_f and back pitch Y_b.

Hence, pole pitch = Z/P = 36/6 = 6

But pole pitch = $(Y_b + Y_f)/2$

Hence, $(Y_b + Y_f)/2 = 6$

$$(Y_b + Y_f) = 12 \quad \text{(i)}$$

But $$Y_b = Y_f \pm 2m$$

(where m = 1 for simplex, 2 for duplex and 3 for triplex)

$$(Y_b - Y_f) = 2 \quad \text{(ii)}$$

Solving Eq. (i) and (ii), we get

$$\boxed{Y_b = 7} \quad \text{and} \quad \boxed{Y_f = 5}$$

Step 2: Now, develop the winding table so as to establish the coil connection in various slots as shown in Table 2.2.

TABLE 2.2 Winding table

S. No.	*At the back* $Y_b = 7$	*At the front* $Y_f = 5$	*S. No.*	*At the back* $Y_b = 7$	*At the front* $Y_f = 5$
1	1 + 7 = 8	8 – 5 = 3	10	19 + 7 = 26	26 – 5 = 21
2	3 + 7 = 10	10 – 5 = 5	11	21 + 7 = 28	28 – 5 = 23
3	5 + 7 = 12	12 – 5 = 7	12	23 + 7 = 30	30 – 5 = 25
4	7 + 7 = 14	14 – 5 = 9	13	25 + 7 = 32	32 – 5 = 27
5	9 + 7 = 16	16 – 5 = 11	14	27 + 7 = 34	34 – 5 = 29
6	11 + 7 = 18	18 – 5 = 13	15	29 + 7 = 36	36 – 5 = 31
7	13 + 7 = 20	20 – 5 = 15	16	31 + 7 = 38(2)	(2)38 – 5 = 33
8	15 + 7 = 22	22 – 5 = 17	17	33 + 7 = 40(4)	(4)40 – 5 = 35
9	17 + 7 = 24	24 – 5 = 19	18	35 + 7 = 42(6)	(6)42 – 5 = 37(1)

Note: Winding table is read horizontally for one set of Y_b and Y_f. For example, on the back 1st conductor is connected to 10th conductor and again on the front, the 10th conductor is connected to 3rd conductor and it repeats as shown in the Table 2.2.

Now, this winding table shows the connection of coils on both front and back pitches. Repeat the steps 1 to 20 as stated in solution of problem to draw the winding diagram.

Note: In this problem armature conductors are of double layer, hence one conductor is placed above the other, i.e., 2 conductors per armature slot, so one of the 2 conductors is represented in dashed lines. Dashed line can be obtained by selecting the line drawn and then selecting the appropriate dashed line format in line tool bar. It is also very important to note that the distance of conductors placed in the same slot should be minimal when compared to the distance between the conductors in the other armature slot.

Figure 2.28 gives the winding diagram along with the sequence diagram.

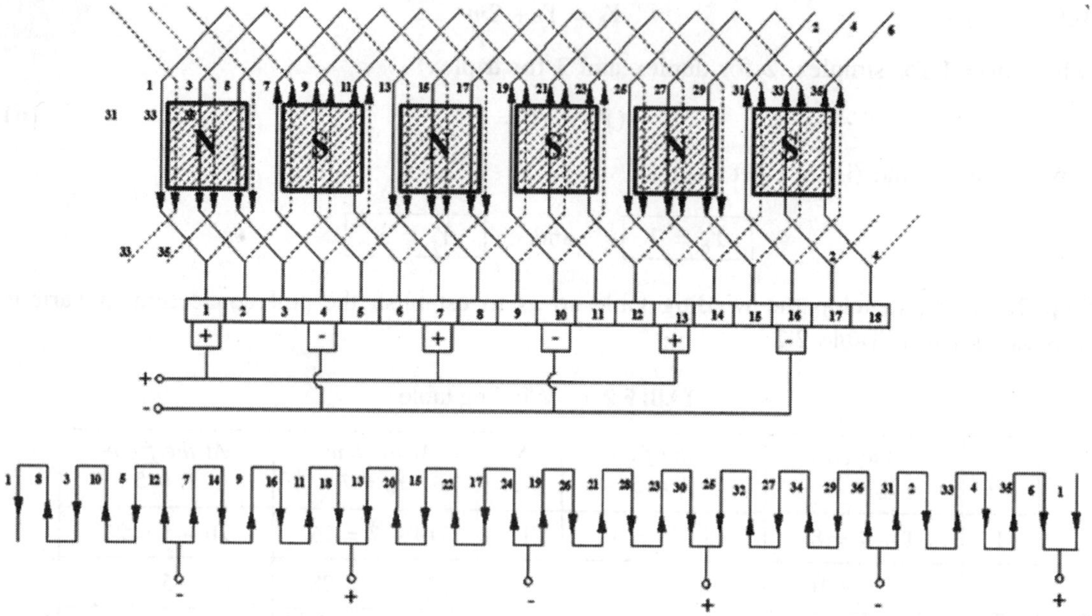

Figure 2.28 Developed winding diagram and sequence diagram (solution for problem 2.2).

PROBLEM 2.3: A DC machine as 28 armature conductors and 4 poles, with one conductor per slot. Develop a progressive simplex lap winding diagram for the DC machine, mark the poles. Also show equaliser ring.

Solution:

Analysing the problem: This particular problem states us to develop a lap winding diagram for a DC machine having 28 armature conductors and 4 poles. Drawing sequence diagram helps us to analyse the flow of current and helps to locate the brushes.

Equalising connection: It is a characteristic of lap winding that all conductors in any parallel path lies under one pair of pole. Each parallel path carries same current when it place exactly under the pole, but due to slight variation in air gap or magnetic property, there is inequalities in flux occurs. Hence, there is always slight imbalance of induced emf in the various parallel paths and also the brushes which carry unequal currents, some brushes will get over loaded. This results in poor commutation and affects the performance of the machine.

In order to overcome the problem of imbalance of induced emf, armature winding must be at equal potential and the difference in brush currents should be diminished. This requires that there should be a whole number of slots per pole pair. For example, if there is a slot under the centre of an N-pole which is connected to the conductor which are in the form of copper rings at the armature back. These rings are called as *equaliser ring*. Hence, the function of equaliser ring is to avoid unequal distribution of the current at the brushes and also helps to get sparkles commutation.

Note: The equaliser rings are not used in wave winding, because there is no imbalance in the emf of the two parallel paths.

Here, m = number of rings

$$\text{Total number of tapping} = m \times \text{pairs of poles} = \frac{m \times P}{2}$$

$$\text{Distance between adjacent tapping } (T_g) = \frac{\text{Total number of coils}}{\text{Total number of tapping}}$$

Given data:

Number of poles (P) = 4

Number of armature slots = number of conductors (Z) = 28

Step 1: First calculate the pole pitch, front pitch Y_f and back pitch Y_b.

Hence, pole pitch = Z/P = 28/4 = 7

But pole pitch = $(Y_b + Y_f)/2$

Hence,

$$(Y_b + Y_f)/2 = 7$$

$$(Y_b + Y_f) = 14 \quad \text{(i)}$$

$$(Y_b - Y_f) = 2 \quad \text{(ii)}$$

Solving Eqs. (i) and (ii), we get

$$\boxed{Y_b = 8} \quad \text{and} \quad \boxed{Y_f = 6}$$

Here, both Y_b and Y_f are even.

Since, both Y_b and Y_f should be odd for lap winding in this particular problem Y_b and Y_f can be considered as follows:

Hence,

$$\boxed{Y_b = 7} \quad \text{and} \quad \boxed{Y_f = 5}$$

Step 2: Now, develop the winding table so as to establish the coil connection in various slots as shown in Table 2.3.

TABLE 2.3 Winding table

S. No.	*At the back* $Y_b = 7$	*At the front* $Y_f = 5$	*S. No.*	*At the back* $Y_b = 7$	*At the front* $Y_f = 5$
1	1 + 7 = 8	8 – 5 = 3	8	15 + 7 = 22	22 – 5 = 17
2	3 + 7 = 10	10 – 5 = 5	9	17 + 7 = 24	24 – 5 = 19
3	5 + 7 = 12	12 – 5 = 7	10	19 + 7 = 26	26 – 5 = 21
4	7 + 7 = 14	14 – 5 = 9	11	21 + 7 = 28	28 – 5 = 23
5	9 + 7 = 16	16 – 5 = 11	12	23 + 7 = 30(2)	30 – 5 = 25
6	11 + 7 = 18	18 – 5 = 13	13	25 + 7 = 32(4)	32 – 5 = 27
7	13 + 7 = 20	20 – 5 = 15	14	27 + 7 = 34(6)	34 – 5 = 29(1)

Now, this winding table shows the connection of coils on both front and back pitches.

Repeat the steps 1 to 20 as stated in solution of problem to draw the winding diagram.

Figure 2.29 shows the developed winding diagram along with the sequence diagram.

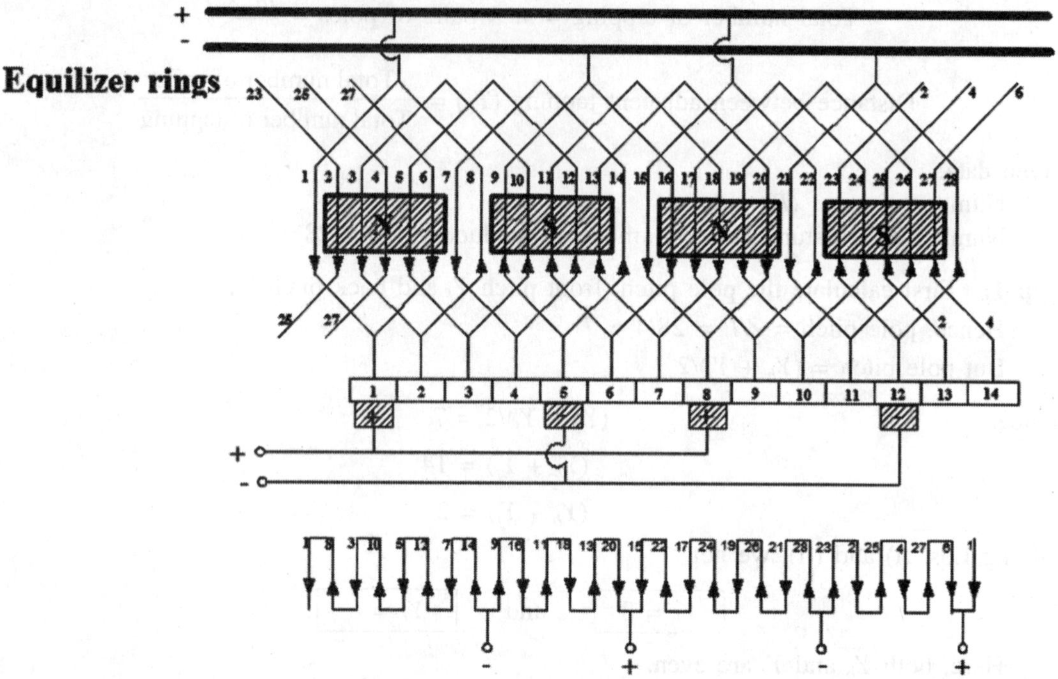

Figure 2.29 Developed winding diagram and sequence diagram (solution for problem 2.3).

PROBLEM 2.4: A DC machine has 32 armature slots and 4 poles, with one conductor per slot. Develop a progressive duplex lap winding diagram for the DC machine.

Solution:

Analysing the problem: This particular problem states us to develop a duplex lap winding diagram for a DC machine having 32 armature conductors and 4 poles.

Step 1: First calculate the pole pitch, front pitch Y_f and back pitch Y_b.

Hence, pole pitch = $Z/P = 32/4 = 8$

But pole pitch = $(Y_b + Y_f)/2$

Hence, $(Y_b + Y_f)/2 = 8$

Calculating Y_b as per the general procedure:

$$(Y_b + Y_f) = 16 \qquad \text{(i)}$$

$$(Y_b - Y_f) = 2 \qquad \text{(ii)}$$

Solving equations (i) and (ii), we get

$$\boxed{Y_b = 9}$$

But $Y_b = Y_f \pm 2m$

(where m = 1 for simplex, 2 for duplex and 3 for triplex)

$$(Y_b - Y_f) = 2 \times 2 = 4 \qquad \text{(iii)}$$

Now, substituting the value of Y_b in equation (iii)

Hence

$Y_b = 9$ and $Y_f = 5$

Step 2: Now, develop the winding table so as to establish the coil connection in various slots as shown in Table 2.4.

TABLE 2.4 Winding table

At the back $Y_b = 9$	*At the front* $Y_f = 5$	*At the back* $Y_b = 9$	*At the front* $Y_f = 5$
1 + 9 = 10	10 – 5 = 5	3 + 9 = 12	12 – 5 = 7
5 + 9 = 14	14 – 5 = 9	7 + 9 = 16	16 – 5 = 11
9 + 9 = 18	18 – 5 = 13	11 + 9 = 20	20 – 5 = 15
13 + 9 = 22	22 – 5 = 17	15 + 9 = 24	24 – 5 = 19
17 + 9 = 26	26 – 5 = 21	19 + 9 = 28	28 – 5 = 23
21 + 9 = 30	30 – 5 = 25	23 + 9 = 32	32 – 5 = 27
25 + 9 = 34(2)	34 – 5 = 29	27 + 9 = 36(4)	36 – 5 = 31
29 + 9 = 38(6)	38 – 5 = 33(1)	31 + 9 = 40(8)	40 – 5 = 35(3)

Now, this winding table shows the connection of coils on both front and back pitches.

Repeat the steps 1 to 20 as stated in solution of problem to draw the winding diagram. Figure 2.30 shows the developed winding diagram for this particular problem.

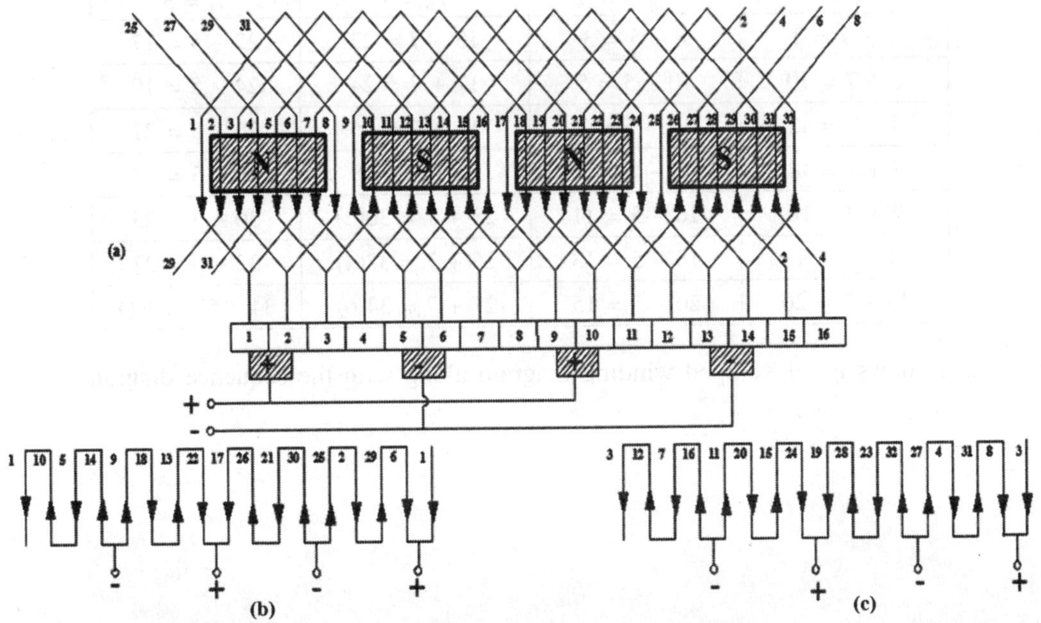

Figure 2.30 (a) Developed duplex winding diagram, (b) Sequence diagram for back pitch and (c) Sequence diagram for front pitch for this particular problem (solution for problem 2.4).

PROBLEM 2.5: Draw the armature winding of a DC machine with 4 poles, 14 slots and double layer progressive lap. Show the position of brush and direction of induced emf. Draw the sequence diagram and equaliser connections. (VTU, June 2013).

Solution:

Given data:

Type of winding = Progressive lap
Number of slots (S) = 14
Number of conductors (Z) = 28
Number of poles (P) = 4
Number of circuits (m) = 1
Number of layers = 2

Calculation:

Pole pitch (Z/P) = 7
$Y_b = 7$
$Y_f = 5$

Now, develop the winding table so as to establish the coil connection in various slots as shown in Table 2.5.

TABLE 2.5 Winding table

At the back $Y_b = 7$	*At the front* $Y_f = 5$	*At the back* $Y_b = 7$	*At the front* $Y_f = 5$
1 + 7 = 8	8 – 5 = 3	15 + 7 = 22	22 – 5 = 17
3 + 7 = 10	10 – 5 = 5	17 + 7 = 24	24 – 5 = 19
5 + 7 = 12	12 – 5 = 7	19 + 7 = 26	26 – 5 = 21
7 + 7 = 14	14 – 5 = 9	21 + 7 = 28	28 – 5 = 23
9 + 7 = 16	16 – 5 = 11	23 + 7 = 30(2)	30 – 5 = 25
11 + 7 = 18	18 – 5 = 13	25 + 7 = 32(4)	32 – 5 = 27
13 + 7 = 20	20 – 5 = 15	27 + 7 = 34(6)	34 – 5 = 29(1)

Figure 2.31 shows the developed winding diagram along with the sequence diagram.

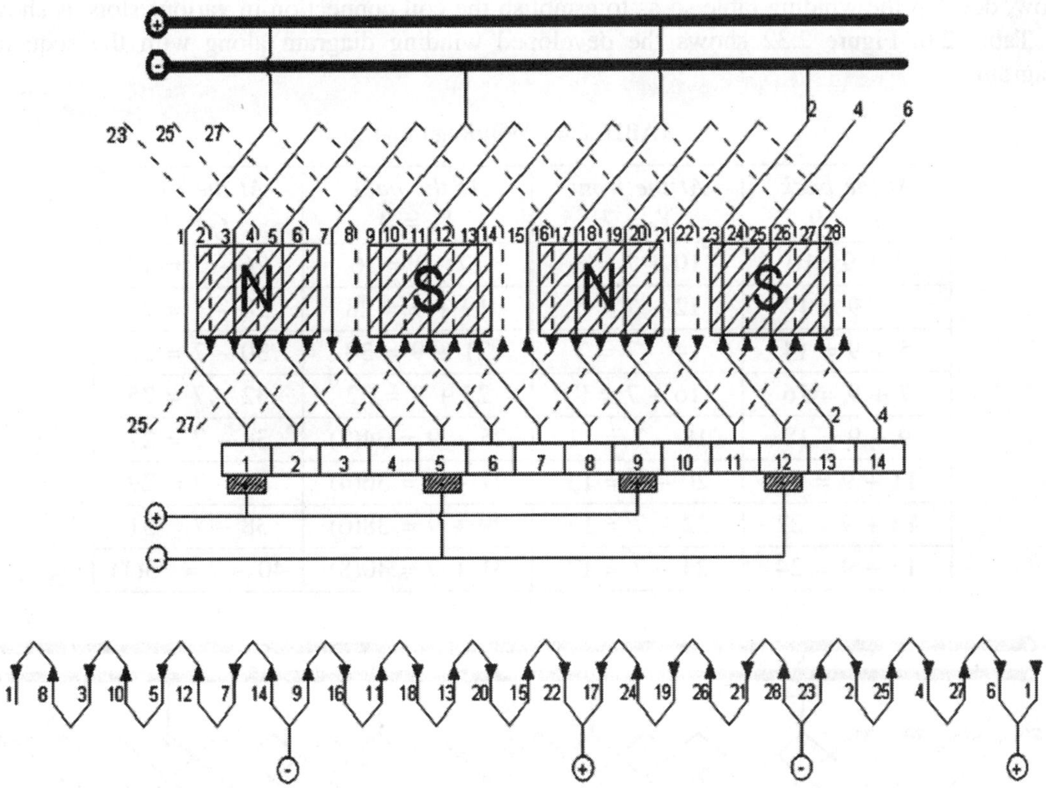

Figure 2.31 Developed winding diagram and sequence diagram (solution for problem 2.5).

PROBLEM 2.6: Develop a double layer winding for a DC machine having 16 slots and 4 poles. Draw the sequence diagram and indicate the position of the brushes. Show the direction of induced emf and give equaliser connection. (VTU, June 2013)

Solution:

Given data:

Type of winding = Progressive lap
Number of slots (S) = 16
Number of conductors (Z) = 32
Number of poles (P) = 4
Number of circuits (m) = 1
Number of layers = 2

Calculation:

Pole pitch (Z/P) = 8
$Y_b = 9$
$Y_f = 7$

Now, develop the winding table so as to establish the coil connection in various slots as shown in Table 2.6. Figure 2.32 shows the developed winding diagram along with the sequence diagram.

TABLE 2.6 Winding table

At the back $Y_b = 9$	*At the front* $Y_f = 7$	*At the back* $Y_b = 9$	*At the front* $Y_f = 7$
1 + 9 =10	10 – 7 = 3	17+ 9 = 26	26 – 7 = 19
3 + 9 = 12	12 – 7 = 5	19 + 9 = 28	28 – 7 = 21
5 + 9 = 14	14 – 7 = 7	21 + 9 = 30	30 – 7 = 23
7 + 9 = 16	16 – 7 = 9	23 + 9 = 32	32 – 7 = 25
9 + 9 = 18	18 – 7 = 11	25 + 9 = 34(2)	34 – 7 = 27
11 + 9 = 20	20 – 7 = 13	27 + 9 = 36(4)	36 – 7 = 29
13 + 9 = 22	22 – 7 = 15	29 + 9 = 38(6)	38 – 7 = 31
15 + 9 = 24	24 – 7 = 17	31 + 9 = 40(8)	40 – 7 = 33(1)

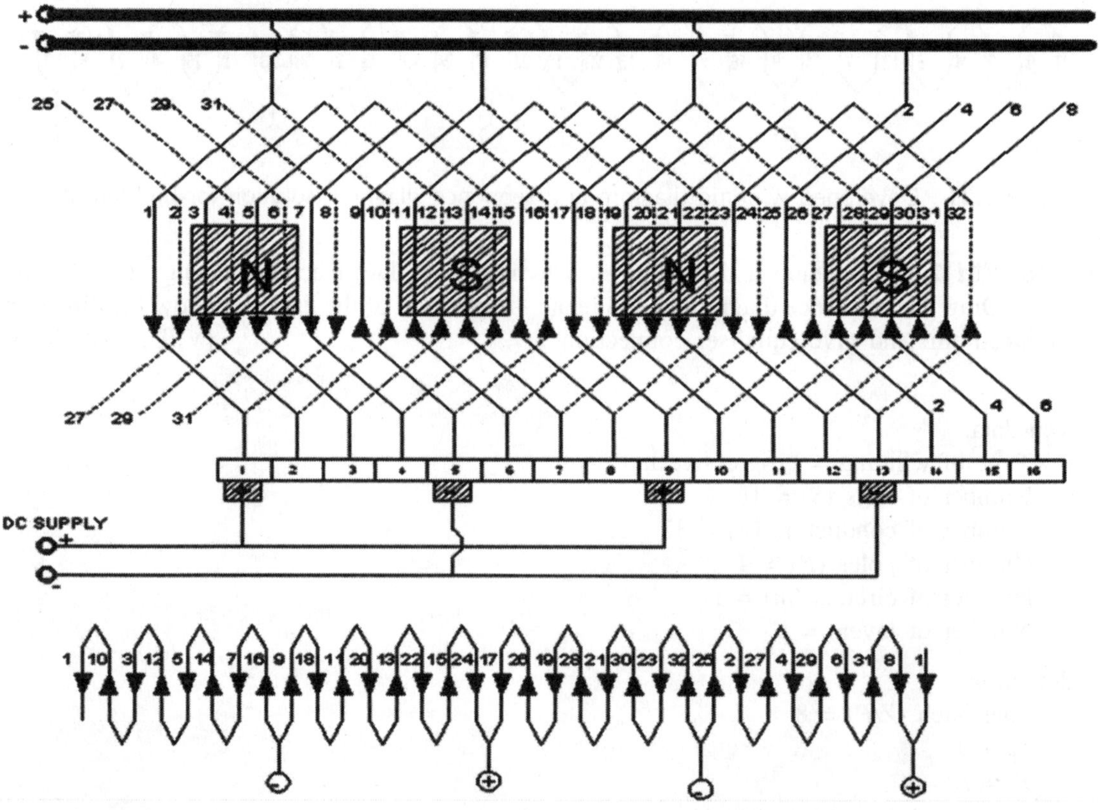

Figure 2.32 Developed winding diagram and sequence diagram (solution for problem 2.6).

PROBLEM 2.7: Design and draw developed duplex winding diagram for 18 slots, double layer, 4 pole and progressive lap winding. Draw the sequence diagram. Show the positions of brush and direction of current. (VTU, June 2013)

Solution:

Given data:

Type of winding = Progressive lap
Number of slots (S) = 18
Number of conductors (Z) = 36
Number of poles (P) = 4
Number of circuits (m) = 2
Number of layers = 2

Calculation:

Pole pitch (Z/P) = 9
$Y_b = 11$
$Y_f = 7$

Now, develop the winding table so as to establish the coil connection in various slots as shown in Table 2.7(a) and 2.7(b). Figure 2.33 shows the developed winding diagram along with the sequence diagram.

TABLE 2.7(a) Winding table: Circuit 1

At the back $Y_b = 11$	*At the front* $Y_f = 7$
1 + 11 = 12	12 − 7 = 5
5 + 11 = 16	16 − 7 = 9
9 + 11 = 20	20 − 7 = 13
13 + 11 = 24	24 − 7 = 17
17 + 11 = 28	28 − 7 = 21
21 + 11 = 32	32 − 7 = 25
25 + 11 = 36	36 − 7 = 29
29 + 11 = 40(4)	40 − 7 = 33
33 + 11 = 44(8)	44 − 7 = 37(1)

TABLE 2.7(b) Winding table: Circuit 2

At the back $Y_b = 11$	*At the front* $Y_f = 7$
3 + 11 = 14	14 − 7 = 7
7 + 11 = 18	18 − 7 = 11
11 + 11 = 22	22 − 7 = 15
15 + 11 = 26	26 − 7 = 19
19 + 11 = 30	30 − 7 = 23
23 + 11 = 34	34 − 7 = 27
27 + 11 = 38(2)	38 − 7 = 31
31 + 11 = 42(6)	42 − 7 = 35
35 + 11 = 46(10)	46 − 7 = 39(3)

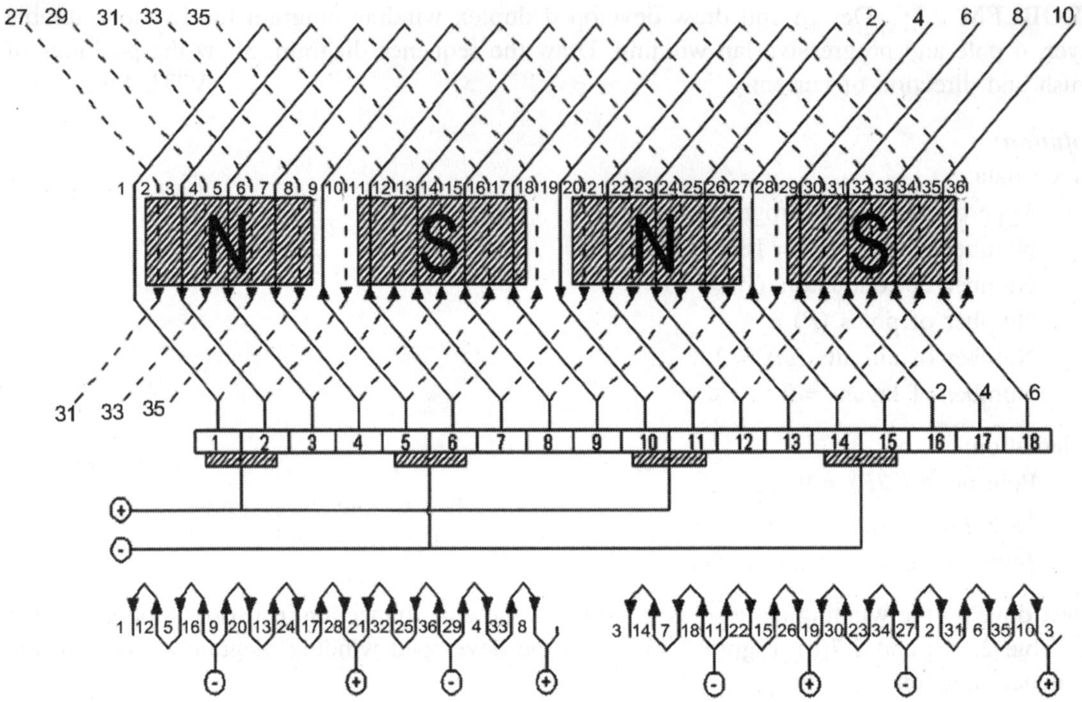

Figure 2.33 Developed winding diagram and sequence diagram (solution for problem 2.7).

PROBLEM 2.8: Design and draw a duplex winding diagram of a DC machine with 32 conductors and 4 poles. Draw the sequence diagram. Fix the position and polarity of brushes. (VTU, June 2013)

Solution:

Given data:

Type of winding = Progressive lap
Number of slots (S) = 16
Number of conductors (Z) = 32
Number of poles (P) = 4
Number of circuits (m) = 2
Number of layers = 2

Calculation:

Pole pitch (Z/P) = 8
$Y_b = 9$
$Y_f = 5$

Now, develop the winding table so as to establish the coil connection in various slots as shown in Table 2.8(a) and 2.8(b). Figure 2.34 shows the developed winding diagram along with the sequence diagram.

TABLE 2.8(a) Winding table: Circuit 1

At the back $Y_b = 9$	*At the front* $Y_f = 5$
1 + 9 = 10	10 – 5 = 5
5 + 9 = 14	14 – 5 = 9
9 + 9 = 18	18 – 5 = 13
13 + 9 = 22	22 – 5 = 17
17 + 9 = 26	26 – 5 = 21
21 + 9 = 30	30 – 5 = 25
25 + 9 = 34(2)	34 – 5 = 29
29 + 9 = 38(6)	38 – 5 = 33(1)

TABLE 2.8(b) Winding table: Circuit 2

At the back $Y_b = 9$	*At the front* $Y_f = 5$
3 + 9 = 12	12 – 5 = 7
7 + 9 = 16	16 – 5 = 11
11 + 9 = 20	20 – 5 = 15
15 + 9 = 24	24 – 5 = 19
19 + 9 = 28	28 – 5 = 23
23 + 9 = 32	32 – 5 = 27
27 + 9 = 36(4)	36 – 5 = 31
31 + 9 = 40(8)	40 – 5 = 35(3)

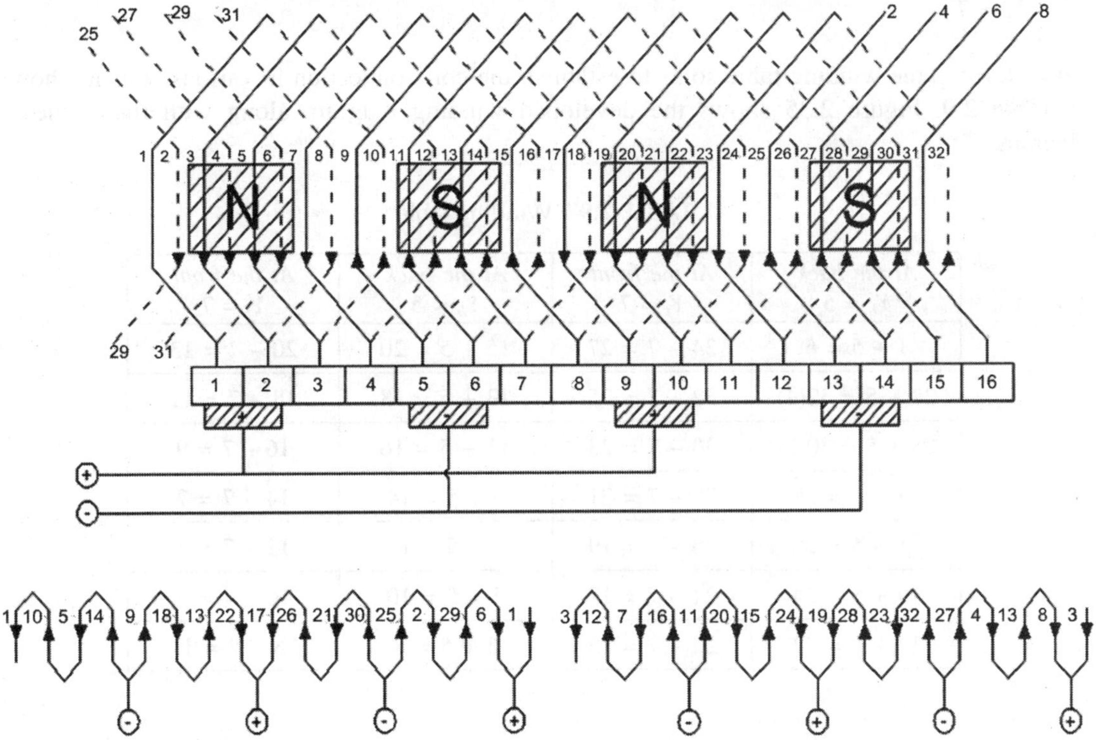

Figure 2.34 Developed winding diagram and sequence diagram (solution for problem 2.8).

PROBLEM 2.9: Draw the armature winding of a DC machine with 4 poles, 14 slots and double layer retrogressive lap. Show the position of brush and direction of induced emf. Draw the sequence diagram, show position of brush and direction of induced emf. Also draw the sequence diagram and show position of brush of current. (VTU, June 2013)

Solution:

Given data:

Type of winding = Retrogressive lap
Number of slots = 14
Number of conductors (Z) = 28
Number of poles (P) = 4
Number of circuits (m) = 1
Number of layers = 2

Calculation:

Pole pitch (Z/P) = 7
$Y_b = 5$
$Y_f = 7$

Now, develop the winding table so as to establish the coil connection in various slots as shown in Table 2.9. Figure 2.35 shows the developed winding diagram along with the sequence diagram.

TABLE 2.9 Winding table

At the back $Y_b = 5$	*At the front* $Y_f = 7$	*At the back* $Y_b = 5$	*At the front* $Y_f = 7$
1 + 5 = 6	34 – 7 = 27	15 + 5 = 20	20 – 7 = 13
27 + 5 = 32(4)	32 – 7 = 25	13 + 5 = 18	18 – 7 = 11
25 + 5 = 30(2)	30 – 7 = 23	11 + 5 = 16	16 – 7 = 9
23 + 5 = 28	28 – 7 = 21	9 + 5 = 14	14 – 7 = 7
21 + 5 = 26	26 – 7 = 19	7 + 5 = 12	12 – 7 = 5
19 + 5 = 24	24 – 7 = 17	5 + 5 = 10	10 – 7 = 3
17 + 5 = 22	22 – 7 = 15	3 + 5 = 8	8 – 7 = 1

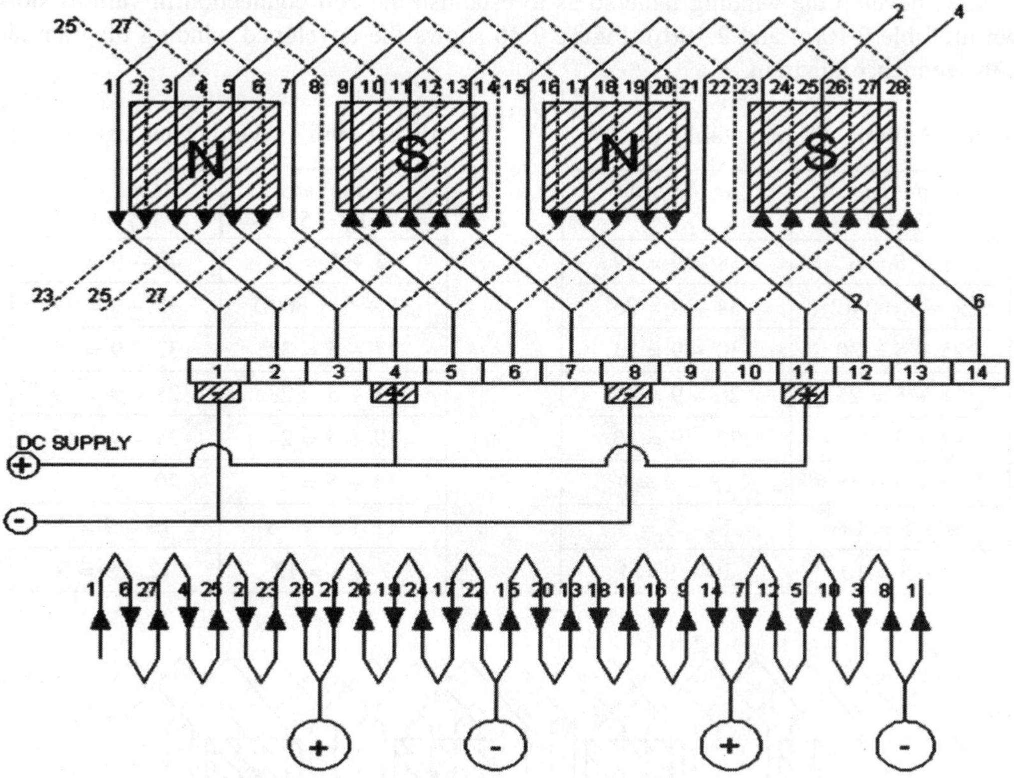

Figure 2.35 Developed winding diagram and sequence diagram (solution for problem 2.9).

PROBLEM 2.10: Draw the armature winding of a DC machine with 4 poles, 16 slots and duplex double layer retrogressive lap. Show the position of brush and direction of induced emf. Draw the sequence diagram, show position of brush and direction of induced emf. Also draw the sequence diagram and show position of brush of current.

Solution:

Given data:

Type of winding = Lap (retrogressive)

Number of slots = 16

Number of conductors (Z) = 32

Number of poles (P) = 4

Number of circuits (m) = 2

Number of layers = 2

Calculation:

Pole pitch (Z/P) = 8

$Y_b = 5$

$Y_f = 9$

Now, develop the winding table so as to establish the coil connection in various slots as shown in Table 2.10(a) and 2.10(b). Figure 2.36 shows the developed winding diagram along with the sequence diagram.

TABLE 2.10(a) Winding table: Circuit 1

At the back $Y_b = 5$	*At the front* $Y_f = 9$
1 + 5 = 6	38 – 9 = 29
29 + 5 = 34(2)	34 – 9 = 25
25 + 5 = 30	30 – 9 = 21
21 + 5 = 26	26 – 9 = 17
17 + 5 = 22	22 – 9 = 13
13 + 5 = 18	18 – 9 = 9
9 + 5 = 14	14 – 9 = 5
5 + 5 = 10	10 – 9 = 1

TABLE 2.10(b) Winding table: Circuit 2

At the back $Y_b = 5$	*At the front* $Y_f = 9$
3 + 5 = 8	40 – 9 = 31
31 + 5 = 36(4)	36 – 9 = 27
27 + 5 = 32	32 – 9 = 23
23 + 5 = 28	28 – 9 = 19
19 + 5 = 24	24 – 9 = 15
15 + 5 = 20	20 – 9 = 11
11 + 5 = 16	16 – 9 = 7
7 + 5 = 12	12 – 9 = 3

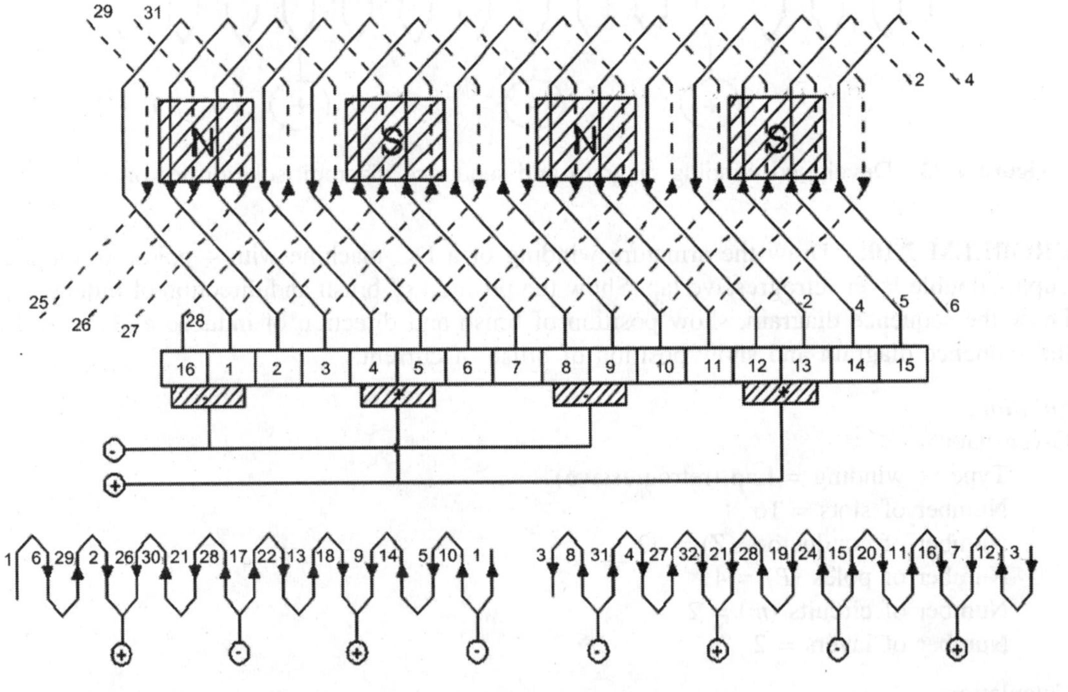

Figure 2.36 Developed winding diagram and sequence diagram (solution for problem 2.10).

PROBLEM 2.11: Draw the armature winding of a DC machine with 6 poles, 21 slots and simplex double layer retrogressive lap. Show the position of brush and direction of induced emf. Draw the sequence diagram, show position of brush and direction of induced emf. Also draw the sequence diagram and show position of brush of current.

Solution:

Given data:

Type of winding = Retrogressive lap
Number of slots = 21
Number of conductors (Z) = 42
Number of poles (P) = 6
Number of circuits (m) = 1
Number of layers = 2

Calculation:

Pole pitch (Z/P) = 7
$Y_b = 7$
$Y_f = 9$

Now, develop the winding table so as to establish the coil connection in various slots as shown in Table 2.11. Figure 2.37 shows the developed winding diagram along with the sequence diagram.

TABLE 2.11 Winding table

At the back $Y_b = 7$	*At the front* $Y_f = 9$	*At the back* $Y_b = 7$	*At the front* $Y_f = 9$
1 + 7 = 8	8 – 9 = (–1)41	21 + 7 = 28	28 – 9 = 19
41 + 7 = 48(6)	48 – 9 = 39	19 + 7 = 26	26 – 9 = 17
39 + 7 = 46(4)	46 – 9 = 37	17 + 7 = 24	24 – 9 = 15
37 + 7 = 44(2)	44 – 9 = 35	15 + 7 = 22	22 – 9 = 13
35 + 7 = 42	42 – 9 = 33	13 + 7 = 20	20 – 9 = 11
33 + 7 = 40	40 – 9 = 31	11 + 7 = 18	18 – 9 = 9
31 + 7 = 38	38 – 9 = 29	9 + 7 = 16	16 – 9 = 7
29 + 7 = 36	36 – 9 = 27	7 + 7 = 14	14 – 9 = 5
27 + 7 = 34	34 – 9 = 25	5 + 7 = 12	12 – 9 = 3
25 + 7 = 32	32 – 9 = 23	3 + 7 = 10	10 – 9 = 1
23 + 7 = 30	30 – 9 = 21		

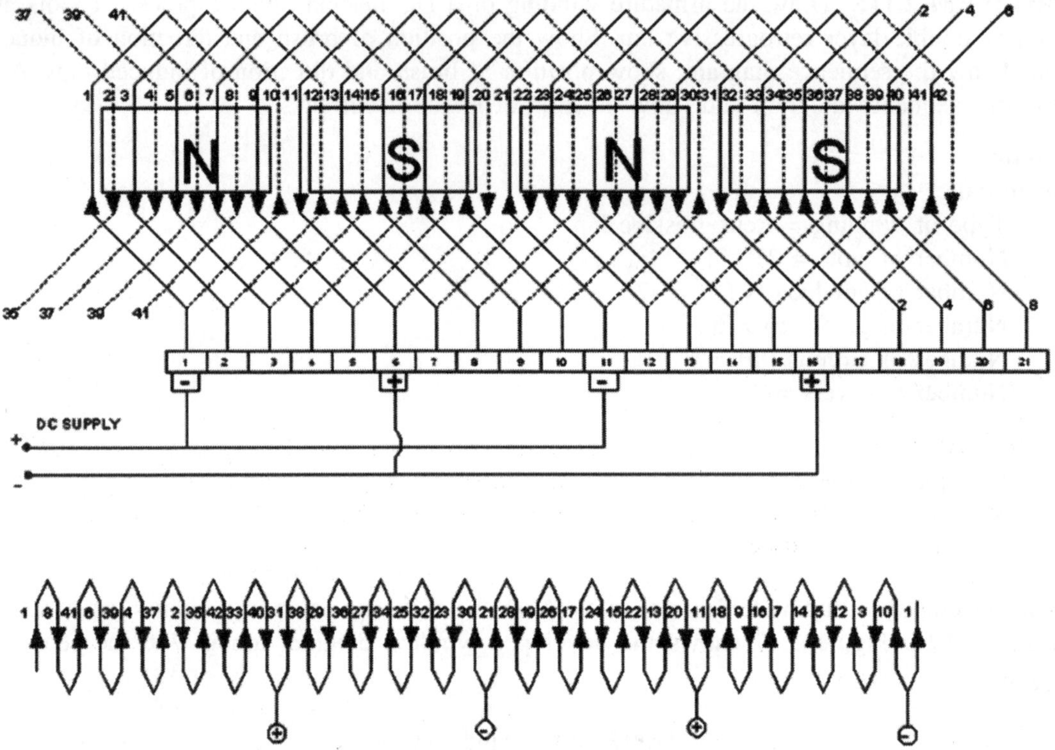

Figure 2.37 Developed winding diagram and sequence diagram (solution for problem 2.11).

PROBLEM 2.12: Draw the armature winding of a DC machine with 2 poles, 12 slots and simplex single layer retrogressive lap. Show the position of brush and direction of induced emf. Draw the sequence diagram, show position of brush and direction of induced emf. Also draw the sequence diagram and show position of brush of current.

Solution:

Given data:

Type of winding = Retrogressive lap
Number of slots = 12
Number of conductors (Z) = 12
Number of poles (P) = 2
Number of circuits (m) = 1
Number of layers = 1

Calculation:

Pole pitch (Z/P) = 6
$Y_b = 5$
$Y_f = 7$

Now, develop the winding table so as to establish the coil connection in various slots as shown in Table 2.12. Figure 2.38 shows the developed winding diagram along with the sequence diagram.

TABLE 2.12 Winding table

S. No.	*At the back* $Y_b = 5$	*At the front* $Y_f = 7$
1	1 + 5 = 6	6 – 7 = (–1)11
2	11 + 5 = 16(4)	16 – 7 = 9
3	9 + 5 = 14(2)	14 – 7 = 7
4	7 + 5 = 12	12 – 7 = 5
5	5 + 5 = 10	10 – 7 = 3
6	3 + 5 = 8	8 – 7 = 1

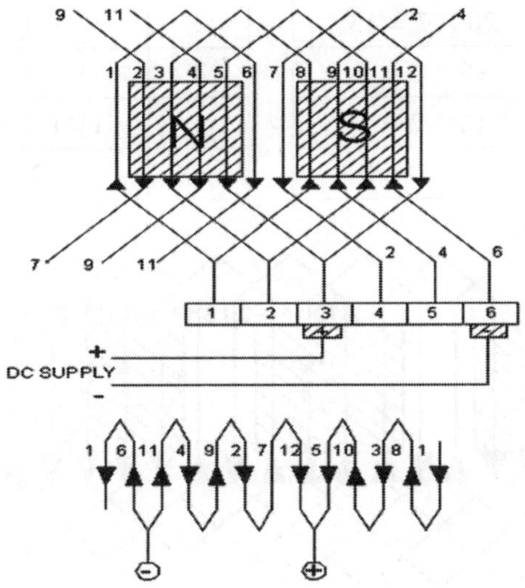

Figure 2.38 Developed winding diagram and sequence diagram (solution for problem 2.12).

PROBLEM 2.13: Draw the armature winding of a DC machine with 4 poles, 24 slots and simplex single layer retrogressive lap. Show the position of brush and direction of induced emf. Draw the sequence diagram, show position of brush and direction of induced emf. Also draw the sequence diagram and show position of brush of current.

Solution:

Given data:

Type of winding = Retrogressive lap

Number of slots = 24

Number of conductors (Z) = 24

Number of poles (P) = 4

Number of circuits (m) = 2

Number of layers = 1

Calculation:

Pole pitch = 6

$Y_b = 3$

$Y_f = 7$

Now, develop the winding table so as to establish the coil connection in various slots as shown in Table 2.13(a) and 2.13(b). Figure 2.39 shows the developed winding diagram along with the sequence diagram.

TABLE 2.13(a) Winding table: Circuit 1

S. No.	*At the back* $Y_b = 3$	*At the front* $Y_f = 7$
1	1 + 3 = 4	4 – 7 = (–3) 21
2	21 + 3 = 24	24 – 7 = 17
3	17 + 3 = 20	20 – 7 = 13
4	13 + 3 = 16	16 – 7 = 9
5	9 + 3 = 12	12 – 7 = 5
6	5 + 3 = 8	8 – 7 = 1

TABLE 2.13(b) Winding table: Circuit 2

S. No.	*At the back* $Y_b = 3$	*At the front* $Y_f = 7$
1	3 + 3 = 6	6 – 7 = (–1)23
2	23 + 3 = 26(2)	26 – 7 = 19
3	19 + 3 = 22	22 – 7 = 15
4	15 + 3 = 18	18 – 7 = 11
5	11 + 3 = 14	14 – 7 = 7
6	7 + 3 = 10	10 – 7 = 3

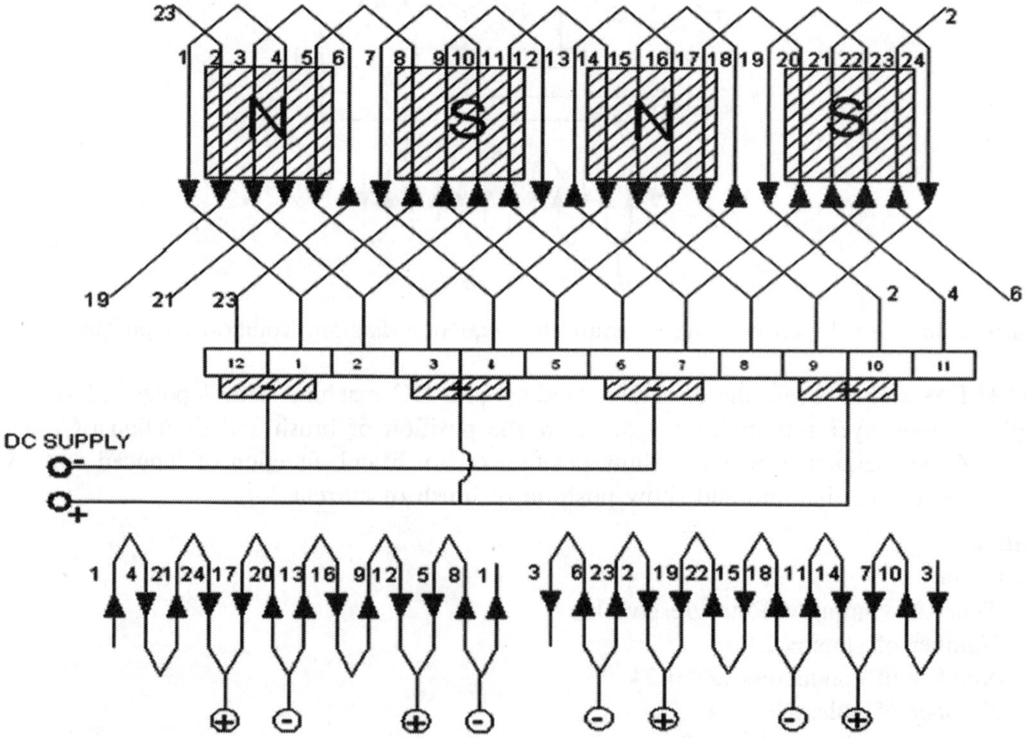

Figure 2.39 Developed winding diagram and sequence diagram (solution for problem 2.13).

SUMMARY

<table>
<tr><th>Winding</th><th>Type</th><th></th></tr>
<tr><td rowspan="2">DC lap winding</td><td>Simplex lap winding</td><td>
• The difference between Y_b and Y_f is always 2. Y_b will be greater than Y_f in progressive winding and vice-versa.
• Both Y_b and Y_f are always odd numbers.
• The number of parallel paths in the armature is always equal to the number of poles in the machine.
• The number of brushes in the machine is also equal to the number of poles and brushes occupy only one commutator segment.
• From the winding table, it can also be seen that the difference is 2 in each row.
• Only one sequence diagram can be drawn referring to the winding table.
• Winding might be single layer, double layer and multi-layer winding.
1. In a single layer winding, the number of conductors is equal to the number of slots in the armature; hence one conductor is placed in each slot of the armature. The number of commutator segments will always be half of the number of conductors in the armature.
2. In a double layer winding, the number of conductors will always be twice as that of number of slots. In this case, one conductor overlaps the other in each slot and hence while representation, one conductor that is visible is represented in thick line and the conductor which is being over lapped is represented in dotted line format. The back and front pitch connection to the conductors represented in dotted line format should also be represented in dotted lines in case of double layer.
Note: Double layer winding and duplex winding are not the same.
3. In a multi-layer winding, there are many conductors in each slot of the armature.
</td></tr>
<tr><td>Duplex lap winding</td><td>
• The difference between Y_b and Y_f is always 4. Y_b will be greater than Y_f in progressive winding and vice-versa.
• Both Y_b and Y_f are always odd numbers.
• The number of parallel paths in the armature is always equal to the number of poles in the machine.
• The number of brushes in the machine is twice the number of poles and brushes occupy two commutator segment.
• From the winding table it can also be seen that the difference is 4 in each row. There are two winding tables formed for this, i.e., if table is started from conductor 1, then the next conductor on back pitch side is 5 and the table ends at 1. Now, the next table will start from the conductor 3 and so on even the sequence diagram drawn will be 2 diagrams referring to the winding table.
• Winding might be single layer, double layer and multi-layer winding.
</td></tr>
</table>

EXERCISES

1. What is lap winding and where is it employed? State the various names of lap winding.
2. State the difference between duplex lap and double layer winding.
3. When is simplex lap and duplex lap utilised?
4. Briefly state the advantages of using equaliser rings in a DC machine.
5. Develop a single turn lap winding diagram for a DC machine having 18 armature slots, two conductors per slot and 6 poles. Mark the poles and draw the sequence diagram. Indicate the position of the brushes and show the direction of induced emf.
6. Develop a simplex parallel winding diagram for DC machine and show the equaliser rings along the direction of induced emf. With 4 poles, flux/pole = 0.366 wb, the speed of the machine is 1500 rpm and induced emf is 220 V. Use 2 equaliser rings.
7. Develop the duplex single layer lap winding diagram for a DC machine having pole pitch = 6 and poles = 4.
8. Develop a duplex double layer parallel winding diagram for a DC machine with 32 conductors and 4 brushes.
9. Develop the duplex lap winding for a DC machine with 26 conductors, 4 brushes and $Y_b < Y_f$.
10. Develop a single layer one turn winding diagram for a DC machine with front pitch = 7 and the back pitch is less than the front pitch. The number of brushes and number of parallel paths is equal to 6.
11. Develop the single layer simplex progressive winding diagram for DC machine. The first conductor is connected to the 6th conductor away from the commutator side. The parallel path and the number of poles in the machine is twice that of the back pitch. Show the direction of induced emf, place the brush and also show equaliser ring and also substantiate the number of equaliser rings.
12. Develop a duplex lap winding table for a DC machine housing 2 conductors per slot. The number of slots in the machine is 32 and pole is 4.
13. Develop a triplex lap winding table for a DC machine housing 4 conductors per slot. The number of slots in the machine is 32 and pole is 4.
14. Develop the duplex winding diagram for a 4 pole DC machine. The 5th conductor is connected to the 14th conductor on the commutator side. The parallel path and the number of poles is one less than that of the connection away from the commutator side. Show the direction of induced emf, place the brush and also show equaliser ring and also substantiate the number of equaliser rings.
15. A DC machine as 18 armature slots with 2 conductors per slot and 6 poles. Develop a lap winding diagram for the DC machine and mark the poles. Draw the sequence diagram and indicate the position of the brushes and also show the direction of induced emf.
16. A 25 kW DC generator has a 6 pole lap connected armature of 312 conductors. How would you change the connections to the commutator to form two armature circuits and what effect would this change have on the voltage, current and output of the machine?

3 DC Wave Winding

Learning Objectives

This chapter illustrates wave winding format employed in DC machines, its design and applications and using the AutoCAD software to develop the wave winding diagrams in a step by step manner.

3.1 INTRODUCTION

Wave winding is usually employed in DC machines in which high voltage and low current is required. Generally, wave winding is employed in DC generators. Unlike the lap winding as illustrated in Chapter 2, here the winding progresses just like a wave as shown in Figure 3.1, hence named as wave winding. When the windings are connected in series, the voltage of each winding adds, but the current capacity remains the same. The two ends of each coil are connected to commutator segments separated by the distance between poles. This configuration allows the series addition of the voltages in all the windings between brushes. When the end connections of the coils are spread apart as shown in Figure 3.1, a wave or series winding is formed. In a wave winding there are only two paths regardless of the number of poles, hence

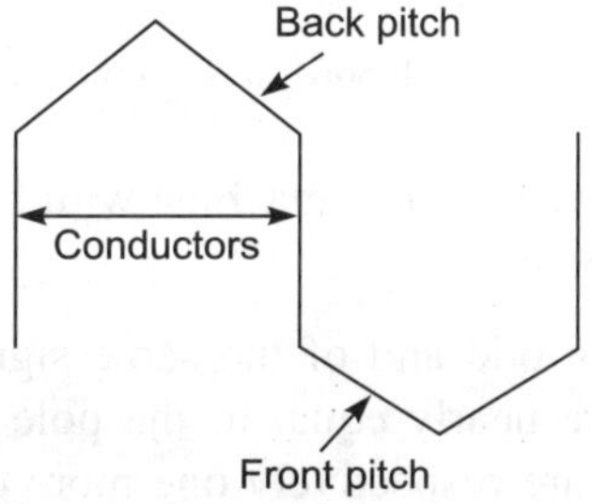

Figure 3.1 Wave winding.

it requires only two brushes but can use as many brushes as poles. Wave winding requires only one pair of brushes, i.e., one positive and one negative brush.

In this type, the winding progresses in one direction round the armature in a series of waves. If after passing once round the armature, the winding falls in a slot to the right of its starting point then winding is said to be progressive wave winding, i.e., if an armature slot is named as 1 to start the winding as shown in Figure 3.2 and once round the armature if the winding falls to the right of the starting point, it is termed as *progressive winding*.

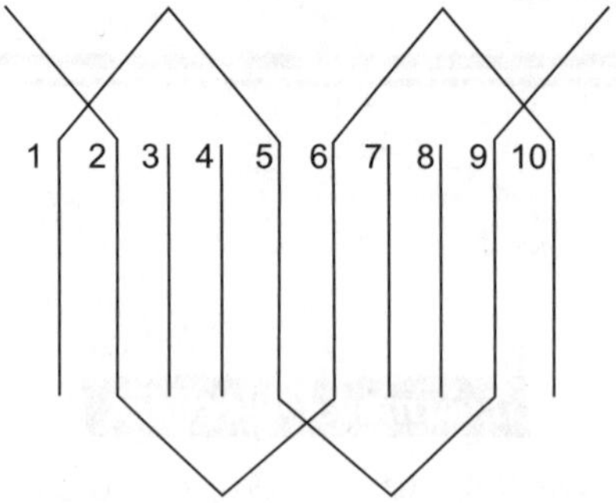

Figure 3.2 Progressive wave winding.

If after passing once round the armature, the winding falls in a slot to the left of its starting point then winding is said to be retrogressive wave winding, i.e., if an armature slot is named as 1 to start the winding as shown in Figure 3.3 and once round the armature if the winding falls to the nth slot or the last slot which is at left of the starting point, then it is termed as *retrogressive winding*.

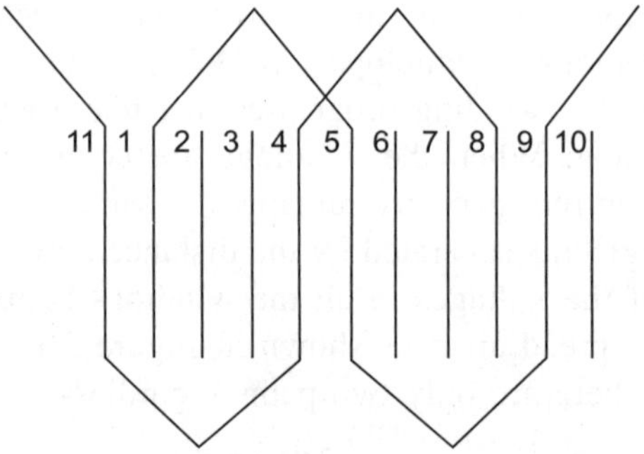

Figure 3.3 Retrogressive wave winding.

While designing wave winding for a DC machine with high voltage rating and low current, following criterions should be noted:

1. Both pitches Y_b and Y_f are odd and of the same sign.
2. Back and front pitches are nearly equal to the pole pitch and may be equal or differ by 2, in which case, they are respectively one more or one less than the average pitch.

3. Resultant pitch $Y_r = Y_f + Y_b$. If this is divisible by 2 and odd then both Y_f and Y_b are equal. If not they are unequal and differ by 2. Also $Y_r = (2C \pm 2)/(P/2)$.
4. Pole pitch $Z/P = (Y_f + Y_b)/2$
5. The average pitch which must be an integer is given by $Y_a = (Z \pm 2)/P$ = (Number of commutator bars ± 1)/Number of poles
6. It is obvious from 5 that for a wave winding, the number of armature conductors with 2 either added or subtracted must be a multiple of the number of poles of the generator. This restriction eliminates many even numbers which are unsuitable for this winding.
7. The number of armature parallel paths = $2m$, where 'm' is the multiplicity of the winding.

3.2 SIMPLEX AND DUPLEX WAVE WINDING

Just similar to lap winding in DC machines, if the difference between back pitch and front pitch is 2 then it is called as simplex wave winding. If the difference is 4 then it is called as duplex wave winding.

3.3 DUMMY COIL IN WAVE WINDING

While performing wave winding in DC machines, a special care is to be taken to see that the commutator pitch Y_c is an integer and not a fraction. If the commutator pitch is a fractional number then at that instance performing wave winding becomes impossible. The commutator pitch can be calculated as given below:

$$Y_c = \frac{C+1}{P/2} \quad \text{or} \quad Y_r/2$$

where, Y_c is the commutator pitch and C is the number of coils.

If Y_c is a fraction then wave winding is not possible and it is necessary to make one coil as dummy or inactive or dead coil.

Dummy coils are nothing but electrically inactive coils which are placed in the slots of the armature but not connected to any other conductor or coil such that they do not carry any current. The terminal of the dummy coil on the commutator side of the armature is cut-off and suitably taped and thus the dummy coil ends are left open.

If the commutator pitch Y_c does not give an integer by value with the given number of coils then Y_c is made an integer by considering one coil as dummy.

For example: If number of coils = 20 and number of poles = 4 then

$$Y_c = \frac{C+1}{P/2}$$

$$Y_c = \frac{20 \pm 1}{4/2} = 21/2 \quad \text{or} \quad (19/2)$$

Now, from the above example, commutator pitch is a fraction, so wave winding is not possible. Hence in this case, make 1 coil as dummy.

$$Y_c = \frac{19+1}{2} = 10 \text{ (+ for progressive)}$$

$$= 9 \text{ (– for retrogressive)}$$

Number of commutator segments = number of active coils

= (*Z*/*P*)(without dummy coils)

= (total number of coils–1)(with dummy coils)

Note: Even though dummy coil does not carry any current, it exists as a prime member in the winding. The main reasons for this are:

- To provide mechanical balancing.
- The number of slots in the machine is always predefined and manufactured depending upon the standards and requirements. Henceforth when wave winding is to be performed on the machine posing standard number of slots, which might result in the commutator pitch being a fraction, then making a coil dummy is very much essential.

3.4 SOLVED PROBLEMS

PROBLEM 3.1: Develop a single layer simplex progressive wave winding for a DC machine with 4 poles and 24 slots. Show the position of brush and direction of induced emf. Draw the sequence diagram, show position of brush and direction of induced emf.

Solution:

Analysing the problem: This particular problem states us to develop a single layer progressive wave winding diagram for a DC machine having 24 armature conductors and 4 poles. Drawing sequence diagram helps us to analyse the flow of current and helps to locate the brushes.

Given data:

Number of poles (P) = 4

In single layer, number of conductors (Z) = slots = 24

Step 1: First calculate the pole pitch, front pitch Y_f and back pitch Y_b.

Hence, pole pitch (Z/P) = 24/4 = 6.

Therefore,

$$\boxed{Y_b = 7} \quad \text{and} \quad \boxed{Y_f = 7}$$

Step 2: Now, develop the winding table so as to establish the coil connection in various slots as shown in Table 3.1.

TABLE 3.1 Winding table

At the back $Y_b = 7$	*At the front* $Y_f = 7$	*At the back* $Y_b = 7$	*At the front* $Y_f = 7$
1 + 7 = 8	8 + 7 = 15	13 + 7 = 20	20 + 7 = 27(3)
15 + 7 = 22	22 + 7 = 29	3 + 7 = 10	10 + 7 = 17
5 + 7 = 12	12 + 7 = 19	17 + 7 = 24	24 + 7 = 31(7)
19 + 7 = 26(2)	2 + 7 = 9	7 + 7 = 14	14 + 7 = 21
9 + 7 = 16	16 + 7 = 23	21 + 7 = 28(4)	4 + 7 = 11
23 + 7 = 30(6)	6 + 7 = 13	11 + 7 = 18	18 + 7 = 25

Now, this winding table shows the connection of coils on both front and back pitches.

Steps to develop the winding diagram using CAD:

Step 1: Click on the AutoCAD icon appearing on the computer screen. A new window of AutoCAD will open.

Step 2: Select FILE in the AutoCAD window and open a new drawing (.dwg) file.

Step 3: In the command window type as UNITS ↵, a new dialog box will pop-up as shown in Figure 3.4. In this dialog box select the precision type, lighting and units as required. Generally, the precision set is 0.00, units to scale inserted are millimetres and lighting selected is International as shown in Figure 3.5.

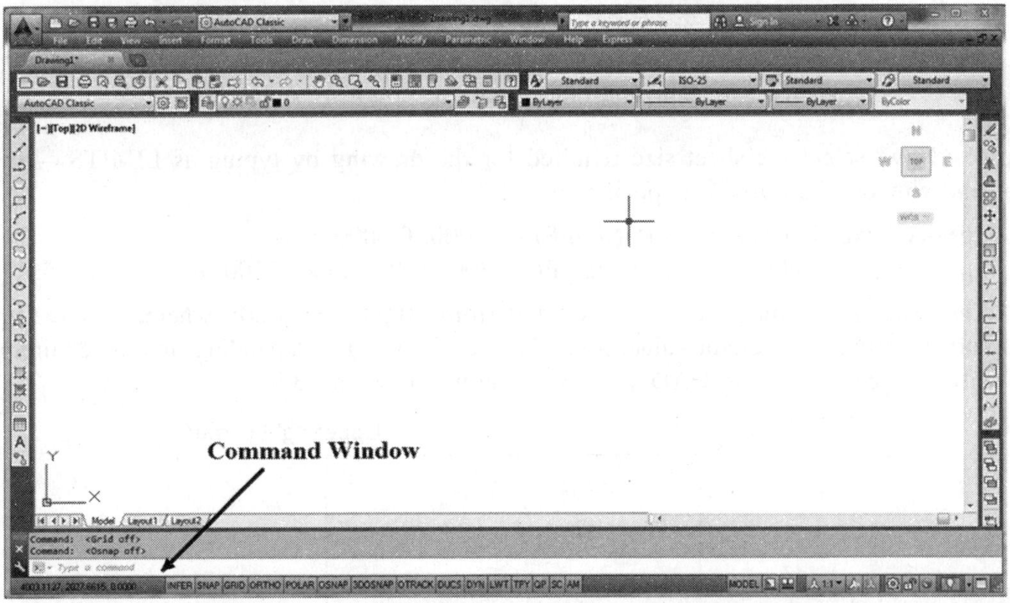

Figure 3.4 Command window, *courtesy:* AutoCAD®.

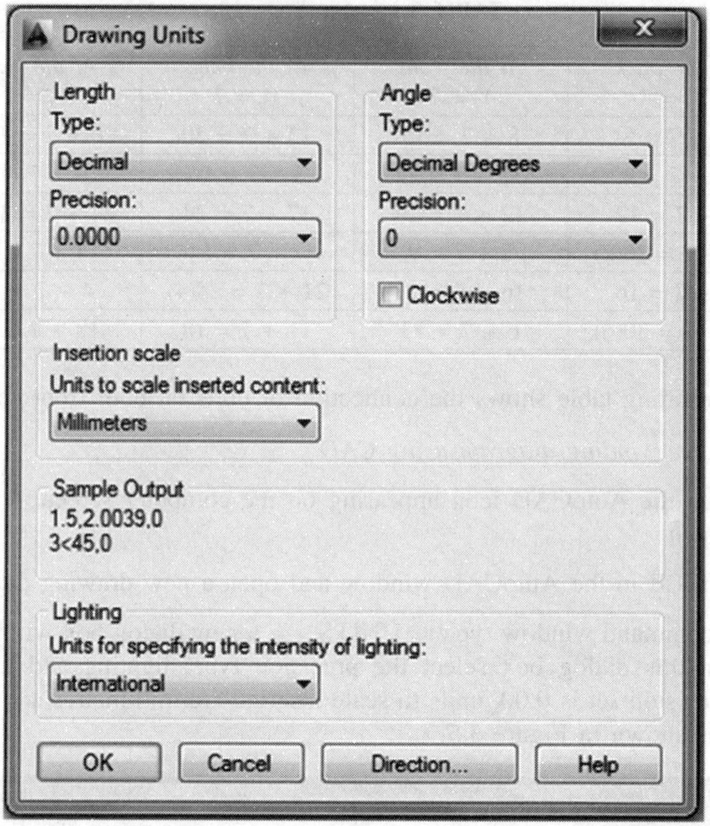

Figure 3.5 Drawing units' window, *courtesy:* AutoCAD®.

Step 4: Now, select the sheet size required for the drawing by typing as LIMITS↵ in the command window, here itself it specifies as:

Specify lower left corner or (ON/OFF) <0.0000, 0.0000>: ↵
Specify upper right corner or (ON/OFF) <300, 300>: 1500, 1500 ↵

The lower left corner should always start from <0.0000, 0.0000> whereas for the upper right corner will have a default value, it can be set to any value depending on our requirement. The setting of page limits in CAD window is shown in Figure 3.6.

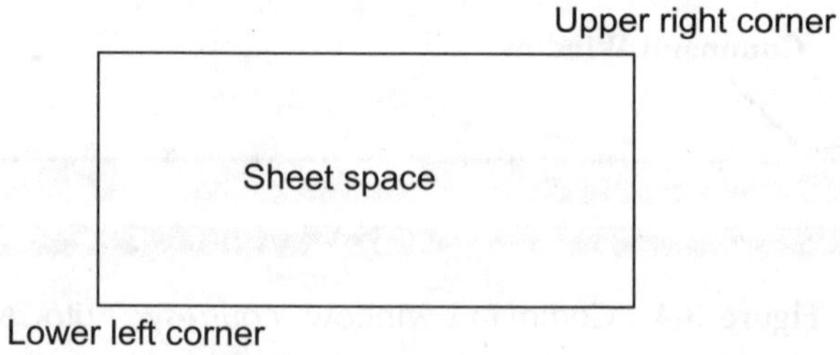

Figure 3.6 Setting of page limits in CAD window.

Step 5: In the command window type as ZOOM↵, it specifies as [All/Centre/Dynamic/Extents/Previous/Scale/Window/Object]<real time>:

Here, specify as All (or shortcut key A)↵. This zooms up the drawing sheet as specified in the limits.

This completes the setting part of the CAD window to the requirement.

Step 6: Select the line icon on the left tool bar of the CAD window. The command window asks to specify the starting point for the line. This can be randomly done by clicking on the CAD window.

Now, command window asks to specify the next point for the line, in the form:

Specify next point or [undo]: @600<90

This should always be done by giving a known dimension for the line and specifying the angle in the above stated manner. Here, 600 represents the length of the line to be drawn and this depends on the limits of the chosen window and < 90 represents the angle at which it is to be drawn as shown in Figure 3.7.

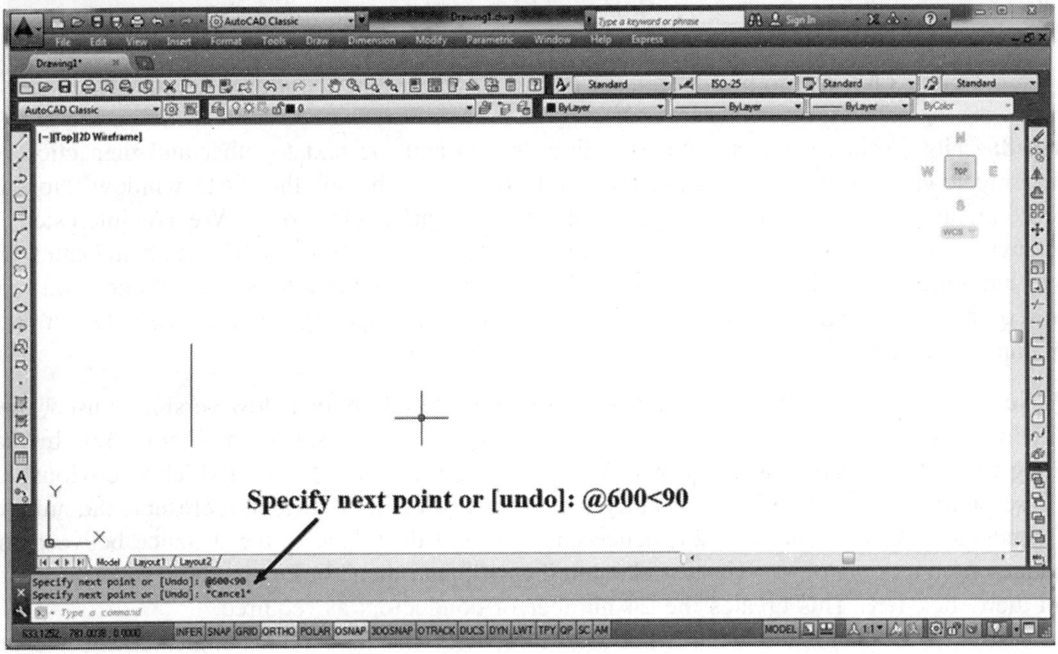

Figure 3.7 Line specifications in command window, *courtesy:* AutoCAD®.

Note: All dimensions are in millimetres (mm). Always ensure that ORTHO is kept on, in order to obtain straight line.

Step 7: Now, click on the icon 'A' available on the toolbar which represents multiline text. Now, select a size and style as shown in Figure 3.8 for the text and then enter the number for the conductor. Then place this number (text) next to the conductor (the line drawn).

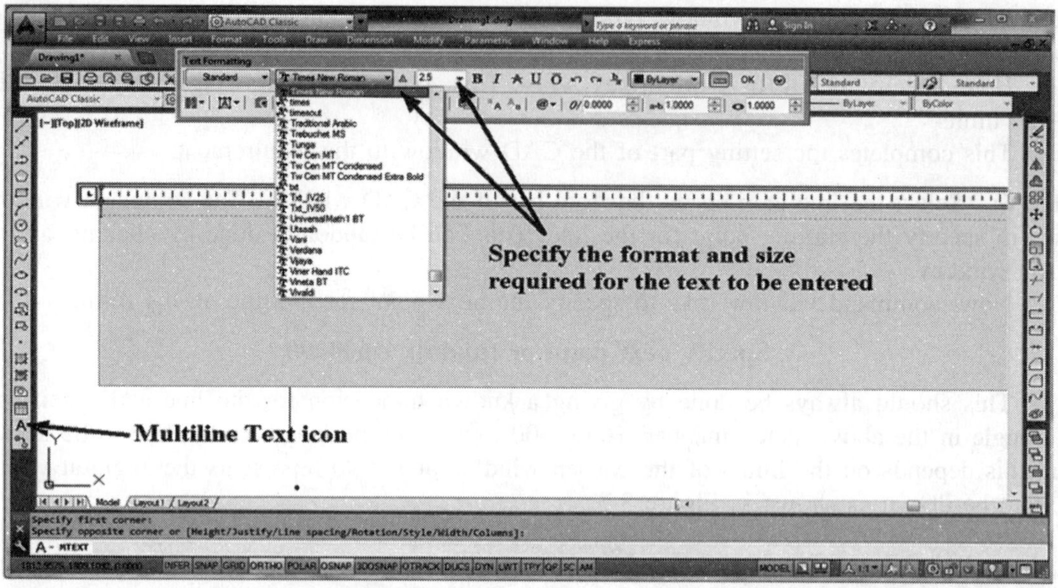

Figure 3.8 Text format to enter a text in CAD window, *courtesy:* AutoCAD®.

Step 8: Now, select the conductor (the line drawn) and the text together and then click on the array icon available on the right hand side of the toolbar of the CAD window. Now in the command window, it asks to specify the base point/ angle/ count. We are interested in rectangular array, hence first select the number of rows, i.e., type as 'r' which indicates the rows and enter as 1, then select or type COL which indicates the number of columns and type the required value which is 24 in this case and enter. Then specify the distance between each column that is 100.

*****Note:** If a lower version of AutoCAD like AutoCAD 2009 or below version is used, then a dialog box will pop-up when array command is selected as shown in Figure 3.9. In that dialog box select rectangular array and then specify the number of rows (which is obviously 1 in case of winding diagrams) then specify the number of columns, which represents the number of conductors. In this case it is 24, hence enter 24 and then specify the distance between the conductors in column offset. Here, it is entered as 100 and then click preview in order to verify and then click OK. This creates the 24 number of conductors as required.

Now in the command window, it asks to specify the base point/ angle/ count. We are interested in rectangular array hence select count, i.e., type ***C*** in command window and enter, and then it asks for the number of rows required and when the value is given it asks for the number of columns required, as soon as the value of columns is given, it asks for the spacing in between the columns, first type as **S** and enter and then give the value.

Step 9: Now, select all the conductors and text and explode it in order to make them individual entity and then click on the text available next to each conductor and edit it in the form of 1, 2, 3, ..., 24 as shown in Figure 3.10.

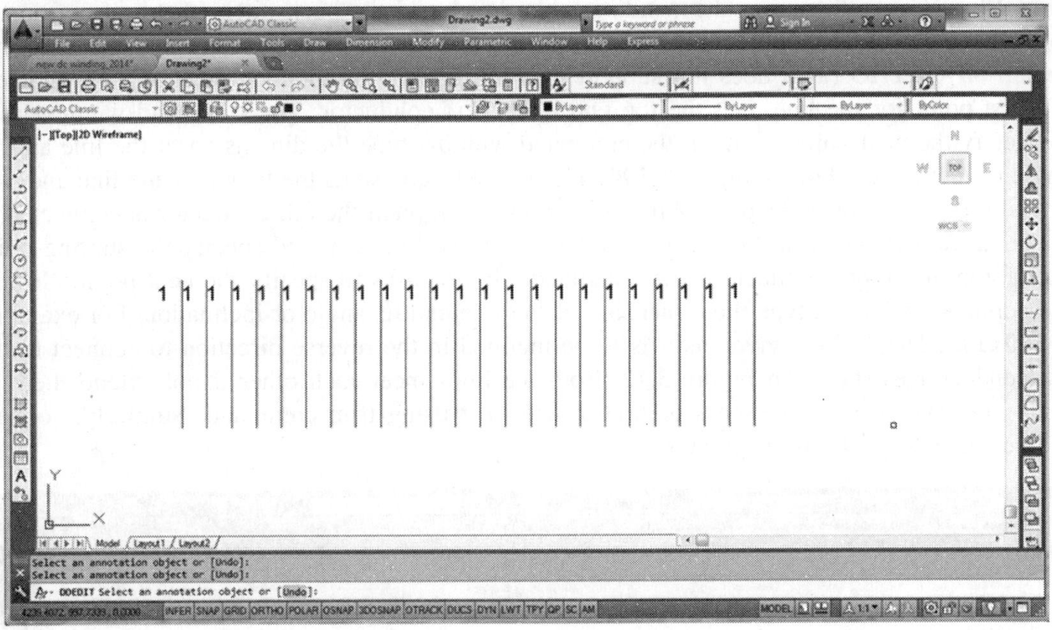

Figure 3.9 Array format to enter an array in CAD window, *courtesy:* AutoCAD®.

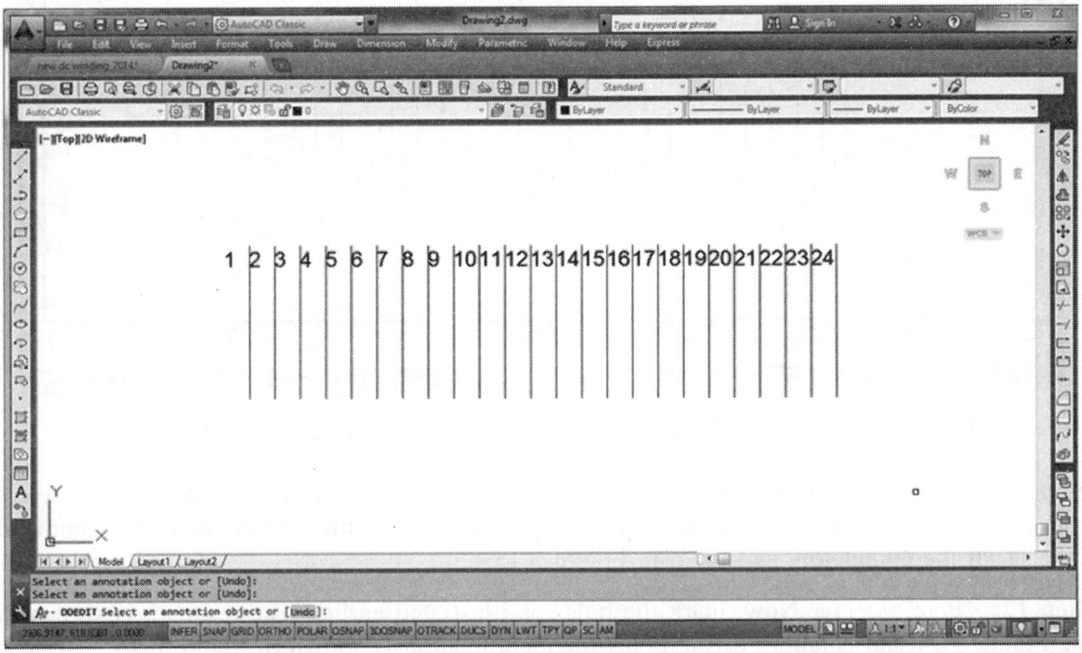

Figure 3.10 Exploding to obtain individual entities from a block in CAD window, *courtesy:* AutoCAD®.

Step 10: Now, referring to the winding table developed the back pitch (that appears on the top) of the 1st conductor is connected to the 8th conductor. Hence, select the line icon and switch off ORTHO (as it does not support drawing lines in an inclined position). Now, select the first point for the line, i.e., the top end of the 1st conductor. The command window asks to specify the next point. Now, in the command window type the dimension of the line and its angle of inclination. For example: **@500<45**, here 500 represents the length of the line and <45 refers to the angle of inclination. After this, in the back pitch the 8th conductor is connected to 1st conductor as shown in Figure 3.11, again select the line icon and specify the starting point on the top of the 8th conductor. The command window asks to specify the next point. Now in the command window, type the dimension of the line and its angle of inclination. For example: **@500<135**. The <135 is given as it is to be inclined in the reverse direction to connect to the 1st conductor as shown in Figure 3.12. Both the lines meet each other if not extend them, if both meet and if there is excess of line then trim it using trim command. Similarly, connect the conductors on the front pitch also.

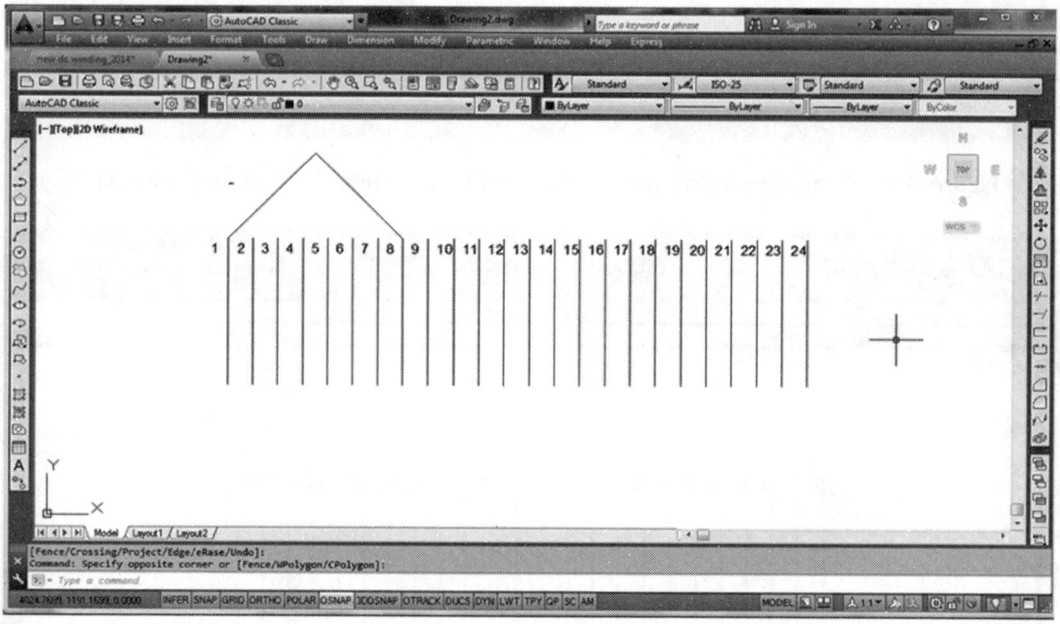

Figure 3.11 Back pitch connection in CAD window, *courtesy:* AutoCAD®.

Step 11: Now, the winding connection for one set of front and back pitch is done. Now, select both the connection of front and back pitch individually and with the help of array command connect all the conductors as shown in Figure 3.13.

Step 12: *Pole placing:* Now, mark the poles as illustrated earlier. The resultant is shown in the Figure 3.14 and hatching of the poles for identification is shown in Figure 3.15.

Step 13: Now, the direction of current is to be assigned. The direction of current in the conductors coming under the influence of North Pole is always towards the downwards whereas in the South Pole, it is in upward direction.

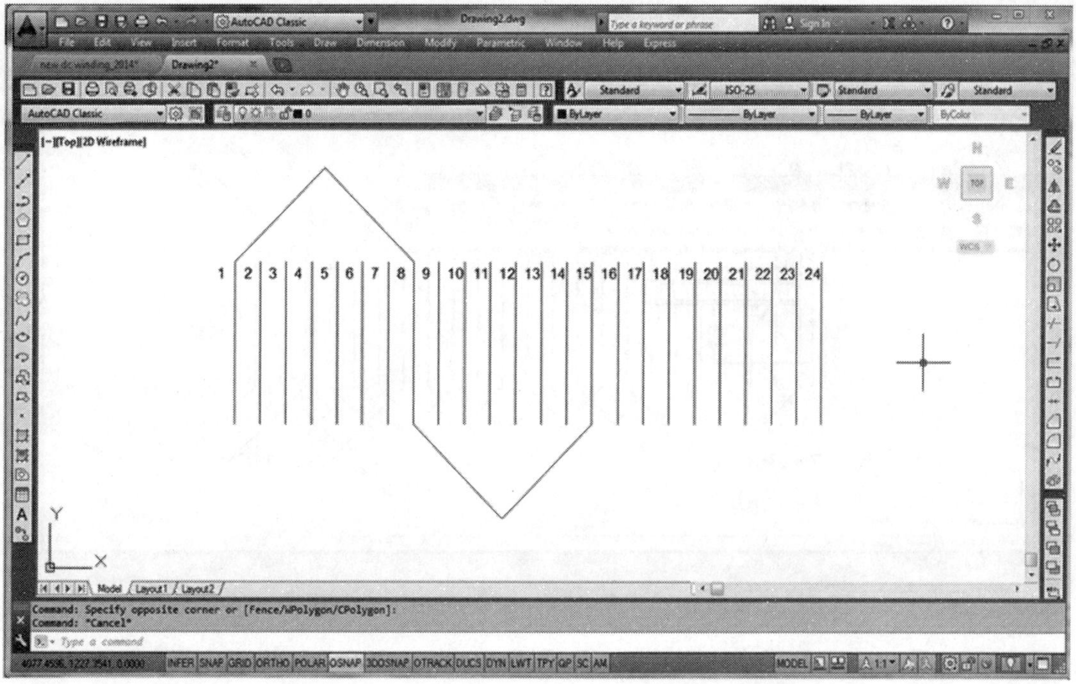

Figure 3.12 Back pitch connection in CAD window, *courtesy:* AutoCAD®.

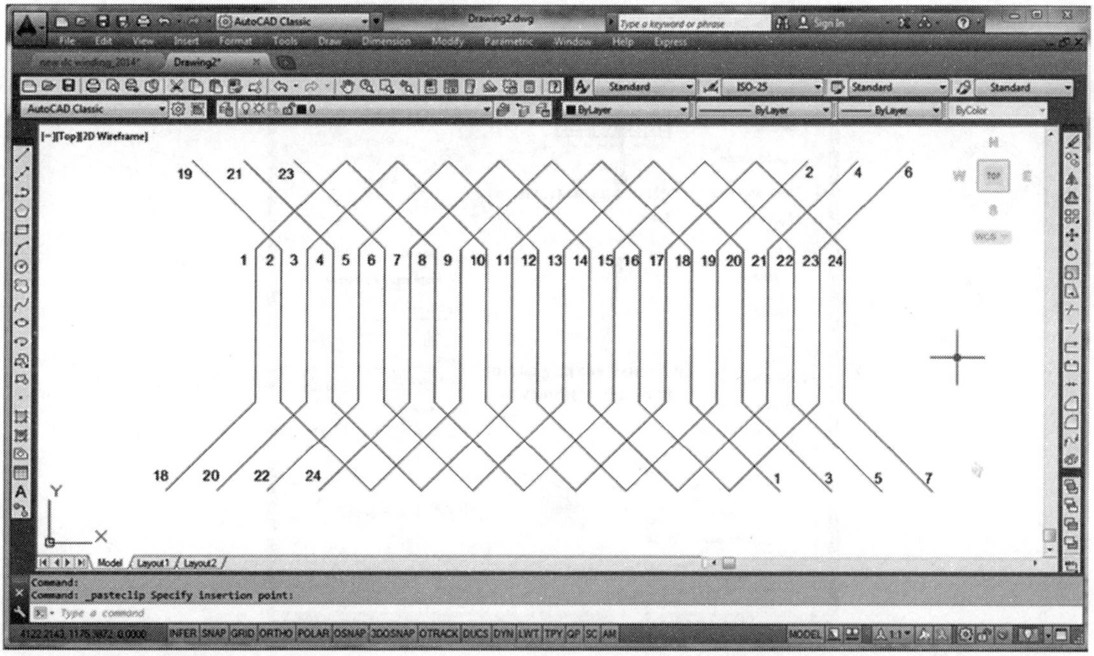

Figure 3.13 Back and front pitch connection in CAD window, *courtesy:* AutoCAD®.

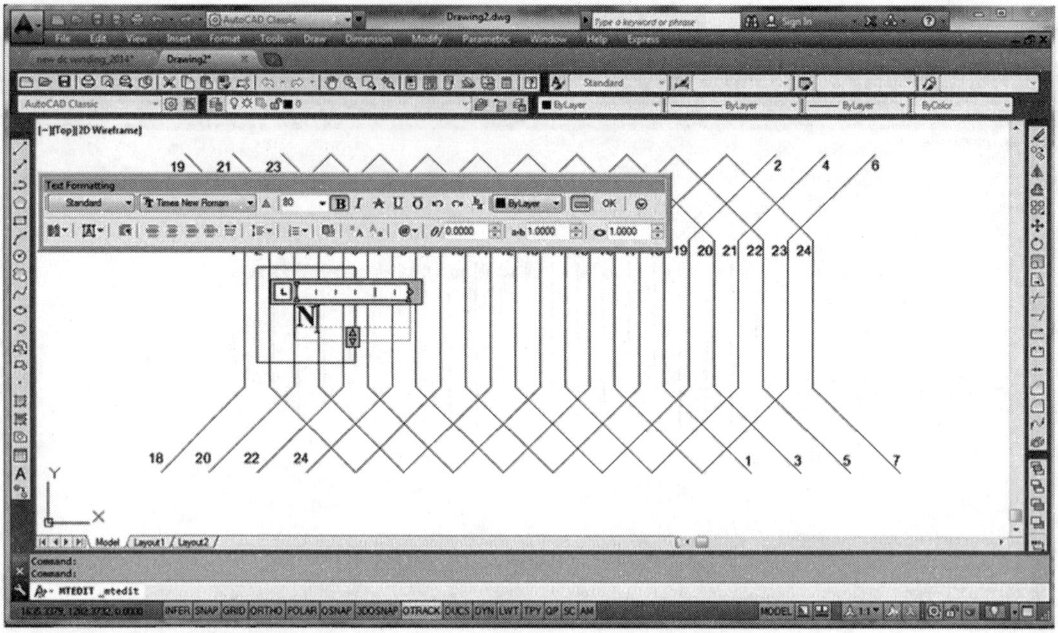

Figure 3.14 Pole placement in CAD window, *courtesy:* AutoCAD®.

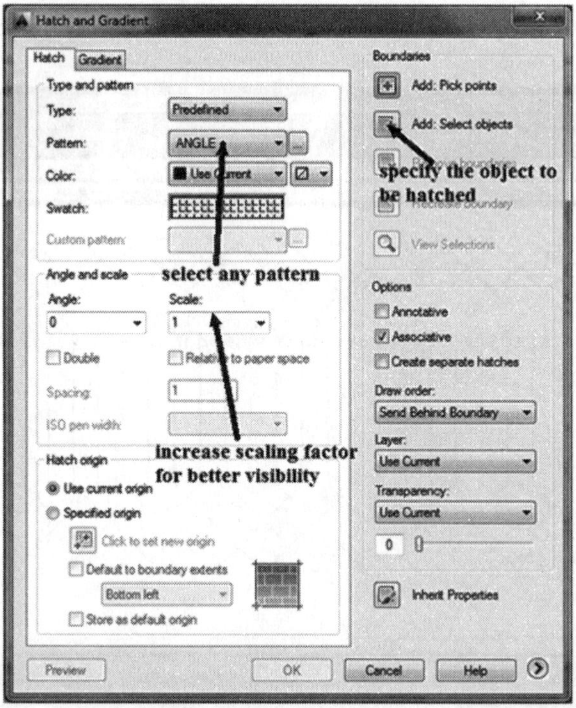

Figure 3.15 Hatching of pole in CAD window, *courtesy:* AutoCAD®.

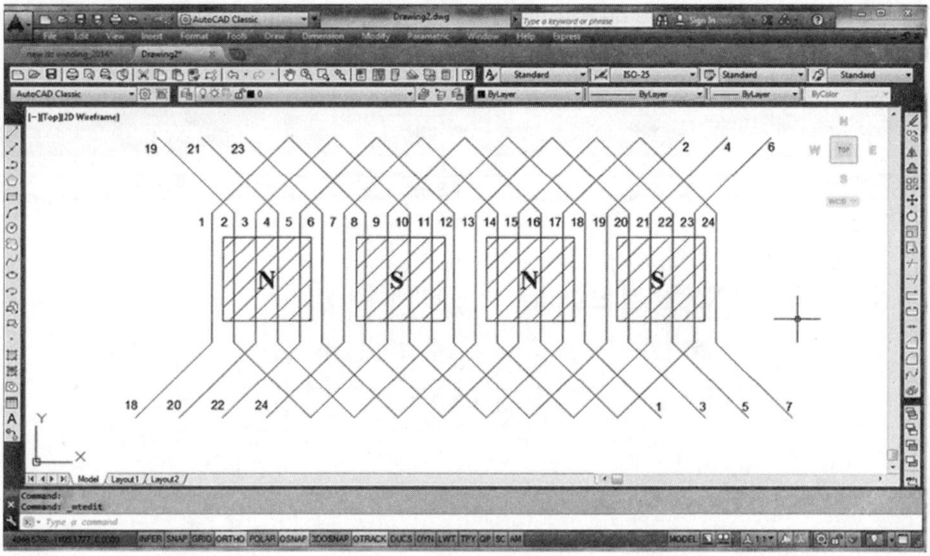

Figure 3.16 Poles in CAD window, *courtesy:* AutoCAD®.

Arrow marks to show the direction of current flow can be drawn in the following manner:

Select the icon polyline in the command window, it asks to specify the starting point. Now, select any point on the screen by just a random click. In the command window it displays as specify next point or [arc/ half width/ undo/width]: w↵.

Command window now asks to specify starting width<0.0000>: 50↵

Specify ending width <0.0000>: 0↵

This creates an arrow which can be used as required. The Figure 3.17 shows the arrow creating and used to show the direction of current in the winding.

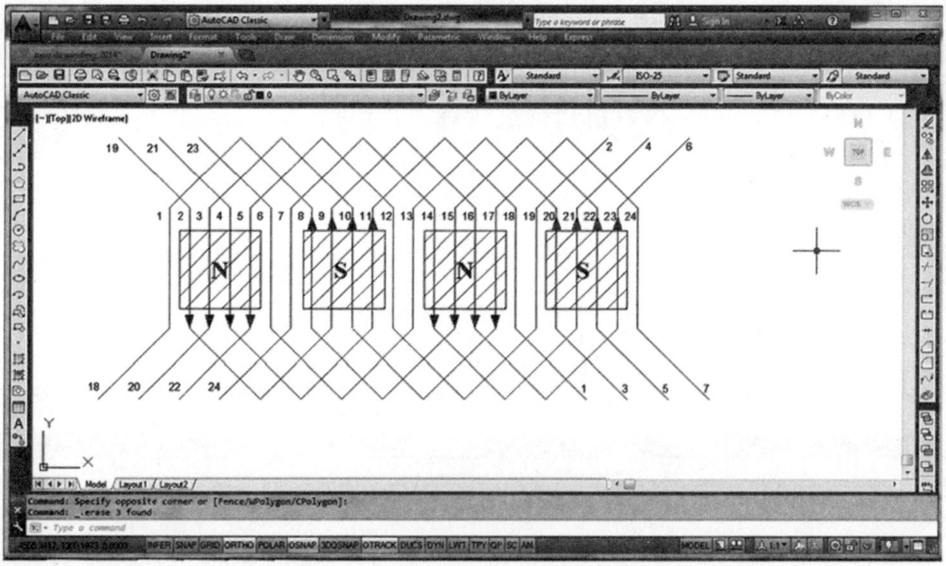

Figure 3.17 Marking of direction of current in CAD window, *courtesy:* AutoCAD®.

Step 14: Now, from each coil take a tapping and connect it to the commutator and number the commutator segments as shown in Figure 3.18(a) and (b).

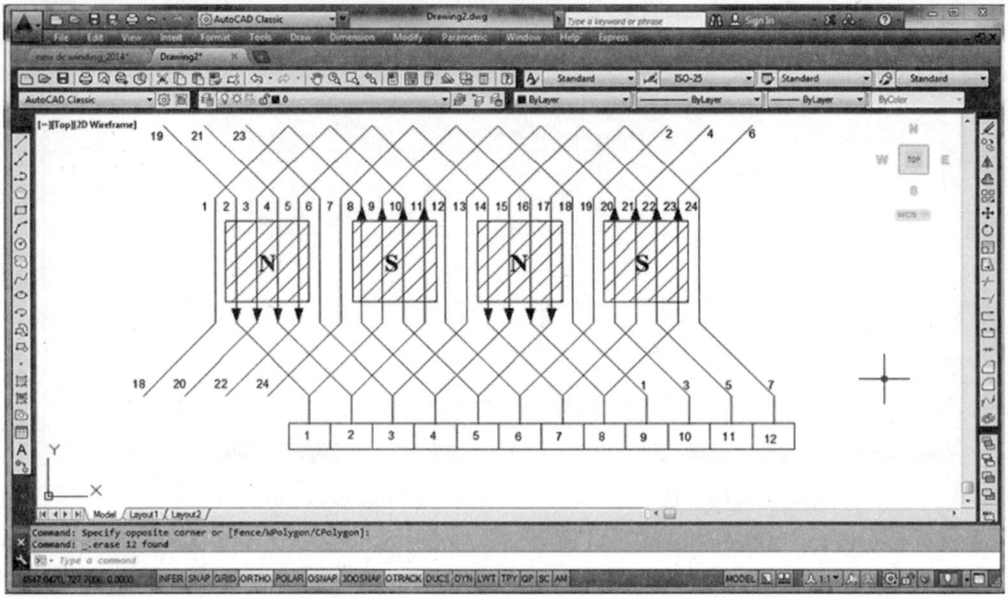

Figure 3.18(a) Commutator segments in CAD window, *courtesy:* AutoCAD®.

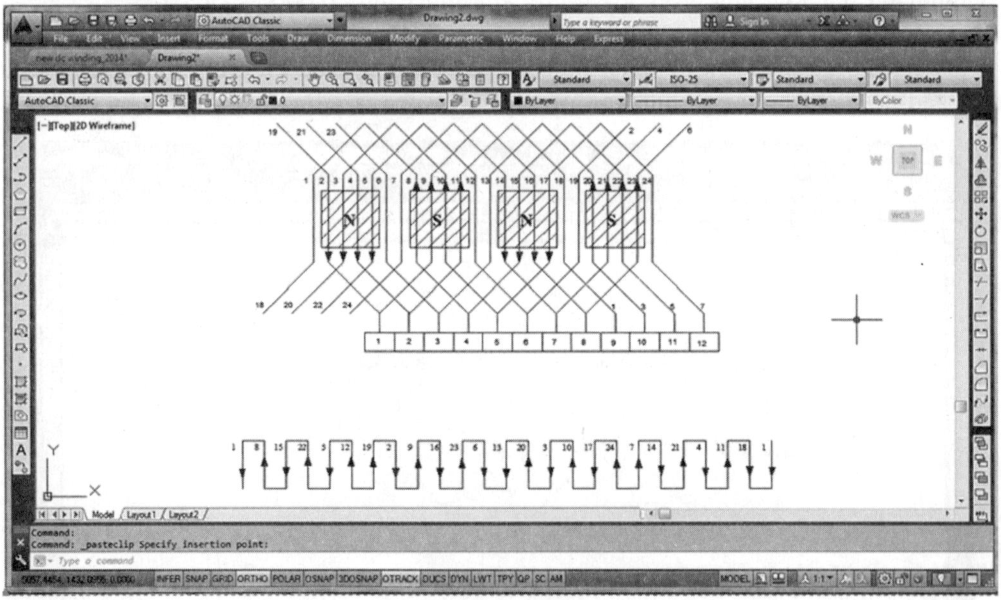

Figure 3.18(b) Commutator segments in CAD window, *courtesy:* AutoCAD®.

Step 15: Draw the sequence diagram to obtain the current and place the brushes. Sequence diagram is drawn using the winding table for each set of Y_b and Y_f as shown in Figure 3.19.

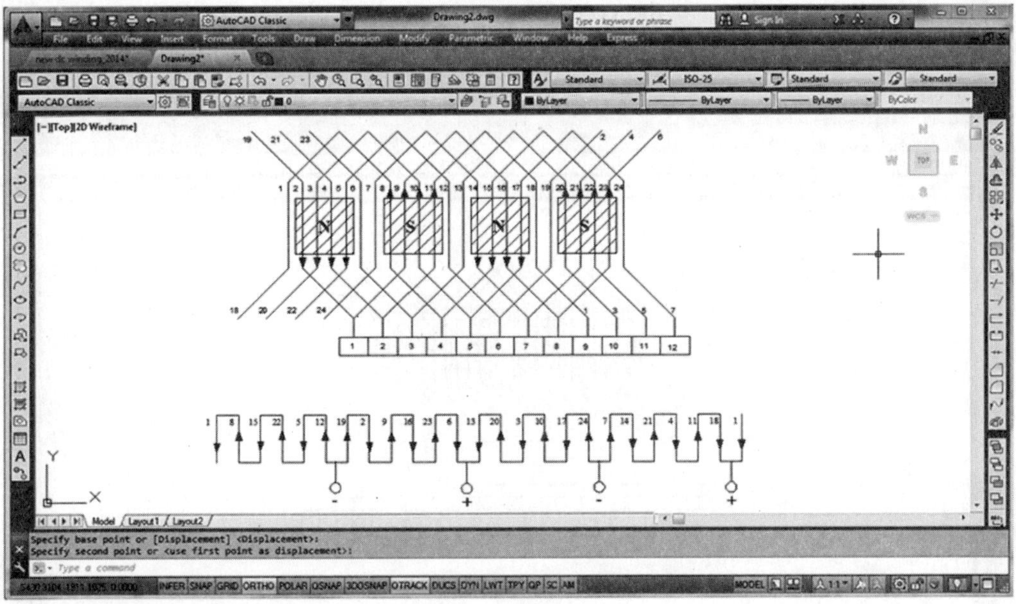

Figure 3.19(a) Sequence diagram in CAD window, *courtesy:* AutoCAD®.

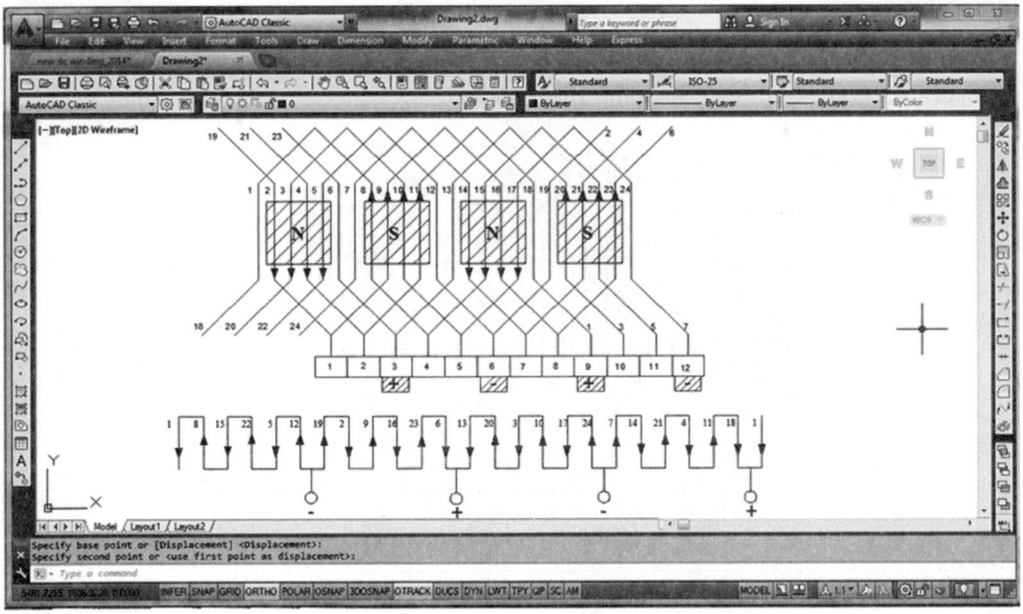

Figure 3.19(b) Sequence diagram with brush placement in CAD window, *courtesy:* AutoCAD®.

Step 16: Now, brushes are to be placed on the commutator. Referring to the sequence diagram, hence a brush is to be placed on this commutator segment. Brush can be drawn using the icon rectangle available on the left tool bar of CAD software and then placed on the segment as shown in Figure 3.20 and then assign the polarity as in the sequence diagram.

Figure 3.20(a) and (b) give the complete wave winding diagram of DC machine having 24 armature conductors and 4 poles with the direction of induced emf.

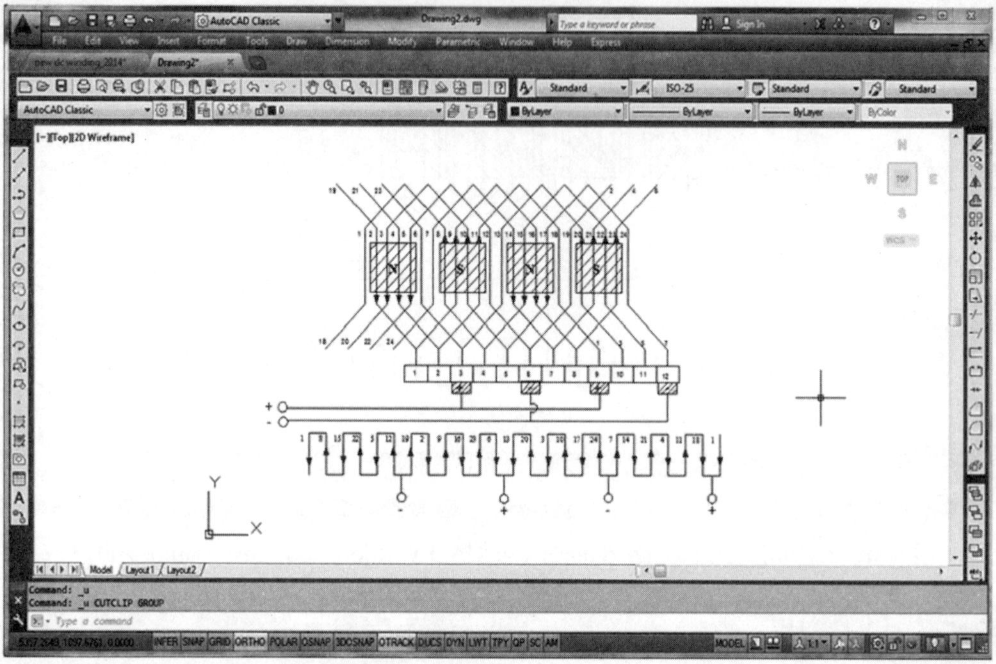

Figure 3.20(a) Complete winding diagram in CAD window, *courtesy:* AutoCAD®.

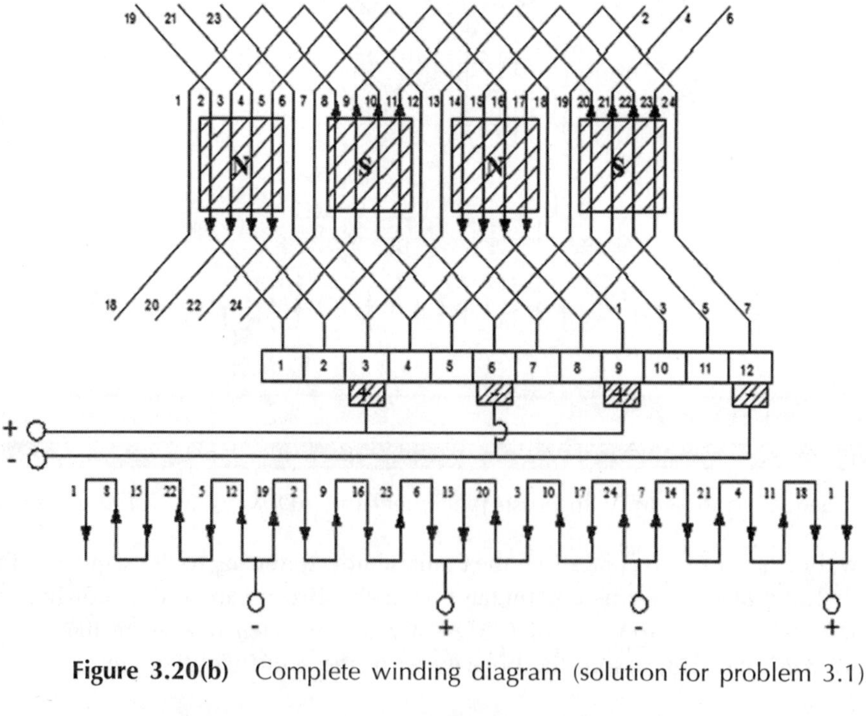

Figure 3.20(b) Complete winding diagram (solution for problem 3.1).

PROBLEM 3.2: Draw the armature winding of a DC machine with 2 poles, 18 slots and single layer retrogressive wave. Draw the sequence diagram and show the position of brush and direction of induced emf. (VTU, June 2013)

Solution:

Given data:

Type of winding = Retrogressive wave
Number of slots = 18
Number of conductor (Z) = 18
Number of poles (P) = 2
Number of circuits (m) = 1
Number of layers = 1

Calculation:

Pole pitch (Z/P) = 9
$Y_b = 7$
$Y_f = 9$

Now, develop the winding table so as to establish the coil connection in various slots as shown in Table 3.2.

TABLE 3.2 Winding table

At the back $Y_b = 7$	*At the front* $Y_f = 9$	*At the back* $Y_b = 7$	*At the front* $Y_f = 9$
1 + 7 = 8	8 + 9 = 17	9 + 7 = 16	16 + 9 = 25(7)
17 + 7 = 24(6)	6 + 9 = 15	7 + 7 = 14	14 + 9 = 23(5)
15 + 7 = 22(4)	4 + 9 = 13	5 + 7 = 12	12 + 9 = 21(3)
13 + 7 = 20(2)	2 + 9 = 11	3 + 7 = 10	10 + 9 = 19(1)
11 + 7 = 18	18 + 9 = 27(9)		

Figure 3.21 shows the developed winding diagram along with the sequence diagram.

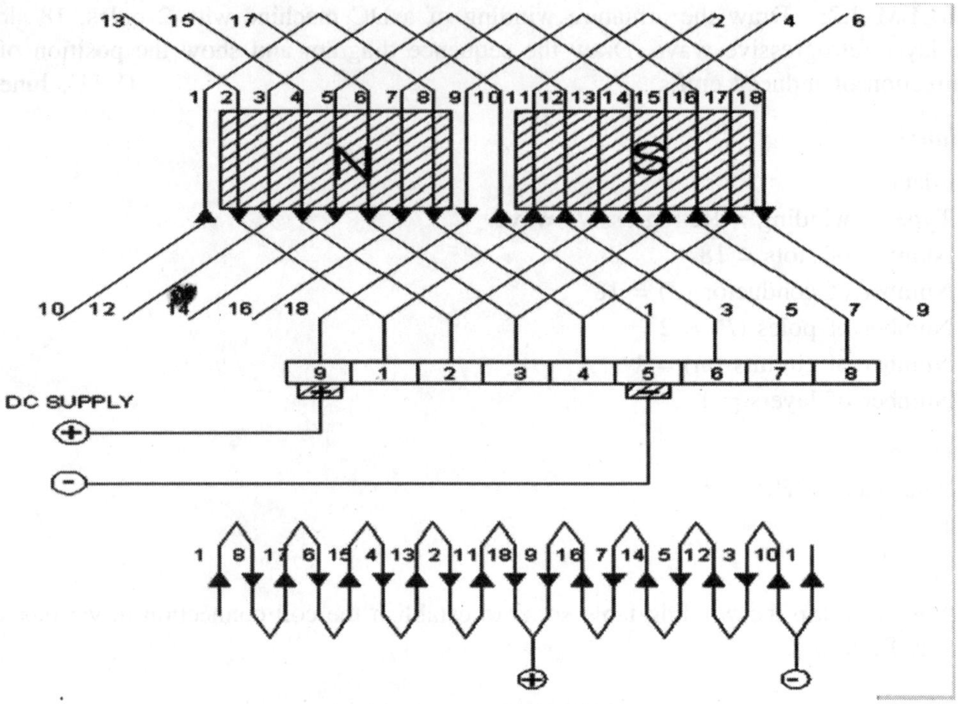

Figure 3.21 Developed winding diagram and sequence diagram for problem 3.2.

PROBLEM 3.3: Draw the armature winding of a DC machine with 4 poles, 13 slots and double layer simplex progressive wave. Show the position of brush and direction of induced emf. (VTU, June 2013)

Solution:

Given data:

Type of winding = Progressive wave

Number of slots = 13

Number of conductor (Z) = 26

Number of poles (P) = 4

Number of circuits (m) = 1

Number of layers = 2

Calculation:

Pole pitch (Z/P) = 6.5 ≅ 6

$Y_b = 7$

$Y_f = 7$

Now, develop the winding table so as to establish the coil connection in various slots as shown in Table 3.3.

Figure 3.22 shows the developed winding diagram along with the sequence diagram.

TABLE 3.3 Winding table

At the back $Y_b = 7$	*At the front* $Y_f = 7$	*At the back* $Y_b = 7$	*At the front* $Y_f = 7$
1 + 7 = 8	8 + 7 = 15	21 + 7 = 28(2)	2 + 7 = 9
15 + 7 = 22	22 + 7 = 29(3)	9 + 7 = 16	16 + 7 = 23
3 + 7 = 10	10 + 7 = 17	23 + 7 = 30(4)	4 + 7 = 11
17 + 7 = 24	24 + 7 = 31(5)	11 + 7 = 18	18 + 7 = 25
5 + 7 = 12	12 + 7 = 19	25 + 7 = 32(6)	6 + 7 = 13
19 + 7 = 26	26 + 7 = 33(7)	13 + 7 = 20	20 + 7 = 27(1)
7 + 7 = 14	14 + 7 = 21		

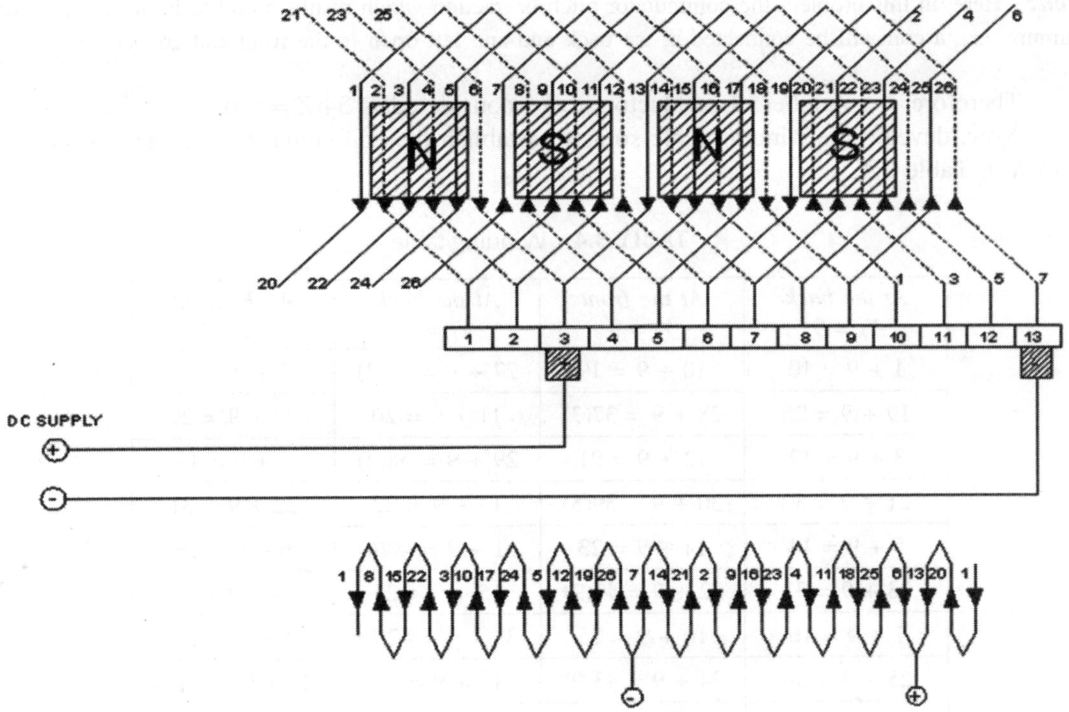

Figure 3.22 Developed winding diagram and sequence diagram for problem 3.3.

PROBLEM 3.4: Draw the armature winding of a DC machine with 4 poles, 18 slots and double layer simplex retrogressive wave. Show the position of brush and direction of induced emf. (VTU, June 2013)

Solution:

Given data:

Type of winding = Retrogressive wave

Number of slots = 18

Number of conductor (Z) = 36

Number of poles (P) = 4

Number of circuits (m) = 1

Number of layers = 2

Calculation:

Pole pitch (Z/P) = 9

$Y_b = 9$

$Y_f = 9$

Note: Here, in this problem the commutator pitch is fraction which results a coil to be made electrical dummy, i.e., a coil will be connected at the back end and left open in the front end connection.

Therefore, the number of conductors to be considered is 34(Z = 34).

Now, develop the winding table so as to establish the coil connection in various slots as shown in Table 3.4.

TABLE 3.4 Winding table

At the back $Y_b = 9$	*At the front* $Y_f = 9$	*At the back* $Y_b = 9$	*At the front* $Y_f = 9$
1 + 9 = 10	10 + 9 = 19	27 + 9 = 36(2)	2 + 9 = 11
19 + 9 = 28	28 + 9 = 37(3)	11 + 9 = 20	20 + 9 = 29
3 + 9 = 12	12 + 9 = 21	29 + 9 = 38(4)	4 + 9 = 13
21 + 9 = 30	30 + 9 = 39(5)	13 + 9 = 22	22 + 9 = 31
5 + 9 = 14	14 + 9 = 23	31 + 9 = 40(6)	6 + 9 = 15
23 + 9 = 32	32 + 9 = 41(7)	15 + 9 = 24	24 + 9 = 33
7 + 9 = 16	16 + 9 = 25	33 + 9 = 42(8)	8 + 9 = 17
25 + 9 = 34	34 + 9 = 43(9)	17 + 9 = 26	26 + 9 = 35(1)
9 + 9 = 18	18 + 9 = 27		

Figure 3.23 shows the developed winding diagram along with the sequence diagram.

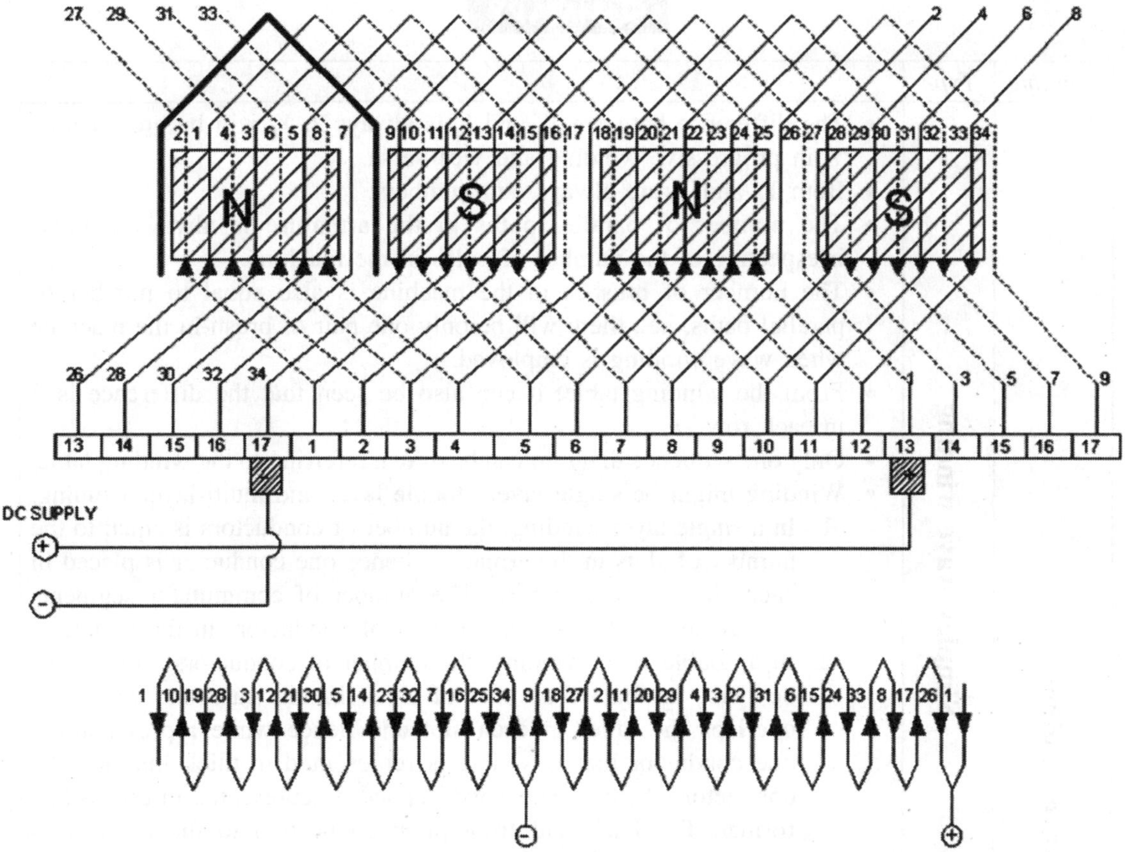

Figure 3.23 Developed winding diagram and sequence diagram for problem 3.4.

SUMMARY

<table>
<tr><th>Winding</th><th>Type</th><th></th></tr>
<tr><td rowspan="2">DC wave winding</td><td>Simplex wave winding</td><td>
• The difference between Y_b and Y_f is always 2. Y_b will be greater than Y_f in progressive winding and vice-versa.
• Both Y_b and Y_f are always odd numbers.
• The number of parallel paths in the armature is always 2 only, irrespective of the number of poles in the machine.
• The number of brushes in the machine is also equal to number of parallel paths, i.e., there will be only one pair of brush in the machine when wave winding is employed.
• From the winding table, it can also be seen that the difference is 2 in each row.
• Only one sequence diagram can be drawn referring to the winding table.
• Winding might be single layer, double layer and multi-layer winding.
1. In a single layer winding, the number of conductors is equal to the number of slots in the armature; hence one conductor is placed in each slot of the armature. The number of commutator segments will always be half of the number of conductors in the armature.
2. In a double layer winding, the number of conductors will always be twice as that of number of slots. In this case one conductor overlaps the other in each slot and hence while representation, one conductor that is visible is represented in thick line and the conductor which is being over lapped is represented in dotted line format. The back and front pitch connection to the conductors represented in dotted line format should also be represented in dotted lines in the case of double layer winding diagrams.
Note: Double layer winding and duplex winding are not the same.
3. In a multi-layer winding, there are many conductors in each slot of the armature.
</td></tr>
<tr><td>Duplex wave winding</td><td>
• The difference between Y_b and Y_f is always 4. Y_b will be greater than Y_f in progressive winding and vice-versa.
• Both Y_b and Y_f are always odd numbers.
• The number of parallel paths in the armature is always 2 irrespective of the number of poles in the machine.
• The number of brushes in the machine is 2 only and brushes occupy two commutator segment.
• From the winding table, it can also be seen that the difference is 4 in each row. There are two winding tables formed for this, i.e., if table is started from conductor 1 then the next conductor on back pitch side is 5 and the table ends at 1. Now, the next table will start from the conductor 3 and so on even the sequence diagram drawn will be 2 diagrams referring to the winding table.
• Winding might be single layer, double layer and multi-layer winding.
</td></tr>
</table>

EXERCISES

1. What is wave winding and where is it employed? Also state the various names of wave winding.
2. When is simplex lap and duplex lap utilised?
3. Develop a simple wave winding for a DC machine having 18 armature slots, double layer and 4 poles.
4. Develop a simplex series winding diagram for a DC machine with 4 poles, flux/pole = 0.366, the speed of the machine is 1500 rpm and induced emf is 220 V.
5. Develop a simple wave winding for a DC machine having 34 armature conductors and 4 poles.
6. Develop the duplex single layer series winding diagram for a DC machine having pole pitch = 6 and poles = 4.
7. Develop the simplex series winding for a DC machine with 26 conductors, 4 brushes and $Y_b < Y_f$.
8. Design a suitable double layer wave winding for a 4 pole 13 slot DC armature with two coil sides per slot. Give the value of pitches and draw the developed winding diagram.
9. A 6 pole DC armature with 36 slots and 2 coil sides per slot is to be wave wound with double layer. Draw the developed winding diagram of the winding.
10. For a 4 pole DC armature with 28 slots and 8 coil sides per slot, find the pitches and the distance between commutator segments.
11. For a 6 pole DC armature with 16 slots having two coil sides per slot and single turn coils, calculate the relevant pitches for a wave winding and develop the winding diagram.

4 AC Winding

Learning Objectives

This chapter illustrates the advantages of AC machines in brief. The various formats of winding followed in AC machines, its description, design, applications and developing of these windings using AutoCAD software in a step by step manner.

4.1 INTRODUCTION

In the recent years, the advent of AC machines has been a boon for the industrial sector. AC machines have widely replaced the use of DC machines in almost all the industries due to their inherent characteristics like:

- High efficiency
- Rugged construction
- Reliability
- Light weight
- Low maintenance

Unlike for the operation of a DC machine, DC supply is required which is not readily available. The practise of transmission is in AC mode and when DC machines are used, the AC supply is to be converted to DC to operate the machine. This disadvantage has made the DC machines to be replaced with AC machines.

Winding is the precise format of arrangement of conductors in which the current can flow. The winding done in AC machines is termed as *AC winding*.

4.2 WINDINGS IN AC MACHINE

Stator: It is the stationary part of the machine. The winding done on the stator of the AC machine is called as *stator winding*.

Rotor: It is the rotating part of the machine. The winding done on the rotor is called as *rotor winding*.

AC winding is designed so as to give a sinusoidal emf as near as possible. The windings in an AC machine can be single phase or poly-phase windings depending upon the type of supply.

In a three phase winding, there are three identical separate windings displaced 120° electrical from each other. The three phase windings are wound for a particular number of poles, depending upon the speed requirement.

Generally the winding format employed in an AC machine can be classified in the manner as shown in the Figure 4.1.

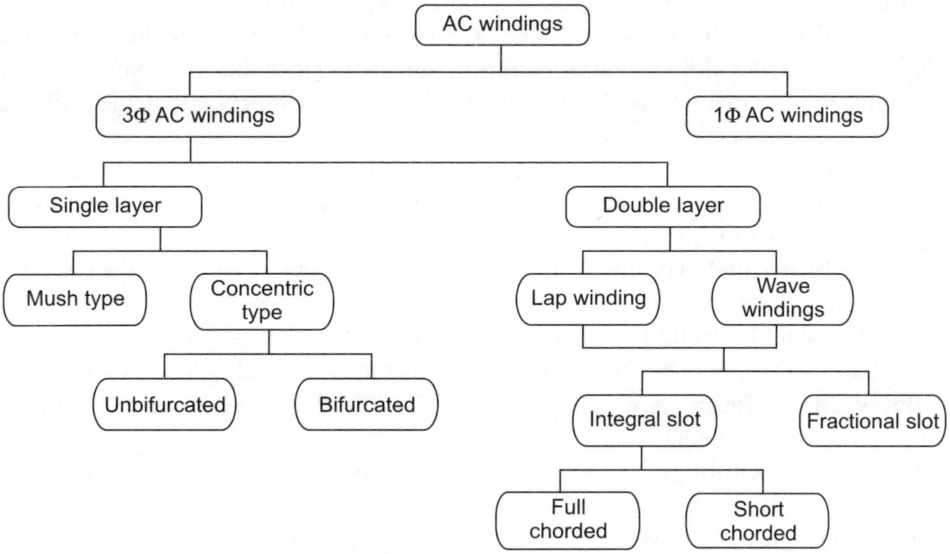

Figure 4.1 Classification of winding formats in AC machines.

1. **Integral slot winding:** If slots per pole per phase are an integer, then winding is called as *integral slot winding*.
2. **Fractional slot winding:** If slots per pole per phase are a fraction, then winding is called as *fractional slot winding*.
3. **Full pitched winding:** A winding is said to be *full pitched winding* if winding pitch is equal to 180°. More precisely in a full pitched winding, one conductor or one coil side of a coil comes under the influence of one pole and the other coil side of the same coil comes under the influence of other pole as shown in Figure 4.2.
4. **Short pitched winding:** A winding is said to be *short pitched winding* if winding pitch is less than 180°. More precisely in a short pitched winding, both conductors or both coil sides of a coil come under the influence of same pole as shown in Figure 4.2.

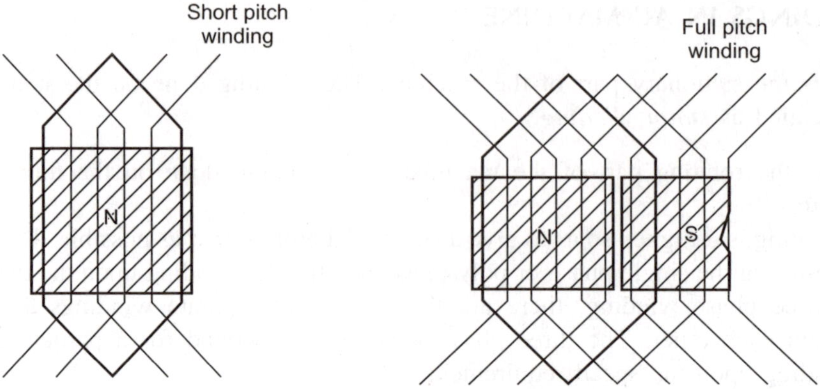

Figure 4.2 Full pitch and short pitch winding.

5. **Mush winding:** In this type of winding, all coils will have the same coil span. One conductor in a coil or one coil side of each coil is longer than the other. The coils are placed in the slots in the armature in such a manner that the long and short coils occupy the alternate slots. In this winding it can be observed that the coil span will be an odd number.
6. **Concentric winding:** It is defined as the winding in which all the coils exist in one side of the coil or in other words, it can be said that all coils containing one coil group is placed in one slot.
   - **Un-bifurcated winding:** In this form of winding, a pair of adjacent pole phase groups forms a concentric coil.
   - **Bifurcated winding:** In this form of winding, each pole phase group is split up into two sets of concentric coils sharing its return coil sides with another such group.
7. **Balanced winding:** A winding is said to be balanced if the number of coils per pole per phase is an integer.
8. **Unbalanced winding:** A winding is said to be unbalanced if the number of coils per pole per phase is not an integer.
9. **Two tier winding:** When performing concentric winding, if the overhang exists in two different planes, it is called as *two-tier winding* or *two plane overhang*. Two tier winding may be of bifurcated or un-bifurcated. Figure 4.3 shows a two tier un-bifurcated concentric winding.

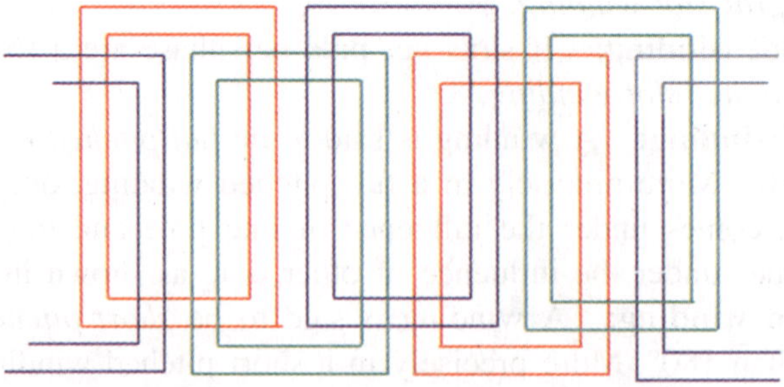

Figure 4.3 Two tier un-bifurcated concentric winding.

10. **Three tier winding:** When performing concentric winding, if the overhang exists in three different planes, it is called as *three-tier winding* or *three plane overhang*. Three tier winding may be of bifurcated or un-bifurcated. Figure 4.4 shows a three tier concentric winding. In the Figure 4.4, it can be clearly seen that all the three phases overhang exists in different planes.

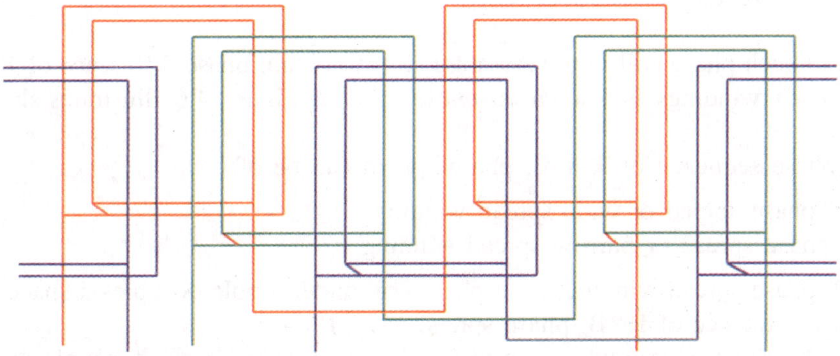

Figure 4.4 A three tier concentric winding.

4.3 SOME GENERAL TERMS RELATED TO AC WINDING

1. **Pole pitch:** It is defined as the distance between the centre of two adjacent poles and is always measured in terms of number of slots as shown in Figure 4.5.

   Pole pitch = (number of slots/pole)

2. **Slots per pole per phase (SPP):** It refers to the number of slots existing in each pole and each phase. If SPP = 3, then one phase group consists of three slots.
3. **Slot angle:** It is always calculated in terms of pole pitch and is in electrical degrees.

   Slot angle = (180°/pole pitch)

4. **Coil pitch:** This is defined as the distance between two active sides of a coil in terms of slots. It is also called as *coil span*. Coil pitch is shown in Figure 4.5.

   Coil span = (winding pitch/slot angle)

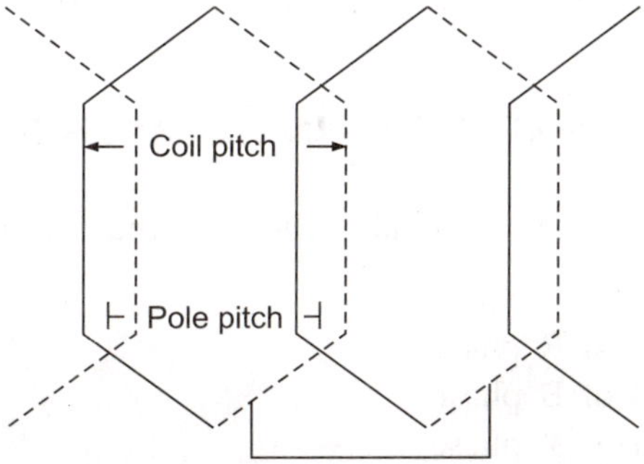

Figure 4.5 Coil pitch and pole pitch.

For full pitched winding:

- Coil span = (180°/slot angle)
- Winding pitch = 180° – (number of slots shorted × slot angle)

4.4 PHASE SPREAD

Distribution of each phase coil in the armature slots to obtain phase difference of 120° between the start of each windings is known as *phase spread*. Figure 4.6 illustrates the concept of phase spread.

For a phase sequence of R-Y-B, phase spread can be of:

- 120° phase spread or wide spread winding
- 60° phase spread or narrow spread winding

In 120° phase spread winding, each phase coil under a pole occupies a space of 120° ele, thus for phase sequence of RYB, phase spread is RYB.

In 60° phase spread winding, each phase coil occupies a space of 60° ele, thus for phase sequence of RYB, phase spread is RBY.

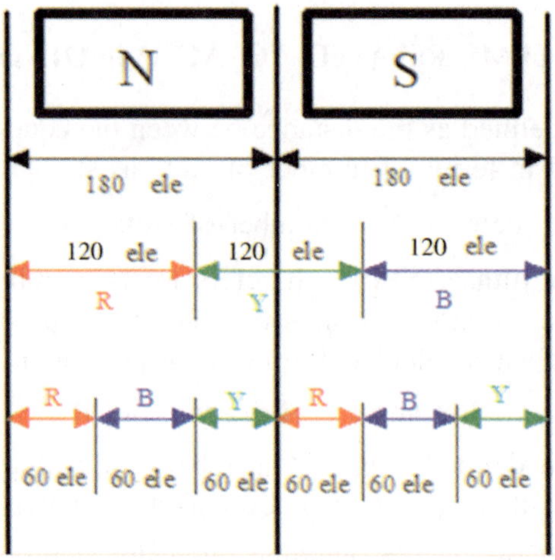

Figure 4.6 The concept of phase spread.

4.5 TERMINALS AND CONNECTIONS IN AC MACHINES

Three phase windings consist of 6 terminals. They are the starting and ending points of the three phases named as:

- R_S: Starting terminal of R phase
- B_S: Starting terminal of B phase
- Y_S: Starting terminal of Y phase
- R_F: Finishing or end terminal of R phase

- B_F: Finishing or end terminal of B phase
- Y_F: Finishing or end terminal of Y phase

In star connection, the terminals R_F, Y_F and B_F are shorted as shown in Figure 4.7(a).

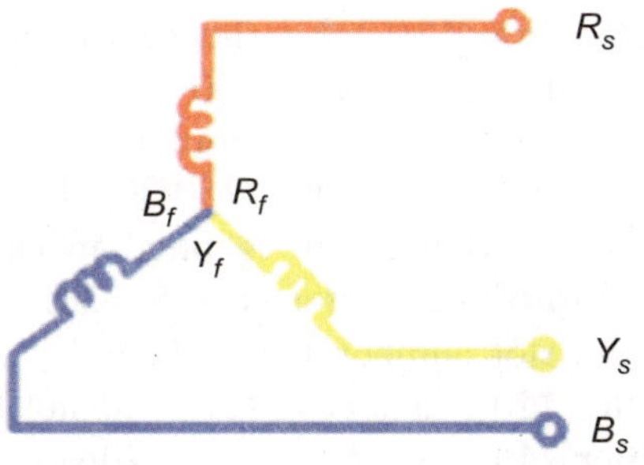

Figure 4.7(a) Star connection in AC machines.

In delta connection, the terminals R_F and Y_S, B_S and Y_F, R_S and B_F are shorted as shown in Figure 4.7(b).

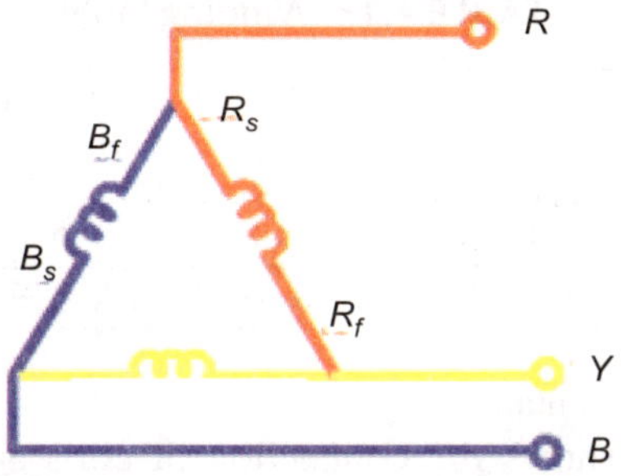

Figure 4.7(b) Delta connection in AC machines.

Note: The yellow phase will not be so visible in drawings and even when print outs are taken; hence the colour green can be used instead of yellow.

4.6 SOLVED PROBLEMS

PROBLEM 4.1: Draw the developed single layer lap winding diagram of a 3 phase star connected AC machine with 4 poles and 24 conductors. The winding is to be short pitched by one slot.

Solution:

Analysing the problem: This particular problem states us to develop a single layer lap winding diagram for an AC machine having 24 conductors and 4 poles.

Given data:

Number of poles = 4

Number of slots = S = Z = number of conductors = 24

Step 1: First calculate all the necessary details like pole pitch, slots/pole, slots/pole/phase, coil span, etc. as given below:

- Pole pitch = number of slots/pole = (24/4) = 6
- Number of slots/pole/phase = (6/3) = 2
- Number of coils/pole/phase = 12/12 = 1 (hence winding is balanced)
- Slot angle = (180/pole pitch) = (180/6) = 30°
- Winding pitch = 180 – (number of slots shorted × slot angle) = 180 – (1 × 30) = 150
- Coil span = (winding pitch/slot angle) = (150/30) = 5
- The winding is balanced and one coil is fitted in each pole per phase. Hence, 1st conductor is connected to 6th conductor (1 + 5 = 6).
- The phase R starts from slot number 1, i.e., $R_S = 1$.
- The phase Y starts after 120°, i.e., $Y_S = 1 + (120/\text{slot angle}) = 1 + (120/30) = 5$.
- The phase B starts after 240°, i.e., $B_S = 1 + (240/\text{slot angle}) = 1 + (240/30) = 9$.

Step 2: Now, develop the winding table so as to establish the coil connection in various slots as shown in Table 4.1.

TABLE 4.1 Winding table

	1st pole	2nd pole	3rd pole	4th pole
R phase	1 + 5 = 6	7 + 5 = 12	13 + 5 = 18	19 + 5 = 24
B phase	3 + 5 = 8	9 + 5 = 14	15 + 5 = 20	21 + 5 = 26(2)
Y phase	5 + 5 = 10	11 + 5 = 16	17 + 5 = 22	23 + 5 = 28(4)

Note: Winding table is read horizontally.

Now, this winding table shows the connection of coils and their phase groups.

Steps to develop the winding diagram using CAD:

Step 1: Click on the AutoCAD icon appearing on the computer screen. A new window of AutoCAD will open.

Step 2: Select FILE in the AutoCAD window and open a new drawing (.dwg) file.

Step 3: In the command window type as UNITS↵, a new dialog box will pop-up. In this dialog box select the precision type, lighting and units as required. Generally, the precision set is 0.00, units to scale inserted are millimetres and lighting selected is International.

Step 4: Now, select the sheet size required for the drawing by typing as LIMITS↵ in the command window, here itself it specifies as:

Specify lower left corner or (ON/OFF) <0.0000, 0.0000>: ↵
Specify upper right corner or (ON/OFF) <300, 300>: 1500, 1500↵

The lower left corner should always start from <0.0000, 0.0000> whereas for the upper right corner will have a default value. It can be set to any value depending on our requirement.

Step 5: In the command window type as ZOOM↵, it specifies as [All/Centre/Dynamic/Extents/Previous/Scale/Window/Object] <real time>:

Here, specify as All (or shortcut key A)↵. This zooms up the drawing sheet as specified in the limits.

This completes the setting part of the CAD window to the requirement.

Step 6: Select the line icon on the left tool bar of the CAD window. The command window asks to specify the starting point for the line; this can be randomly done by clicking on the CAD window.

Now, command window asks to specify the next point for the line, in the form:

Specify next point or [undo]: @600<90

This should always be done by giving a known dimension for the line and specifying the angle in the above stated manner. Here, 600 represents the length of the line to be drawn and this depends on the limits of the chosen window and < 90 represents the angle at which it is to be drawn as shown in Figure 4.8.

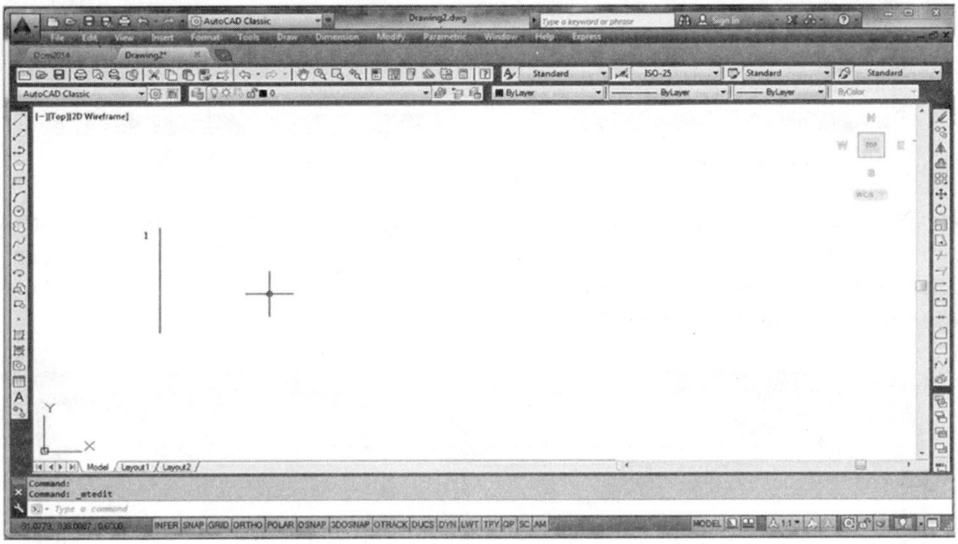

Figure 4.8 Line specifications in command window, *courtesy:* AutoCAD®.

Note: All dimensions are in millimetres (mm). Always ensure that ORTHO is kept on in order to obtain straight line.

Step 7: Now, click on the icon 'A' available on the toolbar which represents multiline text. Now, select a size and style for the text and then enter the number for the conductor. Then place this number (text) next to the conductor (the line drawn).

Step 8: Now, select the conductor (the line drawn) and the text together and then click on the array icon available on the right hand side of the toolbar of the CAD window. A new dialog box will pop-up, in this select rectangular array and then specify the number of rows (which is obviously 1 in case of winding diagrams) then specify the number of columns, which represents the number of conductors. In this case it is 24 hence enter 24 and then specify the distance between the conductors in column offset. This creates the 24 number of conductors as required and names each and every conductor as shown in the Figure 4.9.

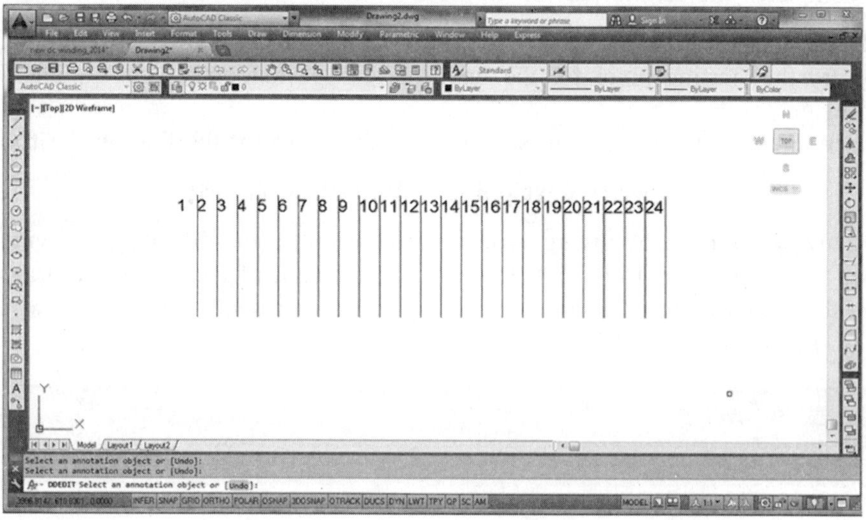

Figure 4.9 Drawing of conductors, *courtesy:* AutoCAD®.

Step 9: Now, select the conductor (the line drawn) and give it the colour of the phase they belong to as per the winding diagram by selecting the conductor, click on the **ByLayer** colour toolbar and select the colour and hence colour all the conductors with respect to their phase groups as shown below in Figure 4.10.

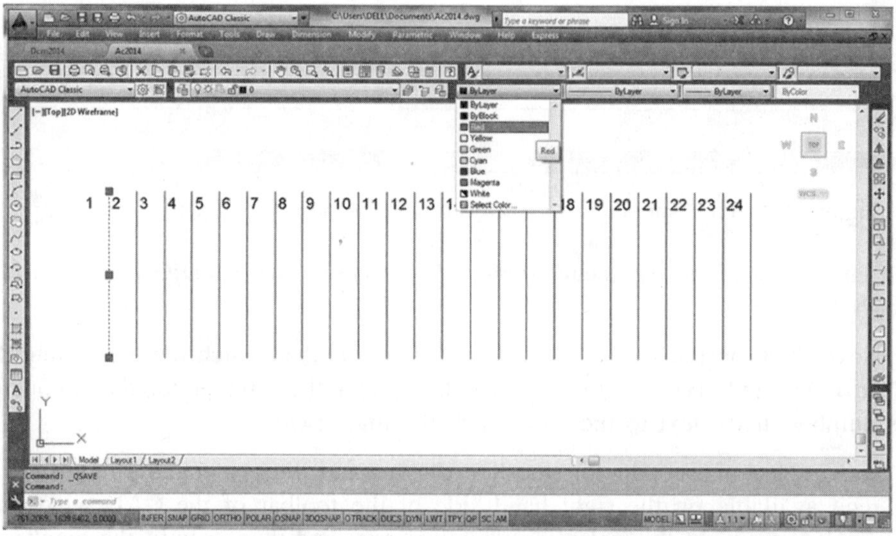

Figure 4.10 Colouring of conductors based on phase group, *courtesy:* AutoCAD®.

Step 10: Once the colouring of conductors or placing the conductors to their respective phase group is completed. Now, with reference to the winding table connect the conductors to form coils as shown in Figure 4.11.

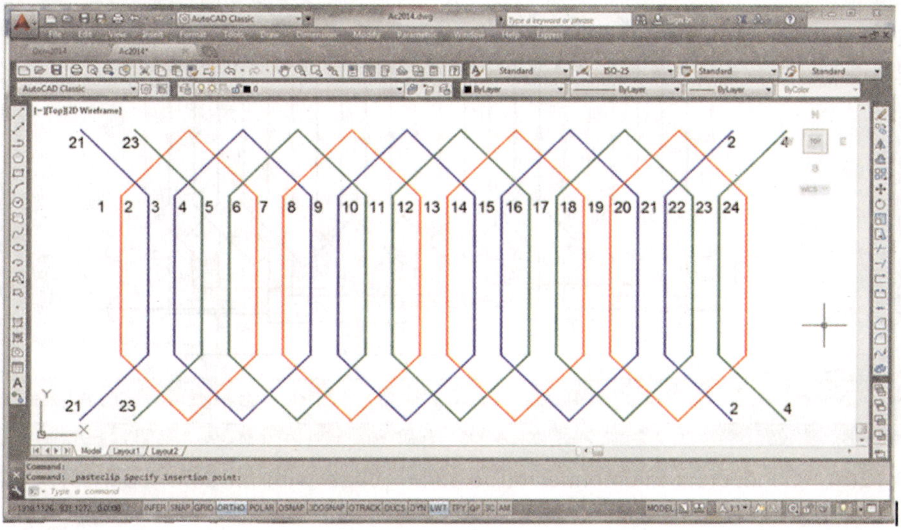

Figure 4.11 Conductors connection to form coils, *courtesy:* AutoCAD®.

Step 11: Now, interconnect the coils of the same phase group as shown in Figure 4.12(a) and (b) and mark the direction of current flow.

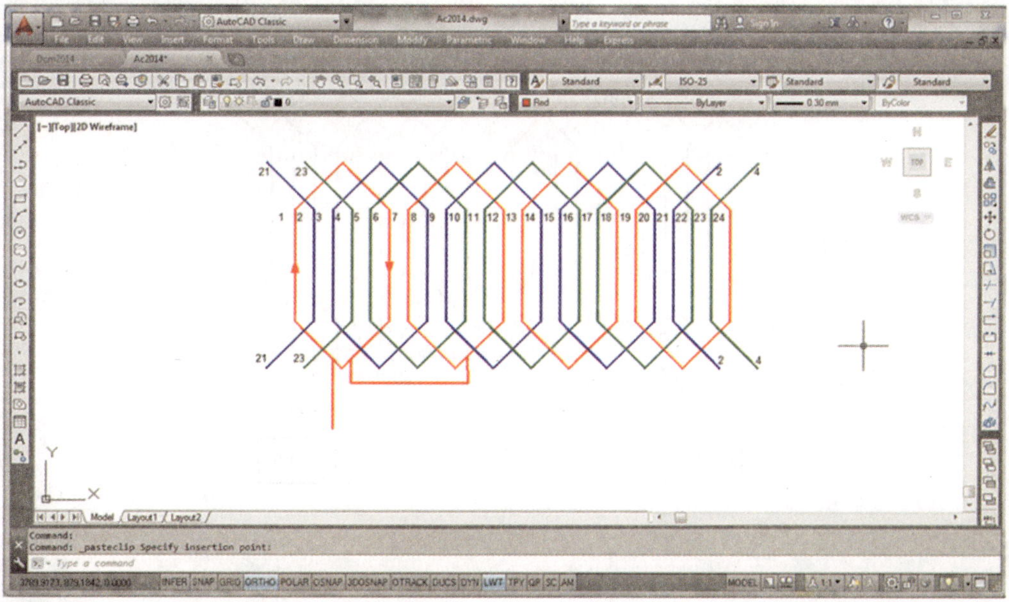

Figure 4.12(a) Conductors interconnected to same phase with one coil, *courtesy:* AutoCAD®.

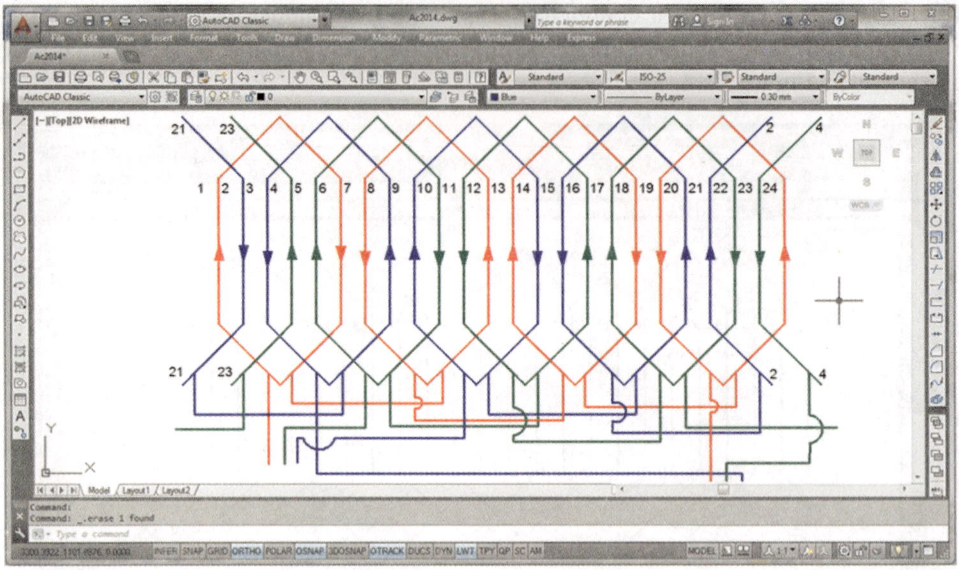

Figure 4.12(b) Conductors interconnected to same phase with all coils, *courtesy:* AutoCAD®.

Step 12: Now, draw the terminal plates as shown in Figure 4.13(a). Draw both starting and finishing terminal plates and name the terminals upon their phases and connect them as shown in Figure 4.13(b).

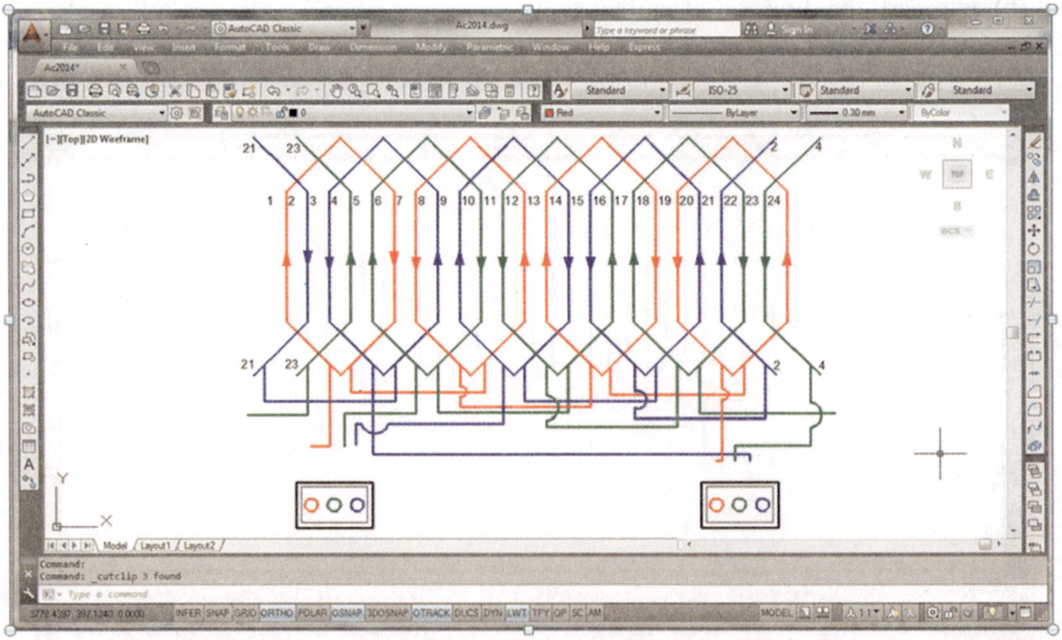

Figure 4.13(a) Terminal plates for connection, *courtesy:* AutoCAD®.

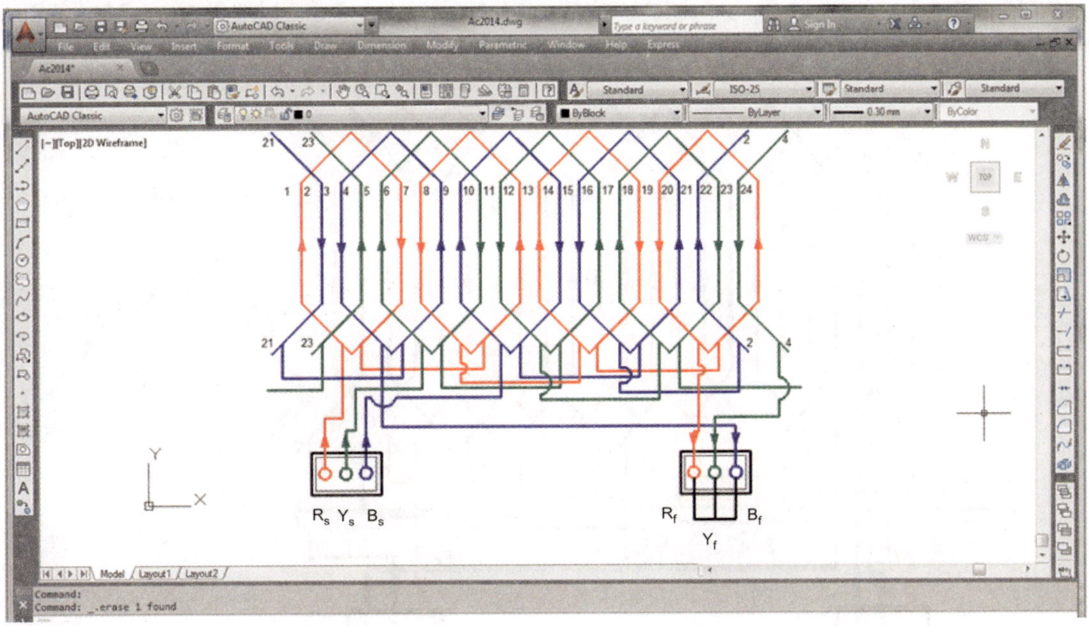

Figure 4.13(b) Terminal plates for connection with terminals marked, *courtesy:* AutoCAD®.

Step 13: As in the problem, it is stated as the machine is star connected, henceforth short the finishing terminals in the terminal plate and indicate the star connection diagram right next to the winding diagram to indicate that the machine is star connected as shown in Figure 4.14(a).

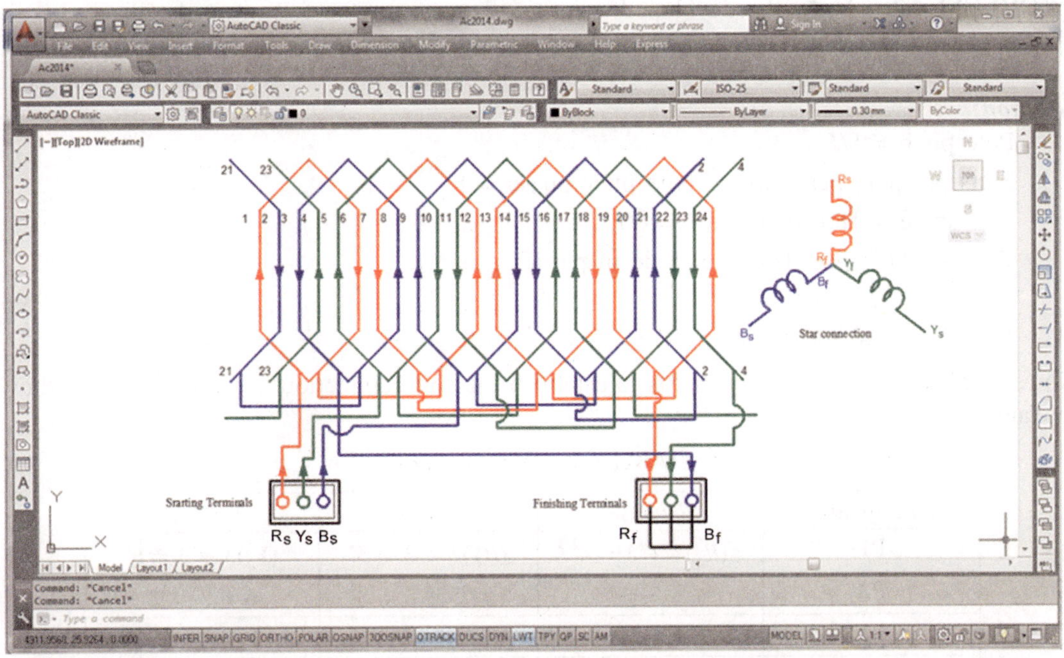

Figure 4.14(a) Completed winding diagram with star connection, *courtesy:* AutoCAD®.

Figure 4.14(b) gives the complete winding diagram of AC machine having 24 armature conductors and 4 poles with the connection details.

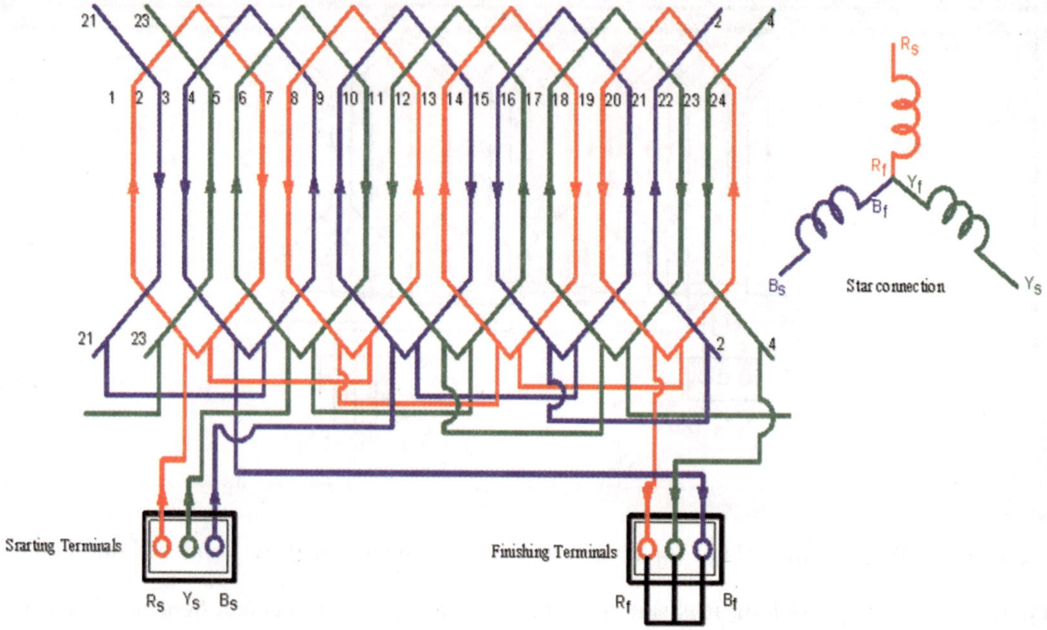

Figure 4.14(b) Complete winding diagram (solution for problem 4.1).

PROBLEM 4.2: Draw the developed winding diagram for the following details:
3 phase AC double layer lap winding, slots = 12, poles = 4 and phase sequence = R Y B.
(VTU, June 2013)

Solution:

Pole pitch = S/P = 3

Slots per pole per phase = pole pitch/phase = 1

Slot angle = 180°/pole pitch = 60°

$R_S = 1^{TCS}$ (TCS = Top Coil Side in particular slot)

$Y_S = 1 + (120°/60°) = 3^{TCS}$

$B_S = 1 + (240°/60°) = 5^{TCS}$

Now, develop the winding table so as to establish the coil connection in various slots as shown in Table 4.2.

TABLE 4.2 Winding table

Poles/phases	*R phase*	*B phase*	*Y phase*
P1	$(R_S)1 + 3 = 4'$	$(B_F)2 + 3 = 5'$	$(Y_S)3 + 3 = 6'$
P2	$4 + 3 = 7'$	$(B_S)5 + 3 = 8'$	$6 + 3 = 9'$
P3	$7 + 3 = 10'$	$8 + 3 = 11'$	$9 + 3 = 12'$
P4	$(R_F)10 + 3 = 13'$	$11 + 3 = 14'$	$(Y_F)12 + 3 = 15'$

Figure 4.15 gives the complete winding diagram of AC machine having 12 slots and 4 poles with the connection details.

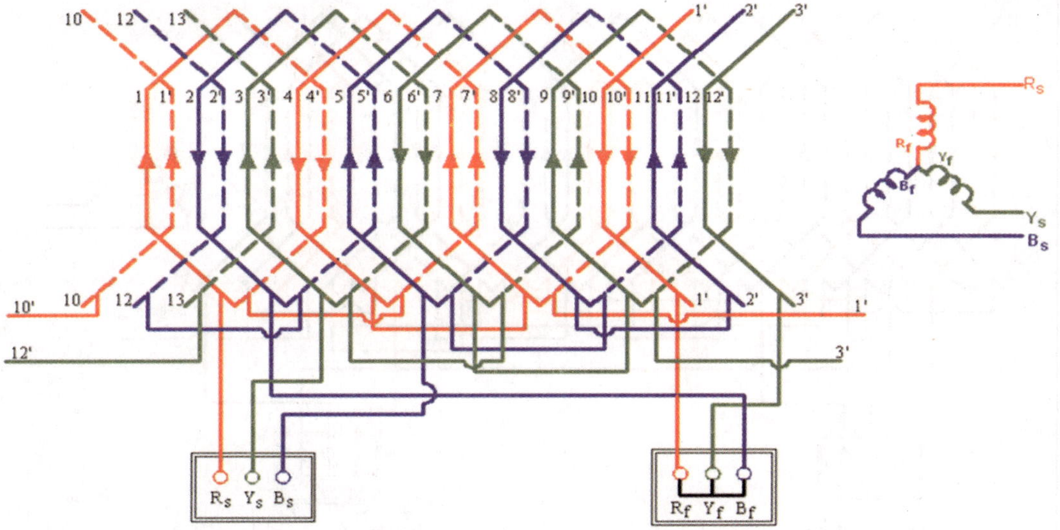

Figure 4.15 Complete winding diagram (solution for problem 4.2).

PROBLEM 4.3: Develop the winding diagram for a 3 phase AC machine with 18 slots and 6 poles. Assume it is star connected and phase sequence is RYB. (VTU, June 2013)

Solution:

Pole pitch = S/P = 18/6 = 3

Slots per pole per phase = pole pitch/phase = 1

Slot angle = 180°/pole pitch = 60°

$R_S = 1^{TCS}$ (TCS = Top Coil Side in particular slot)

$Y_S = 1 + (120°/60°) = 3^{TCS}$

$B_S = 1 + (240°/60°) = 5^{TCS}$

Now, develop the winding table so as to establish the coil connection in various slots as shown in Table 4.3.

TABLE 4.3 Winding table

Poles/phases	*R phase*	*B phase*	*Y phase*
P1	(**R_S**)1 + 3 = 4′	(**B_F**)2 + 3 = 5′	(**Y_S**)3 + 3 = 6′
P2	4 + 3 = 7′	(**B_S**)5 + 3 = 8′	6 + 3 = 9′
P3	7 + 3 = 10′	8 + 3 = 11′	9 + 3 = 12′
P4	10 + 3 = 13′	11 + 3 = 14′	12 + 3 = 15′
P5	13 + 3 = 16′	14 + 3 = 17′	15 + 3 = 18′
P6	(**R_F**)16 + 3 = 1′	17 + 3 = 2′	(**Y_F**)18 + 3 = 3′

Figure 4.16 gives the complete winding diagram of AC machine having 18 slots and 6 poles with the connection details.

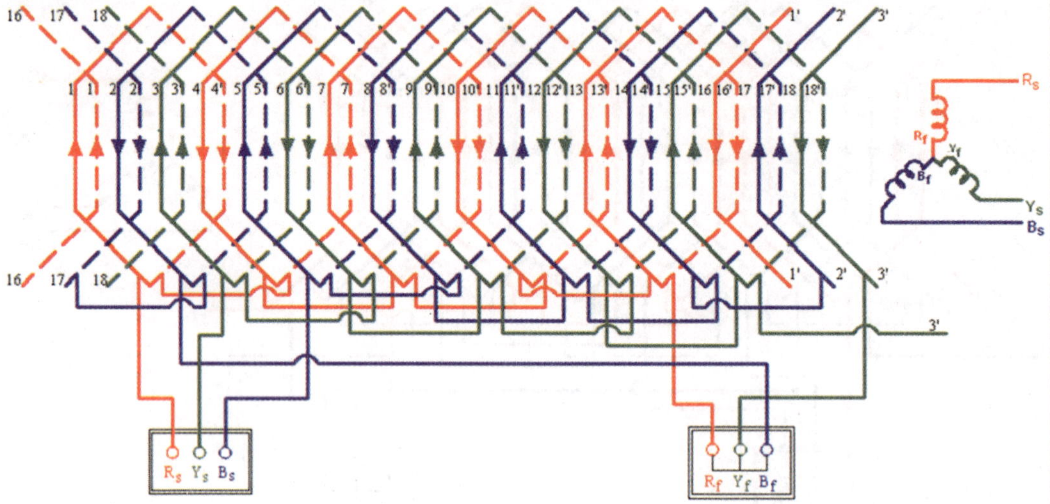

Figure 4.16 Complete winding diagram (solution for problem 4.3).

PROBLEM 4.4: Design and draw the developed 3 phase AC lap winding diagram for 24 slots, double layer lap connected, 4 poles and one slot to be chorded. Also show the winding in star connection.

Solution:

Pole pitch = S/P = 6

Slots per pole per phase = pole pitch/phase = 2

Slot angle = 180°/pole pitch = 30°

$R_S = 1^{\text{TCS}}$ (TCS = Top Coil Side in particular slot)

$Y_S = 1 + (120°/30°) = 5^{\text{TCS}}$

$B_S = 1 + (240°/30°) = 9^{\text{TCS}}$

Actual coil span = pole pitch – number of coils to be chorded = 6 – 1 = 5

Now, develop the winding table so as to establish the coil connection in various slots as shown in Table 4.4.

TABLE 4.4 Winding table

Poles/phases	*R phase*	*B phase*	*Y phase*
P1	(R_S)1 + 5 = 6′ 2 + 5 = 7′	3 + 5 = 8′ 4 + 5 = 9′	5 + 5 = 10′ 6 + 5 = 11′
P2	7 + 5 = 12′ 8 + 5 = 13′	9 + 5 = 14′ 10 + 5 = 15′	11 + 5 = 16′ 12 + 5 = 17′
P3	13 + 5 = 18′ 14 + 5 = 19′	15 + 5 = 20′ 16 + 5 = 21′	17 + 5 = 22′ 18 + 5 = 23′
P4	19 + 5 = 24′ 20 + 5 = 25′(1′)	21 + 5 = 26′(2′) 22 + 5 = 27′(3′)	23 + 5 = 28′(4′) 24 + 5 = 29′(5′)

Figure 4.17 gives the complete winding diagram of AC machine having 24 slots and 4 poles with the connection details.

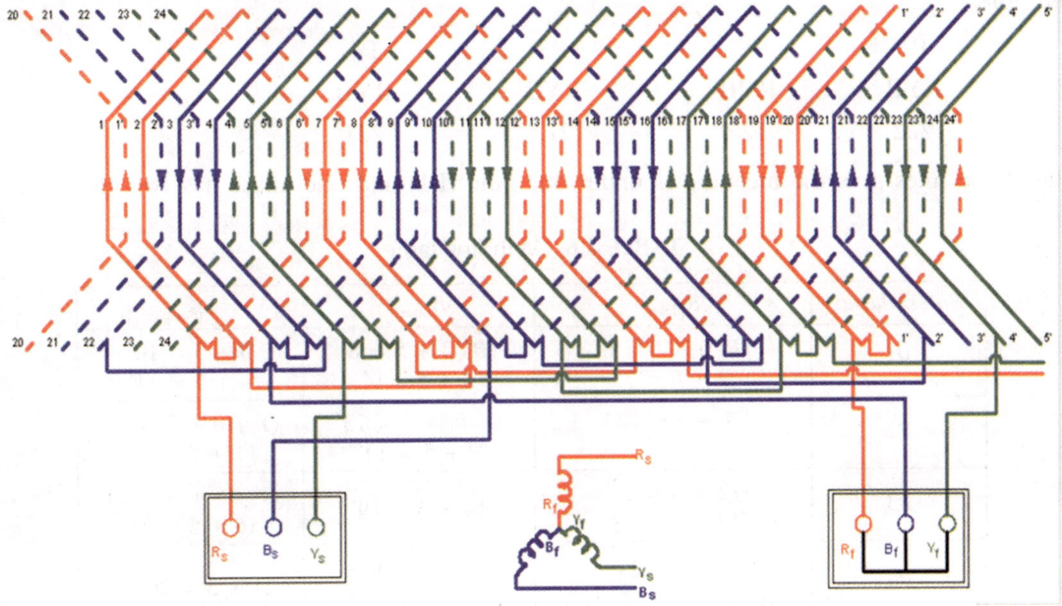

Figure 4.17 Complete winding diagram (solution for problem 4.4).

PROBLEM 4.5: Develop the winding of an alternator of 21 slots, 4 poles, RYB phase sequence and double layer.

Solution:

Pole pitch = S/P = 21/4 = 5.25

Slots per pole per phase = pole pitch/phase = 18/12 = 1.5

The pole pitch can rewrite as (21/4), i.e., m/d. Here, 'm' is termed as number of columns and 'd' is termed as number of rows.

Slot angle = 180°/pole pitch = 34.2857°

$R_S = 1^{TCS}$ (TCS = Top Coil Side in particular slot)

$Y_S = 1 + (120°/34.2857°) = 4.5^{TCS}$

$B_S = 1 + (240°/34.2857°) = 8^{TCS}$

Before preparing the actual Winding Table 4.6, let us know the actual number of slots per phase by using the given Table 4.5.

TABLE 4.5 Actual number of slots per phase

	R							*B*							*Y*						
P1	☆				☆				☆				☆				☆				☆
P2				☆				☆				☆				☆				☆	
P3			☆				☆				☆				☆				☆		
P4		☆				☆				☆				☆				☆			

From the above Table 4.5, here the square box next to P1 is conductor 1 and it increases in ascending order and the star mark corresponds that particular conductor falls under that phase and pole.

P1	P2	P3	P4
RYB	RYB	RYB	RYB
222	122	212	221

The above lines give the meaning is under one pole (P1) and one phase has two slots.

TABLE 4.6 Winding table

Poles/phases	R_{phase}	B_{phase}	Y_{phase}
P1	$(R_S)1 + 5 = 6'$ $2 + 5 = 7'$	$(B_F)3 + 5 = 8'$ $4 + 5 = 9'$	$5 + 5 = 10'$ $6 + 5 = 11'$
P2	$7 + 5 = 12'$	$(B_S)8 + 5 = 13'$ $9 + 5 = 14'$	$(Y_F)10 + 5 = 15'$ $11 + 5 = 16'$
P3	$12 + 5 = 17'$ $13 + 5 = 18'$	$14 + 5 = 19'$	$(Y_S)15 + 5 = 20'$ $16 + 5 = 21'$
P4	$17 + 5 = 22'(1')$ $(R_F)18 + 5 = 23'(2')$	$19 + 5 = 24'(3')$ $20 + 5 = 25'(4')$	$21 + 5 = 26'(5')$

Figure 4.18 gives the complete winding diagram of an alternator having 21 slots and 4 poles with the connection details.

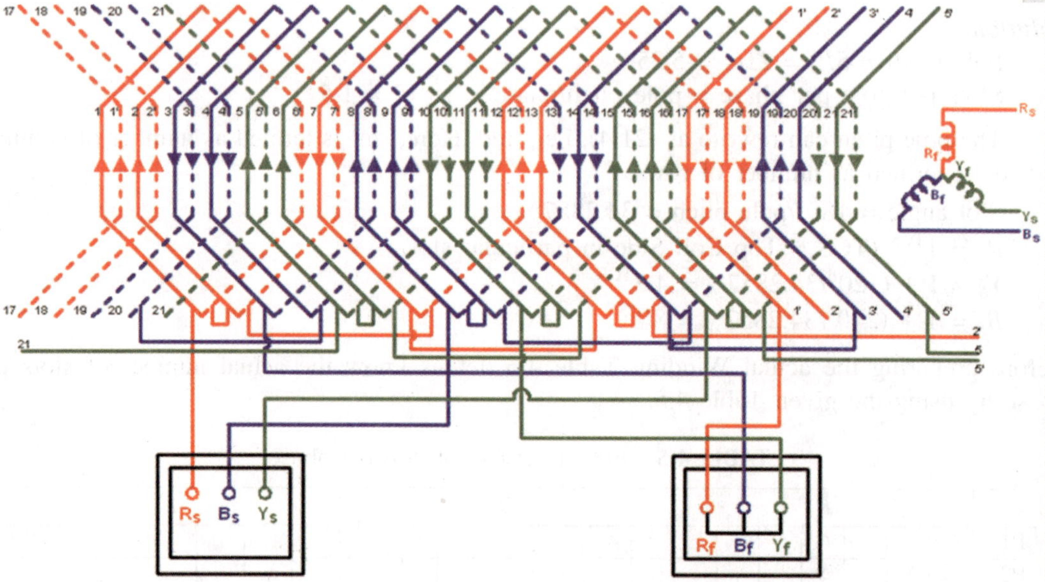

Figure 4.18 Complete winding diagram (solution for problem 4.5).

PROBLEM 4.6: Develop and draw the wave winding diagram for the following details: Slots = 12, poles = 4, single layer, phase sequence is RYB and delta connected.

Solution:

Pole pitch = S/P = 3

Slots per pole per phase = pole pitch /phase = 1

Slot angle = 180°/ pole pitch = 60°

$R_S = 1^{\text{TCS}}$

$Y_S = 1 + (120°/60°) = 3^{\text{TCS}}$

$B_S = 1 + (240°/60°) = 5^{\text{TCS}}$

The coil span is 6, hence the Y_B and $Y_F = 6$

R_S conductor in $1^{\text{TCS}} = 1$ (TCS = Top Coil Side in particular slot)

Y_S conductor in $3^{\text{TCS}} = 5$

B_S conductor in $5^{\text{TCS}} = 9$

Now, develop the winding table so as to establish the coil connection in various slots as shown in Table 4.7.

TABLE 4.7 Winding table

R_S 1 + 6 = 7	7 + 6 = 13	13 + 6 = 19	19 + 6 = 25(1)
2 + 6 = 8	8 + 6 = 14	14 + 6 = 20	R_F 20 + 6 = 26(2)
Y_S 5 + 6 = 11	11 + 6 = 17	17 + 6 = 23	23 + 6 = 29(5)
6 + 6 = 12	12 + 6 = 18	18 + 6 = 24	Y_F 24 + 6 = 30(6)
B_S 9 + 6 = 15	15 + 6 = 21	21 + 6 = 27(3)	3 + 6 = 9
10 + 6 = 16	16 + 6 = 22	22 + 6 = 28(4)	B_F 4 + 6 = 10

Figure 4.19 gives the wave complete winding diagram having 12 slots and 4 poles with the connection details.

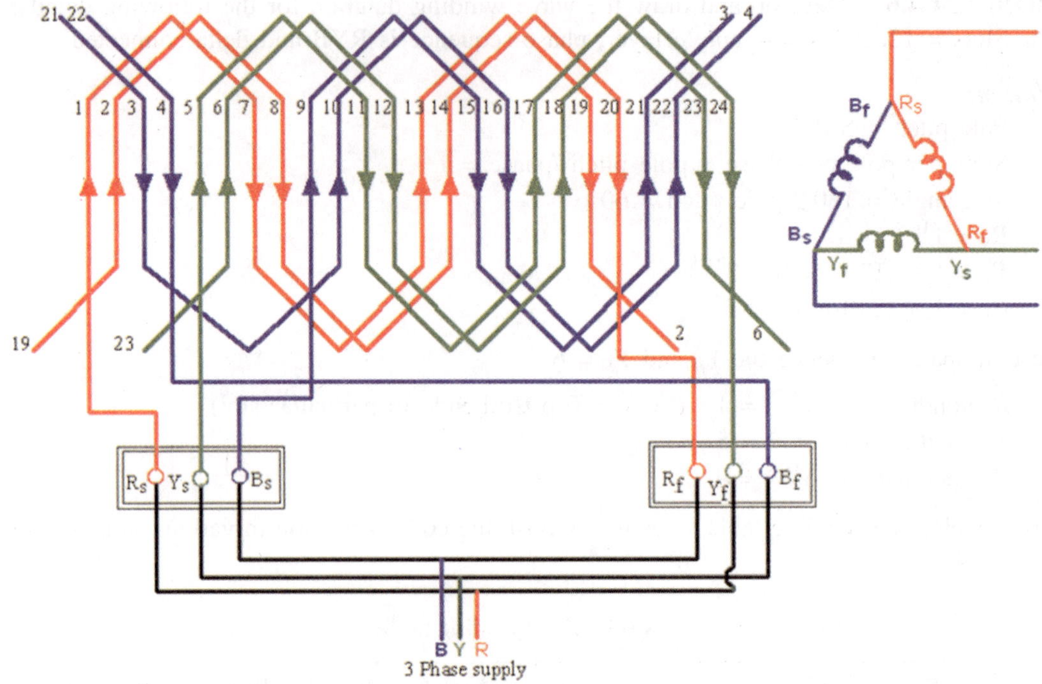

Figure 4.19 Complete winding diagram (solution for problem 4.6).

PROBLEM 4.7: For the following details draw the mush winding diagram.

Number of slots = 12, number of poles = 4 and number of phases = 3.

Solution:

Slots per pole per phase (SPP) = 12/(4 × 3) = 1

Coil span = pole pitch = 12/4 = 3 slots

Slot angle = 180°/pole pitch = 60°

$R_S = 1^{TCS}$ (TCS = Top Coil Side in particular slot)

$Y_S = 1 + (120°/60°) = 3^{TCS}$

$B_S = 1 + (240°/60°) = 5^{TCS}$

In the mush winding, the coil sides are arranged like long and short coil sides alternatively. If the coil span is **odd** then the mush winding is possible and **longer** coil side of first coil is placed in first slot.

If the coil span is **even** then the mush winding is not possible, then make the coil span reduced by one, i.e., **actual coil span** – 1 (for example, 6 – 1 = 5). Now, the mush winding is possible and **shorter** coil side of first coil is placed in first slot.

Figure 4.20 gives the complete mush winding diagram having 12 slots and 4 poles with the connection details.

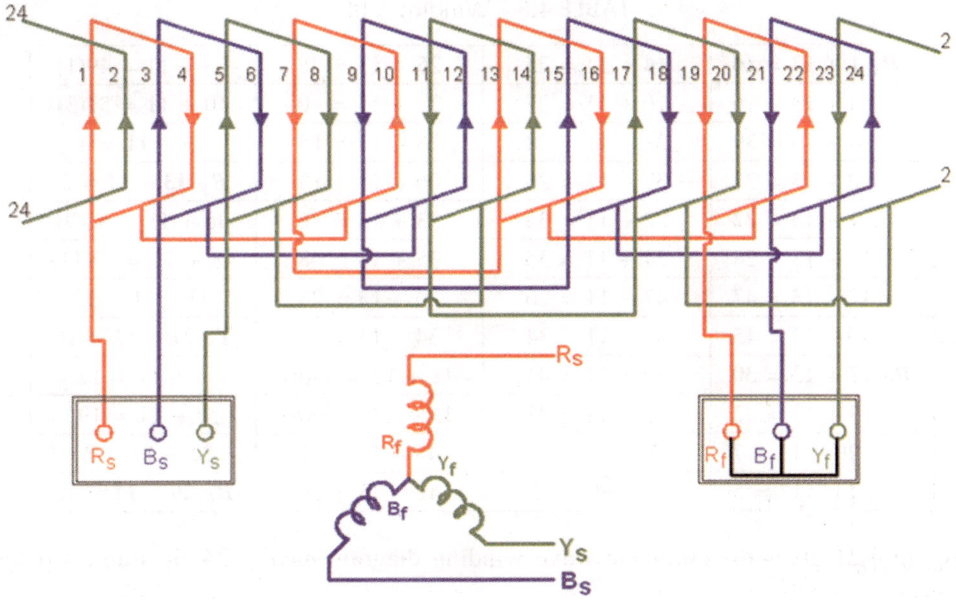

Figure 4.20 Complete winding diagram (solution for problem 4.7).

PROBLEM 4.8: Develop the wave winding for the stator of an induction motor having 24 slots, 4 poles, RYB phase sequence and double layer.

Solution:

Pole pitch = S/P = 6

Slots per pole per phase = pole pitch/phase = 2

Slot angle = 180°/pole pitch = 30°

$R_S = 1^{\text{TCS}}$ (TCS = Top Coil Side in particular slot)

$Y_S = 1 + (120°/30°) = 5^{\text{TCS}}$

$B_S = 1 + (240°/30°) = 9^{\text{TCS}}$

The total winding pitch $Y = Y_B + Y_F = 12 \times 2 = 24$ coil

$Y_B = 13$ and $Y_F = 11$

R_S conductor in $1^{\text{TCS}} = 1$ (TCS = Top coil side in particular slot)

Y_S conductor in $5^{\text{TCS}} = 9$

B_S conductor in $9^{\text{TCS}} = 17$

Now, develop the winding table so as to establish the coil connection in various slots as shown in Table 4.8.

TABLE 4.8 Winding table

R_S **1 + 13 = 14**	14 + 11 = 25	25 + 13 = 38	38 + 11 = 49(1)
3 + 13 = 16	16 + 11 = 27	27 + 13 = 40	40 + 11 = 51(3)
4 – 13 = 39	39 – 11 = 28	28 – 13 = 15	15 – 11 = 4
2 – 13 = 37	37 – 11 = 26	26 – 13 = 13	R_F **13 – 11 = 2**
Y_S **9 + 13 = 22**	22 + 11 = 33	33 + 13 = 46	46 + 11 = 57(9)
11 + 13 = 24	24 + 11 = 35	35 + 13 = 48	48 + 11 = 59(11)
12 – 13 = 47	47 – 11 = 36	36 – 13 = 23	23 – 11 = 12
10 – 13 = 45	45 – 11 = 34	34 – 13 = 21	Y_F **21 – 11 = 10**
B_S **17 + 13 = 30**	30 + 11 = 41	41 + 13 = 54(6)	6 + 11 = 17
19 + 13 = 32	32 + 11 = 43	43 + 13 = 56(8)	8 + 11 = 19
20 – 13 = 7	7 – 11 = 44	44 – 13 = 31	31 – 11 = 20
18 – 13 = 5	5 – 11 = 42	42 – 13 = 29	B_F **29 – 11 = 18**

Figure 4.21 gives the complete wave winding diagram having 24 slots and 4 poles with the connection details.

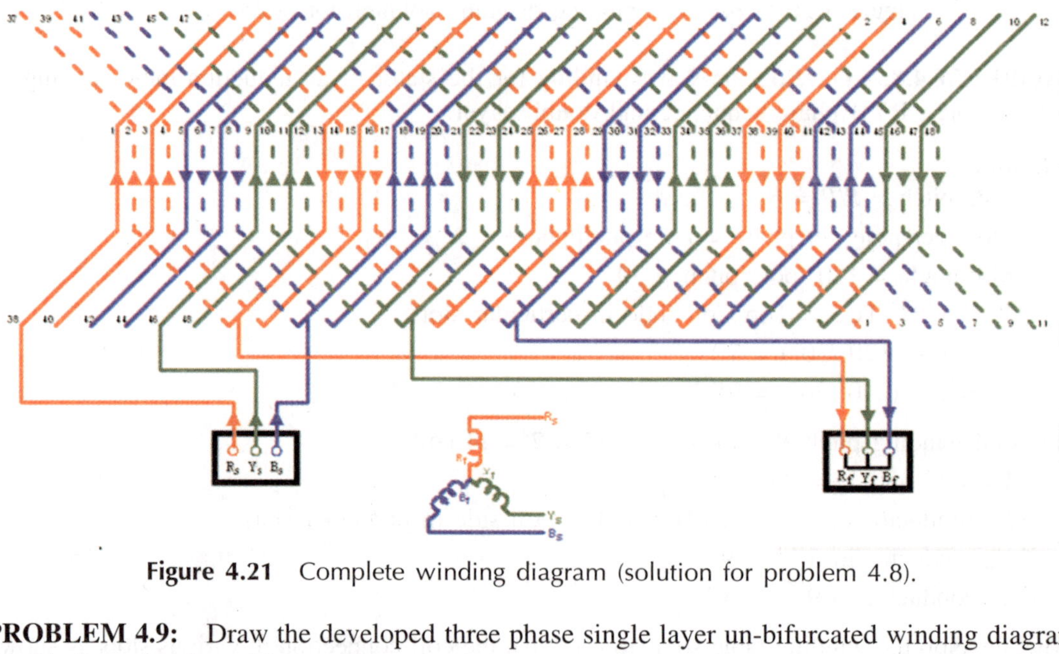

Figure 4.21 Complete winding diagram (solution for problem 4.8).

PROBLEM 4.9: Draw the developed three phase single layer un-bifurcated winding diagram for 24 slots, 4 poles with two plane overhang.

Solution:

Slots per pole per phase (SPP) = 24/(4 × 3) = 2

Coil span = pole pitch = 24/4 = 6 slots

Slot angle = 180°/pole pitch = 30°

$R_S = 1^{TCS}$ (TCS = Top Coil Side in particular slot)

$Y_S = 1 + (1200/300) = 5^{TCS}$

$B_S = 1 + (2400/300) = 9^{TCS}$

The given number of pole pairs is even; therefore it will overhang in two planes.

Figure 4.22 gives the complete un-bifurcated winding diagram having 24 slots and 4 poles with the connection details.

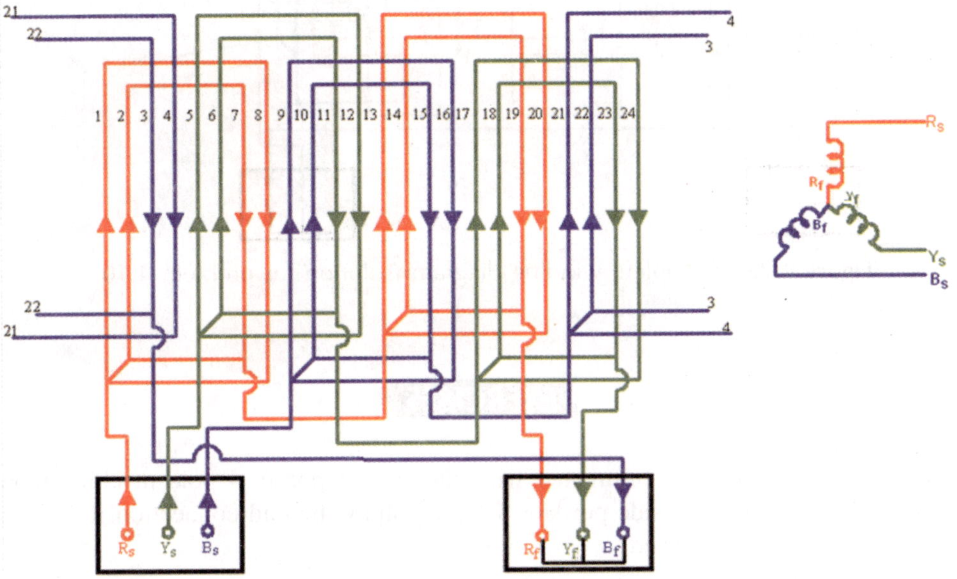

Figure 4.22 Complete winding diagram (solution for problem 4.9).

PROBLEM 4.10: Develop a two plane overhang winding diagram for three phase AC machine with 36 slots and 6 poles.

Solution:

Slots/pole/phase (SPP) = $36/(6 \times 3) = 2$

Coil span = pole pitch = $36/6 = 6$ slots

Slot angle = $180°/\text{pole pitch} = 30°$

$R_S = 1^{TCS}$ (TCS = Top Coil Side in particular slot)

$Y_S = 1 + (120°/30°) = 5^{TCS}$

$B_S = 1 + (240°/30°) = 9^{TCS}$

The given number of pole pairs is odd, therefore it will overhang in two planes and also results one coil group as cranked coil.

Figure 4.23 gives the complete two plane overhang winding diagram having 36 slots and 6 poles with the connection details.

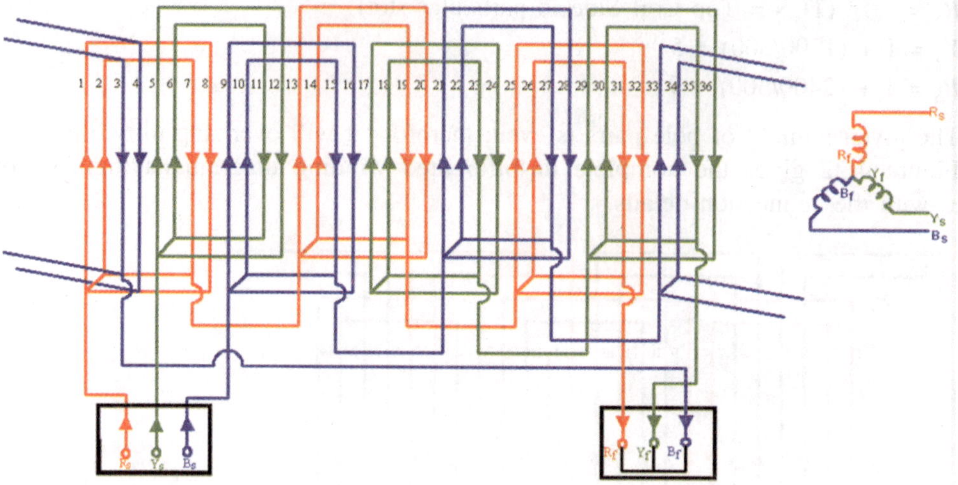

Figure 4.23 Complete winding diagram (solution for problem 4.10).

EXERCISES

1. Draw a single layer un-bifurcated winding for a 3 phase, 4 pole machine having 24 slots. Assume one coil side per slot. Clearly, show the end connection if a continuous chain arrangement is used.
2. Draw the developed winding diagram for the following details: 3 phase AC lap winding, slots = 24, poles = 4, phase sequence = RBY and double layer.
3. A 3 phase AC machine has 24 slots and 6 poles. Draw the developed winding diagram and assume it is delta connected and phase sequence is RYB.
4. Draw a single layer bifurcated winding for a 3 phase, 4 pole machine having 24 slots. Assume one coil side per slot. Clearly, show the end connection if a continuous chain arrangement is used. Is it possible to have a bifurcated winding, if the slots are changed from 24 to 36, if not state the reason?
5. Draw the developed 3 phase AC winding diagram for 24 slots, double layer, full pitched wave connected and 4 poles. Also, show the winding in delta connection.
6. A 3 phase, 10 poles and 50 Hz machine has 72 armature slots. Construct the winding table for fractional slot winding. Draw the winding diagram with a coil span of seven slots.
7. A 3 phase machine has 4 poles and 48 armature slots. If the coils are chorded by one slot, draw the double layer winding diagram. State the reason as why that chording more than 1/3 pole pitch is not used in practise.

8. Develop the winding of an alternator of 27 slots, 4 poles, RBY phase sequence and double layer.
9. Develop and draw the wave winding diagram for the following details:
Slots = 14, poles = 4, double layer, phase sequence is RYB and star connected.
10. Draw the mush winding diagram for a 3 phase AC machine having number of slots = 18 and number of poles = 4.
11. Develop the wave winding for an induction motor with 18 slots, 4 poles, RBY phase sequence and double layer.
12. Develop a two plane overhang winding diagram for 3 phase, 26 slots and 4 poles.

5 Single Line Diagrams and Substations

Learning Objectives

This chapter enumerates the various modes of power generation done in practise, the transmission and distribution of power to the consumers and understand the various components used in transmission and distribution of electric power and their representation in single line diagram.

5.1 INTRODUCTION

Usually, the power is generated in a remote place away from residential or industrial areas or urban places. For example, hydroelectric power station is located at a place where there is availability of water to generate power and this power generated in such station is to be transmitted to other residential or industrial areas or urban places in order to fulfil the energy demand.

The power generated in the generating stations cannot be directly transmitted to meet the consumer's needs. Hence, the power generated will be first stepped up depending on the requirement then transmitted and this power is received in a power station where, again it is stepped up or down and later it is distributed to the consumers. This station, where the power is stepped up or down is called as *substation*.

Right from the generating station to receiving station and to the consumers, there are numerous electrical apparatus involved in order to cater to the energy demand of the consumers. It is always necessary to have a pictorial representation of the flow of power from generating station to the consumers but drawing all the components becomes difficult and hasty. Hence, a diagram with only the representations of the symbols can be drawn and this sort of a diagram which gives the complete information is called as a '*single line diagram*'.

These diagrams or representations are extensively used and the location or identification of electrical faults is also easier by the help of these diagrams.

5.2 GENERATING STATION

Generating station refers to the place where the electricity is generated. For examples, hydroelectric generating station, nuclear station, thermal, diesel, etc., usually these stations are located away from urban or densely populated areas and where the resources are available in plenty. Usually, the electricity generated is around 11 kV in a hydroelectric generating station. This generated electricity is to be transmitted to the urban areas or to the consumers. When this generated voltage of 11 kV is transmitted, then due to transmission losses, at the receiving end we might not receive the suitable voltage and the very same might not be used by all the consumers. Henceforth as soon as the power is generated, the voltage thus generated should be stepped up.

5.3 SUBSTATION

Substation refers to the place where the electricity generated in the generating station is stepped up or down for transmission purpose depending upon the requirement. The station or the location where the electricity is stepped down for distribution purpose to the consumer is known as *distribution substation*. Figure 5.1 gives the classification of substation.

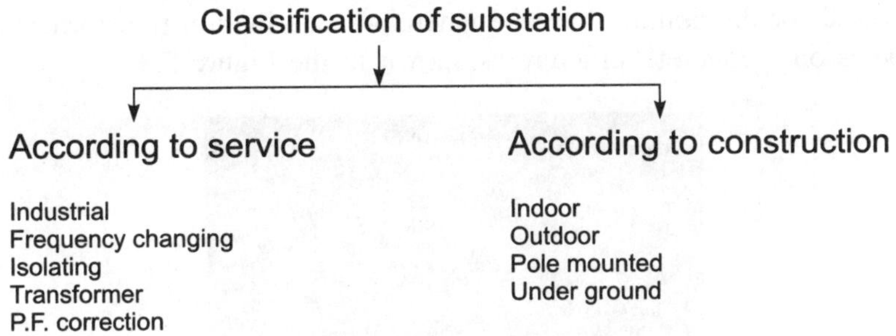

Figure 5.1 The classification of substation.

MUSS: Refers to **Master Unit Sub Station**

5.3.1 Pole Mounted Substation

This is mainly used for distribution purpose wherein a distribution transformer is mounted on the pole or in between two poles with the help of supporting rails as shown in Figure 5.2.

Figure 5.2 Pole mounted substation, *Courtesy:* Bescom.

5.3.2 Plinth Mounted Substation

This is mainly used for distribution purpose wherein a distribution transformer is mounted in between two poles on a concrete structure as shown in the Figure 5.3.

Figure 5.3 Plinth mounted substation, *Courtesy:* Bescom.

***Note:* The transformers used in both pole and plinth mounted substations are distribution transformers, which are of shell type in construction and their essential duty is to step down the voltage from the lines and transmit it to the consumers.

5.4 RECEIVING STATION

Receiving station refers to the place which is usually located in an urban area or a place which is nearer to the consumer. The power generated from the generating station is stepped up in a substation and is then transmitted via transmission lines; this power is received in the receiving stations. The consumer requirement differs from consumer to consumer. Consumers are mainly of two kinds, they are domestic and commercial consumers. A commercial consumer refers to industries and domestic consumers refer to household purposes. Thus, receiving stations are mainly responsible to receive power from a generating station and then depending on requirement transmit it to distribution substations for distribution of power to the consumers.

5.5 REPRESENTATION OF VARIOUS ELECTRICAL APPARATUS

The Table 5.1 gives the various electrical apparatus used in representing the single line diagram.

TABLE 5.1 Representation of electrical apparatus

S.No.	*Representation*	*Description*
1		*AC generator*: It is responsible for generating sinusoidal or alternating voltage.
2		*Lightning arrestor* (LA) with grounded: Where all the transmission line is exposed to sunlight, at such places lightning arrestors should be provided compulsorily.
3		*Wave trap* (WT): This is used to eliminate any unwanted radiations like the radio frequency and electromagnetic radiations abrupting the transmission process.
4		*Current transformer* (CT): This is used to measure the current flowing in the transmission line and is always connected in series with the transmission line.
5	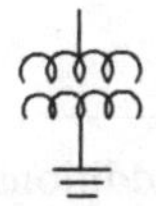	*Potential transformer* (PT): This is used to check the voltage flowing in the transmission line and is always connected in parallel with the transmission line.
6		*Coupling condenser* (CC):

S.No.	Representation	Description
7		*Earthing switch* (ES): This is a normal switch but when connected along with ground then it is called as earthing switch. It is used to eliminate stray charges.
8	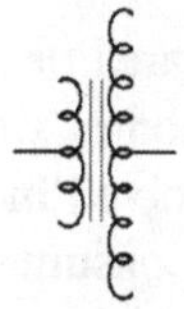	*Step up transformer*: It is used to step up the voltage.
9	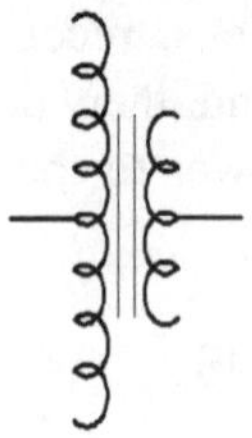	*Step down transformer*: It is used to step down the voltage.
10	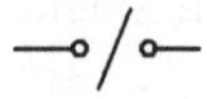	*Isolator*: This is nothing but a switch.
11	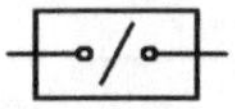	*Bus coupler* (BC): It is used to couple 2 bus bars.
12		*Oil circuit breaker* (OCB): It is used in places where the voltage level is high.
13	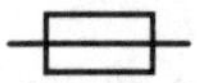	*Low tension oil circuit breaker* (LT OCB): It is used in places where the voltage level is low.
14		*Transformer with delta star connection*: In a star delta transformer the primary is connected in star connection and secondary in delta connection and vice versa.
15		*Feeder*: A feeder is structure resembling bus bar responsible for feeding or providing power to consumers.
16		*Bus bar*: This is a thick conductor. It can be used either vertically or horizontally. It is used to distribute power.

Note: In a substation, along with the main bus bar there is always one more additional bus bar used just along the main or original bus bar known as the *duplicate bus bar*. Both the original or main and the duplicate bus bars are coupled or connected together by a bus coupler. The main aim of using this duplicate bus bar is that in case of a fault or failure of the main bus bar, the main bus bar is isolated from the healthy system and the supply to the consumers is restored by the duplicate bus bar, thereby the consumer receives uninterrupted power supply.

5.6 LIST OF GENERATING STATIONS IN KARNATAKA

5.6.1 Nonrenewable

Table 5.2 shows the thermal power plants in Karnataka with their locations, units rating and capacities.

TABLE 5.2 Thermal power plants

Name	*Location*	*Unit rating*	*Capacity (MW)*
Raichur Thermal Power Station	Raichur	7 × 210, 1 × 250	1720
Bellary Thermal Power Station	Kudatini	1 × 500	500
JSW EL-SBU-I Power Plant	Vijayanagar	2 × 130	260
JSW EL-SBU-II Power Plant	Vijayanagar	2 × 300	600
Udupi Thermal Power Plant	Nandikoor	1 × 600	600

Table 5.3 shows the nuclear power plant in Karnataka with its location, reactor unit and installed capacity.

TABLE 5.3 Nuclear power plant

Power station	*Location*	*Reactor unit* (MW)	*Installed Capacity* (MW)
Kaiga nuclear power plant	Kaiga	4 × 220	880

Table 5.4 shows the diesel power plant in Karnataka with its location, unit rating and capacity.

TABLE 5.4 Diesel power plant

Power station	*Location*	*Units rating*	*Capacity (MW)*
Yelahanka Diesel Power Station	Yelahanka	6 × 21.32	127.92
Mallapura Mini	Mallapura	2 × 4.5	9
Sirwar Mini	Sirwar	1 × 1	1

5.6.2 Renewable

Table 5.5 shows the hydroelectric power plants in Karnataka with their generator units and capacities.

TABLE 5.5 Hydroelectric power plants

Station	*Generator unit*	*Capacity* (MW)
Sharavathi	10 × 103.5, 2 × 27.5, 4 × 60	1,469
Kalinadi	2 × 50, 1 × 135, 5 × 150, 3 × 50, 3 × 40	1,240
Linganamakki Dam	1 × 55	55
Gerusoppa	4 × 60	240
MGHE-1	4 × 13.2	52.8
MGHE-2	4 × 21.6	86.4
Bhadra right bank-1	1 × 7.2	7.2
Bhadra right bank-2	1 × 6	6
Bhadra left bank-1	2 × 12	24
Bhadra left bank-2	1 × 2	2
Supa dam	2 × 50	100
Nahjhari-1	2 × 135	270
Nagjhari-2	4 × 150	600
Kadra dam	3 × 50	150
Kodasalli dam	3 × 40	120
Varahi river	4 × 115	460
Mani	2 × 4.5	9
Ghataprabha	2 × 16	32
Almatti-1	1 × 15	15
Almatti-2	5 × 55	275
Shivanasamudra-1	4 × 6	24
Shivanasamudra-2	6 × 3	18
Shimsahpura	2 × 8.6	17.2
Munirabad-1	2 × 9	18
Munirabad-2	1 × 10	10

Table 5.6 shows the wind power plants in Karnataka with their locations and total capacities.

TABLE 5.6 Wind power plants

Power Plant	*Location*	*Total capacity* (MW)
Saundatti	Belgaum	84
Nuziveedu Seeds	Bhimasamudra	50.40
Jogmatti BSES	Chitradurga Dist	14
Harapanahalli	Davanagere	40
Kappadagudda-1	Kappadagudda	9 × 0.225 = 2.025
Kappadagudda-2	Kappadagudda	11 × 0.230 = 2.53

Table 5.7 shows the solar power plants in Karnataka with their locations, generator units and capacities.

TABLE 5.7 Solar power plants

Power Plant	*Location*	*Generator unit*	*Capacity (MW)*
Yalesandra Solar PV Plant	Kolar	1 × 3	3
Itnal Solar PV Plant	Belgaum	1 × 3	3

***Data courtesy of Karnataka Power Corporation website*

5.7 SOLVED PROBLEMS

PROBLEM 5.1: Draw a neat single line diagram using I.S.I. symbols for a 110 kV/11 kV M.U.S.S. with the following details:

- Incoming lines: Two, 110 kV
- Lines: Two, OCB 110 kV
- Transformers: Two, step down 110 kV/11 kV
- LT OCBs for transformers: Two
- Duplicate bus bars on high tension (HT) and low tension (LT) sides to be indicated
- Bus coupler on HT side only
- Feeders: Six, 11 kV at LT bus
- LT circuit breakers for feeders: Six
- Station supply transformer: 11 kV/415 V to be shown at LT side

Indicate earthing switch, coupling condensers, lightning arrestors, wave traps, PTs and CTs at appropriate places.

Solution:

Analysing the problem: According to the above stated problem, we have to draw the single line representation of a master unit substation which converts 110 kV to 11 kV. Here, the incoming lines are of 110 kV and there are 2 lines. There should be a facility such that whenever during maintenance, the incoming line is to be disconnected; henceforth we can use a switch

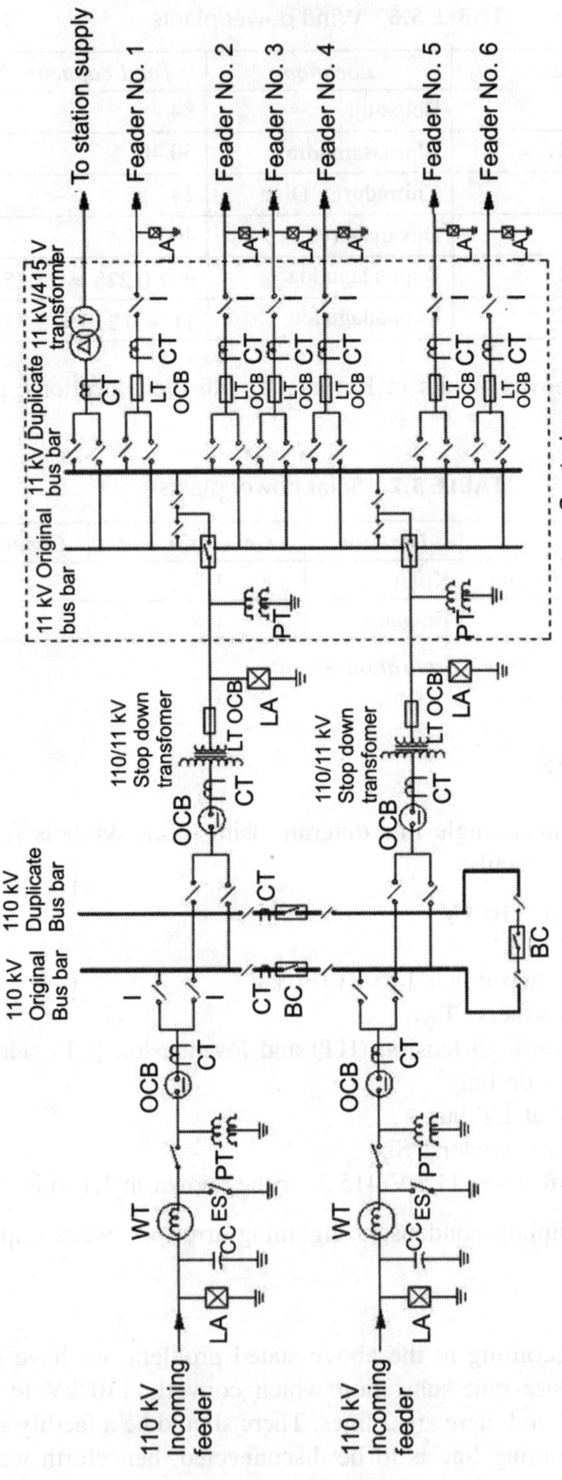

Figure 5.4 Single line diagram (solution for problem 5.1).

for control purpose. As this incoming line is exposed to sunlight, it should be provided with a lightning arrestor and a wave trap.

Note: Please don't be of the opinion that only 2 OCBs are to be used as stated in the problem. Protective devices and other equipment can be used number of times for safety purpose and should be placed at the right places.

While drawing a single line diagram, it is always recommended that the representation of all the equipment is drawn first and used as number of times required in order to save time. Although a few of representation is readily available in the AutoCAD library, it is necessary to draw equipment like lightning arrestor, oil circuit breaker, bus coupler, CT, PT, etc.

Set the units and limits in the CAD window as stated earlier.

Procedure to draw various representation of equipment in CAD:

- ***Lightning arrestor:*** Select the rectangular icon available in the left side drawing toolbar of the AutoCAD window and draw a rectangle. Now, switch off ORTHO command and switch on the OSNAP command and then select the line icon and draw 2 diagonals inside the rectangle intersecting each other. Now, draw to vertical lines to the rectangle as shown in Table 5.1 and connect one line to the GND.
- ***Drawing GND symbol:*** Type as DC in the command window and press enter. A design centre library box will pop-up. In this window select electrical or electronic components and then select blocks, when this is done, there are number of electrical symbols available. Select GND symbol in it and right click on it, and select insert and redefine which gives rise to new dialog box. There select as uniform scale and give a value for example, 25 and press ok and then place the symbol wherever required in the AutoCAD window.
- ***Current transformer:*** Type DC in command window and select inductance symbol and place it on the AutoCAD screen. Now, select the inductance symbol and explode it to break it into individual entities. Now, select the unwanted part and delete it such that we have only one turn and draw straight lines as shown in the symbol of current transformer in the Table 5.1.
- ***Oil circuit breaker:*** This representation is not available in the design centre window of AutoCAD henceforth it is to be drawn using circles and lines.

PROBLEM 5.2: Draw the single line diagram of a substation having the following equipment:

(i) Incoming lines: Two, 110 kV, 50 Hz
(ii) Outgoing lines: One, 110 kV, 50 Hz
Three, 11 kV, 50 Hz
(iii) Transformers: Two, 5 MVA, 110 kV/11 kV, 3 phase, Δ/Δ
One, 15 MVA, 110/220 kV, 3 phase, Δ/Δ
(iv) Auxiliary station transformer: One, 500 kVA, 11 kV/400 V, 3 phase, Δ/Y
(v) The station is connected to another substation through the 15 MVA transformer of 110/220 kV.

Show the positions of CT, PT, isolating switches, lightning arrestors and circuit breakers.

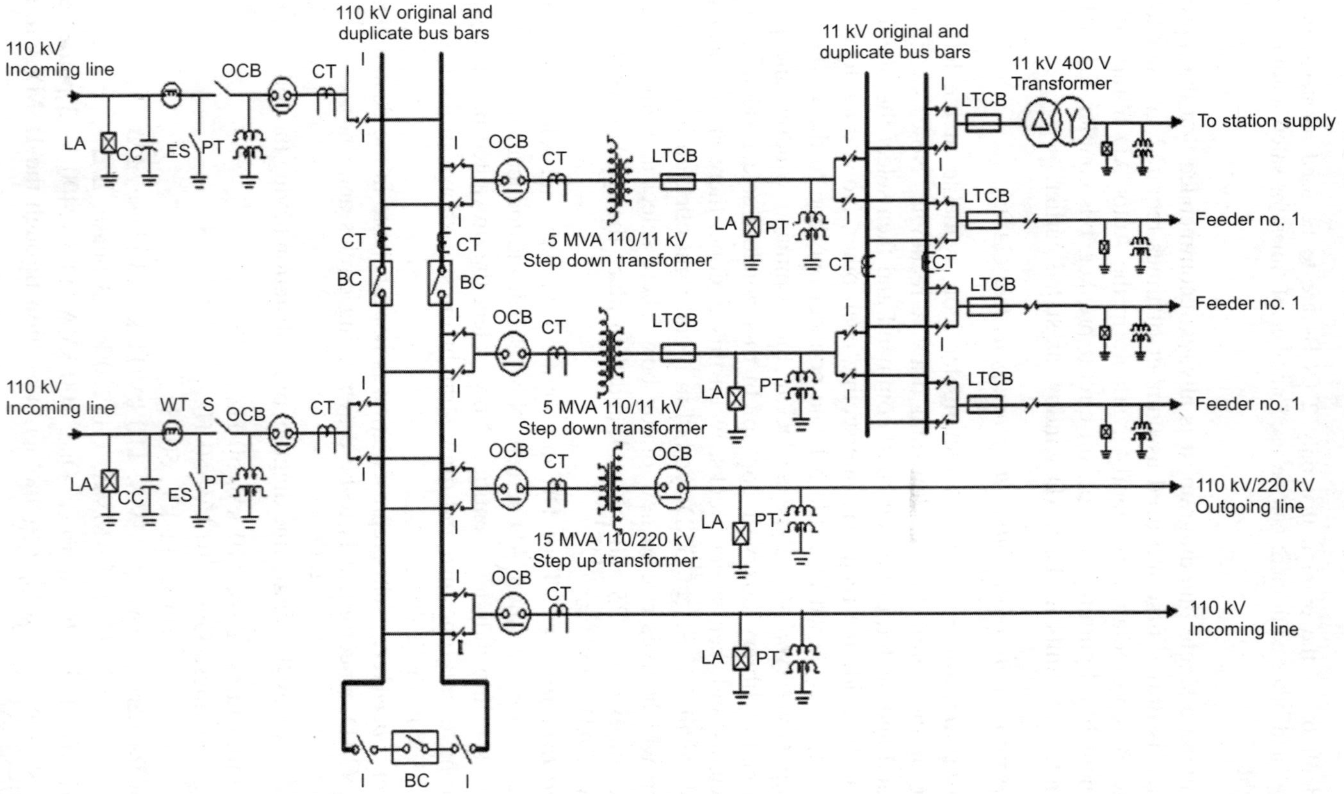

Figure 5.5 Single line diagram (solution for problem 5.2).

Solution:

Analysing the Problem: According to the above stated problem, we have to draw the single line representation of a substation which has the above stated equipment.

Here, the incoming lines are of 110 kV and there are 2 lines. There should be a facility such that whenever during maintenance, the incoming line is to be disconnected; henceforth we can use a switch for control purpose. As this incoming line is exposed to sunlight it should be provided with a lightning arrestor and a wave trap and the same procedure stated in the Problem 5.1 may be followed.

EXERCISES

1. Draw the single line diagram of a substation having the following equipment:
(a) Incoming lines: Two, 110 kV, 50 Hz
(b) Outgoing lines: Four, 33 kV, 50 Hz
(c) Transformers: Two, 110/33 kV, 3 phase, Y/Δ
(d) Bus bars: One, 110 kV
Two, 33 kV
Show the positions of CT, PT, isolating switches, lightning arrestors and circuit breakers. (VTU, June 2013)

2. Draw the single line diagram of a substation having the following equipment:
(a) Incoming lines: Two, 220 kV, 50 Hz
(b) Outgoing lines: Four, 33 kV, 50 Hz
Two, 66 kV, 50 Hz
(c) Transformers: Two, 220/33 kV, 3 phase, Y/Δ
Two, 220/66 kV, 3 phase, Y/Δ
(d) Bus bars: One, 220 kV
Two, 33 kV
Two, 66 kV
Show the positions of CT, PT, isolating switches, lightning arrestors and circuit breakers.

3. Draw the single line diagram of a substation having the following equipment:
(a) Incoming line: One, 110 kV, 50 Hz
(b) Outgoing lines: Three, 13.2 kV, 50 Hz
Four, 11 kV, 50 Hz
(c) Transformer: One, 15 MVA, 110/13.2 kV, 3 phase
(d) Auxiliary station transformer: One, 750 kVA, 11 kV/400 V
(e) Bus bars: One, 110 kV
One, 13.2 kV
One, 11 kV
Show the positions of CT, PT, isolators, lightning arrestors and circuit breakers. (VTU, June 2013)

4. Draw the single line diagram of a 66 kV MUSS with the following details:
   (a) Coming lines: Two, 66 kV
   (b) Step down transformers: Two, 66 kV/11 kV
   (c) OCBs for transformer bank on LT side: Two
   (d) Duplicate bus bars for HT and LT side: Two
   (e) Bus coupler for HT side only
   (f) Feeders: Four, 11 kV radiating from LT bus
   (g) LT circuits breakers for feeders: Four

   Position of lighting arrestors, isolators, CTs and PTs are to be indicated.
   (VTU, June 2013)

5. Draw the single line diagram of a generating station having the following details:
   (a) Generators: Two, 50 MVA, 11 kV, 3 phase
   (b) Transformers: Two, 50 MVA, 11/132 kV, 3 phase
   (c) Transformers (auxiliary): Two, 50 MVA, 11 kV/440 V
   (d) Transformer (reverse): One, 1 MVA, 132/11 kV
   (e) Outgoing lines: Two, 132 kV, 3 phase

   Also indicate the position of CT, PT, isolating switches, lightning arrestor and circuit breakers. (VTU, June 2013)

6. Draw the single line diagram of a 66 kV MUSS with the following details:
   (a) Incoming line: Two, 66 kV
   (b) Step down transformers: Two, 66 kV/11 kV
   (c) OCBs for transformer bank on LT side: Two
   (d) Duplicate bus bars for HT and LT side to be provided
   (e) Bus coupler for HT side only
   (f) Feeders: Four, 11 kV radiating from LT bus
   (g) LT circuits breakers for feeders: Four

   Position of lighting arrestors, isolators, CTs and PTs are to be indicated.
   (VTU, June 2013)

7. Draw the single line diagram of a generating station having the following details:
   (a) Generators: Two, 50 MVA, 11 kV, 3 phase
   (b) Transformers: Two, 50 MVA, 11/132 kV, 3 phase
   (c) Transformers (auxiliary): Two, 500 kVA, 11 kV/400 V
   (d) Transformers (reverse): One, 1 MVA, 132/11 kV
   (e) Outgoing lines: Two, 132 kV, 3 phase

   Also indicate positions of CTs, PTs, isolating switches, lighting arrestors and circuit breakers. (VTU, June 2013)

8. Draw the single line diagram of a 66 kV MUSS and indicate all the devices.

9. Draw the single line diagram of a pole mounted substation.

10. Draw the single line diagram of a plinth mounted substation.

11. Draw the block diagram of the following generating stations:

(a) Nuclear power station
(b) Low, medium and high head hydroelectric power station
(c) Thermal power station
(d) Diesel power plant

12. Draw an 11 kV pin type insulator.

6 DC Machine Assembly

Learning Objectives

This chapter illustrates the importance of DC machine, its types and various parts with the importance of each part along with its characteristics, use and assembly using AutoCAD software in a step by step manner.

6.1 INTRODUCTION

DC machines are known for their uniqueness. Although the DC supply is not readily available, many industries and applications employ DC machines. Just by connecting the field winding to the armature in various combinations, DC machines can be operated as shunt, series and compound machines. They provide a wide range of voltage and current ratios along with a smooth control of speed.

DC machines are characterised by their versatility. By means of various combinations of shunt, series and separately-excited field windings, they can be designed to display a wide variety of volt-ampere or speed-torque characteristics for both dynamic and steady state operation. Because of the ease with which they can be controlled, systems of DC machines have been frequently used in applications requiring a wide range of motor speeds or precise control of motor output.

There are mainly two basic circuits used in any DC motor, the *armature* (the device that rotates sometimes referred to as a rotor) and the *field* (the stationary part, sometimes referred to as a stator). The two components magnetically interact with one another to produce rotation.

The armature rotates as a result of the repelling motion created by the magnetic flux of the armature, in opposition to the magnetic flux created by the field winding. The windings are placed in the slots of the armature.

There are many coils (windings) around the armature to allow for maximum generation of torque. The polarity of the armature coils must be reversed at the precise time to ensure that the repelling action continues. This action is called *commutation* and takes place when properly aligned brushes are contacting the commutator.

The parts of a DC machine may look slightly different, depending on manufacturer but all DC motors will have following components:

A DC Machine consists of:

Stator: Stationary part of the machine.

It consists of:

(a) Yoke/Frame
(b) Pole cores and pole shoes
(c) Field coils

Rotor: Rotating part of the machine.

It consists of:

(a) Armature core and windings
(b) Commutator
(c) Carbon brushes

Other than that there are following several subsidiary parts:

1. *Armature core*: Central mass of iron on which windings are mounted.
2. *Armature slots*: Hollow spaces on core in which windings are placed.
3. *Shaft*: Circular supporting structure on which the entire armature section is balanced.
4. *Spider*: A metallic frame upon which armature laminations are assembled or mounted.
5. *Collar*: A metallic supporting structure which holds end plates supporting the laminations intact.
6. *Hexagonal nut*: Another metallic structure which holds the second end plate.
7. *Flange*: A metallic structure which secures the laminations intact which is bolted on either side.

6.2 CONSTRUCTION OF A DC MACHINE

Figure 6.1 shows the cross section of a TEFC (totally enclosed fan cooled) DC machine with all the parts. In a small machine, the armature is directly mounted on the shaft whereas in a large machine, the armature is mounted on a frame called as *spider*.

Figure 6.2 shows the cross section of the DC machine with armature core separated from the machine, with commutator and carbon brush.

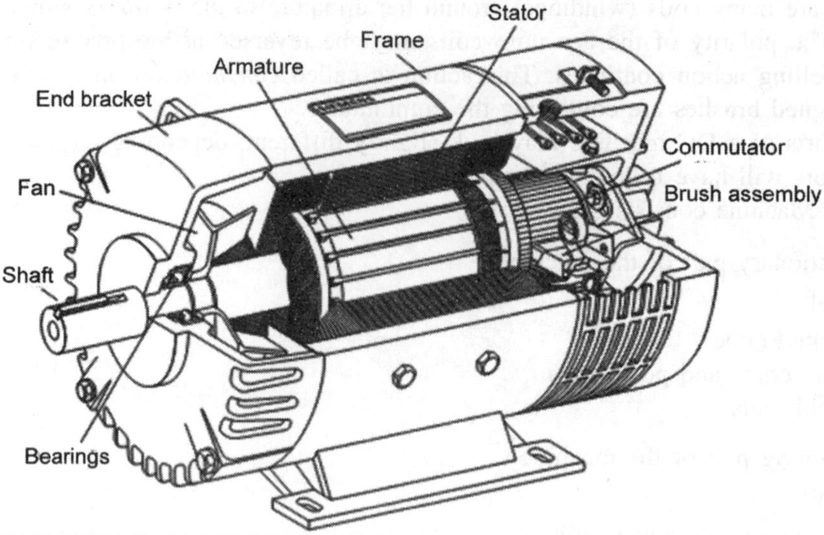

Figure 6.1 Cross section of a DC machine showing all the parts.

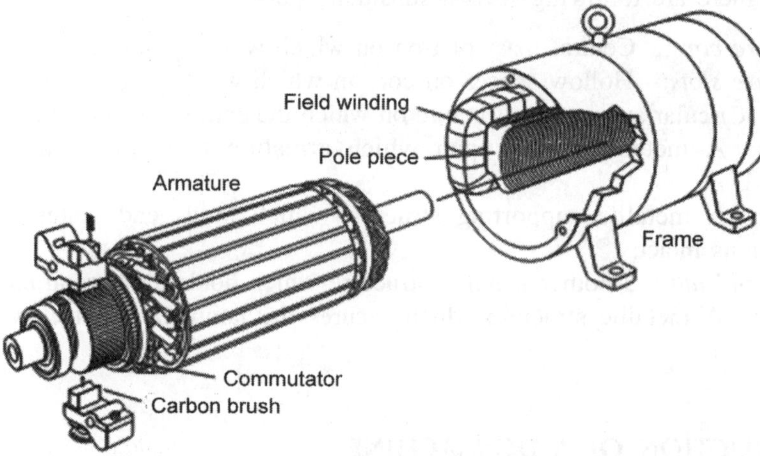

Figure 6.2 Cross section of a DC machine.

Figure 6.3 and 6.4 shows the armature with shaft, commutator and bearings. The winding on the armature is not directly placed, instead of which they are placed in slots provided along with insulation so that the windings do not get misplaced or worn out when the machine is operating.

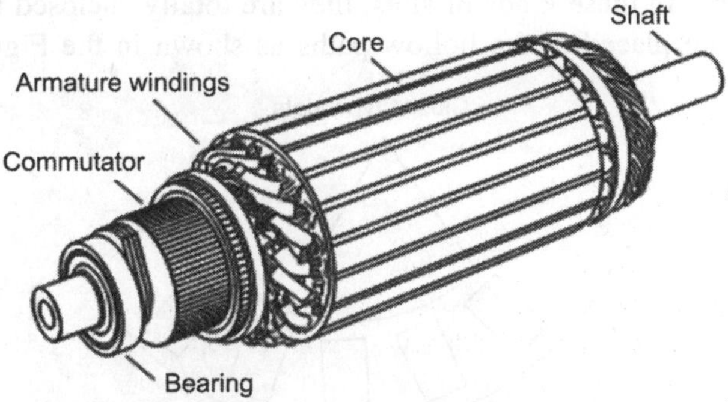

Figure 6.3 Armature core.

Figure 6.4 Armature core.

6.2.1 Slots

Slots are the paths or places in the armature where the conductors are placed to form the armature winding. They are mainly classified based on their appearance on the armature core and their application.

The slots in a machine are mainly of the following types:

1. ***Open type***: In this type of slots, the slots are open as shown in the Figure 6.5(a). The conductors are placed in these windings.

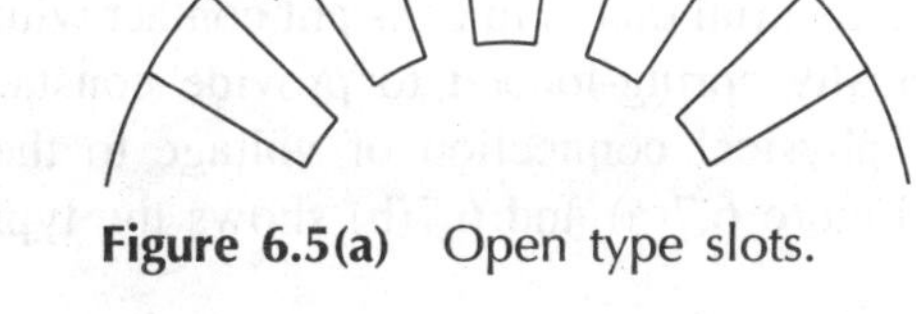

Figure 6.5(a) Open type slots.

2. ***Closed type:*** In these kinds of slots, they are totally enclosed in the armature and the conductors are placed in the hollow paths as shown in the Figure 6.5(b).

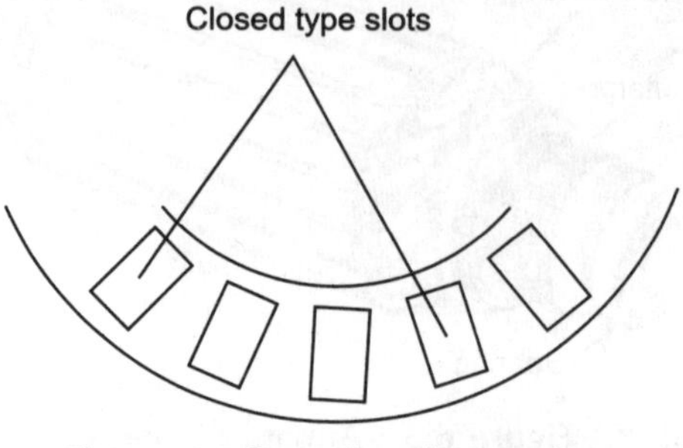

Figure 6.5(b) Closed type slots.

3. ***Semi-enclosed or semi-open type:*** In these kinds of slots, they are neither completely open nor closed as shown in the Figure 6.5(c).

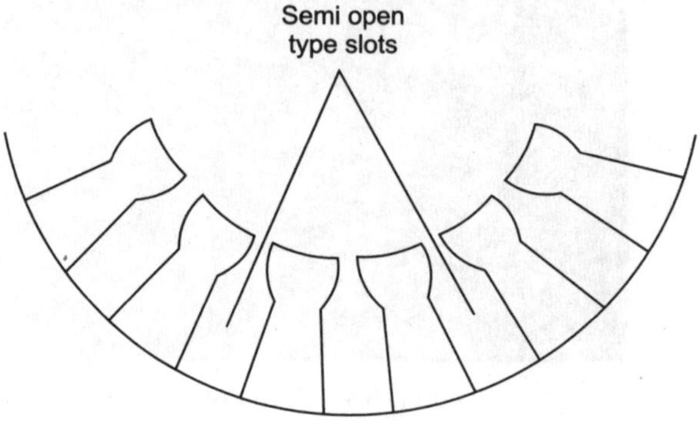

Figure 6.5(c) Semi-enclosed or semi-open type slots.

6.2.2 Commutator

The armature has an integral part, called a *commutator*. The commutator acts as an electrical switch, always switching the polarity of the magnetic flux to ensure that a 'repelling' force taking place. Commutator of a DC machine is shown in Figure 6.6.

6.2.3 Brush

Brushes are made of a carbon material that is in constant contact with the armature's commutator plates. The brushes are typically spring-loaded to provide constant pressure of the brush to the commutator plates. The physical connection of voltage to the armature is accomplished by a device called brushes. Figure 6.7(a) and 6.7(b) shows the typical brush arrangement in a 4 pole DC machine.

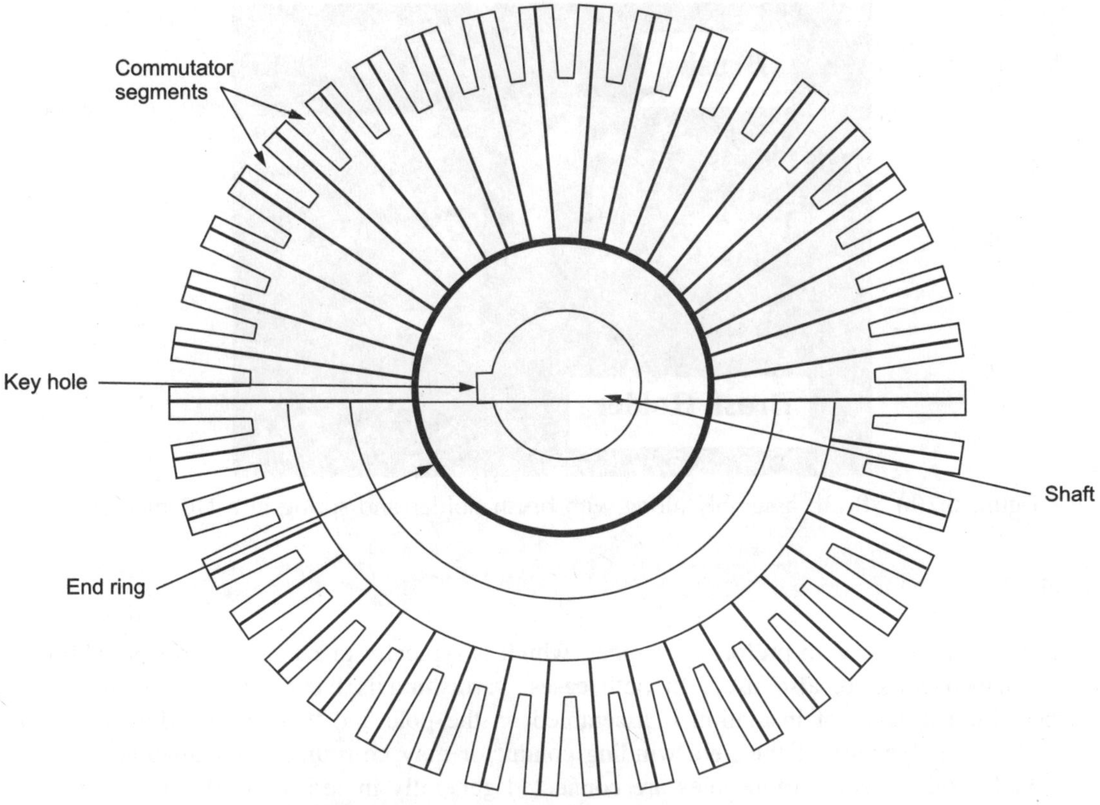

Figure 6.6 Commutator of a DC machine.

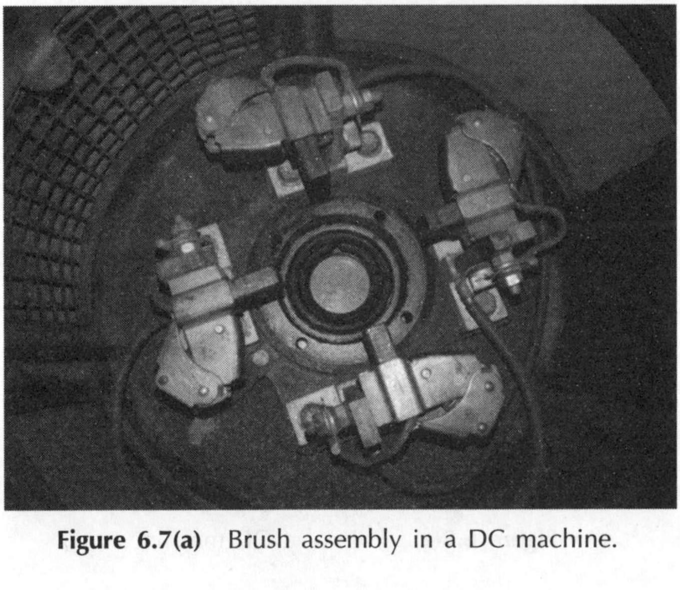

Figure 6.7(a) Brush assembly in a DC machine.

Figure 6.7(b) Brush assembly along with brush holder and spring in a DC machine.

6.2.4 Pole

The poles are wound with preformed copper, which is typically of rectangular shape, although round shaped coils are also used. In both cases, varnishing is the most common insulation method. First, a layer of insulation is assembled on the pole and then the winding is wound on it. The cross section of the field winding conductor may be round or rectangular.

Field coils placed on the poles are connected generally in series and designed for 80 to 85% of excitation voltage. The following Figure 6.8(a), (b), (c) and (d) shows the sectional views of pole and pole coil.

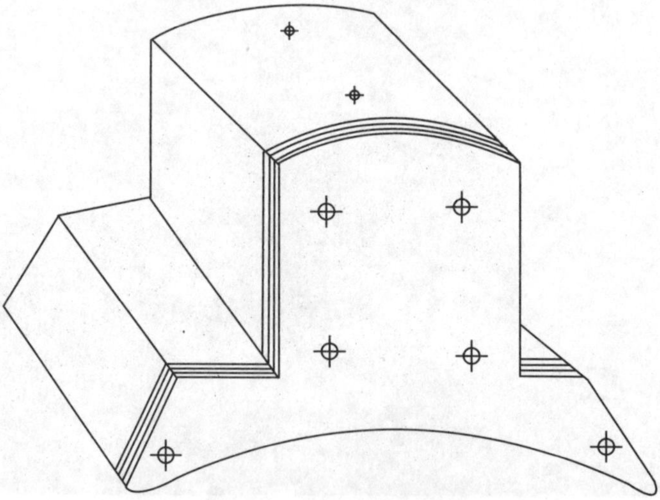

Figure 6.8(a) Pole of a DC machine.

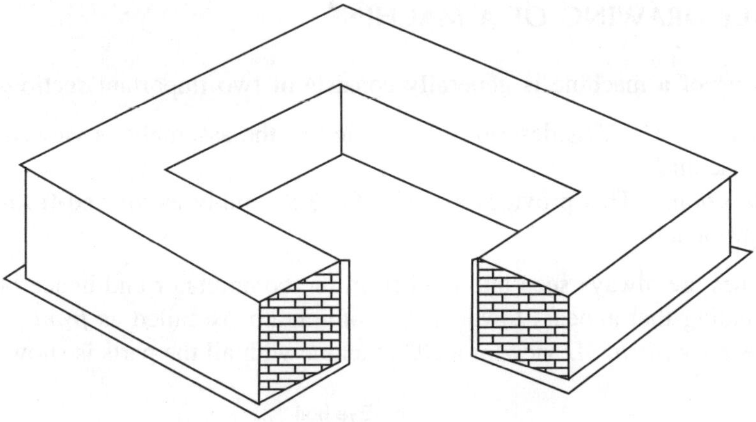

Figure 6.8(b) Pole coil of a DC machine.

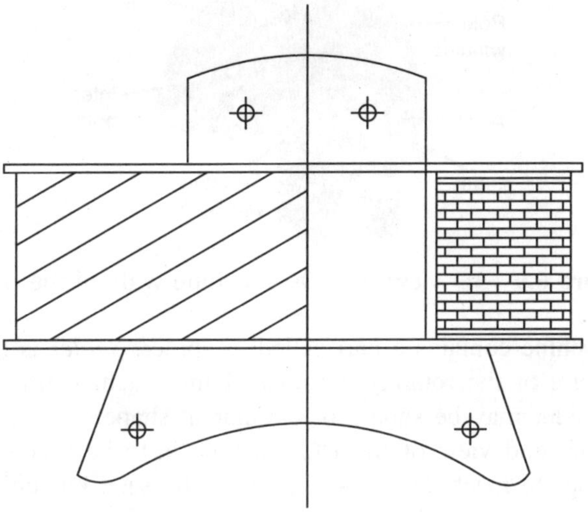

Figure 6.8(c) Right half sectional end view pole of a DC machine.

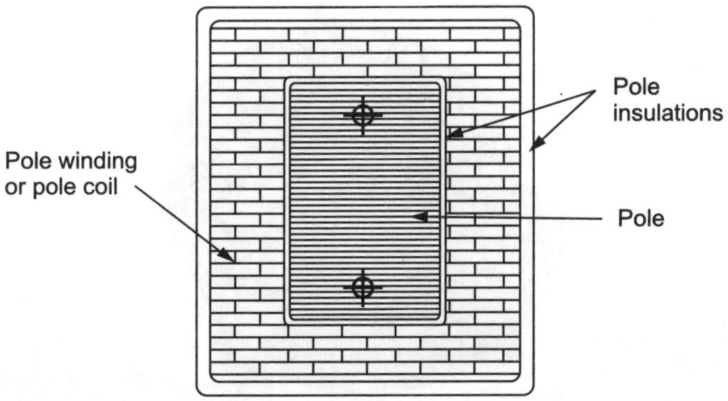

Figure 6.8(d) Sectional view pole coil of a DC machine.

6.3 ASSEMBLY DRAWING OF A MACHINE

Assembly drawing of a machine is generally consists of two important sections:

1. *Front elevation:* This describes the section of the assembly as viewed from the front of the machine.
2. *End elevation:* This provides a view of the assembly as viewed from its either end, i.e., right or left.

DC machines are always seen and read from the commutator end henceforth the pitch in the armature winding that appears towards the commutator is called as *front pitch* and that is away is called as *back pitch*. 3D view of a DC machine with all the parts is shown in Figure 6.9.

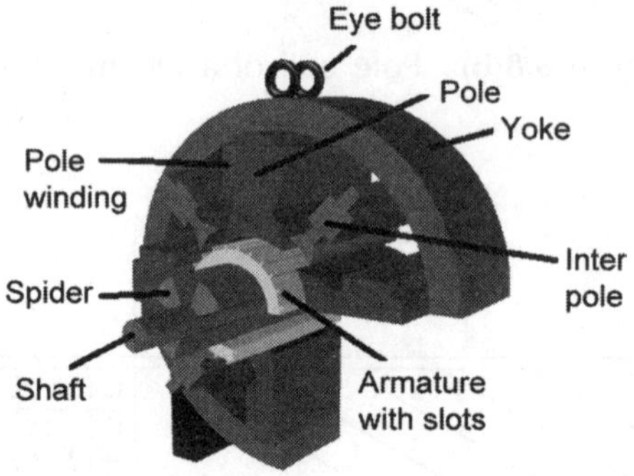

Figure 6.9 3D view of a DC machine with all the parts.

******Note*:** A large machine contains a part called as spider. *Spider* is the part in the machine which holds the armature or the rotating member of the machine firmly to the shaft through dove tail joints. The spider may be square or circular in shape.

When the sectional end view of the DC machine is to be represented, it is not always necessary that the complete machine's end view is to be seen but only the cover in the top half, right half, left half and bottom half is seen only because of the reason that even the other

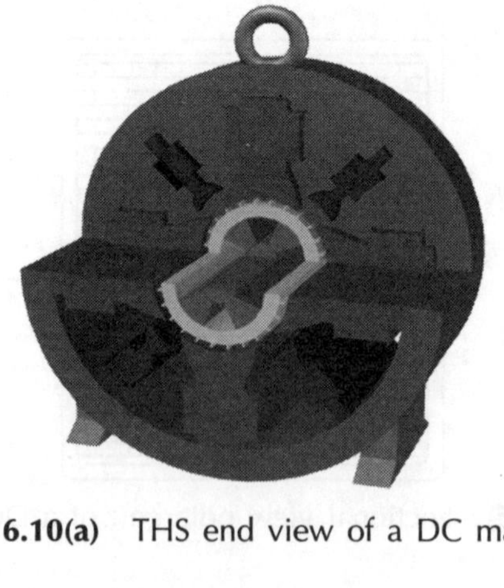

Figure 6.10(a) THS end view of a DC machine.

part which is not visible or seen will also be the same due to symmetry. The Figure 6.10(a) gives the top half in section (THS) end view of a DC machine.

The Figure 6.10(b) shows the left half in section (LHS) of a DC machine whereas the Figure 6.10(c) shows the right half in section (RHS) end view of the DC machine.

Figure 6.10(b) LHS end view.

Figure 6.10(c) RHS end view.

6.4 SOLVED PROBLEMS

PROBLEM 6.1: Draw a suitable scale end view elevation with top half in section of a DC machine, with the following details:

Yoke:

Outside diameter = 92 cm
Inner diameter = 86.5 cm
Axial length = 600 cm

Armature:

Diameter = 52.1 cm
Slot type = Open type
Slot dimension = 20 × 38 mm

Main pole:

Number of poles = 4
Total height = 15.5 cm
Width = 21.4 cm
Air gap = 3 mm

Inter pole:

Number of poles = 4
Total height = 15.5 cm
Width = 2.2 cm
Air gap = 3 mm

Shaft diameter = 50 mm

Dimension of the base plate is 23.1 × 16 cm, assume the missing data.

(VTU, June 2013)

Solution:

Analysing the problem: In this particular problem, we have to draw the end view and the elevation of a DC machine with the details stated in the problem. Firstly, we have to draw the sectional end view of the machine and then elevate it to obtain the complete machine.

Follow the steps below to assemble the DC machine. (Solution procedure for problem 6.1)

Steps to develop the DC machine assembly drawing using CAD:

Step 1: Click on the AutoCAD icon appearing on the computer screen. A new window of AutoCAD will open.

Step 2: Select FILE in the AutoCAD window and open a new drawing (.dwg) file.

Step 3: In the command window type as UNITS↵, a new dialog box will pop-up as shown in Figure 6.11. In this dialog box select the precision type, lighting and units as required. Generally, the precision set is 0.00, units to scale inserted are millimetres and lighting selected is International as shown in Figure 6.12.

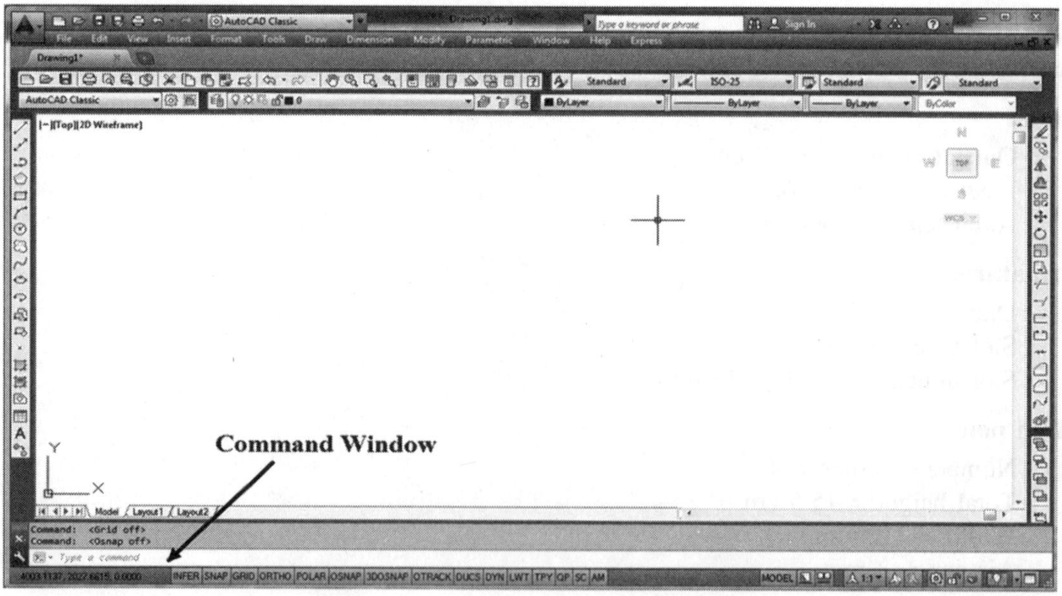

Figure 6.11 AutoCAD command window, *courtesy:* AutoCAD®.

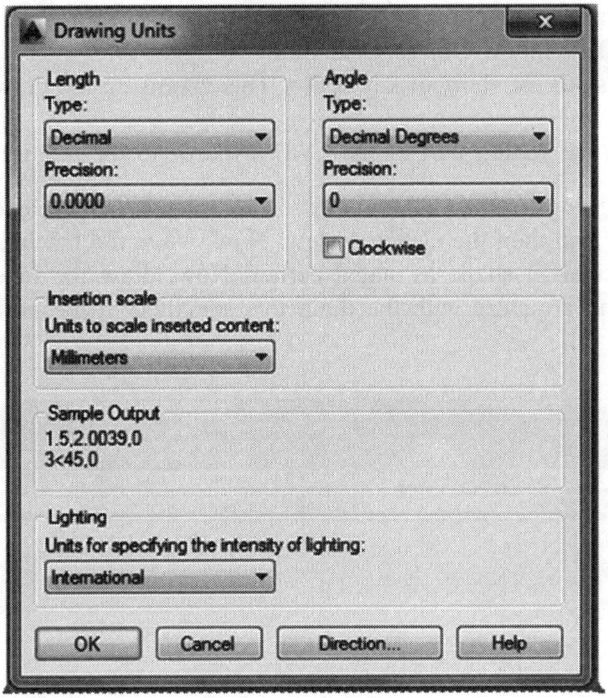

Figure 6.12 Drawing units in AutoCAD, *courtesy:* AutoCAD®.

Step 4: Now, select the sheet size required for the drawing by typing as LIMITS↵ in the command window, here itself it specifies as:

Specify lower left corner or (ON/OFF) <0.0000, 0.0000>: ↵

Specify upper right corner or (ON/OFF) <300, 300>: 2500, 2500 ↵

The lower left corner should always start from <0.0000, 0.0000> whereas for the upper right corner will have a default value. It can be set to any value depending on our requirement. The setting of page limits in CAD window is shown in Figure 6.13.

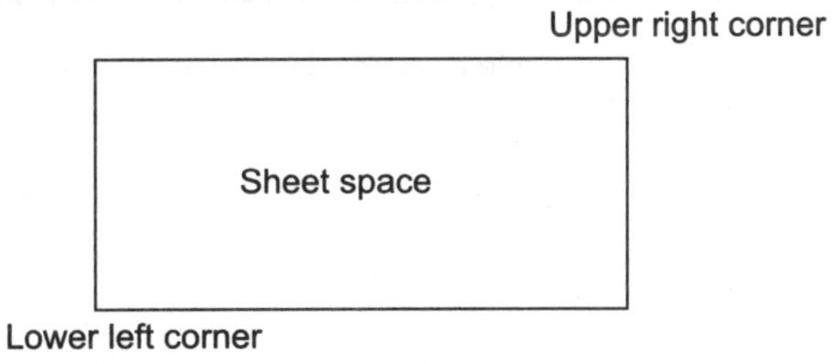

Figure 6.13 Setting of page limits in CAD window.

Step 5: In the command window type as ZOOM↵, it specifies as [All/Centre/Dynamic/Extents/Previous/Scale/Window/Object]<real time>:

Here, specify as All (or shortcut key A)↵. This zooms up the drawing sheet as specified in the limits.

This completes the setting part of the CAD window to the requirement.

Step 6: Once the settings of the CAD window is completed then the end view of the machine is to be drawn firstly and then the elevated view. Now, when the machine is seen from its end view, it appears circular in shape as stated earlier. Now, draw the inner and outer diameter of the yoke, shaft and armature with the diameters specified in the problem as shown in the Figure 6.14.

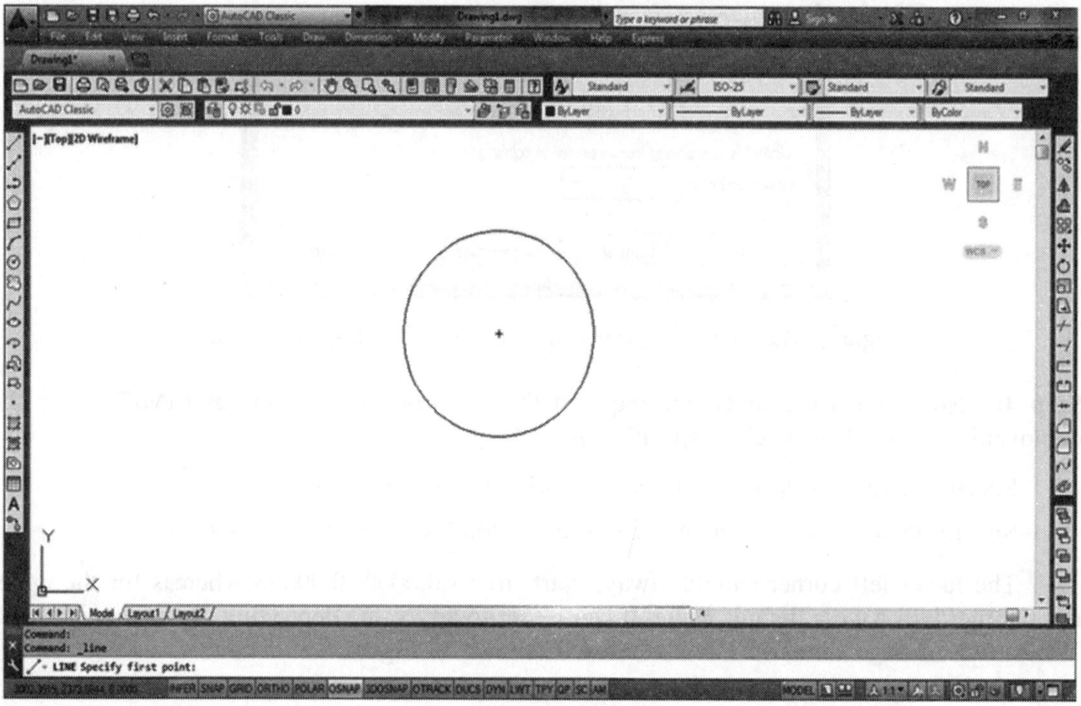

Figure 6.14(a) Drawing of yoke using circle command with specified outer diameter in AutoCAD, *courtesy:* AutoCAD®.

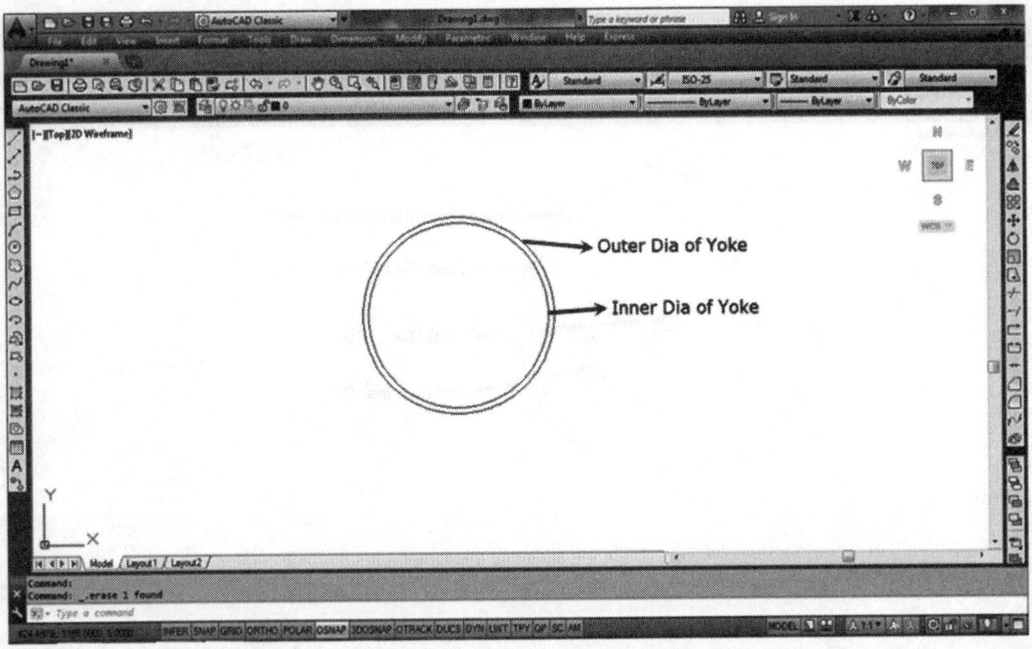

Figure 6.14(b) Drawing of yoke using circle command with specified inner diameter in AutoCAD, *courtesy:* AutoCAD®.

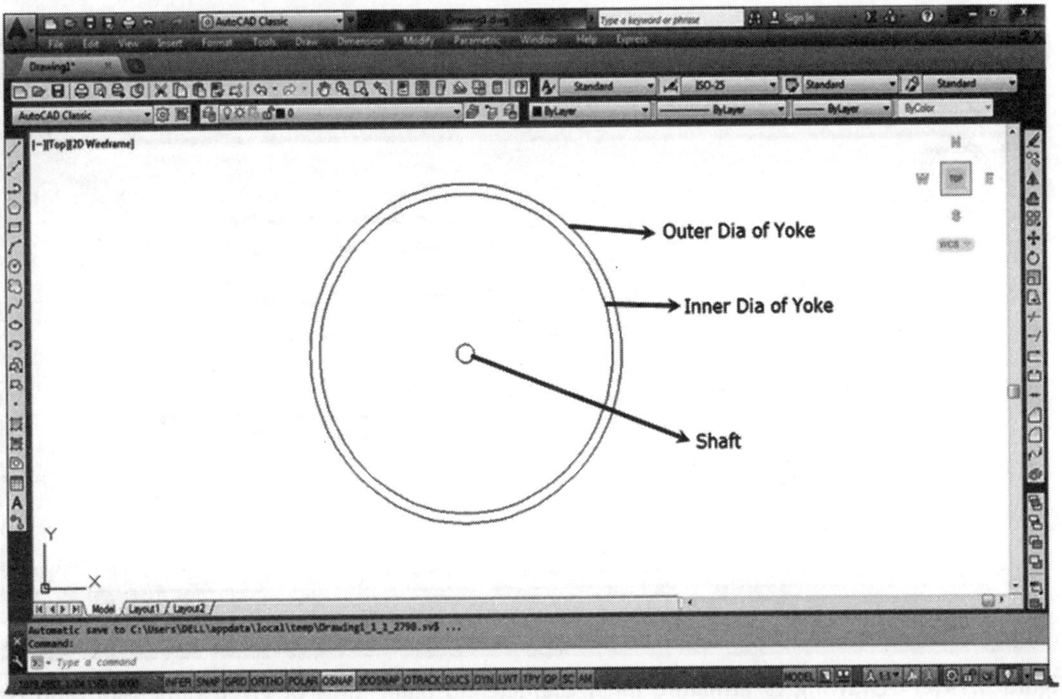

Figure 6.14(c) Drawing of shaft using circle command with specified diameter in AutoCAD, *courtesy:* AutoCAD®.

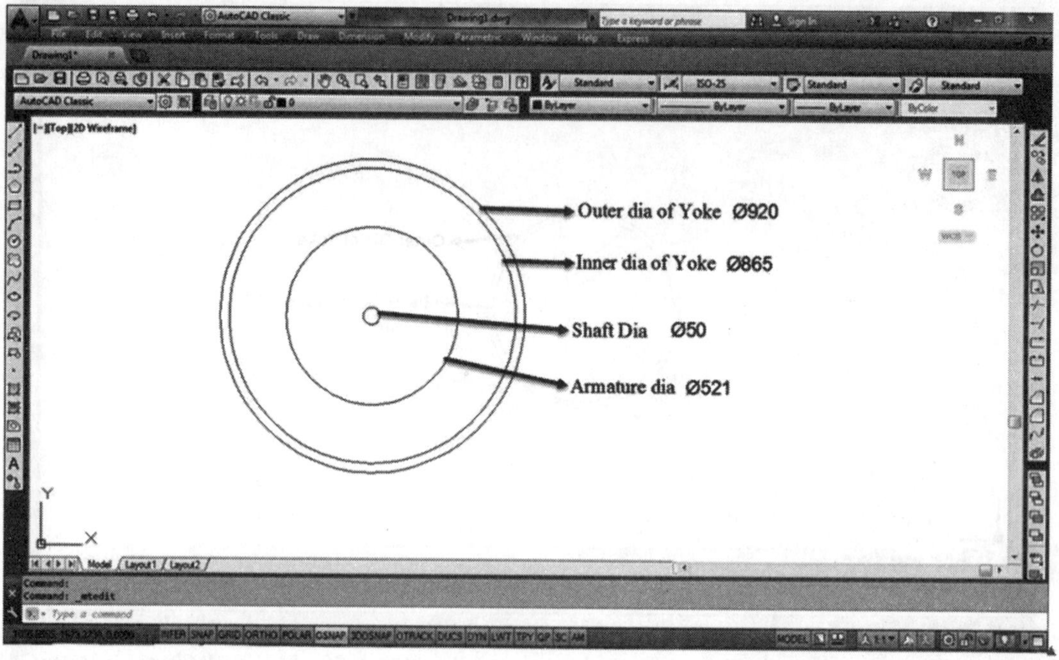

Figure 6.14(d) Drawing of armature using circle command with specified diameter in AutoCAD, *courtesy:* AutoCAD®.

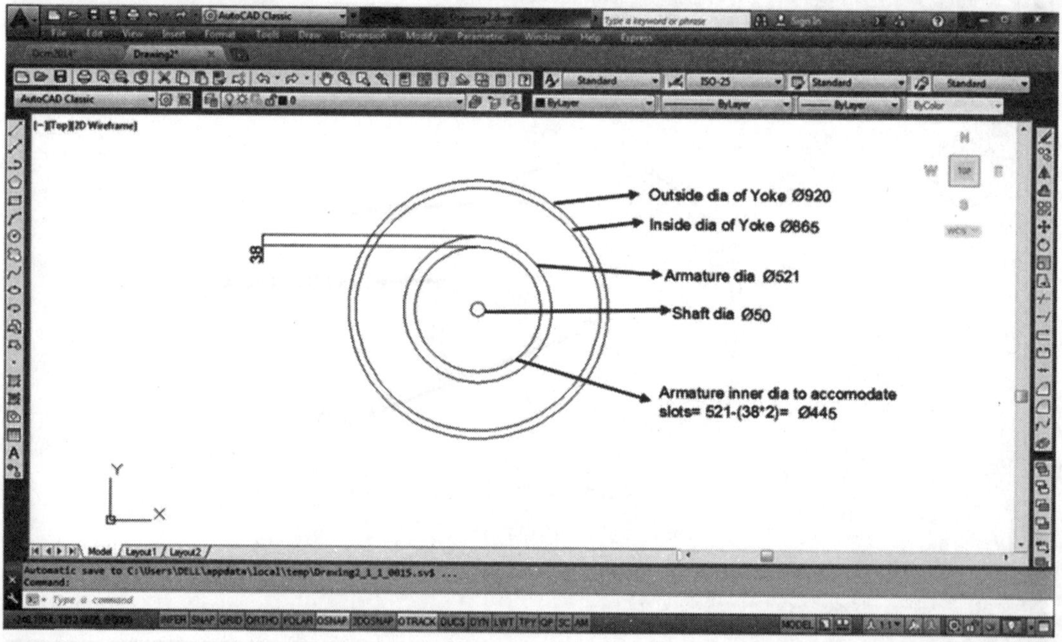

Figure 6.14(e) Drawing of armature inner diameter to place slots of given dimension and type using circle command in AutoCAD, *courtesy:* AutoCAD®.

***Note:** If the dimensions of the slots are not provided, then the dimension of the slot may be assumed suitably and the slots to be of open type.

Step 7: After drawing the yoke, shaft and armature outlines, now draw axis lines as shown in Figure 6.15 so that the placing of poles becomes easier and convenient.

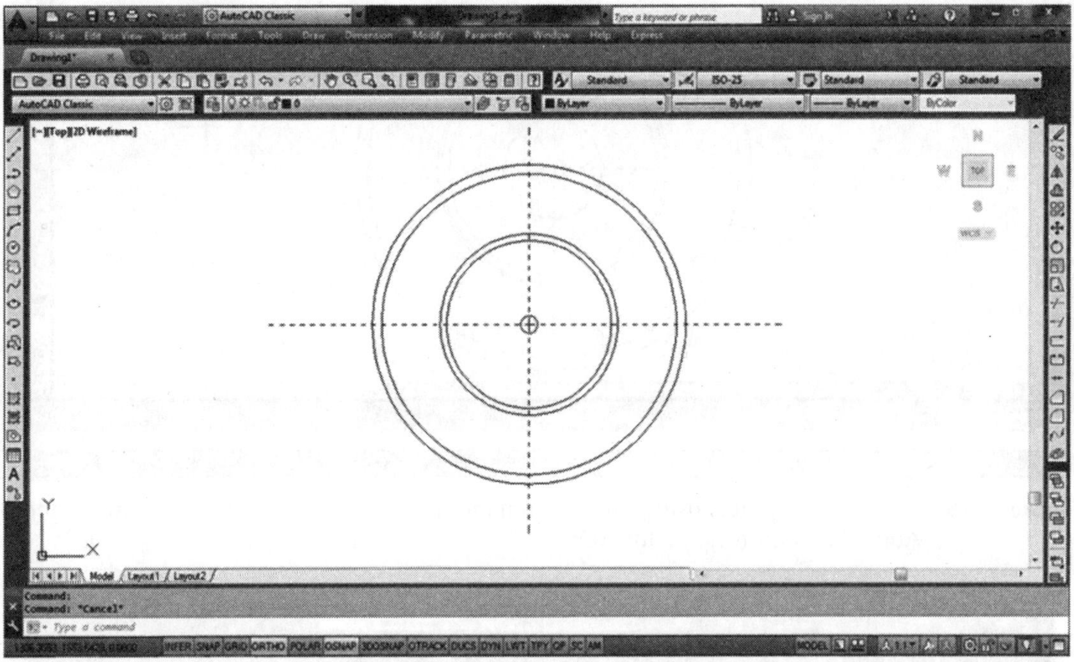

Figure 6.15 Drawing of axis lines in AutoCAD, *courtesy:* AutoCAD®.

Step 8: The pole is to be drawn now. In sectional end view, the poles width can be seen and not the length. In this problem, the height of pole is given as 155 mm. Here the air gap is 3 mm, hence add the air gap value to the outside diameter of armature, i.e., 521 + (3 × 2) = 527 mm and then draw a circle with diameter 527 mm as shown in Figure 6.16. Now, draw the height of the pole as stated in the problem taking inner diameter of the yoke as reference. Now, divide the pole width into two equal parts, i.e., 214 mm/2 = 107 mm and then mark the pole as shown in Figure 6.16, with the help of line command such that 107 mm lies on either side of the axis line. Now, from the end point of the pole draw an arc to the circle of diameter 527 mm depending on the pole pitch which results in the height of pole shoes also.

Step 9: To draw the pole shoes in the form of an arc, the ARC command may be used. If the pole arc is given then the data may be used to draw the pole shoes. If not, it is always recommended to calculate the pole pitch and then draw the arc or pole shoes as shown in Figure 6.17.

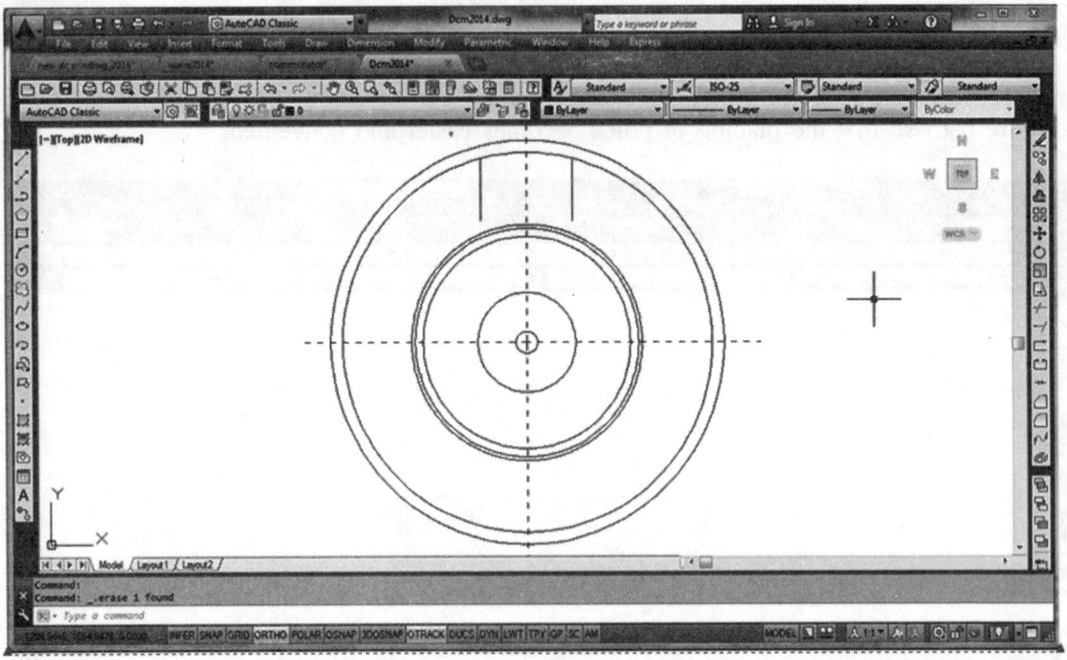

Figure 6.16 Marking of poles using line command and air gap using circle command in AutoCAD, *courtesy:* AutoCAD®.

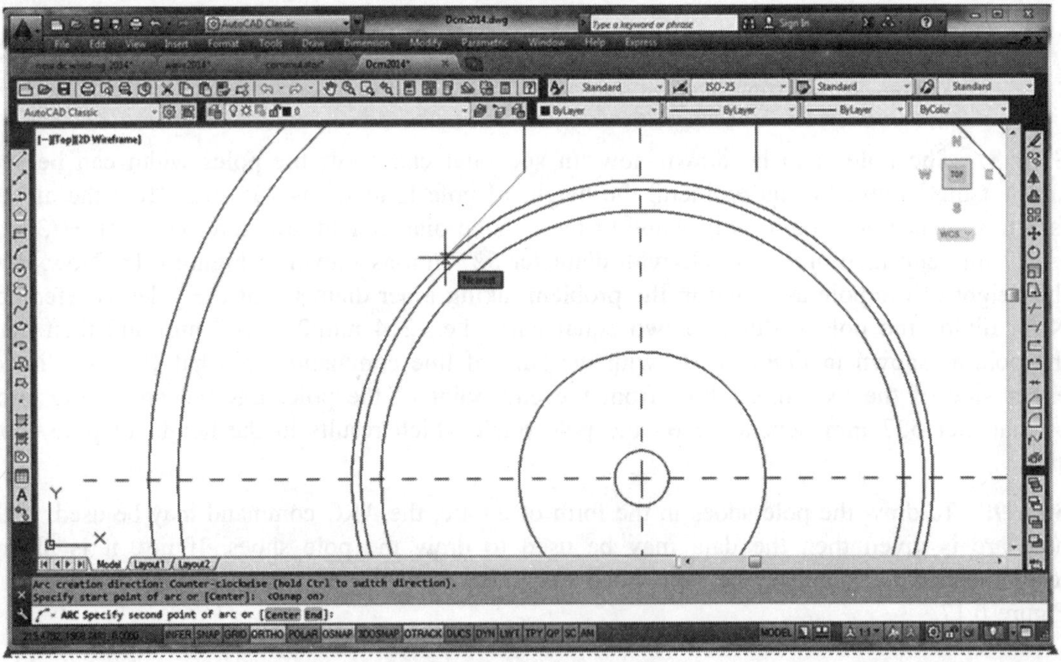

Figure 6.17(a) Marking of pole arc using ARC command in AutoCAD, *courtesy:* AutoCAD®.

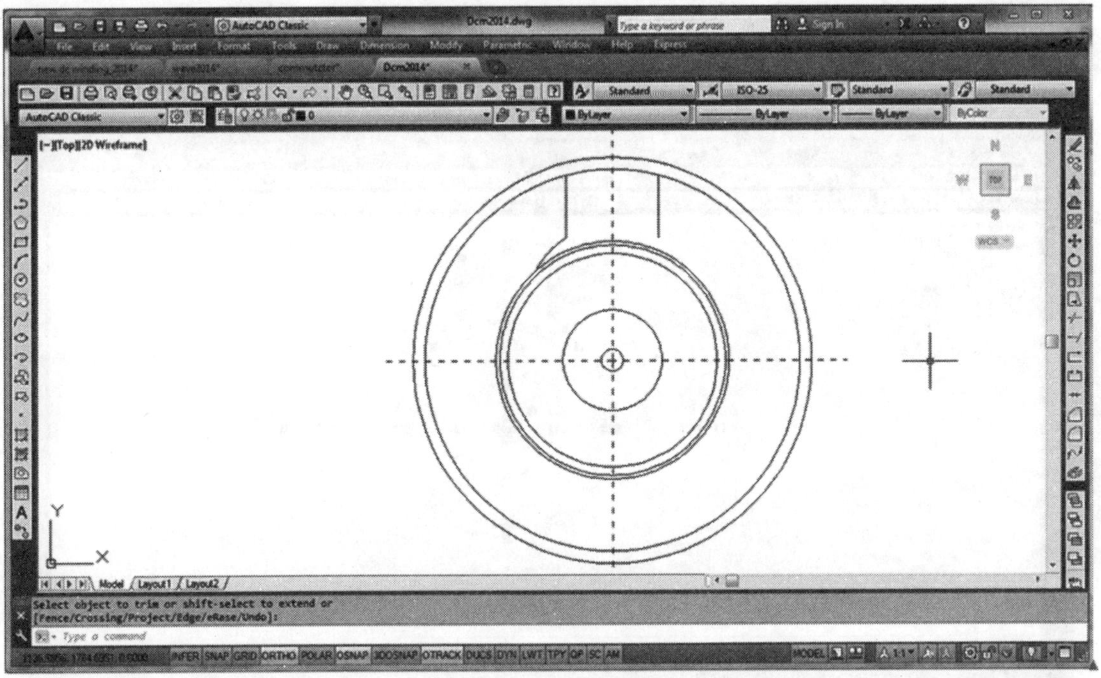

Figure 6.17(b) Marking of pole arc using ARC command in AutoCAD, *courtesy:* AutoCAD®.

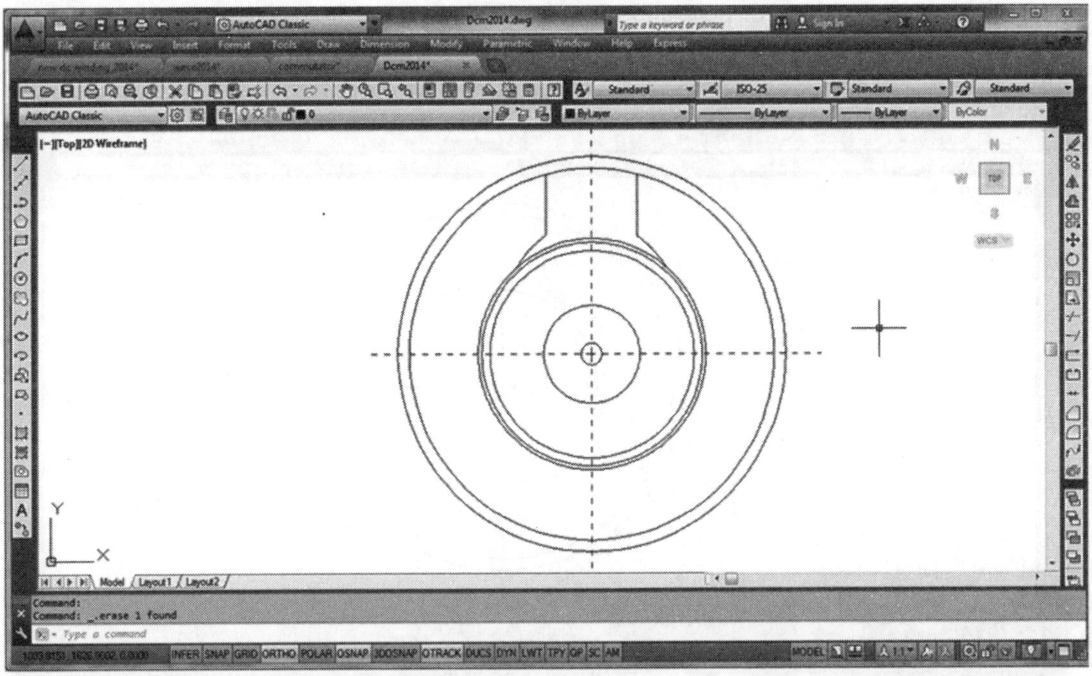

Figure 6.17(c) Pole with pole shoes drawn using ARC command in AutoCAD, *courtesy:* AutoCAD®.

Step 10: After drawing the pole arc, select the necessary things and delete all unwanted lines and arcs using the trim command as shown in the Figure 6.18.

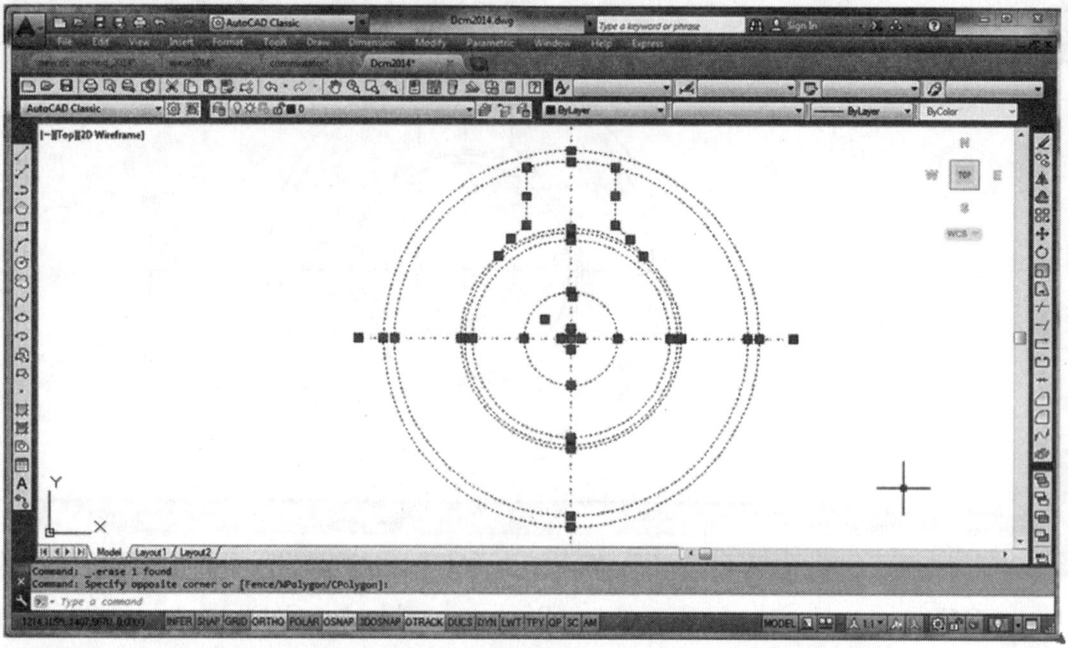

Figure 6.18(a) Marking of pole and trimming the unwanted lines, *courtesy:* AutoCAD®.

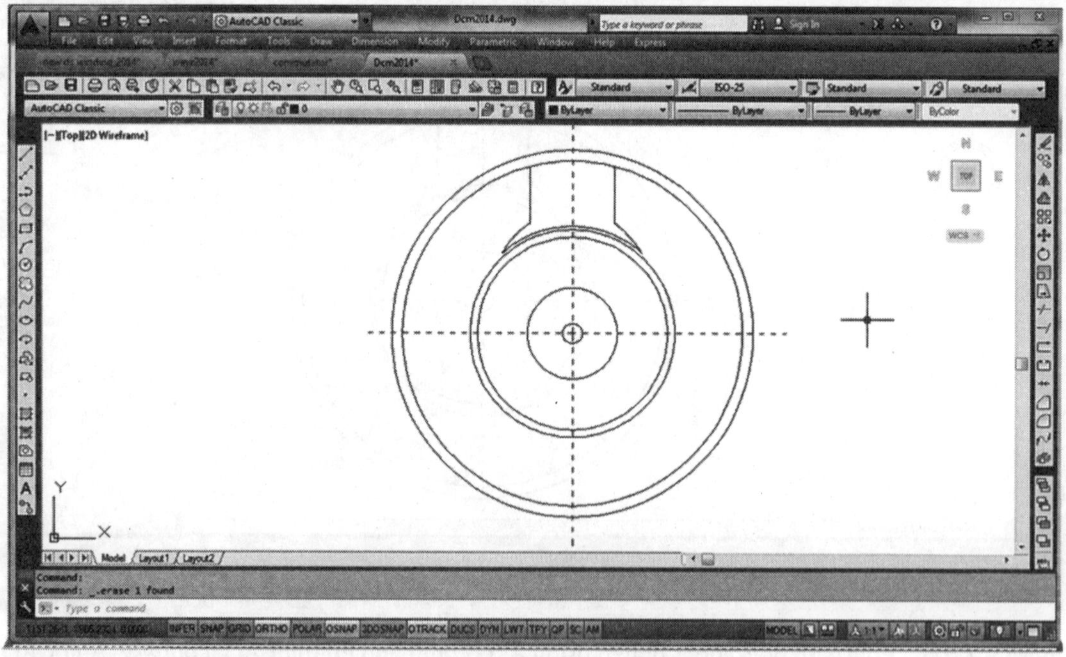

Figure 6.18(b) Pole and pole shoes, *courtesy:* AutoCAD®.

Step 11: Now, draw the pole windings on either side of the pole as shown in the Figures below using the line command and then hatch the pole winding suitably using the hatch command. Draw the pole winding exactly according to the dimensions as stated in the problem. After drawing the pole, now use the array command to obtain the number of poles required. Use polar array here and place the poles only in the top half section as stated in the problem and as shown in Figures 6.19(a), (b), (c), (d), (e) and (f). Mark the inter pole also as shown in the Figure 6.19(g) and (h).

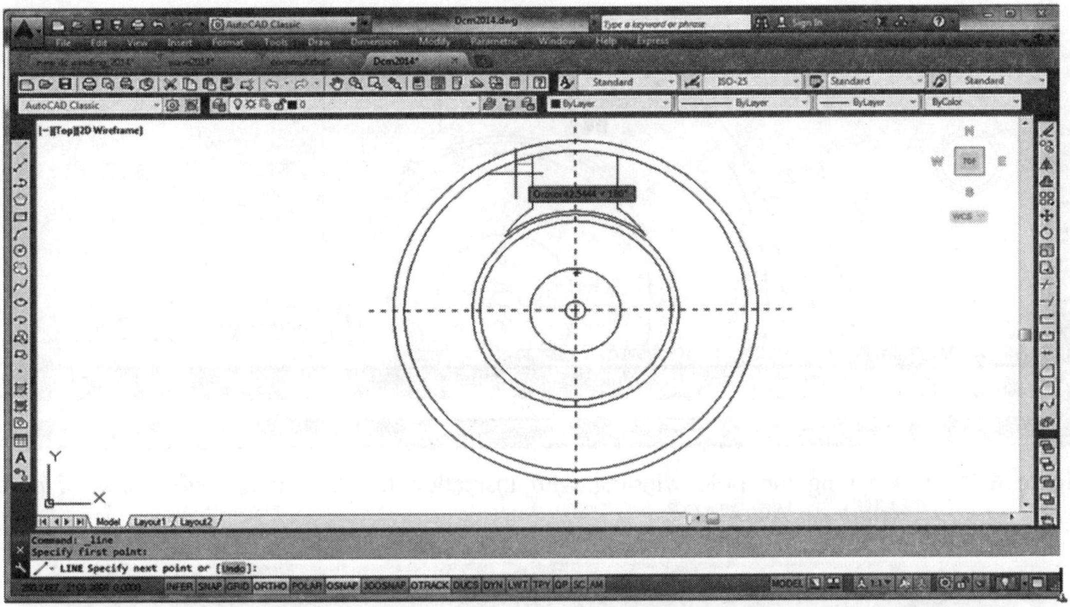

Figure 6.19(a) Making the pole winding using line command, *courtesy:* AutoCAD®.

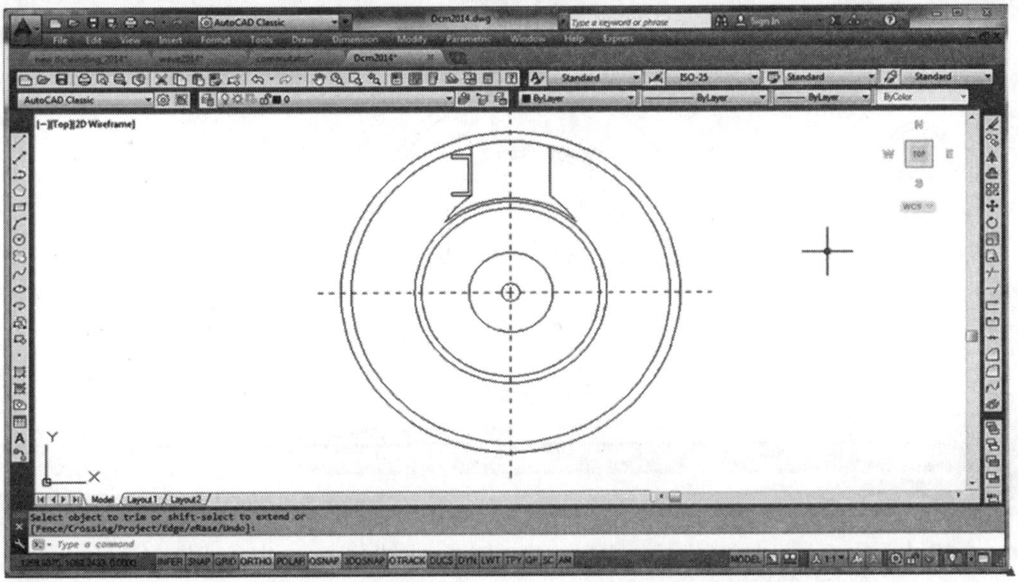

Figure 6.19(b) Making the pole winding insulation using line command, *courtesy:* AutoCAD®.

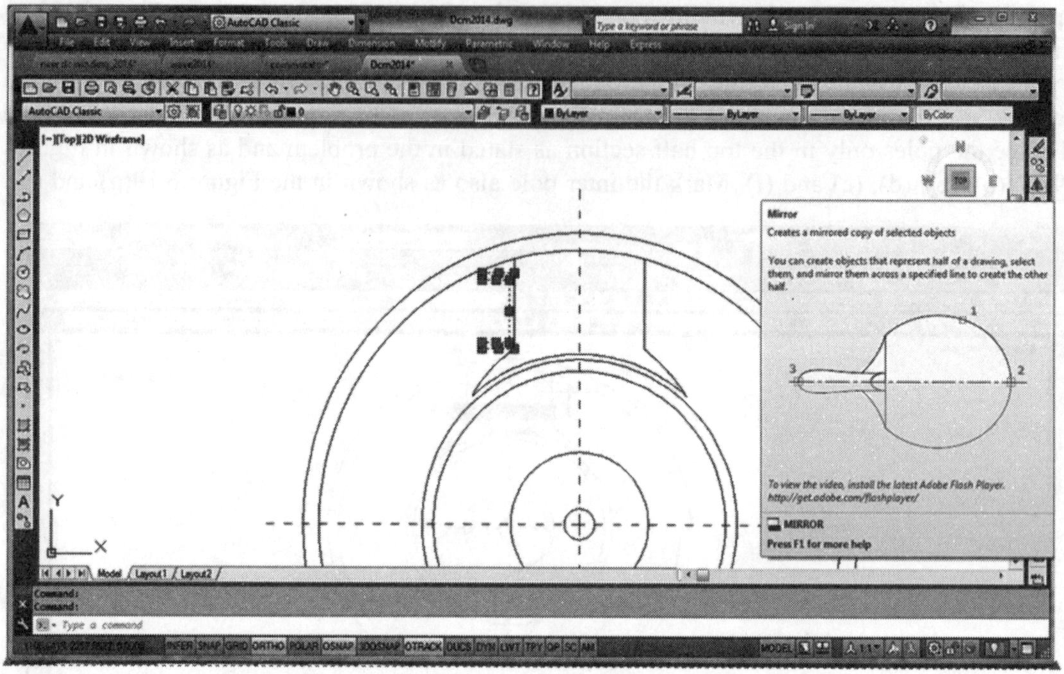

Figure 6.19(c) Copying the pole winding with insulation to place it on either side of pole, *courtesy:* AutoCAD®.

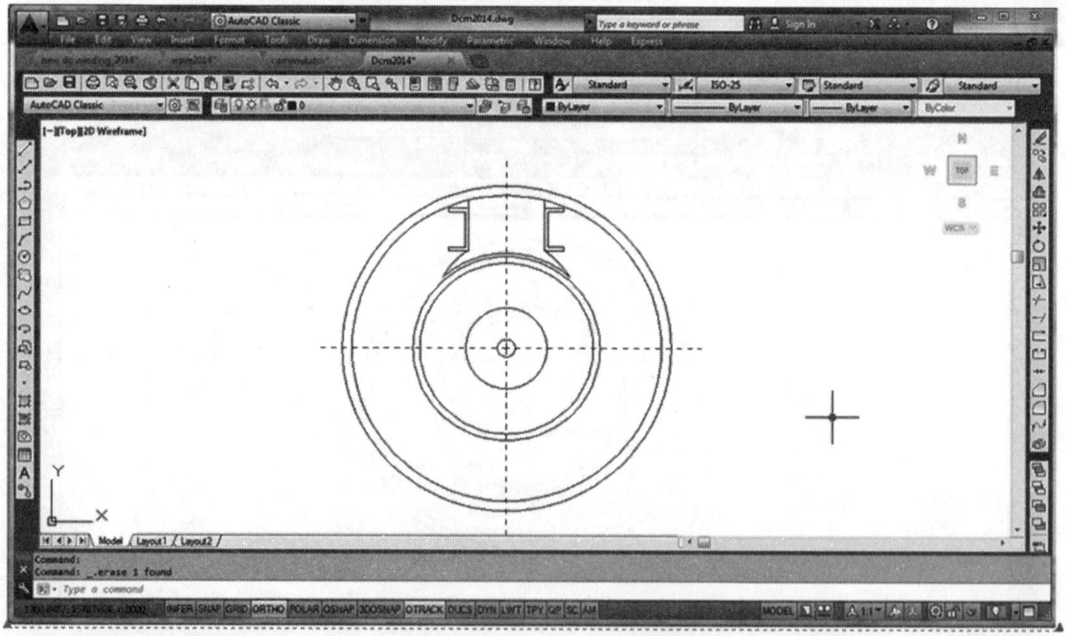

Figure 6.19(d) Copying the pole insulation to place winding on either side of pole, *courtesy:* AutoCAD®.

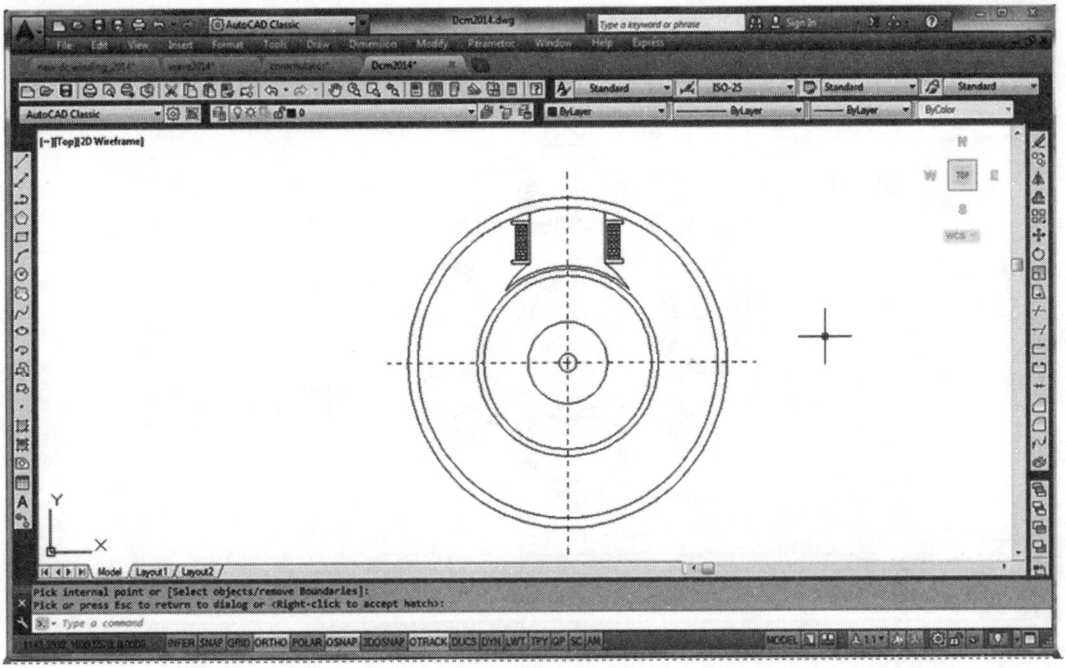

Figure 6.19(e) Pole winding on either side of pole, *courtesy:* AutoCAD®.

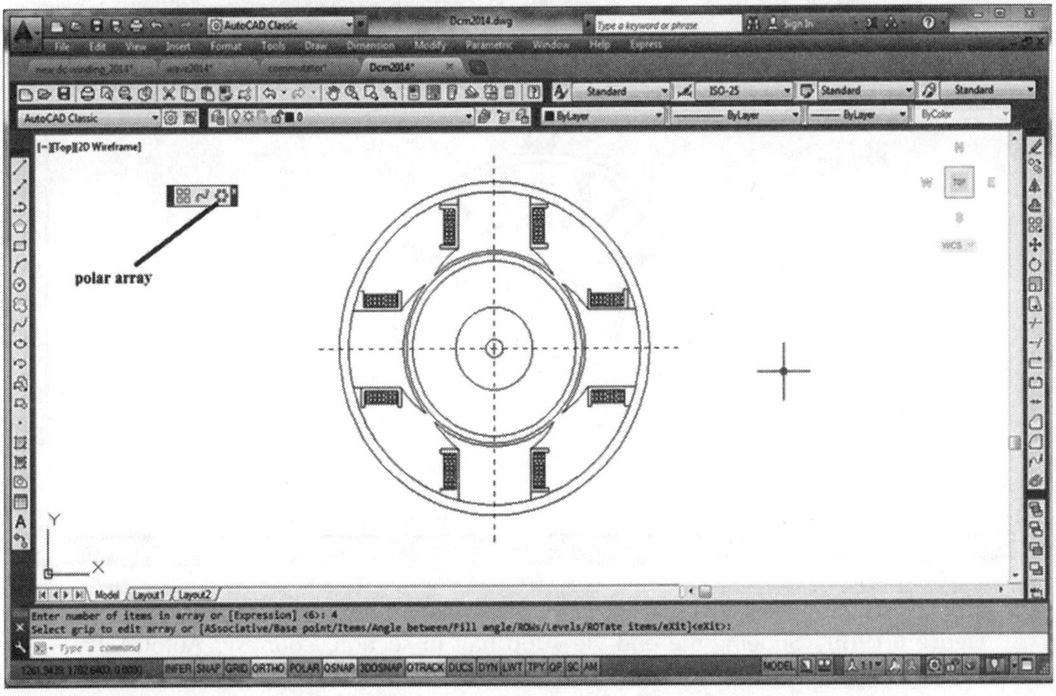

Figure 6.19(f) Arraying the number of poles required, *courtesy:* AutoCAD®.

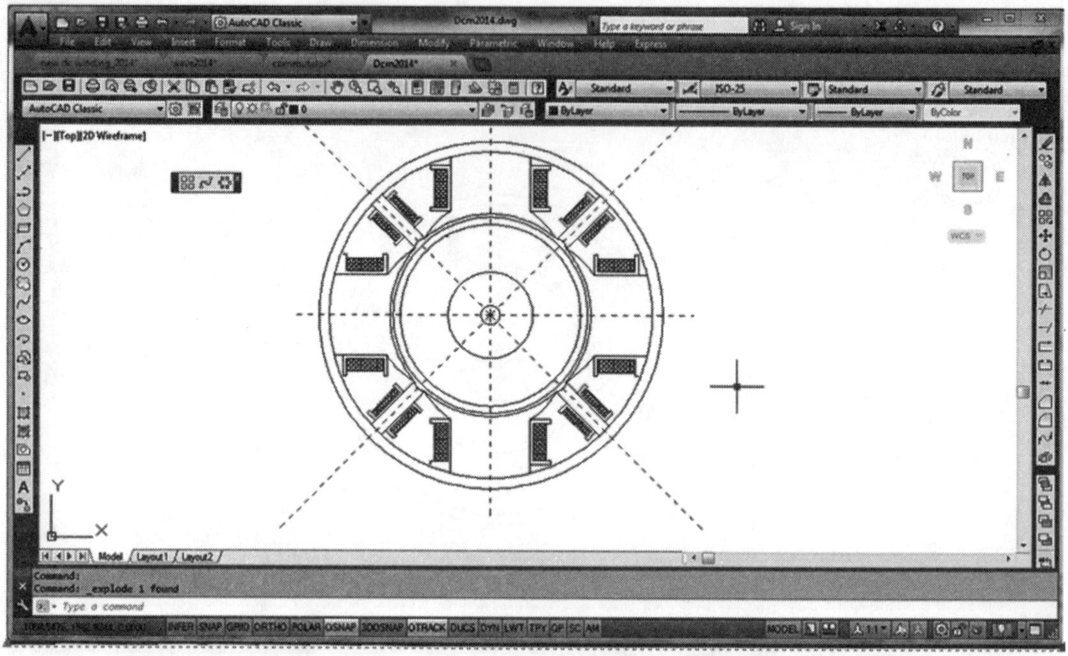

Figure 6.19(g) Inter pole and its windings, *courtesy:* AutoCAD®.

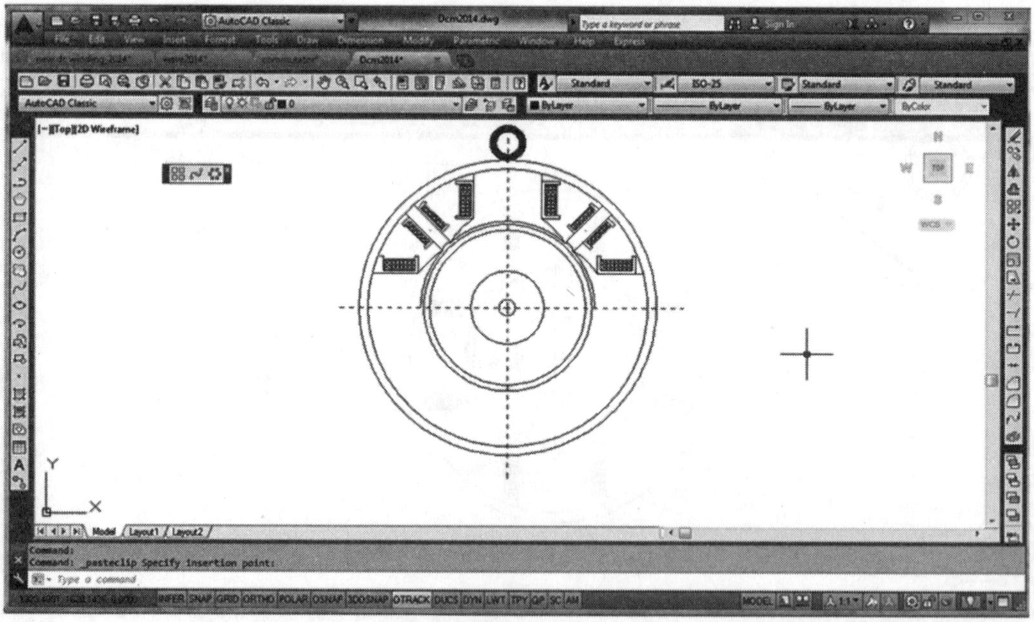

Figure 6.19(h) Shoeing the end view top half in section, *courtesy:* AutoCAD®.

Step 12: Now using the axis line as reference, provide the base plate to the machine such that it is mountable on a flat surface as shown in the Figure 6.20(a).

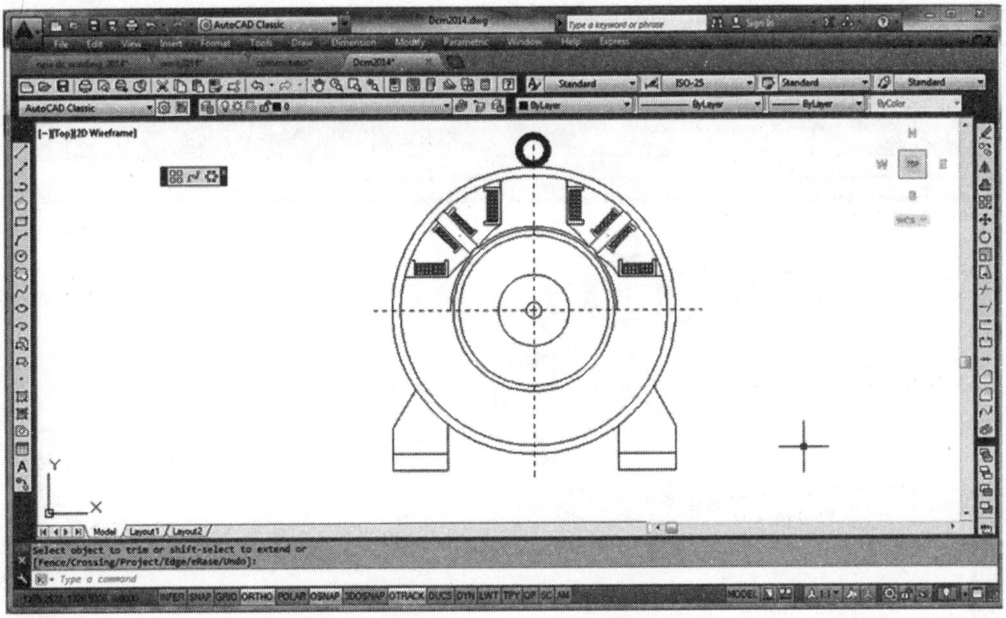

Figure 6.20(a) Base plate drawing and eye bolt, *courtesy:* AutoCAD®.

According to this problem, only the top half in section is to be shown. The bottom cover of the machine is not removed; henceforth provide the ventilating ducts to the machine as shown in the Figure 6.20(b).

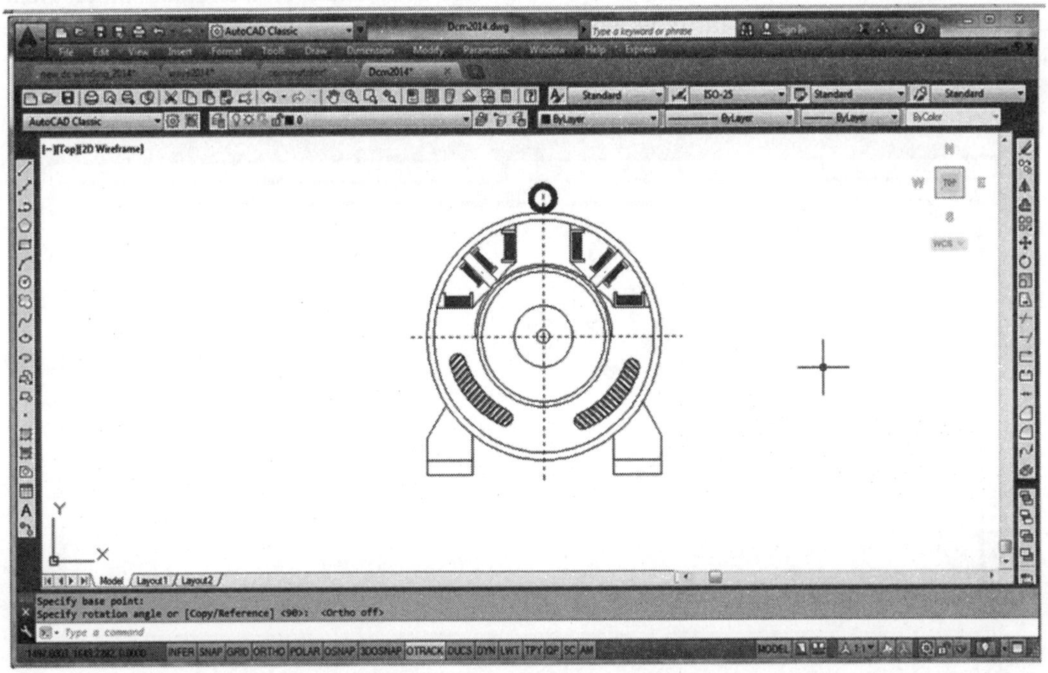

Figure 6.20(b) Making of ventilating ducts, *courtesy:* AutoCAD®.

Step 13: Now, provide the armature slots for the machine and exhibit the slots only in the top half portion of the machine as shown in the Figure 6.21.

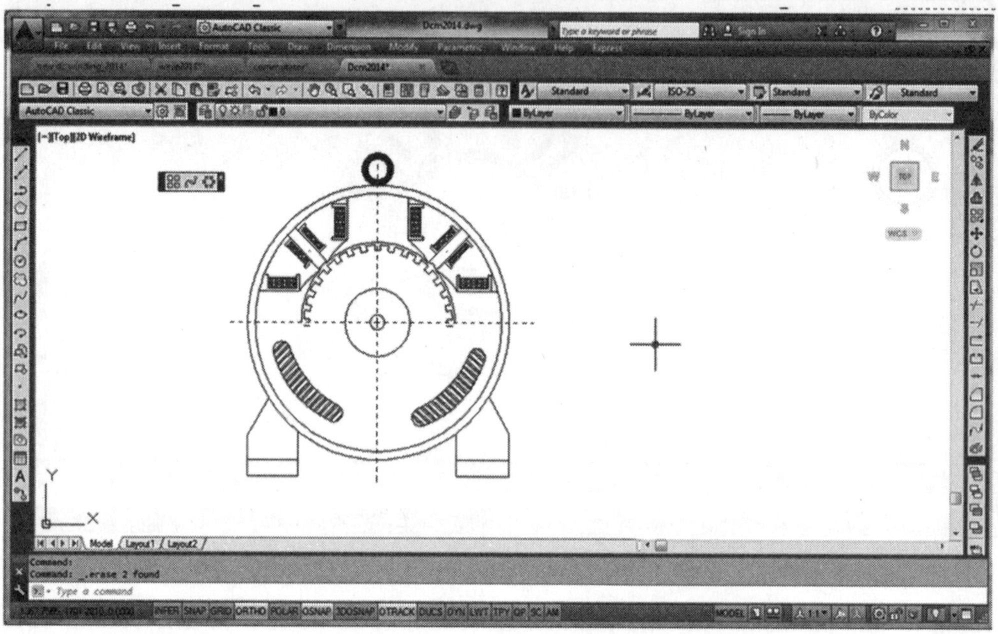

Figure 6.21 Drawing of armature slots, *courtesy:* AutoCAD®.

Step 14: In this problem, it is stated that the armature is mounted on a circular spider. Hence, provide spider on the shaft with dove tail joints to accommodate the armature and hatch the spider to differentiate it from the shaft and the armature as shown in the Figure 6.22(a).

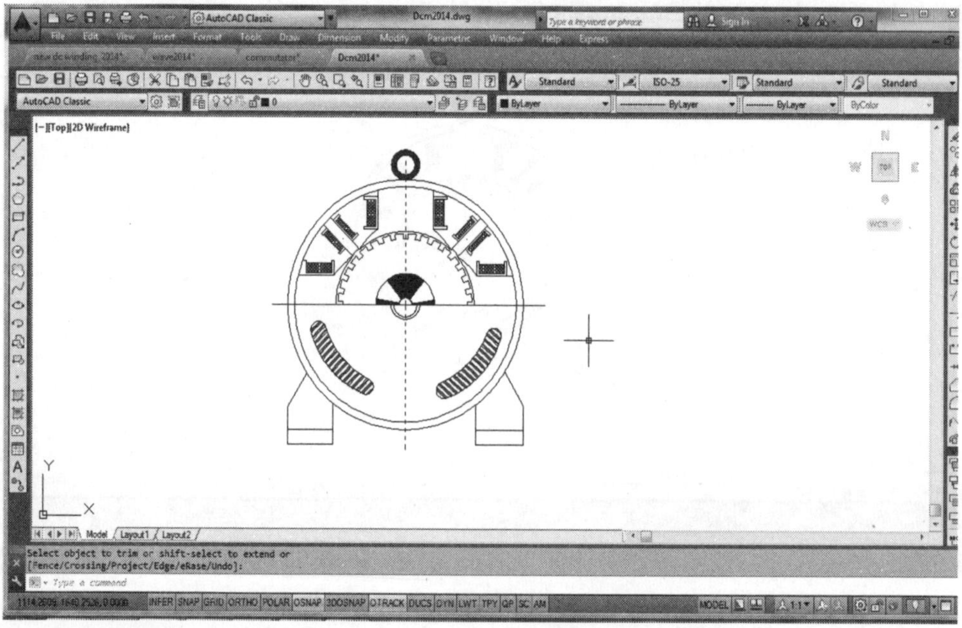

Figure 6.22(a) Drawing of spider with dove tail joint, *courtesy:* AutoCAD®.

Step 15: Show the dimension of each part using the dimension command and also name each part if necessary. This completes the top half sectional end view of the DC machine. Figure 6.22(b) gives the top half sectional end view of the DC machine.

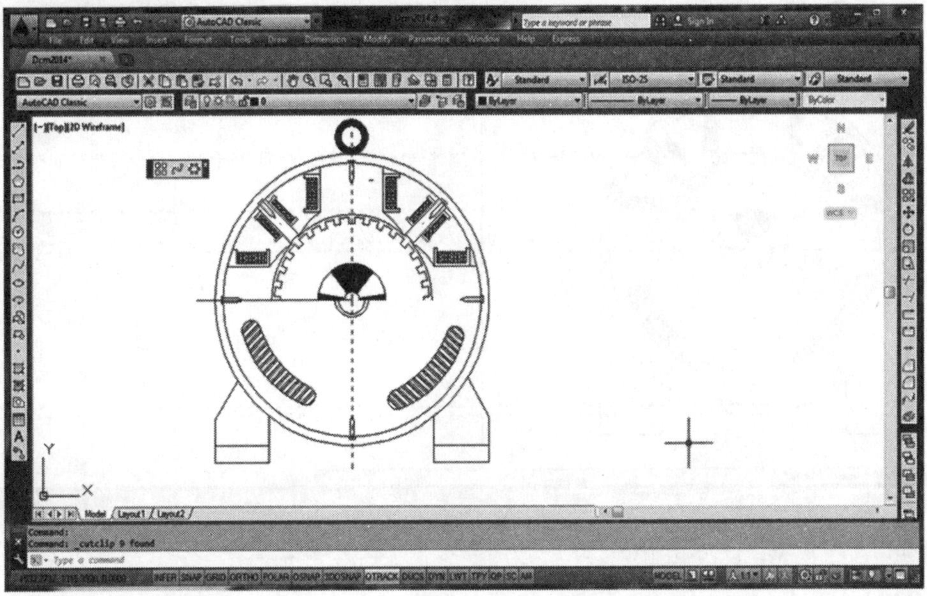

Figure 6.22(b) The complete top half in section end view of the machine, *courtesy:* AutoCAD®.

Step 16: Now, the elevation of the machine is to be done taking the sectional view as reference. Firstly, take projections from each part towards the right hand side and then depending on the length of the machine or the length of the shaft and length of the armature, draw the machine as shown in the Figure 6.23(a), (b), (c), (d), (e), (f), (g), (h), (i), (j), (k) and (l).

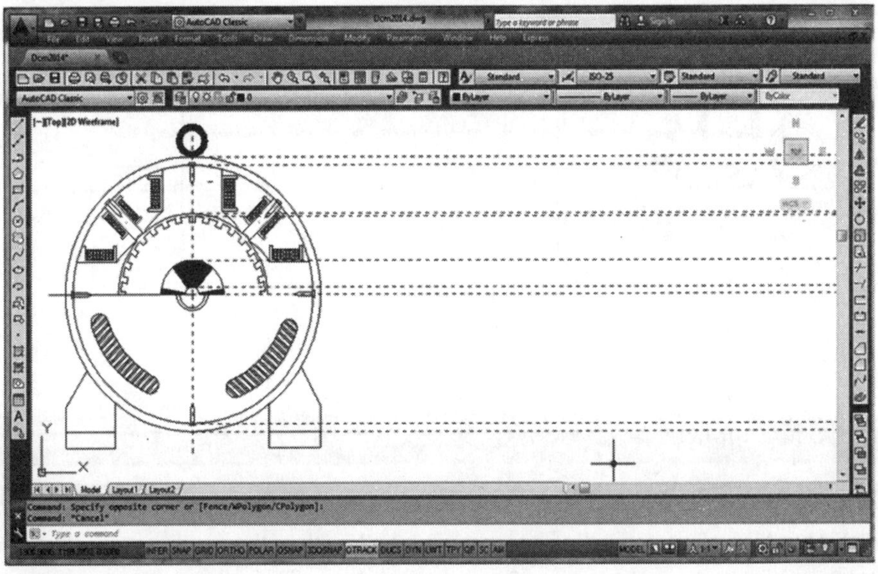

Figure 6.23(a) Marking of reference lines to draw the elevation, *courtesy:* AutoCAD®.

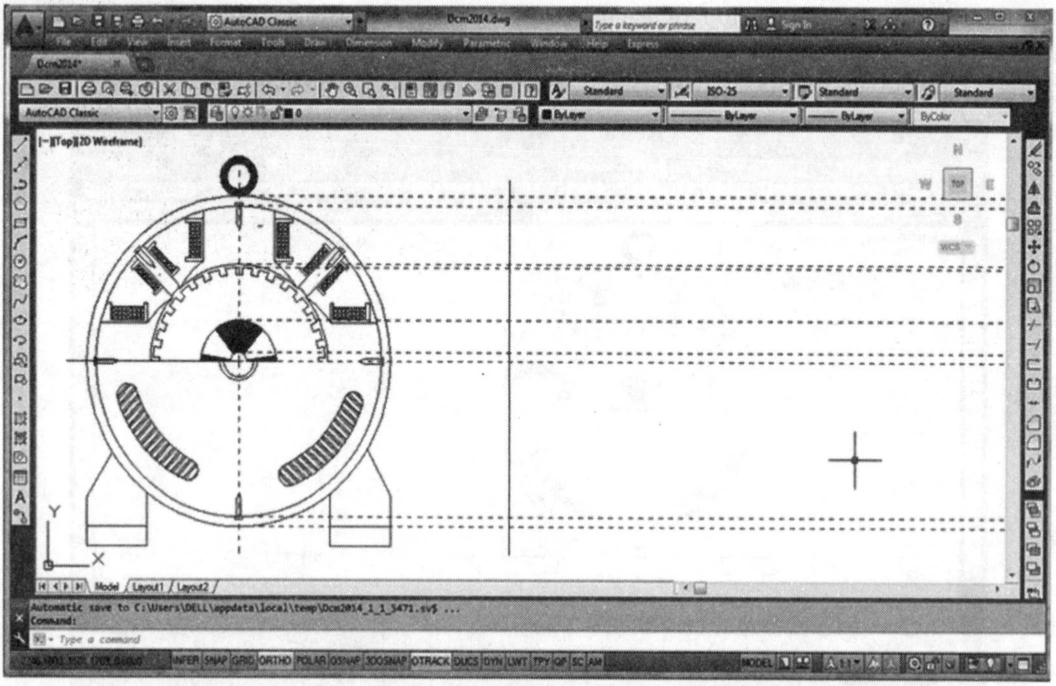

Figure 6.23(b) Marking of reference line according to the length of the machine, *courtesy:* AutoCAD®.

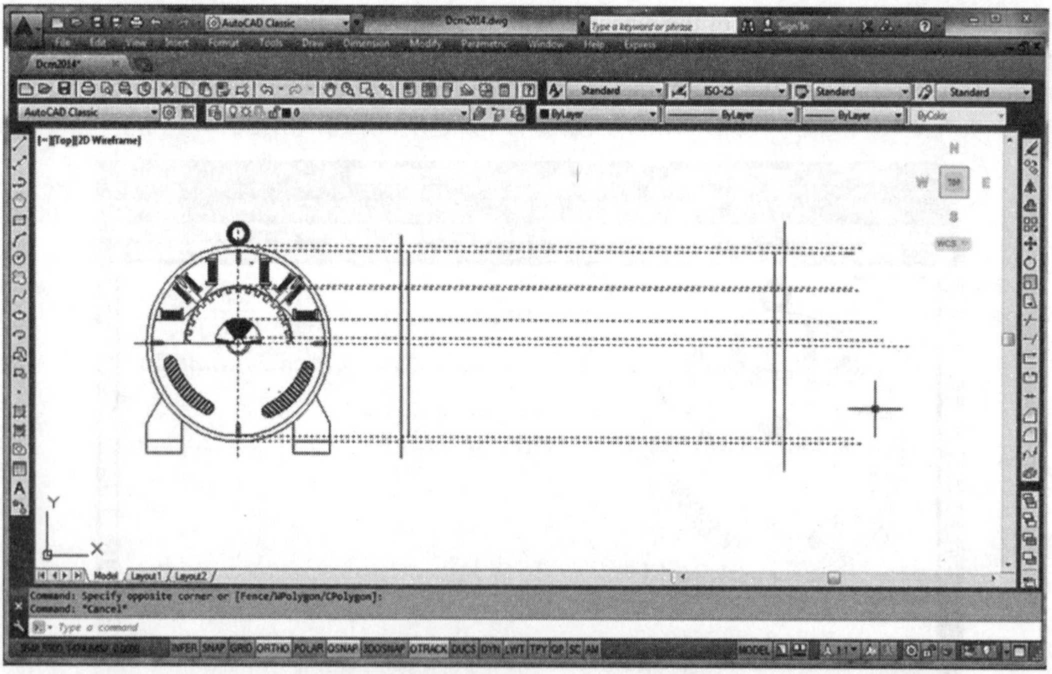

Figure 6.23(c) Marking of reference line according to the length of the machine, *courtesy:* AutoCAD®.

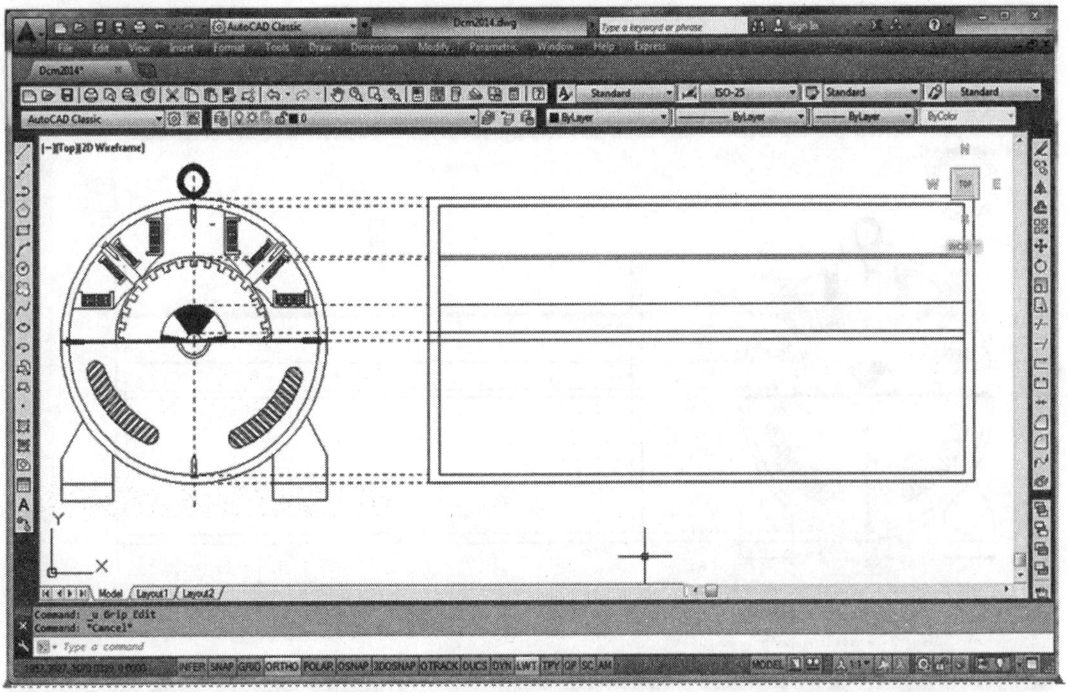

Figure 6.23(d) Elevation of yoke, *courtesy:* AutoCAD®.

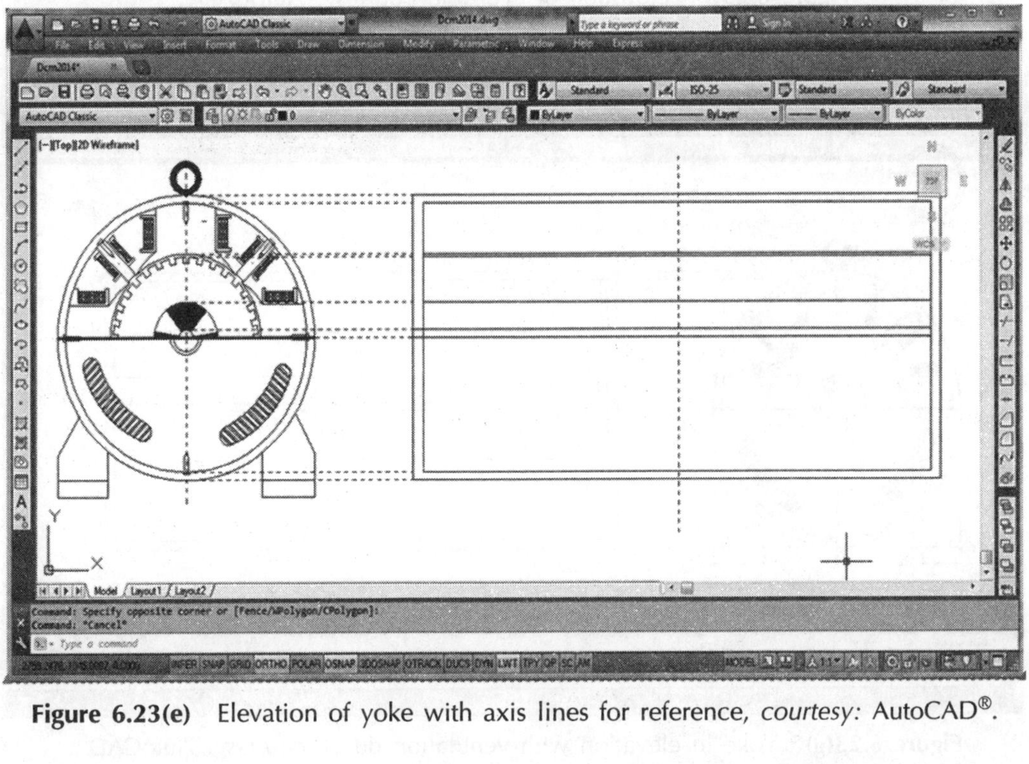

Figure 6.23(e) Elevation of yoke with axis lines for reference, *courtesy:* AutoCAD®.

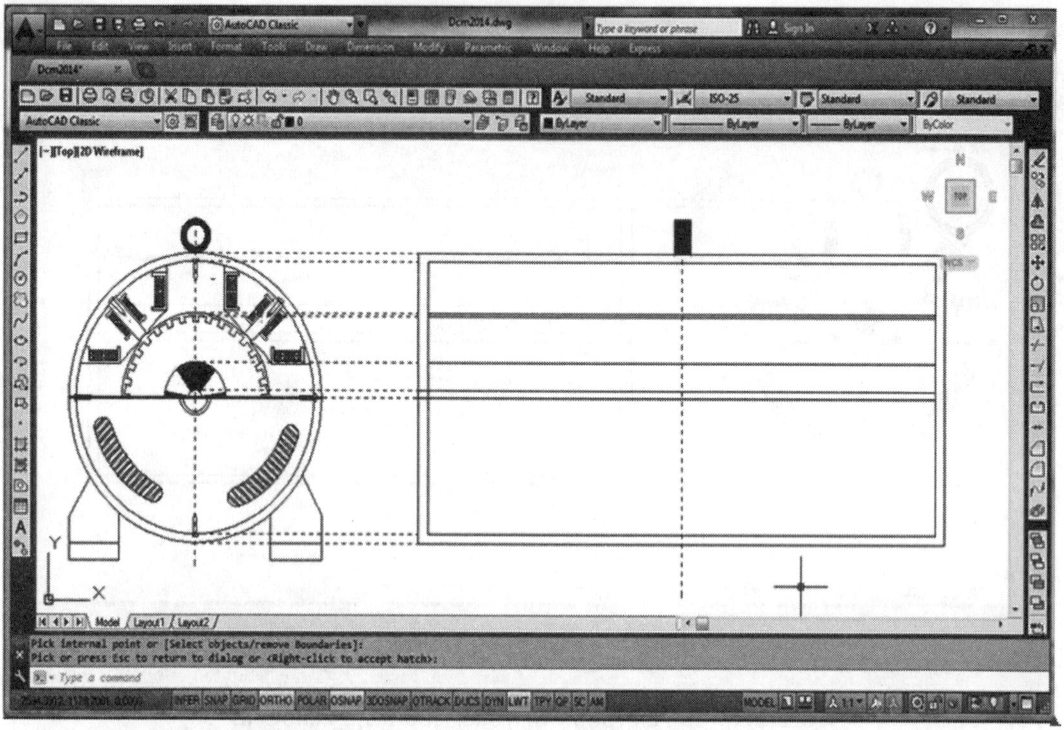

Figure 6.23(f) Elevation of eye bolt, *courtesy:* AutoCAD®.

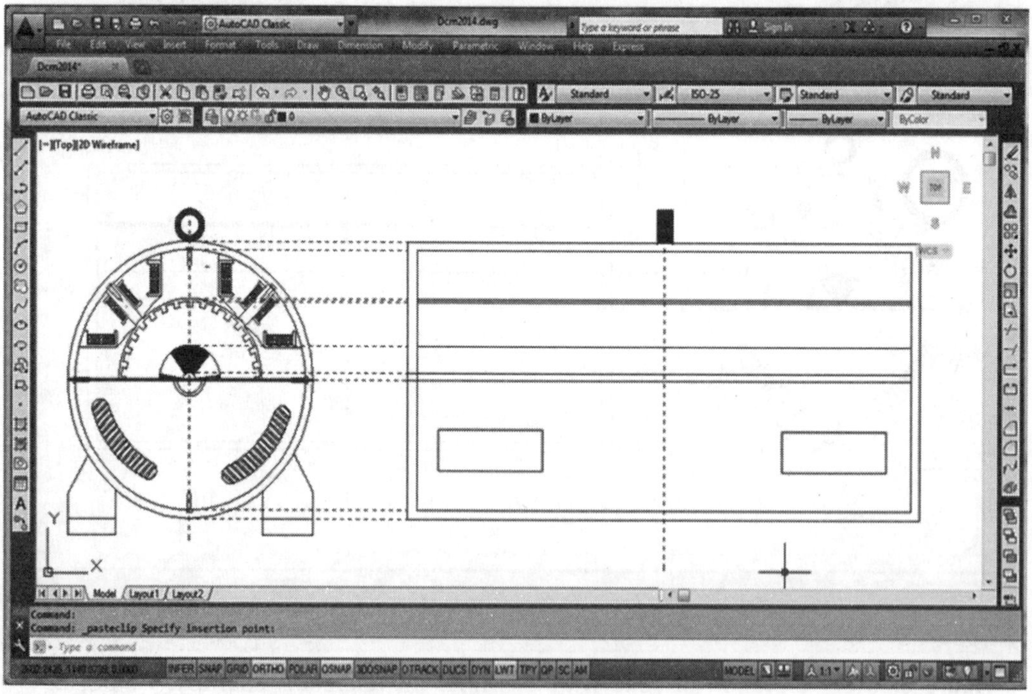

Figure 6.23(g) Yoke in elevation with ventilation ducts, *courtesy:* AutoCAD®.

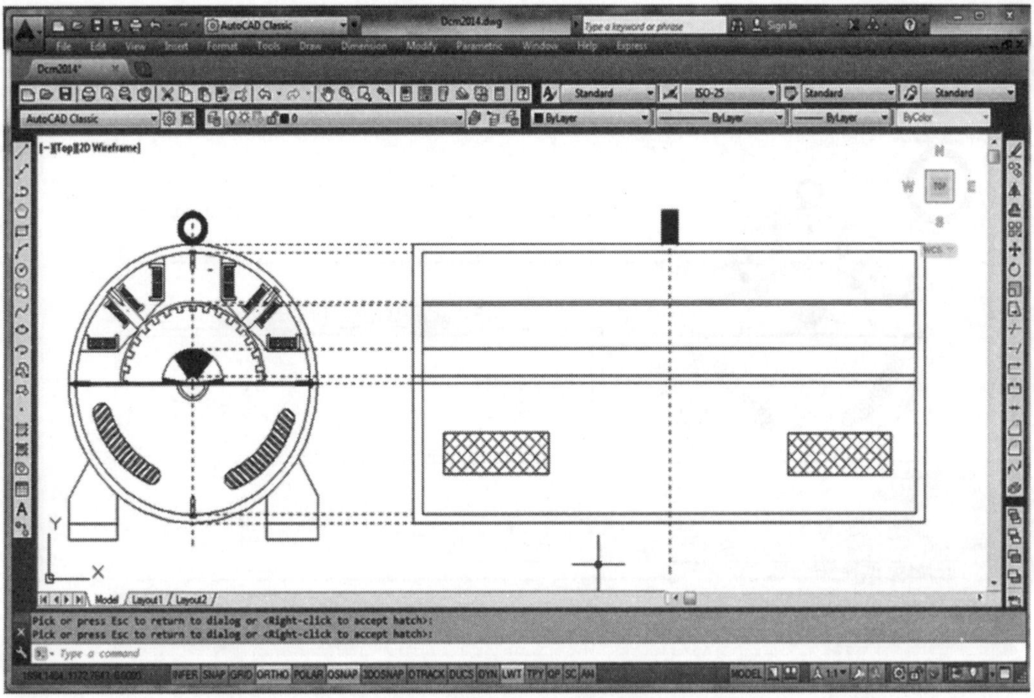

Figure 6.23(h) The ventilating ducts in bottom half of the machine in elevated view with hatching, *courtesy:* AutoCAD®.

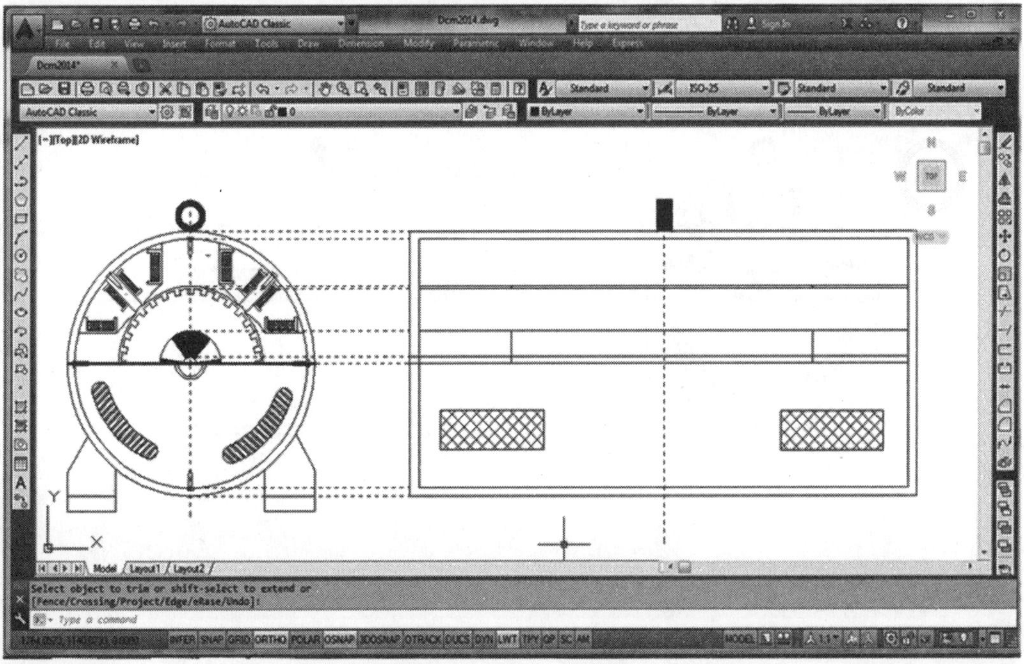

Figure 6.23(i) Spider assembly elevation mounted on the shaft throughout the length of the armature, *courtesy:* AutoCAD®.

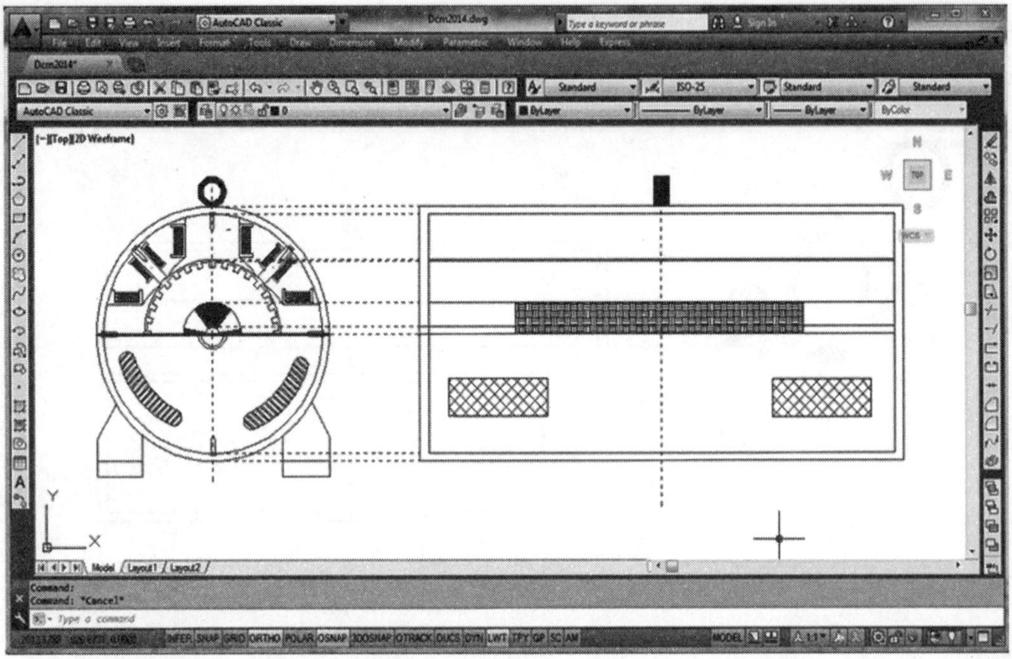

Figure 6.23(j) Spider assembly elevation mounted on the shaft throughout the length of the armature with hatching, *courtesy:* AutoCAD®.

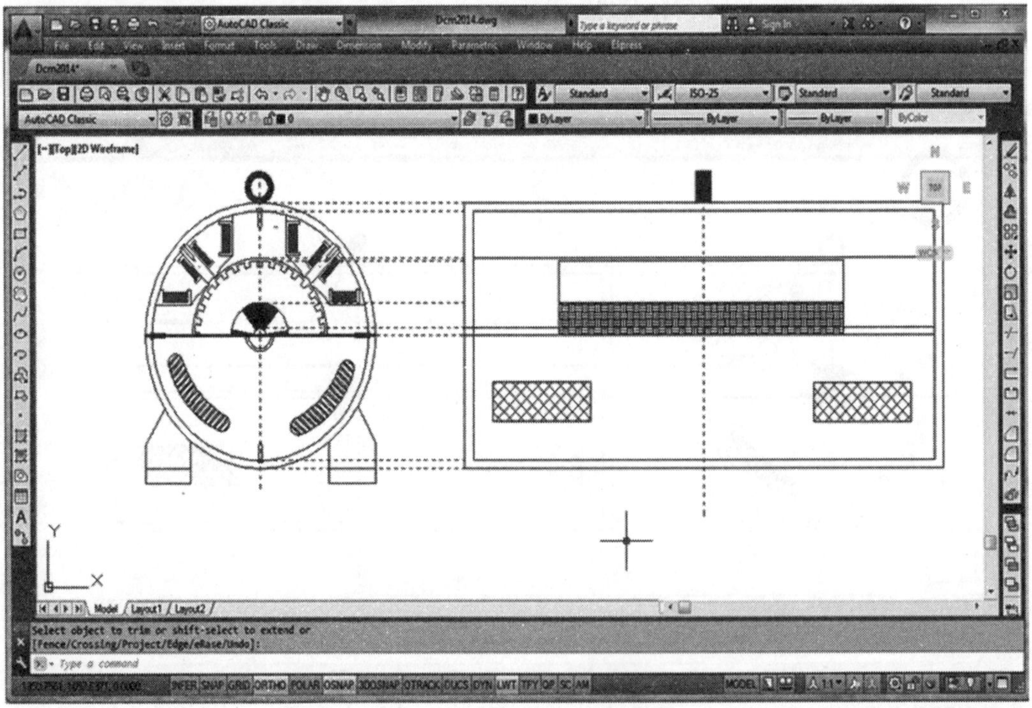

Figure 6.23(k) Armature elevation mounted on shaft with spider, *courtesy:* AutoCAD®.

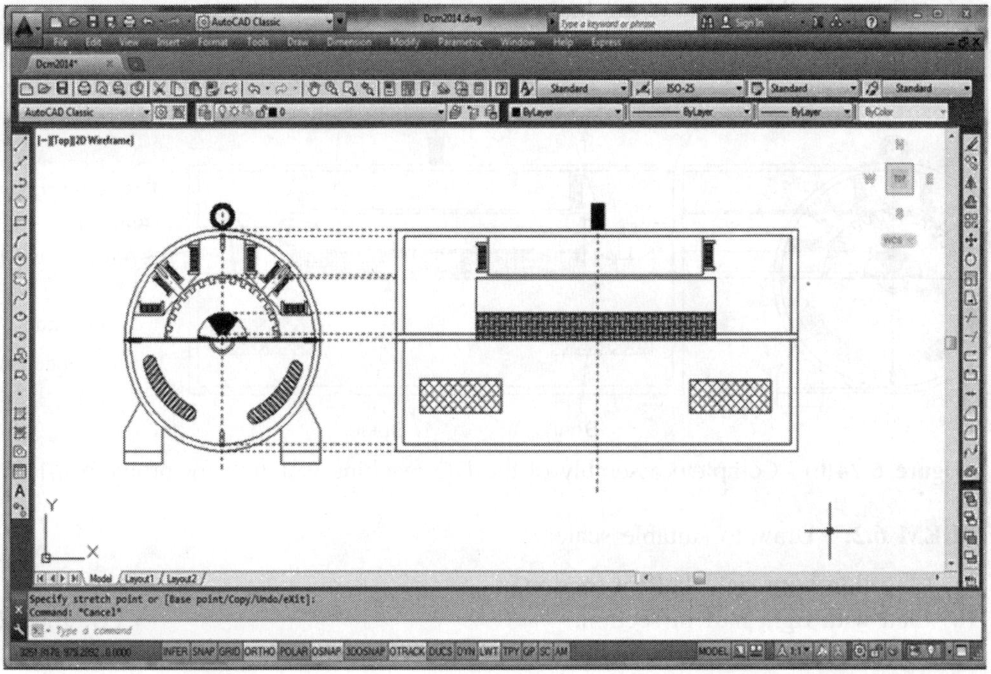

Figure 6.23(l) Pole elevation, *courtesy:* AutoCAD®.

Step 17: Once the elevation of parts is completed, then draw the commutator, brush and fan as shown in the Figure 6.24. It shows the dimensions of all parts in the elevation.

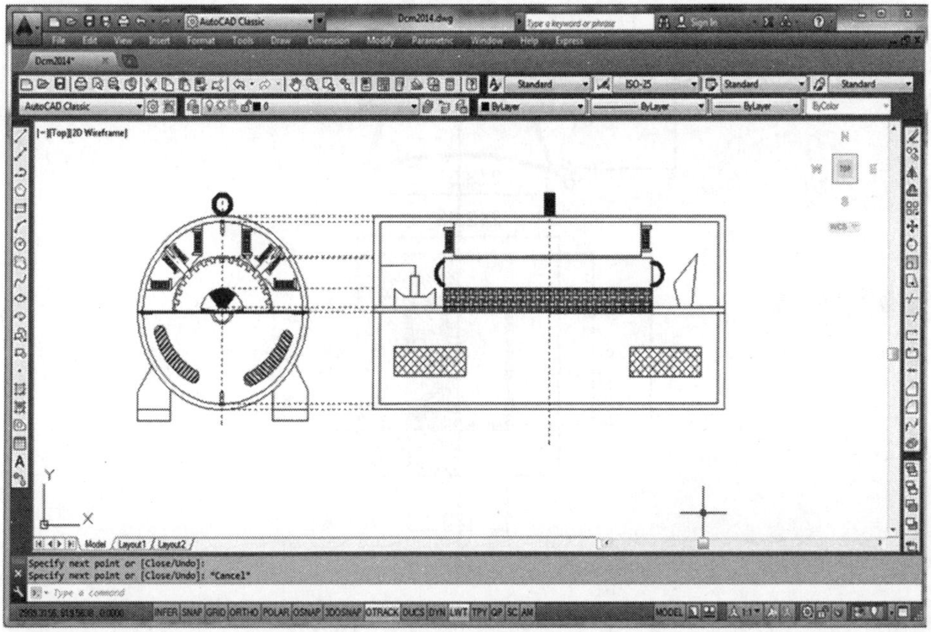

Figure 6.24(a) Commutator assembly with brush and fan mounted on the shaft, *courtesy:* AutoCAD®.

Figure 6.24(b) gives the complete top half in section end view of the DC machine along with its elevation.

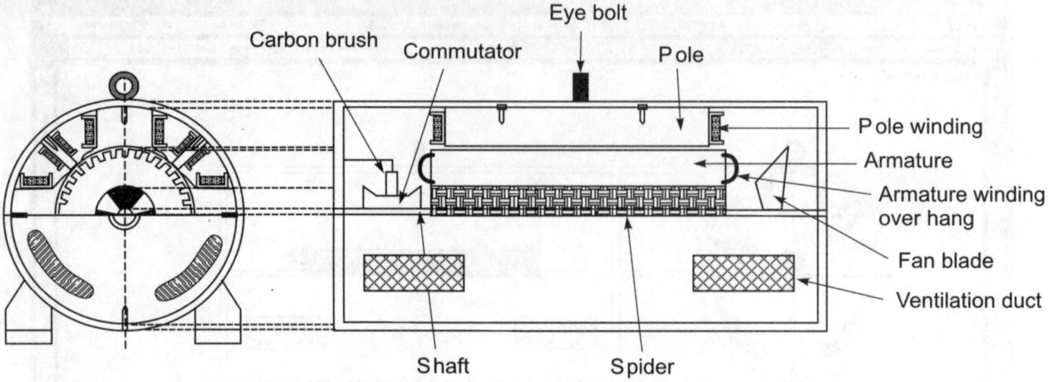

Figure 6.24(b) Complete assembly of the DC machine (solution for problem 6.1).

PROBLEM 6.2: Draw to suitable scale:

(a) Elevation with right half in section.
(b) Plan with right half in section. (VTU, June 2013)

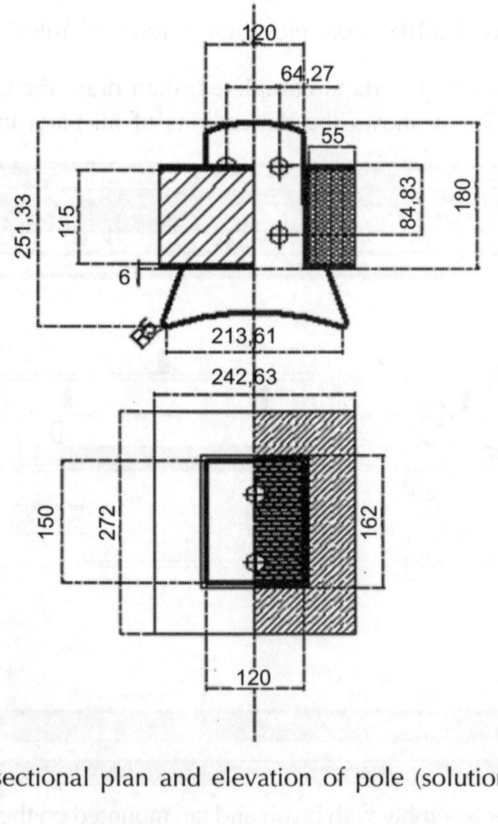

Figure 6.25 The sectional plan and elevation of pole (solution for problem 6.2).

Following are the details of a main pole of a DC machine:

(i) Number of poles = 4
(ii) Height of pole = 180 mm
(iii) Width of the pole = 120 mm
(iv) Length of the pole = 150 mm
(v) Armature diameter = 400 mm
(vi) Pole arc/pole pitch = 0.67
(vii) Number of turns/pole = 1890
(viii) Conductor area = 1.77 mm^2
(ix) Depth of the winding = 55 mm
(x) Height of the winding = 115 mm

PROBLEM 6.3: Draw to a suitable scale end view elevation with top half in section of a DC machine, with the following details:

(VTU, June 2013)

Yoke:

Outside diameter = 49.6 cm
Inner diameter = 40 cm
Axial length = 16 mm

Main pole:

Number of poles = 4
Total height = 12.6 cm
Width = 6.5 cm
Air gap = 3 mm

Inter pole:

Number of poles = 4
Total height = 11 cm
Width = 10 cm
Air gap = 3 mm

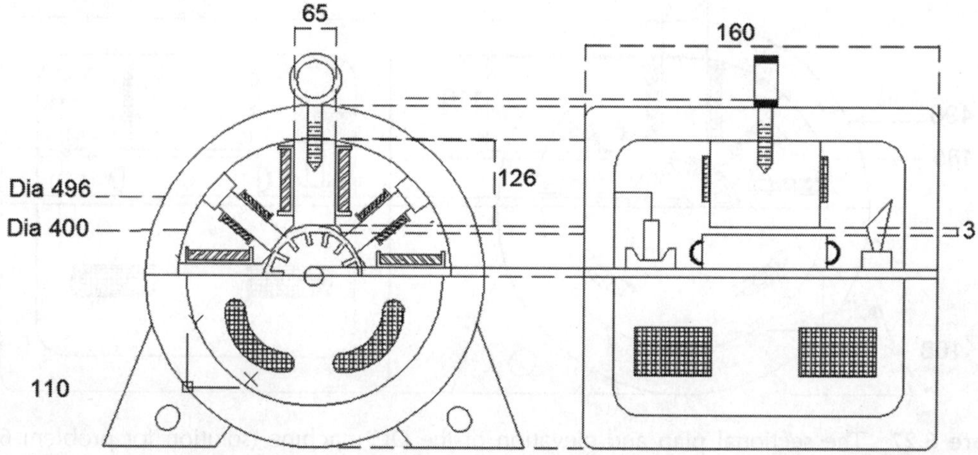

Figure 6.26 The sectional plan and elevation of the DC machine (solution for problem 6.3).

PROBLEM 6.4: Draw to a suitable scale half sectional end view and longitudinal end view of a 60 HP, 4 pole DC shunt motor, with the following details: (VTU, June 2013)

Armature:

Outside diameter = 18.5 cm
Length = 13.5 cm
Number of slots = 24
Size of slot = 0.7 cm × 2 cm

Inter pole (solid):

Size = 2 × 10.8 cm^2
Length = 11 cm

Brush:

Total number of spindles = 4

Winding:

Main pole = 2 cm thick (shunt winding)
Inter pole winding = 1 cm thick

Main pole (laminated):

Total height = 11 cm
Width = 7 cm
Pole arc = 10 cm
Length of the pole = 14 cm
Air gap = 0.5 cm

Commutator:

Diameter = 13 cm
Length = 10 cm

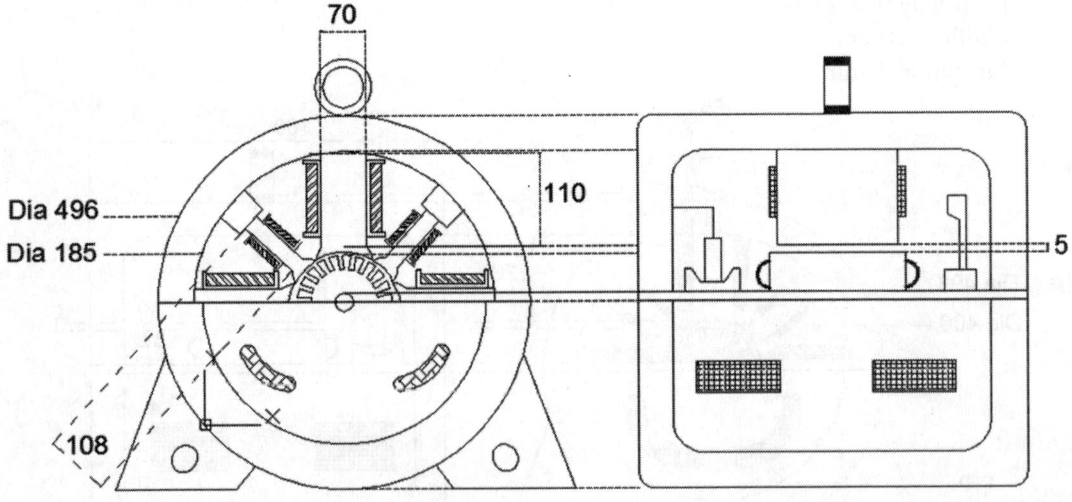

Figure 6.27 The sectional plan and elevation of the DC machine (solution for problem 6.4).

PROBLEM 6.5: Draw to scale

(a) Half sectional end view and

(b) Front view of alternator with the following data:

(i) Diameter of shaft = 1.6 cm
(ii) Height of pole = 11 cm
(iii) Diameter of frame (outer) = 92 cm
(iv) Length of yoke = 22 cm
(v) Diameter of the rotor = 46 cm
(vi) Outer diameter of the stator = 76 cm
(vii) Number of poles = 10
(viii) Length of stator = 16 cm

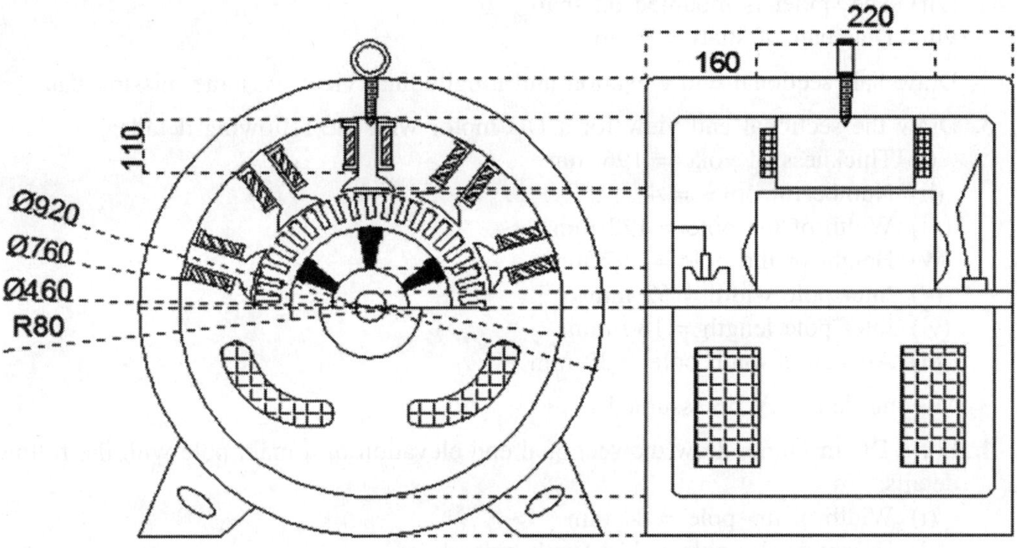

Figure 6.28 The sectional plan and elevation of the DC machine (solution for problem 6.5).

EXERCISES

1. Draw the neat sketch of a DC generator for the following details:

(i) Number of slots = 39
(ii) Size of slots = 8 × 2.4 cm^2
(iii) Number of poles = 4
(iv) Height of main pole = 32 cm
(v) Width of the main pole = 24 cm
(vi) Inter pole width = 9 cm
(vii) Height of inter pole = 30 cm
(viii) Air gap at main pole = 0.7 cm
(ix) Thickness of yoke = 13.6 cm

(x) Diameter of shaft = 18 cm
(xi) Outer diameter of armature stamping = 84 cm
(xii) Inner diameter of armature stamping = 40 cm

Draw quarter half in sectional end view. Missing data may be assumed.

2. Draw the neat sketch of a DC generator with the following details:
(i) Thickness of armature = 20.5 cm
(ii) Length of the armature = 62 cm
(iii) Number of slots = 36
(iv) Width of the slot = 1.2 cm
(v) Height of the slot = 3.8 cm
(vi) The diameter of spider = 16.3 cm
(vii) The spider is mounted on shaft
(viii) Diameter of shaft = 9 cm

Draw half sectional end elevation and longitudinal view. Assume missing data.

3. Draw the sectional end view for a DC motor with the following details:
(i) Thickness of yoke = 196 mm
(ii) Number of poles = 4
(iii) Width of the pole = 122 mm
(iv) Height of the pole = 192 mm
(v) Inter pole width = 52 mm
(vi) Inter pole length = 180 mm
(vii) Air gap at main pole = 32 mm

Missing data may be assumed.

4. For a DC machine, draw the sectional end elevation of a main pole with the following details:
(i) Width of the pole = 84 mm
(ii) Height of the pole = 114 (with pole shoe)
(iii) Pole arc = 120
(iv) Thickness of yoke = 57

Missing data may be assumed.

5. Draw (a) half sectional end view and (b) front elevation of commutator of a DC machine. Missing data may be assumed.
Given data:
(i) Commutator diameter = 41.75 cm
(ii) Length of the commutator = 43 cm
(iii) Shaft diameter = 14.6 cm
(iv) Length of the riser = 5 cm
(v) Width of the riser = 2.5 cm
(vi) Segment pitch with mica = 2.5 cm
(vii) Thickness of mica = 0.625 cm
(viii) Height of the segment = 9.5 cm
(ix) Outer diameter of sleeve = 39 cm

6. For the following details of a DC machine, draw the end view and elevation (right of in section):

(i) Outer diameter of yoke = 99.2
(ii) Inner diameter of yoke = 80
(iii) Axial length = 32
(iv) Number of poles = 4
(v) Size of the pole = 25.2 × 12
(vi) Air gap = 1.6
(vii) Number of inter poles = 4
(viii) Size of the pole = 22 × 19
(ix) Air gap = 2.5

All dimensions are in cm.

7. With the following details, draw left half sectional end elevation and longitudinal view for a DC machine:

(i) Armature thickness = 153.8 mm
(ii) Armature length = 46.5 mm
(iii) Number of slots = 36
(iv) Slots size = 19 mm × 9 mm
(v) The diameter of spider = 12.2 mm
(vi) The spider is mounted on shaft
(vii) Diameter of shaft = 6.8 cm

Assume the missing data.

8. Draw the neat sketch of a DC generator for the following details:

(i) Number of slots = 28
(ii) Size of slots = 4 × 2.4 cm^2
(iii) Number of poles = 4
(iv) Height of main pole = 16 cm
(v) Width of the main pole = 12 cm
(vi) Inter pole width = 4.5 cm
(vii) Height of inter pole = 15 cm
(viii) Air gap at main pole = 0.5 cm
(ix) Thickness of yoke = 7 cm
(x) Diameter of shaft = 9 cm
(xi) Outer diameter of armature stamping = 42 cm
(xii) Inner diameter of armature stamping = 20 cm

Draw quarter half in sectional end view. Missing data may be assumed.

9. Draw the main pole DC machine of the given data:

(i) Number of poles = 4
(ii) Pole height = 70 mm
(iii) Width of the pole = 63.5 mm

(iv) Length of the pole = 85 mm
(v) Diameter of the armature = 200 mm
(vi) Ratio of pole/pole pitch = 0.335
(vii) Depth of the winding = 22.5 mm
(viii) Height of the winding = 55 mm

Missing data may be assumed.

10. For the following details of a DC machine, draw the sectional end elevation (left half in section):

(i) Thickness of yoke = 20 cm
(ii) Number of main poles = 4
(iii) Height of the main pole = 56 cm (including pole shoe)
(iv) Width of the pole = 48 cm
(v) Air gap = 1.6 cm
(vi) Pole arc = 63% of the pole pitch
(vii) Outer diameter of armature stamping = 152 cm
(viii) Inner diameter of armature stamping = 80 cm
(ix) Number of slots = 32
(x) Width of the slot = 6 cm
(xi) Height of the slot = 14 cm
(xii) Shaft diameter = 24 cm

Assume any missing data.

11. Draw to suitable scale:

(a) End view with quarter half in section.
(b) Front elevation with top half in section.

Following main dimensions of a commutator are used for DC machine:

(i) Commutator diameter = 83.5
(ii) Length of riser = 10
(iii) Thickness of mica = 1.25
(iv) Segment pitch with mica = 5
(v) Height of segment = 19
(vi) Length of commutator = 86
(vii) Width of the riser = 5.1
(viii) Shaft diameter = 29.2
(ix) Outer diameter of sleeve = 78

Sleeve is fixed by V ring and collar. All dimensions are in mm. (VTU, June 2013)

7 AC Machine Assemby

Learning Objectives

This chapter illustrates the importance of AC machines, its advantages over DC machines. The various types of AC machine, its parts and assembly using AutoCAD software in a step by step manner.

7.1 INTRODUCTION

AC machines are widely used in almost all the places right from our houses to each and every industry. The design, structure, characteristics, cost, maintenance, speed control and flexibility of the machine to suit any environment, efficiency and reliability have made these machines to replace the DC machines in the industrial sector. The mode of power transmission in our nation is in AC; hence this reason also makes it the best choice when compared to DC machines since the AC power is not required to be converted into DC to operate AC machines.
AC machines can be classified into mainly 2 kinds as shown in Figure 7.1.

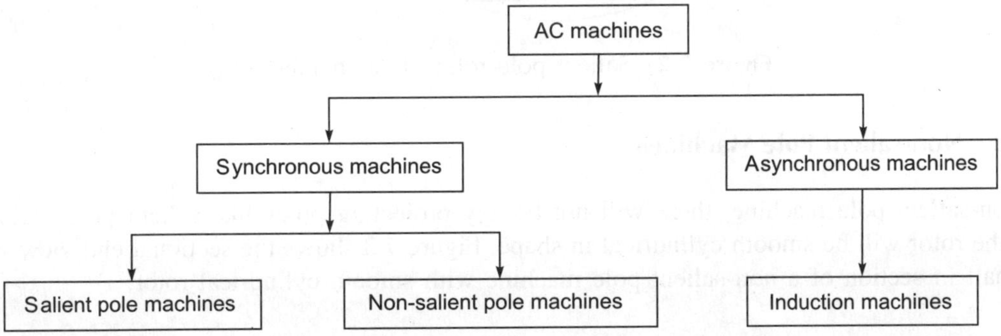

Figure 7.1 Classification of AC machines.

7.2 SYNCHRONOUS MACHINES

In these kinds of machines, the currents to the rotor winding are supplied directly from the stationary frame through a rotating contact.

In synchronous motors, the torque can be produced at synchronous speed by a field winding which is generally wound on the rotor and is excited by a DC supply such that it produces a rotor flux which is relatively static to the rotor. Hence, this results in the rotation of the rotor at synchronous speed *Ns* such that its field travels in step with the stator field axis. At speeds other than *Ns*, the rotor pole will approach alternately a stator 'north' pole field, then a 'south' pole field, changing the resulting torque from a positive to a negative value at a frequency related to the speed difference, the mean torque being zero.

Synchronous machines can be broadly classified into two kinds depending upon its rotor construction as salient pole machines and non-salient pole machines.

7.2.1 Salient Pole Machines

In a salient pole machines, the rotor will pose a number of projecting poles resulting in uneven air gap symmetry as shown in the Figure 7.2.

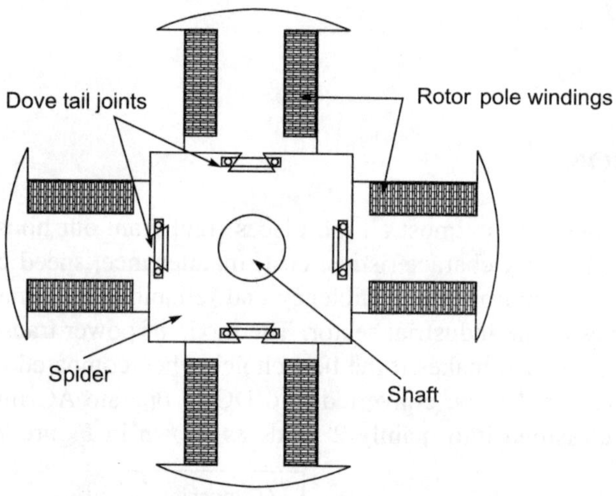

Figure 7.2 Salient pole rotor of AC machine.

7.2.2 Non-salient Pole Machines

In non-salient pole machine, there will not be any projecting poles like salient pole machine and the rotor will be smooth cylindrical in shape. Figure 7.3 shows the sectional end view with top half in section of a non-salient pole machine with smooth cylindrical rotor.

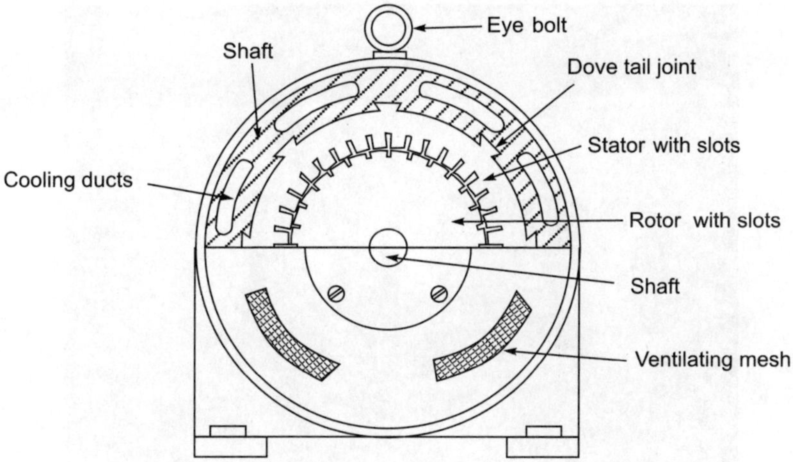

Figure 7.3 Non-salient pole rotor of AC machine with top half in section.

7.3 ASYNCHRONOUS MACHINES/INDUCTION MACHINES

The operating speed of the asynchronous machine is slightly less than the synchronous speed henceforth it is called as an *asynchronous machine*, because of its rigid characteristics in almost all the cases, these machines are used as induction motors for different applications.

Induction machines are considered as a boon to the industrial sector. The machine gains its name as induction machine as it works on the same principle as a transformer. These machines are also addressed as *rotating transformers*. In these machines, the rotor currents get induced in the rotor windings by a combination of the time-variation of the stator currents and the motion of the rotor relative to the stator. Rotor is not at all connected to any electrical supply but the rotor current is a result of induction effect. Only the stator is fed with the electrical supply in an induction machine.

Depending upon the rotor construction, induction machines can be classified into 2 different kinds, namely:

- Squirrel cage rotor
- Phase wound rotor or slip ring rotor

7.3.1 Squirrel Cage Rotor

Induction machines which employ squirrel cage rotors, the speed variation is not possible since the rotor winding is completely shorted and accessing the rotor at any point of time is impossible. Here, the rotor windings are solid aluminium bars which are placed and moulded into the slots of the rotor and are shorted together on both the ends by cast aluminium rings. Figure 7.4(a) shows squirrel cage rotor with aluminium bars and Figure 7.4(b) shows squirrel cage induction motor in an induction machine.

Figure 7.4(a) Squirrel cage rotor with Al bars in an induction machine.

Induction machines with cage rotor are relatively inexpensive and highly reliable.

Figure 7.4(b) Squirrel cage induction motor in an induction machine.

7.3.2 Slip Ring Induction Machine

In slip ring induction machine, the connection in the rotor is star connected such that one end is completely shorted and at the other end it is connected to the Cu rings placed on the shaft of the machine to which external resistance can be conducted and the speed of the induction machine be varied by varying the resistance. The Figure 7.5(a) and (b) show the slip rings in an induction machine.

Figure 7.5(a) Slip rings induction in a machine.

Figure 7.5(b) Slip rings placed on the shaft of the machine.

******Note:*** The steps to draw the assembly drawing of AC machines is just similar to that of DC machines and the very same may be followed except for drawing some special parts like stator, slip rings and terminal boxes.

7.4 SOLVED PROBLEMS

PROBLEM 7.1: Draw the following view of a 7 HP, 400 V, 50 Hz, 3 phase, 1440 RPM slip ring induction motor:

- Half section front elevation.
- Half section end view.

The main dimensions have been given below:

Outer diameter of the stator stamping is 28.8 cm
Stator core length is 10 cm
Thickness of the stator frame is 2.5 cm

Slot:

Type-open type
Number of slots is 36
Size is 14 mm × 6 mm
Air gap is 4 mm

Outer diameter of the rotor stampings is 21.2 cm
Inside diameter of the rotor stamping is 3.6 cm
Rotor core length 10 cm

Slot:

Type-open type
Number of slots is 36
Size is 14 mm × 5 mm

Shaft diameter is 3.6 cm

Base plate thickness is 5 mm, with bolt dimension 24 mm × 66 mm.
The stator frame has eight and rotor stamping have four equally spaced ducts for ventilation.
Inside diameter of the stator stamping is 21.6 cm. (VTU June 2013)

Solution: Figure 7.6 shows the top half in section end view and elevated view of slip ring induction machine with the dimensions given above.

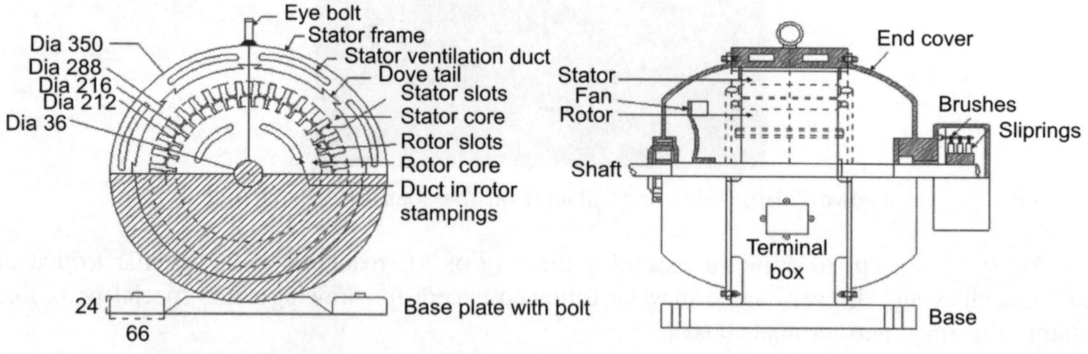

Figure 7.6 Top half in section end view and elevated view of slip ring induction machine (solution for problem 7.1).

PROBLEM 7.2: Draw the following view of a 6.5 HP, 400 V, 50 Hz, 3 phase, 3000 RPM slip ring induction motor:

- Half section end view.
- Half section front elevation.

The main dimensions have been given below:

Outer diameter of the stator stamping is 23 cm
Inside diameter of the stator stamping is 16.4 cm
Stator core length is 11 cm
Thickness of the stator frame is 3 cm

Slot:

Type-open type
Number of slots is 36
Size is 18 mm × 10 mm
Air gap is 2 mm

Outer diameter of the rotor stampings is 16 cm
Inside diameter of the rotor stamping is 3 cm
Rotor core length is 11 cm

Slot:

Type-open type
Number of slots is 18
Size is 18 mm × 6 mm

Shaft diameter is 3.0 cm
Base plate thickness is 5 mm, with bolt dimension 20 mm × 40 mm.
The stator frame has eight and rotor stamping have four equally spaced ducts for ventilation.

Solution: Figure 7.7 shows the top half in section end view and elevated view of slip ring induction machine with the dimensions given above.

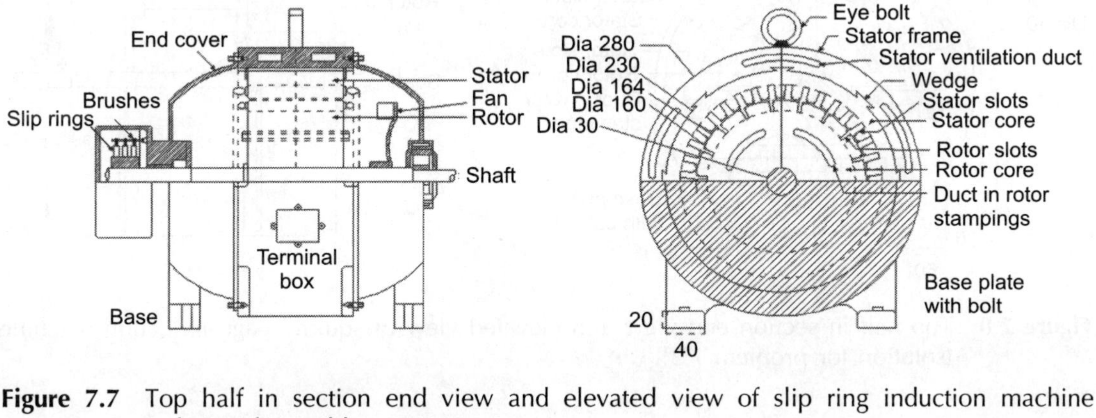

Figure 7.7 Top half in section end view and elevated view of slip ring induction machine (solution for problem 7.2).

PROBLEM 7.3: Draw the following view of a 3.5 HP, 400 V, 50 Hz, 3 phase, 1440 RPM squirrel cage induction motor:

- Half section front elevation.
- Half section end view.

The main dimensions have been given below:

Outer diameter of the stator stamping is 38 cm
Inside diameter of the stator stamping is 32.4 cm
Stator core length is 14 cm
Thickness of the stator frame is 2.5 cm

Slot:

Type-open type
Number of slots is 36
Size is 18 mm × 10 mm
Air gap is 7 mm

Outer diameter of the rotor stampings is 18.4 cm
Inside diameter of the rotor stamping is 4 cm
Number of rotor slots is 18
Shaft diameter is 2 cm

The rotor has totally closed type slots and contains bare conductors which are short circuited at both sides.

Base plate thickness is 5 mm, with bolt dimension 20 mm × 60 mm.

Solution: Figure 7.8 shows the top half in section end view and elevated view of squirrel cage induction machine with the dimensions given above.

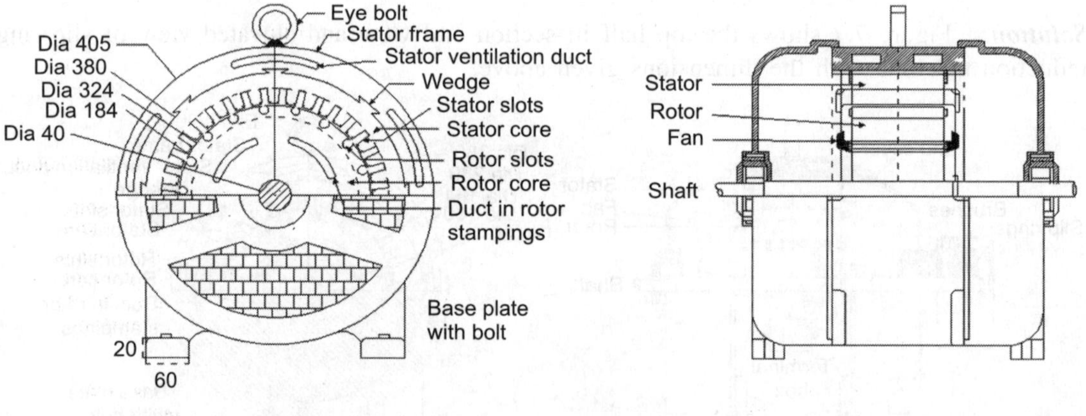

Figure 7.8 Top half in section end view and elevated view of squirrel cage induction machine (solution for problem 7.3).

PROBLEM 7.4: Draw the following view of a 3 HP, 400 V, 50 Hz, 3 phase, 1440 RPM squirrel cage induction motor:

- Half section front elevation.
- Half section end view.

The main dimensions have been given below:

Outer diameter of the stator stamping is 20 cm
Inside diameter of the stator stamping is 16 cm
Stator core length is 10 cm
Thickness of the stator frame is 2.5 cm

Slot:

Type-open type
Number of slots is 36
Size is 12 mm × 8 mm
Air gap is 7 mm

Outer diameter of the rotor stampings is 14.6 cm
Inside diameter of the rotor stamping is 6 cm
Number of rotor slots is 36
Shaft diameter is 4 cm

The rotor has totally closed type slots and contains bare conductors which are short circuited at both sides.

Base plate thickness is 5 mm, with bolt dimension 24 mm × 66 mm.

Solution: Figure 7.9 shows the top half in section end view and elevated view of squirrel cage induction machine with the dimensions given above.

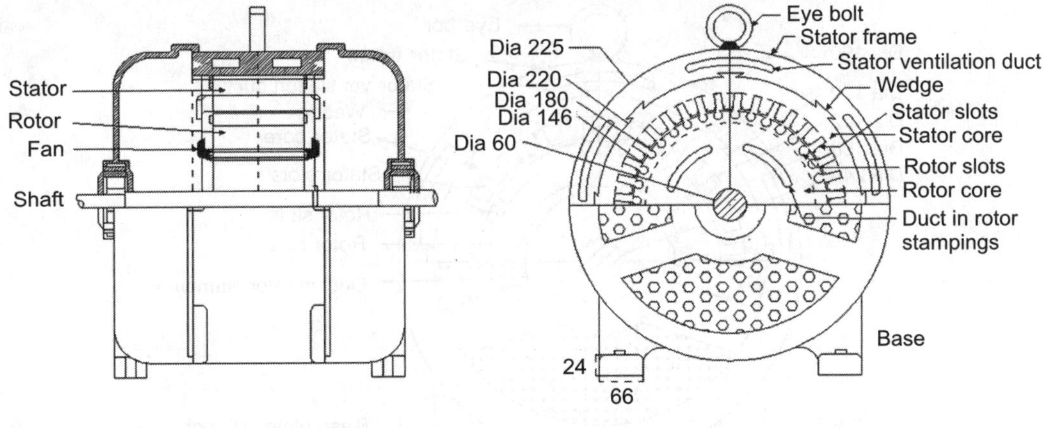

Figure 7.9 Top half in section end view and elevated view of squirrel cage induction machine (solution for problem 7.4).

PROBLEM 7.5: Draw the following view of a 2 HP, 400 V, 50 Hz, 3 phase, 1440 RPM squirrel cage induction motor:

- Half section front elevation.
- Half section end view.

The main dimensions have been given below:

Outer diameter of the stator stamping is 17 cm
Inside diameter of the stator stamping is 14.2 cm
Stator core length is 8 cm
Thickness of the stator frame is 2 cm

Slot:

Type-open type
Number of slots is 36
Size is 10 mm × 6 mm
Air gap is 1.75 mm

Outer diameter of the rotor stampings is 10.8 cm
Inside diameter of the rotor stamping is 2.4 cm
Number of rotor slots is 16
Shaft diameter is 1.8 cm

The rotor has totally closed type slots and contains bare conductors which are short circuited at both sides.

Base plate thickness is 5 mm, with bolt dimension 24 mm × 40 mm.

Solution: Figure 7.10 shows the top half in section end view of squirrel cage induction machine with the dimensions given above.

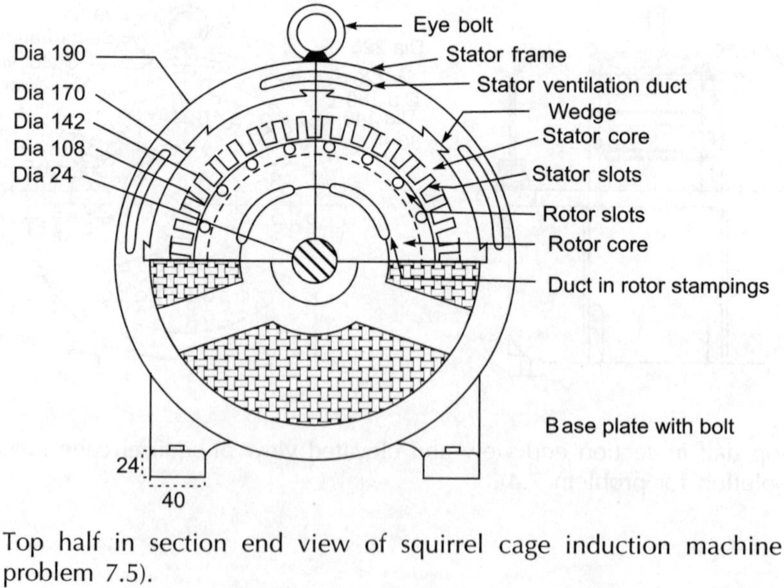

Figure 7.10 Top half in section end view of squirrel cage induction machine (solution for problem 7.5).

7.5 PHOTOGRAPHS OF MACHINES

Figure 7.11 A typical squirrel cage rotor of an induction machine.

Figure 7.12 A typical squirrel cage rotor of an induction machine (used in ceiling fan).

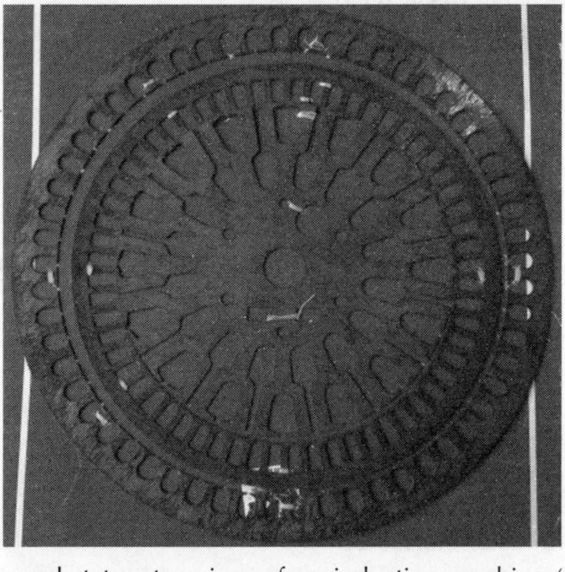

Figure 7.13 A rotor and stator stampings of an induction machine (used in ceiling fan).

EXERCISES

1. Draw the end and front elevation of top half in section of three phase induction motor with the following details:
   - (i) Diameter of shaft = 26.6 cm
   - (ii) Outer diameter of stator = 186.6 cm
   - (iii) Inner diameter of stator = 133.3 cm
   - (iv) Thickness of yoke = 19 cm
   - (v) Length of the core = 110 cm
   - (vi) Number of stator slots = 24
   - (vii) Size of stator slots = 20 cm × 6.5 cm
   - (viii) Air gap = 1.5 cm
   - (ix) Outer diameter of rotor = 130.6 cm
   - (x) Inner diameter of rotor = 23.4 cm
   - (xi) Length of rotor stamping = 110 cm
   - (xii) Number of rotor slots = 36
   - (xiii) Size of rotor slots = 18 cm × 5.32 cm

   Assume the missing data.
2. Draw the end view of top half in section of three phase induction motor with the following details:
   - (i) Outer diameter of stator stamping = 172.5 cm
   - (ii) Inner diameter of stator stamping = 123.23 cm
   - (iii) Length of the stator core = 90.75 cm
   - (iv) Thickness of stator frame = 18.75 cm
   - (v) Number of slots (open type) = 36
   - (vi) Slot size = 11.25 cm × 13.5 cm
   - (vii) Air gap = 1.2 cm
   - (viii) Outer diameter of rotor = 120.75 cm
   - (ix) Inner diameter of rotor = 25.9 cm
   - (x) Diameter of shaft = 25.9 cm

   Rotor has closed type slots and other missing data may be suitably assumed.
3. Draw the half sectional end view of a squirrel cage rotor with the following details:
   - (i) Thickness of the yoke = 6 cm
   - (ii) Diameter of shaft = 3 cm
   - (iii) Outer diameter of rotor = 15 cm
   - (iv) Width of the rotor slot = 0.5 cm
   - (v) Height of the rotor slot = 1 cm
   - (vi) Number of rotor slots = 30
   - (vii) Air gap = 0.3 mm
   - (viii) Number of stator slots = 36

(ix) Width of the stator slot = 0.6 cm
(x) Height of the stator slot = 3 cm

Assume missing data if any.

4. Draw the right half in section of end view of alternator with the following details:

(i) Outer diameter of stator = 213 mm
(ii) Size of the pole including pole shoe = 28.8 mm × 28.8 mm
(iii) Pole arc = 56.3 mm
(iv) Air gap = 4.65 mm
(v) Outer diameter of rotor = 144.3 mm
(vi) Width of pole winding = 18.34 mm and 5.74 mm
(vii) Height pole winding = 9.6 mm

Assume any missing data.

5. Draw the quarter section end view and elevation of the squirrel cage rotor with the following details:

(i) Length of the rotor = 128 cm
(ii) Thickness of the rotor = 156 cm
(iii) Shaft diameter = 32 cm
(iv) Number of rotor (semi closed type) = 38
(v) Size of rotor slot = 6 cm × 1.5 cm
(vi) Outer diameter of the rotor = 155 cm
(vii) Inner diameter of the rotor = 142 cm

Assume missing data if any.

6. Sketch the end view and elevation (bottom half section) of the stator core as per the given data of induction motor:

(i) Number of slots = 36
(ii) Slot size = 5.8 cm × 1.9 cm
(iii) Depth of the iron behind the stator size = 8 cm
(iv) Length of the stator core = 27 cm
(v) Inside diameter of the stator = 36 cm

Assume missing data if any.

7. The following details are given for induction motor for which draw the end view and front elevation (top half in section). All dimensions are in cm.

(i) Squirrel cage rotor
(ii) Outer diameter of rotor = 45
(iii) Axial length of the rotor core = 36
(iv) End ring cross section = 3 × 3
(v) Diameter of the shaft = 7.62
(vi) Number of slots = 30 (rectangular)
(vii) Slot width = 1.5
(viii) Height of the slot = 3

8. Draw the half sectional view and half sectional elevation of the rotor of a three phase induction motor with the following details:

(i) Shaft diameter = 70 mm
(ii) Distance between the end ring and core = 10 mm
(iii) Cooling duct size = 10 mm wide
(iv) Diameter of rotor = 357.6 mm
(v) Length of the rotor = 270 mm
(vi) Conductor size = 18 mm

Assume any missing data.

9. Draw the quarter sectional end view for 10 HP induction motor with the following details:

(i) Number of stator slots = 36
(ii) Number of rotor slots = 31
(iii) Size of stator slots = 4.75 × 14.5
(iv) Diameter of rotor slots = 1 and is mounted on the shaft directly
(v) Air gap = 0.3
(vi) Diameter of shaft = 25
(vii) Inside diameter of stator = 90
(viii) Outside diameter of stator = 160

All dimensions are in cm.

10. Draw the left half sectional end view of a 6 pole alternator with the following dimensions:

(i) Outer diameter of stator = 283 mm
(ii) Outer diameter of rotor = 192.4 mm
(iii) Air gap = 6.2 mm
(iv) Width of the pole = 38.4 mm
(v) Height of the pole = 38.4 mm with pole shoe
(vi) Pole arc = 75 mm
(vii) Pole winding in 3 steps
(viii) Width = 24.45 mm and 7.65 mm
(ix) Height = 12.8 mm

Assume suitable any other missing data required.

8 Transformer Assembly

Learning Objectives

This chapter illustrates the importance of transformers, its types and various parts with the importance of each part, its use and assembly using AutoCAD software in a step by step manner.

8.1 INTRODUCTION

A *transformer* is a static electrical apparatus which transfers power from one circuit to the other which are electrically not connected but mutually coupled.

Transformer is considered as the heart of the power system as it is the main device in the process of transmission and distribution. A power system can never exist without a transformer. Depending on the usage, transformers are basically classified into two types namely:

- ***Power transformer:*** These are the transformers used for transmission purposes.
- ***Distribution transformer:*** These are the transformers used for distribution purposes, i.e., distribution of power to the consumer.

Transformer is a job specific (tailor made) product and requires effort in its design and drafting, even if a single parameter is changed. Standardisation of the specification and design parameters of this vital equipment of energy transport will not only help in ensuring optimal deployment of available resources but also go a long way in economising the capital costs.

The efficiency of a transformer is usually very high when compared to other electrical machines and is of the range 90–95%, as the losses are minimal in the transformer. Theoretically, there exists a transformer which provides 100% efficiency and is known as *ideal transformer*.

Assembly refers to the detailed complete view of an object with all its parts assembled together. Assembly drawing is also known as detailed drafting and is necessary for fitting all the parts or assembling different parts of the item or machine together. Assembly is the area which deals with the complete dimension of the machine and its parts, which in turn helps to produce the various parts which constitutes the machine. It also gives a clear idea of which part is to be connected to which part, where and how so that it results in a complete faultless machine. It is always necessary to give the complete information to the lay man so as to obtain the machine.

8.2 CLASSIFICATION OF TRANSFORMERS

Classification of transformers is shown in Figure 8.1.

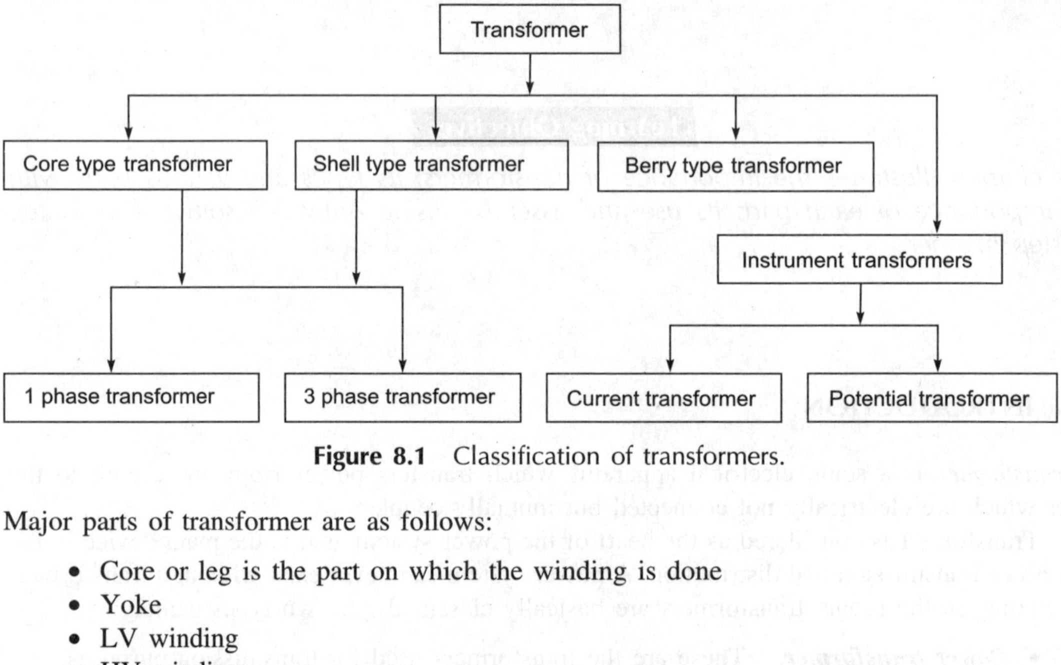

Figure 8.1 Classification of transformers.

Major parts of transformer are as follows:

- Core or leg is the part on which the winding is done
- Yoke
- LV winding
- HV winding
- Conservator
- Breather
- Bushings

8.2.1 Core of a Transformer

When voltage is applied to the exciting or primary winding of the transformer, a magnetising current flows in the primary winding. This current produces the flux in the core. The flow of flux in magnetic circuits is analogous to the flow of current in electrical circuits.

When the flux flows in the steel core, losses are occur. There are two components of this loss, which are termed 'eddy' and 'hysteresis' losses. *Hysteresis loss* is caused by the cyclic reversal of flux in the magnetic circuit and can be reduced by metallurgical control of the steel. *Eddy loss* is caused by eddy currents circulating within the steel induced by the flow of magnetic flux normal to the width of the core and it can be controlled by reducing the thickness of the steel lamination or by applying a thin insulating coating.

If a solid core were used in a power transformer, the losses would be very high and the temperature would be excessive. For this reason, cores are laminated from very thin sheets, such as 0.23 mm and 0.28 mm sheets, to reduce the thickness of the individual sheets of steel normal to the flux and thereby reducing the losses. Each sheet is coated with a very thin material to prevent shorts between the laminations.

Core steel can be hot or cold rolled, grain oriented or non-grain oriented, and even laser scribed for additional performance. The core cross section can be circular or rectangular, with circular cores commonly referred to as cruciform construction. Rectangular cores are used for smaller ratings and as auxiliary transformers used within a power transformer. Rectangular cores use a single width of strip steel, while circular cores use a combination of different strip widths to approximate a circular cross section. Just like other components in the transformer, the heat generated by the core must be adequately dissipated. While the steel and coating may be capable of withstanding higher temperatures, it will come in contact with insulating materials with limited temperature capabilities. In larger units, cooling ducts are used inside the core for additional convective surface area, and sections of laminations may be split to reduce localised losses.

The core is held together by, but insulated from mechanical structures and is grounded to a single point in order to dissipate electrostatic build up. The core ground location is usually some readily accessible point inside the tank, but it can also be brought through a bushing on the tank wall or top for external access. Core construction of a transformer is shown in Figure 8.2.

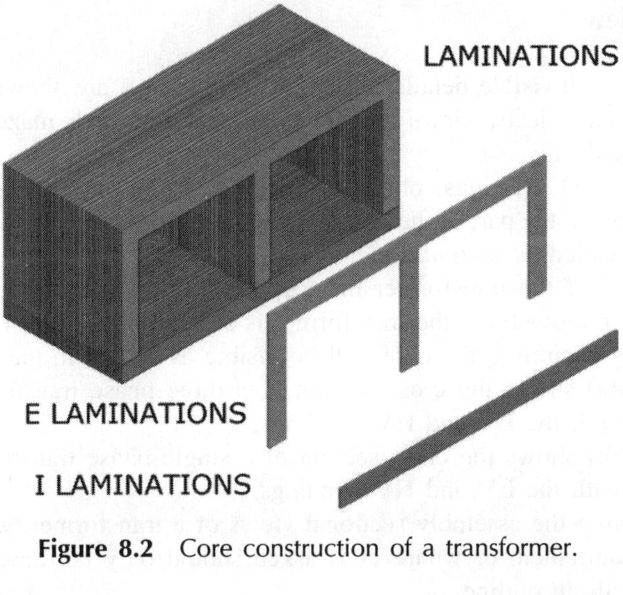

Figure 8.2 Core construction of a transformer.

There are two basic types of core construction used in power transformer: (i) core form and (ii) shell form.

(i) In *core form* construction, there is a single path for the magnetic circuit. For single phase applications, the windings are typically divided on both core legs. In three phase applications, the windings of a particular phase are typically on the same core leg. Figure 8.2 shows what is referred to as the 'E' and 'I' assembly of a three phase core form core during assembly.

(ii) In *shell form* construction, the core provides multiple paths for the magnetic circuit. Variations of three phase shell form construction include five and seven legged cores, depending on size and application.

8.2.2 Windings

The windings consist of the current carrying conductors wound around the sections of the core and these must be properly insulated, supported and cooled to withstand operational and test conditions. Copper and aluminium are the primary materials used as conductors in power transformer windings.

8.3 SECTIONAL VIEWS AND ELEVATIONS OF TRANSFORMERS

This section gives us a brief idea of how the transformer can be seen through different angles. Basically, there are two types of views in which a transformer can be analysed. They are sectional view and elevation.

8.3.1 Sectional View

In drawing, the interior invisible details of objects to be drawn are shown by dotted lines but in case of complicated objects, views are drawn in section which makes the drawing more clear with its interior details.

In making sectional drawings, object is imagined to be cut by a plane in a particular position and direction and the part of the object is removed. The projected view of the remaining part of the object is called as *sectional view*.

This is the view of the transformer that can be seen from the top, i.e., when the yoke of the transformer is removed and the transformer is seen from the top. In this view, only the core and the winding encircling the core will be visible as shown in the Figure 8.3(a).

The Figure 8.3(a) shows the cross section of a three phase transformer with 3 stepped core in detail along with the LV and HV windings.

The Figure 8.3(b) shows the cross section of a single phase transformer with 3 stepped core in detail along with the LV and HV windings.

Whenever drawing the assembly sectional views of a transformer, whatever is necessary depending on the requirement or whatever is asked should only be drawn and the remaining should be notified with an outline.

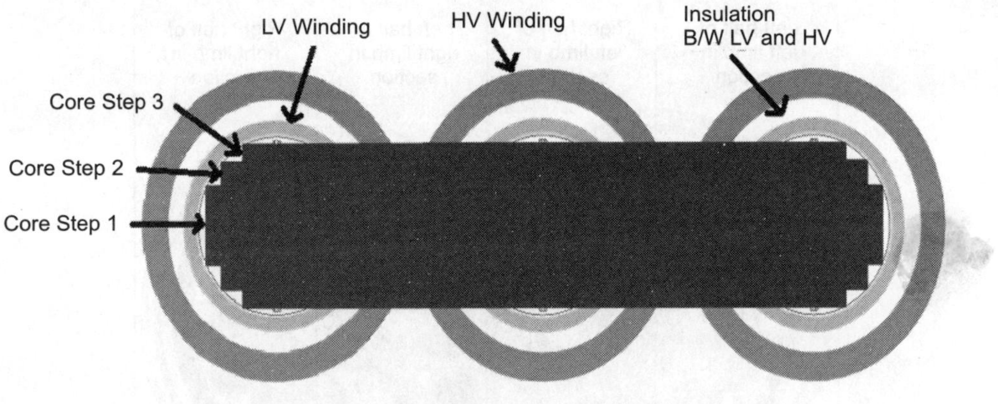

Figure 8.3(a) Sectional view of 3 phase transformer.

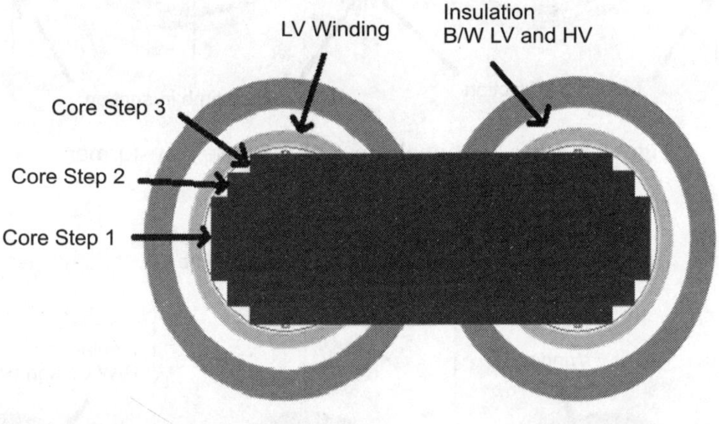

Figure 8.3(b) Sectional view of 1 phase transformer.

For example, the below stated Figure 8.4(a) and (b) give a clear idea about the various views of both single phase and three phase transformer.

With reference to Figure 8.4 (a), if it is asked to draw the sectional view of right half of right limb of the single phase transformer, only the right half of right limb is to be indicated with all the details like HV and LV winding, insulation etc. and the remaining part like the left limb, core and yoke should be only outlined. This is also applicable to three phase transformers and the above stated Figure 8.4(b) can be considered for reference.

8.3.2 Elevation

This refers to the view of the transformer as seen from the front and side but with its outer cover opened and all the necessary parts and details are available as shown in Figure 8.5.

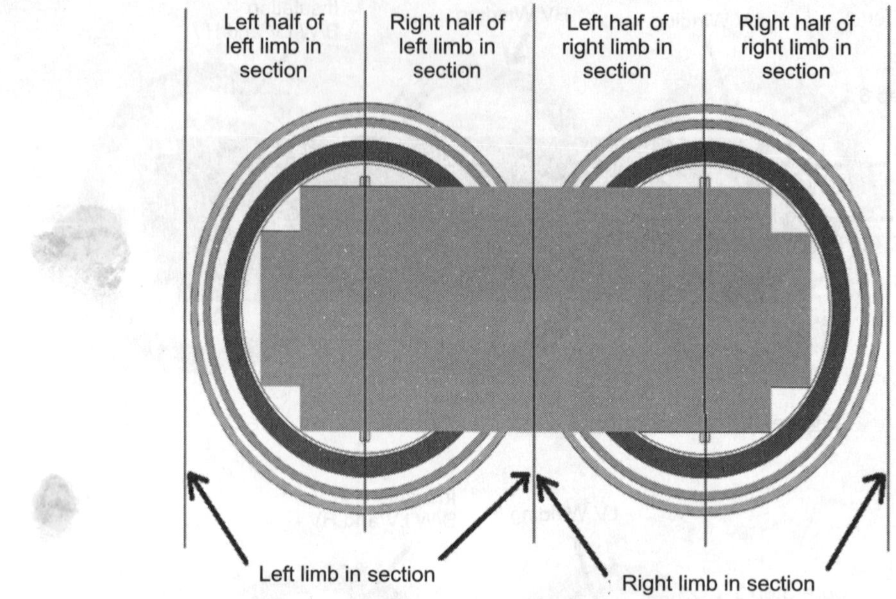

Figure 8.4(a) Sectional view of 1 phase transformer.

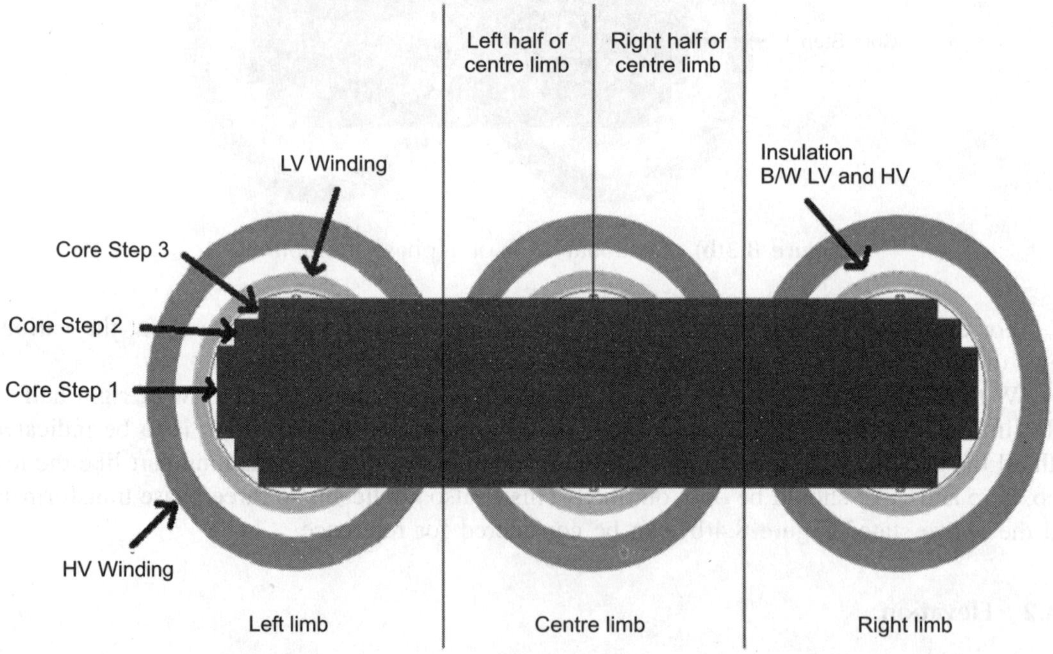

Figure 8.4(b) Sectional view of 3 phase transformer.

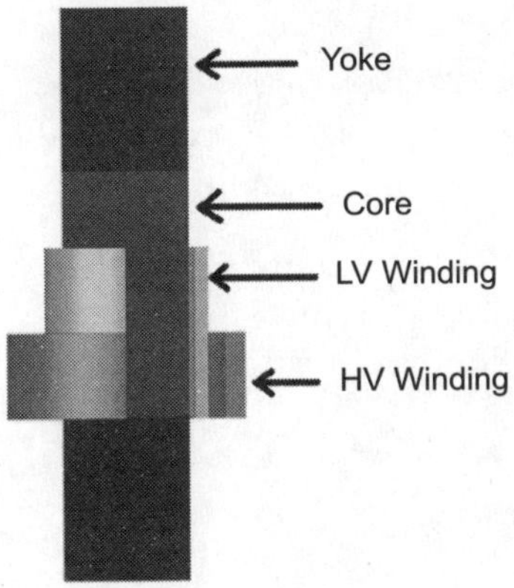

Figure 8.5(a) Side elevation of a transformer.

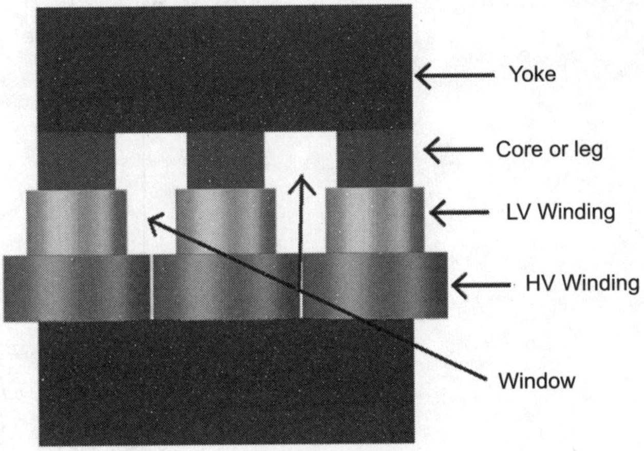

Figure 8.5(b) Front elevation of a transformer.

8.4 CORE SECTIONAL DETAILS OF TRANSFORMERS

Figure 8.6 shows the conventional views of the transformer and Figure 8.7 shows the sectional and elevated view of a single step core also known as *square core*. This type of core is used for low rating transformers. The LV winding encircles the core and the dimension of the core will be 0.71 times the diameter of the circle.

$$a = 0.71 \times D$$

where,

a = width of largest stamping
D = diameter

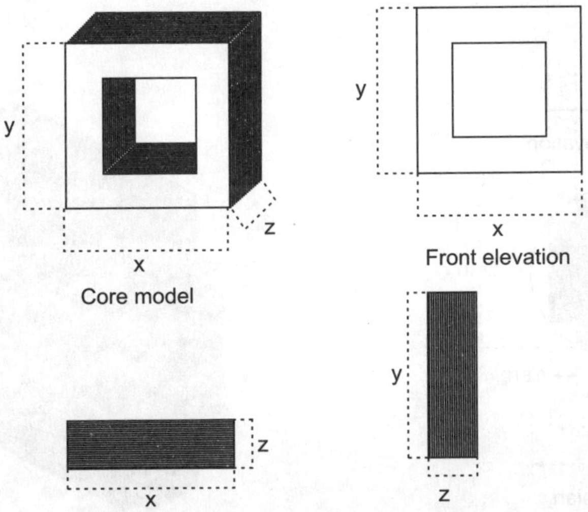

Figure 8.6 Conventional views of a transformer.

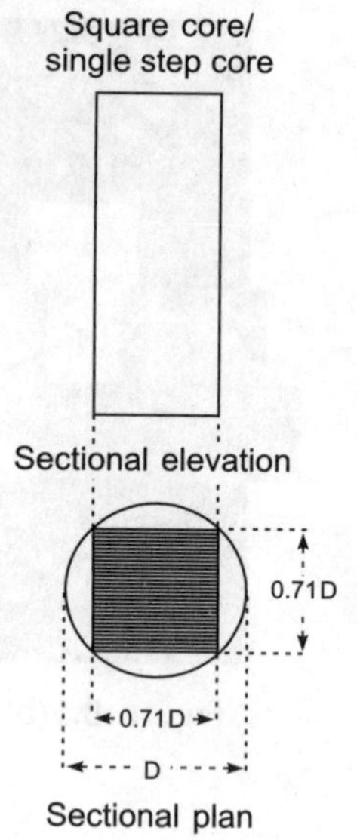

Figure 8.7 Leg section of single step core of a transformer.

Figure 8.8(a) shows the sectional and elevated view of a two-step core also known as *rectangular core*. This type of core is used for low rating transformers. The LV winding encircles the core and the dimension of the core will be 0.71 times the diameter of the circle.

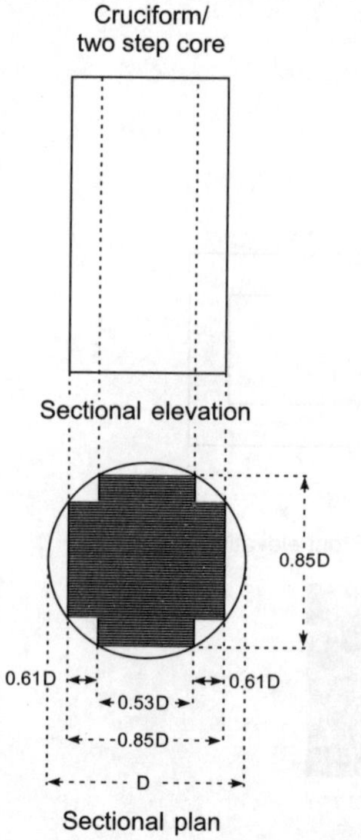

Figure 8.8(a) Leg section of a two-step core of a transformer.

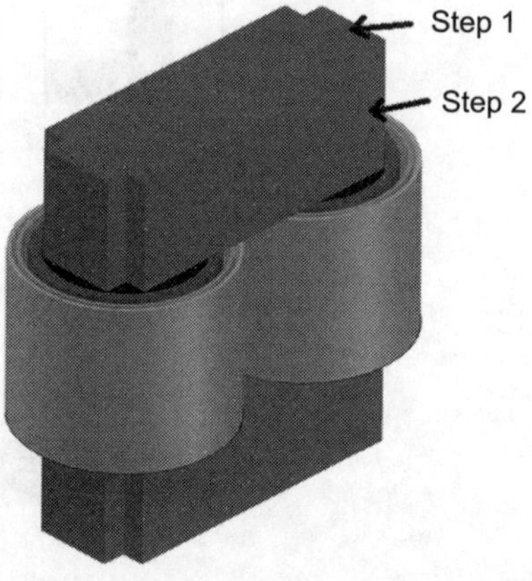

Figure 8.8(b) Two stepped core of a transformer.

$$a = 0.85 \times D$$

$$b = 0.53 \times D$$

where,

a = width of largest stamping
b = width of smallest stamping
D = diameter

Figure 8.8(b) shows the 3 dimensional view of a two stepped core transformer with windings.

Figure 8.9 shows the sectional and elevated view of a three-step core. The LV winding encircles the core and the dimension of the core will be as given below:

$$a = 0.9 \times D$$

$$b = 0.42 \times D$$

where,

a = width of largest stamping
b = width of smallest stamping
D = diameter

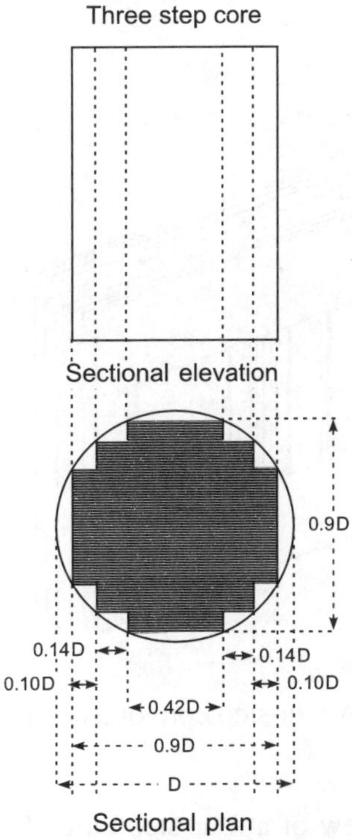

Figure 8.9(a) Leg section of a three-step core of a transformer.

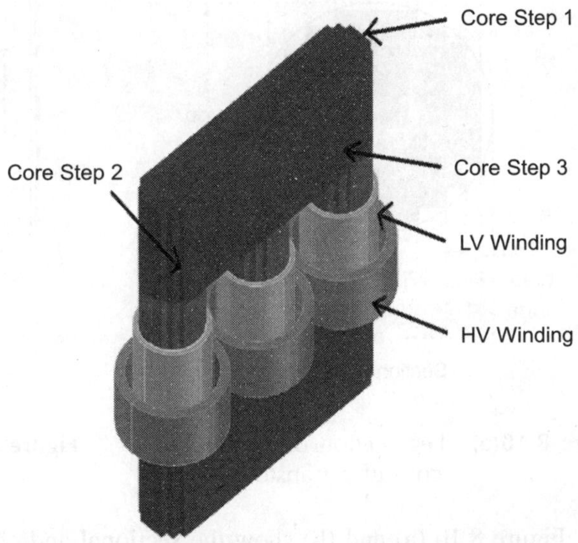

Figure 8.9(b) Leg section of a three-step core of a transformer.

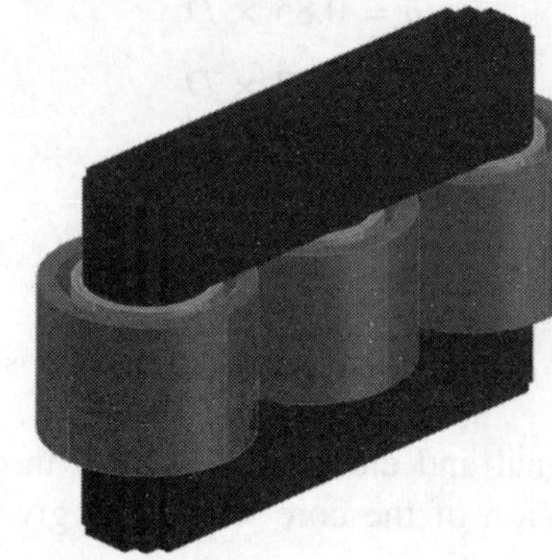

Figure 8.9(c) Three step core of a transformer.

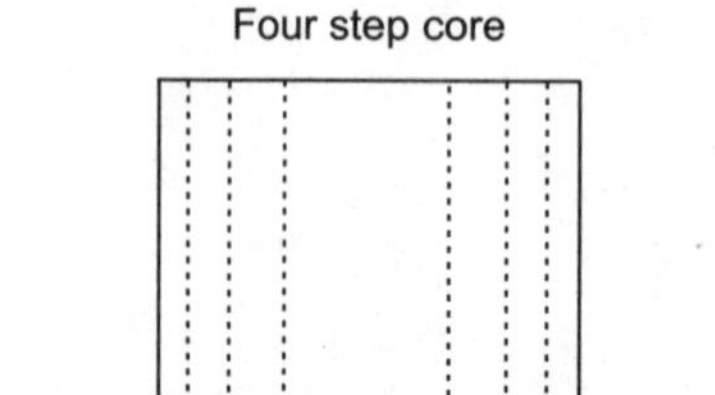

Figure 8.10(a) Leg section of a four-step core of a transformer.

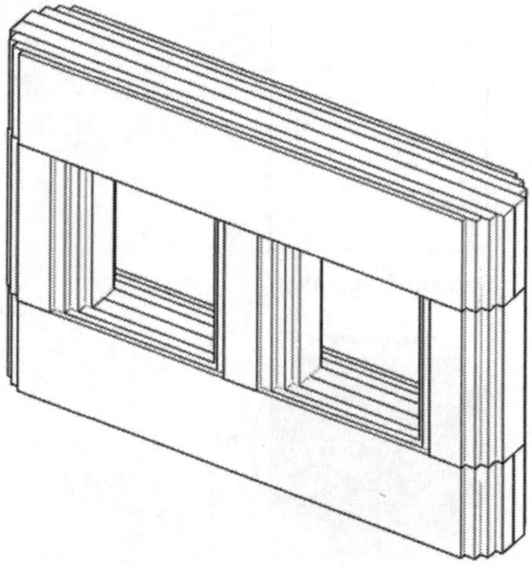

Figure 8.10(b) A four-step core of a transformer.

Figure 8.10 (a) and (b) show the sectional and elevated view of a four-step core. The LV winding encircles the core and the dimension of the core will be as given below:

$$a = 0.91 \times D$$

$$b = 0.36 \times D$$

where,

a = width of largest stamping

b = width of smallest stamping

D = diameter

8.5 SOLVED PROBLEMS

PROBLEM 8.1: Design and draw the assembly of single phase core type transformer with the following details:

Core details:

3 stepped core

Distance between core centres = 48 cm

Diameter of circumscribing circle = 24 cm

Height of the core = 50 cm

Winding details:

LV winding:

Outer diameter of first LV layer = 28.3 cm

Inner diameter of first LV layer = 25 cm

Outer diameter of second LV layer = 34.3 cm

Inner diameter of second LV layer = 29.3 cm

HV winding:

Outer diameter of HV layer = 43 cm

Inner diameter of HV layer = 35.3 cm

Solution:

Analysing the problem: In this particular problem, it is required to depict or to show the LV and HV windings of a single transformer and its sectional view and elevation.

A single phase core type transformer has only two cores or legs around which the LV and HV windings are done. The cores are joining together by the yoke.

In this problem the core is 3 stepped core, hence we have to first calculate the core dimensions. Now, let us assume that the first layer of LV winding is encircling the core, the core dimensions can be calculated as follows:

$a = 0.9 \times D$

$a = 0.9 \times 240 = 216$ mm

$b = 0.42 \times D$

$b = 0.42 \times 240 = 108$ mm

Steps to develop the transformer assembly using CAD:

Step 1: Click on the AutoCAD icon appearing on the computer screen. A new window of AutoCAD will open.

Step 2: Select FILE in the AutoCAD window and open a new drawing (.dwg) file.

Step 3: In the command window type as UNITS↵, a new dialog box will pop-up. In this dialog box select the precision type, lighting and units as required. Generally, the precision set is 0.00, units to scale inserted are millimetres and lighting selected is International.

Step 4: Now, select the sheet size required for the drawing by typing as LIMITS↵ in the command window, here itself it specifies as:

Specify lower left corner or (ON/OFF) <0.0000, 0.0000>: ↵
Specify upper right corner or (ON/OFF) <300, 300>: 2500, 2500 ↵

The lower left corner should always start from <0.0000, 0.0000> whereas for the upper right corner will have a default value. It can be set to any value depending on our requirement.

Step 5: In the command window type as ZOOM↵, it specifies as [All/Centre/Dynamic/Extents/Previous/Scale/Window/Object]<real time>:

Here, specify as All (or shortcut key A)↵. This zooms up the drawing sheet as specified in the limits.

This completes the setting part of the CAD window to the requirement.

Step 6: Once the settings part is finished. Now, first the sectional view of the transformer is to be drawn. As stated earlier, this sectional view is the view in which the transformer is seen from the top after the transformer cover is removed. The windings will be encircling the core hence the sectional view of a core type transformer appears like a circle.

Henceforth now select the circle command available in the left side toolbar of the CAD window as shown in Figure 8.11.

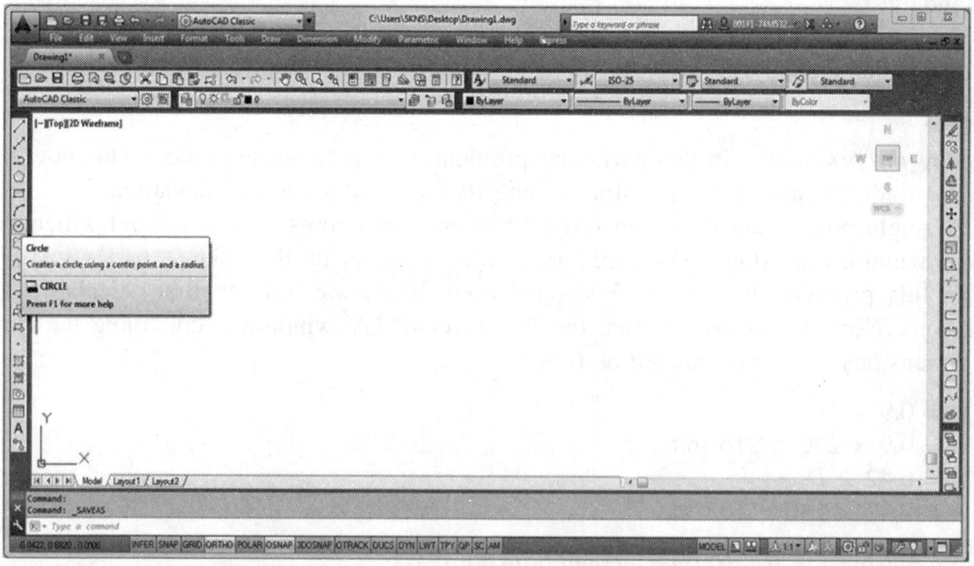

Figure 8.11 Selecting circle command in AutoCAD, *courtesy:* AutoCAD®.

Step 7: Now in the problem, the diameter of the circumscribing circle, i.e., the winding or insulation encircling the core is given to be of diameter = 240 mm. Hence in the command window, select the diameter to be 240 mm, which will result in a circle of the stated diameter as shown in the Figure 8.12.

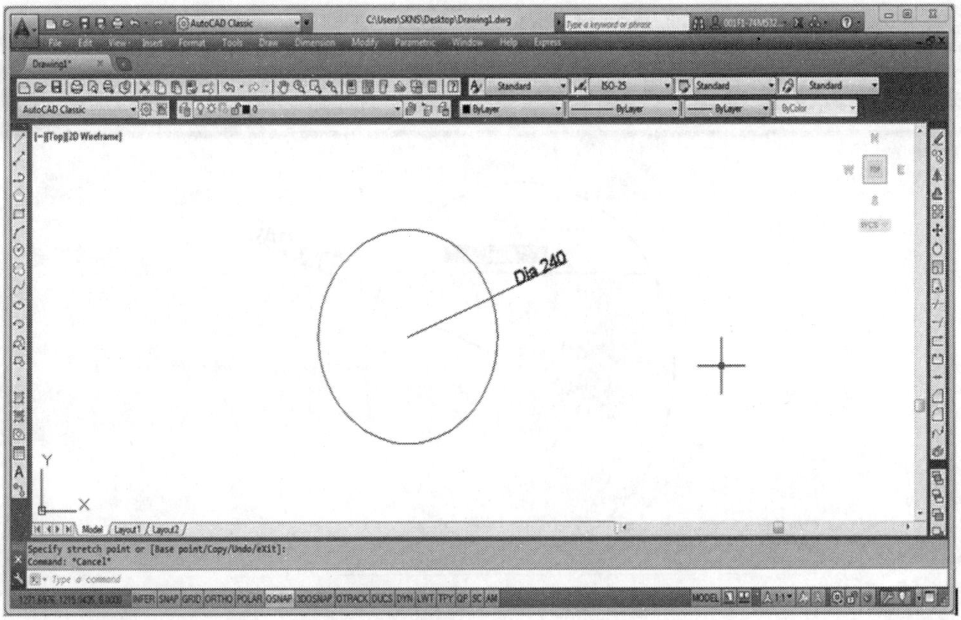

Figure 8.12 Drawing circle of specified diameter and showing the dimension in AutoCAD, *courtesy:* AutoCAD®.

Step 8: Once the circle is drawn, now the core part is to be drawn inside this circle, such that the circle drawn will be circumscribing the core. The dimensions of the core are calculated as stated above and by knowing the width of largest, smallest and intermediate stampings of the core; it can be drawn using lines as illustrated in the Figure 8.13 or by using the rectangle command and placing the rectangle inside the drawn circle exactly.

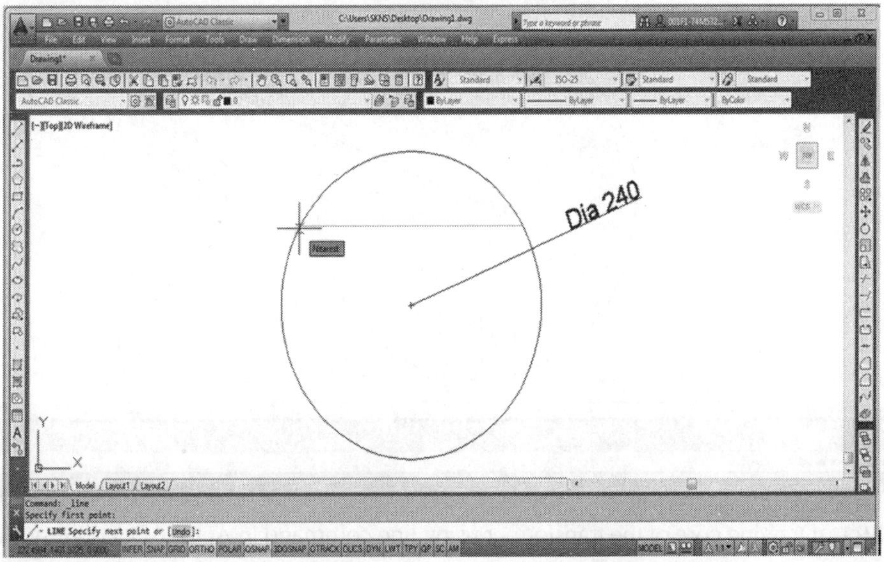

Figure 8.13(a) Drawing core of the transformer using line command in AutoCAD, *courtesy:* AutoCAD®.

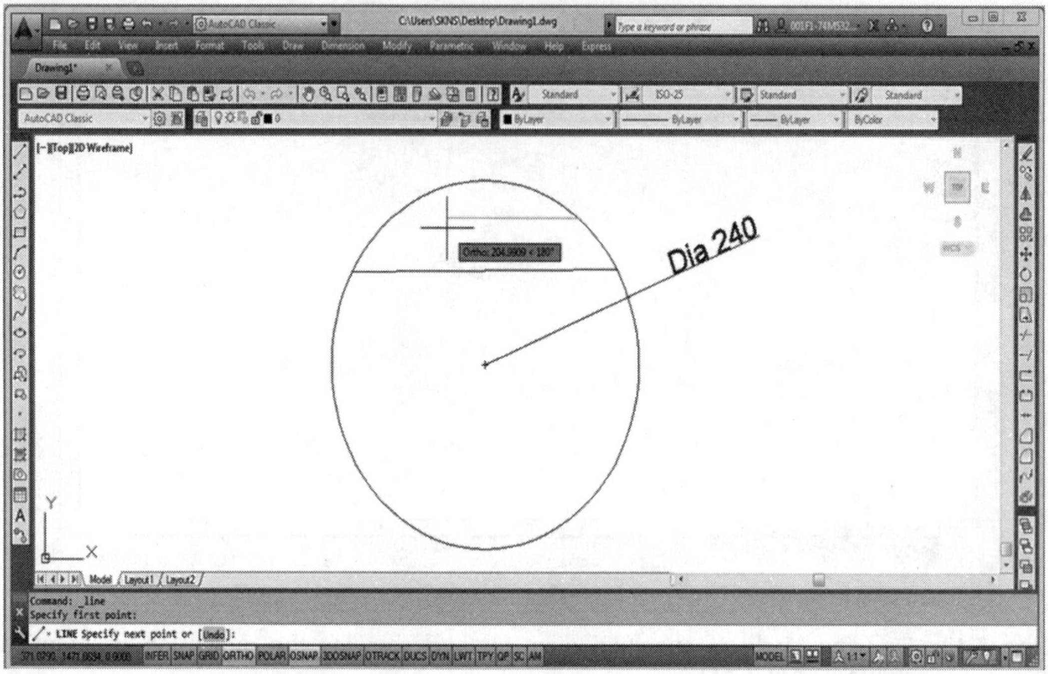

Figure 8.13(b) Drawing core of the transformer using line command in AutoCAD, *courtesy:* AutoCAD®.

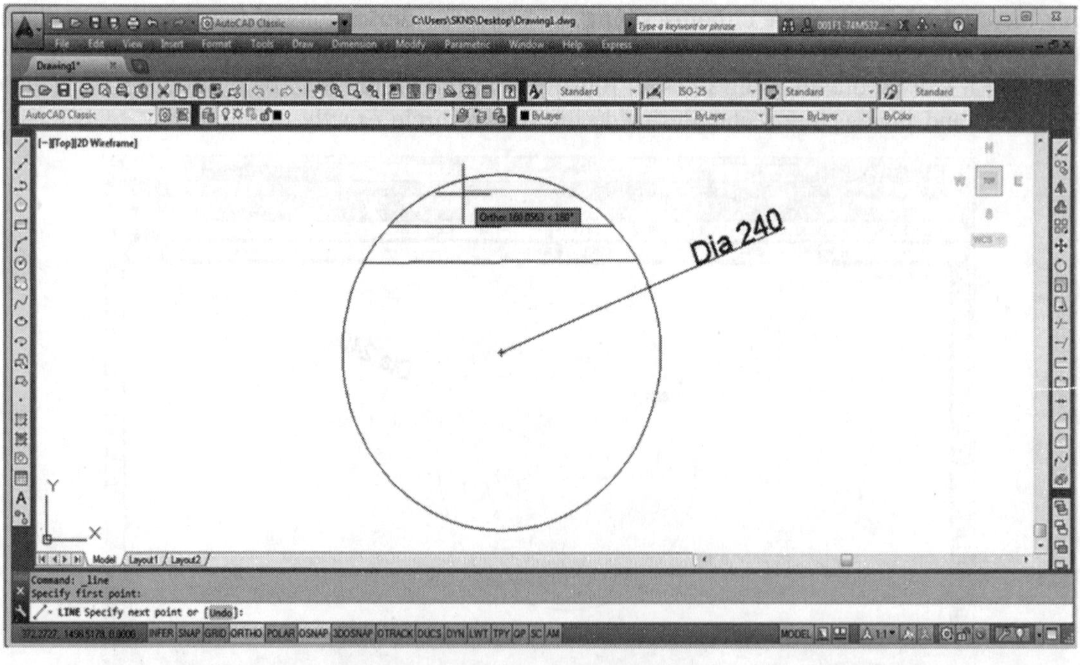

Figure 8.13(c) Drawing core of the transformer using line command in AutoCAD, *courtesy:* AutoCAD®.

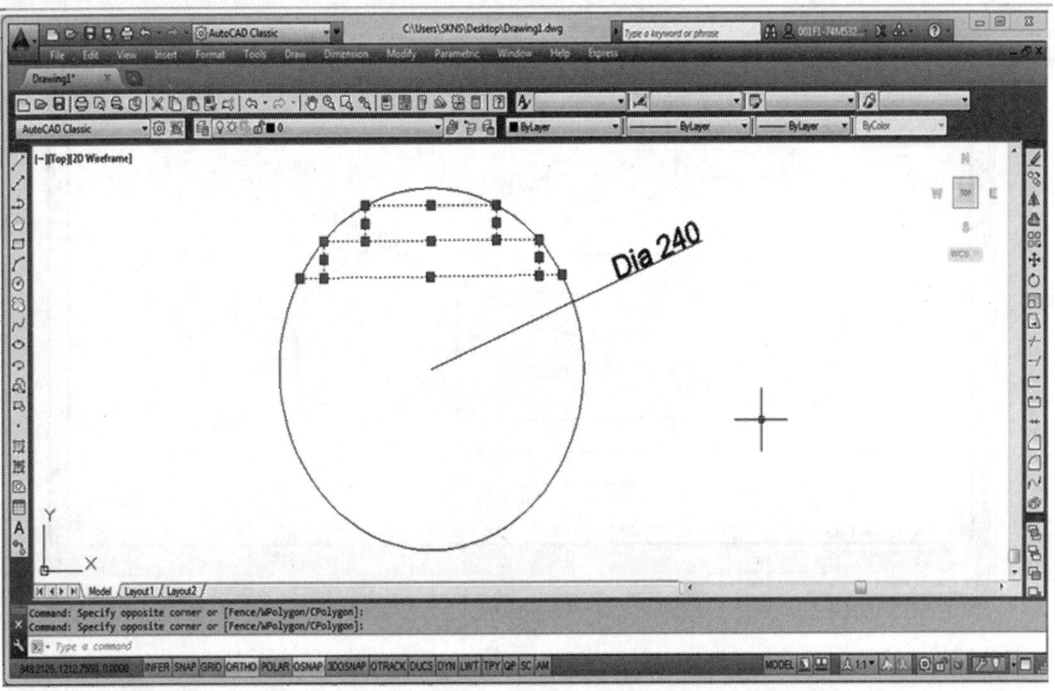

Figure 8.13(d) Drawing core of the transformer using line command in AutoCAD, *courtesy:* AutoCAD®.

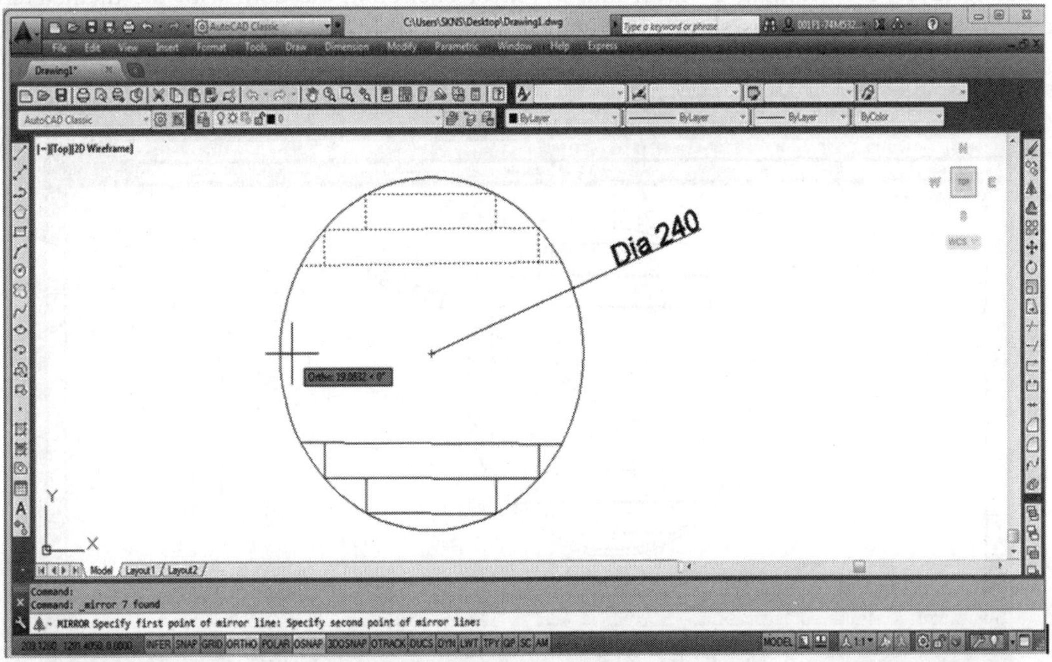

Figure 8.13(e) Drawing core of the transformer using line command in AutoCAD, *courtesy:* AutoCAD®.

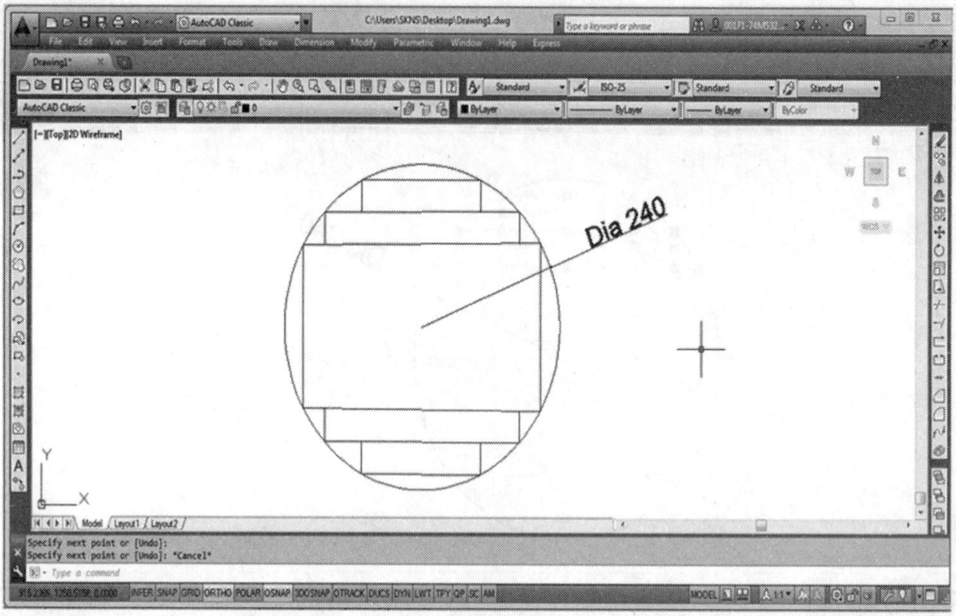

Figure 8.13(f) Drawing core of the transformer using line command in AutoCAD, *courtesy:* AutoCAD®.

Step 9: Once the core is drawn completely as shown in the above figures, then draw the insulating layer, LV winding 1st layer and 2nd layer encircling the core with the diameters as stated in the problem and as shown in Figure 8.14(a), (b), (c) and (d).

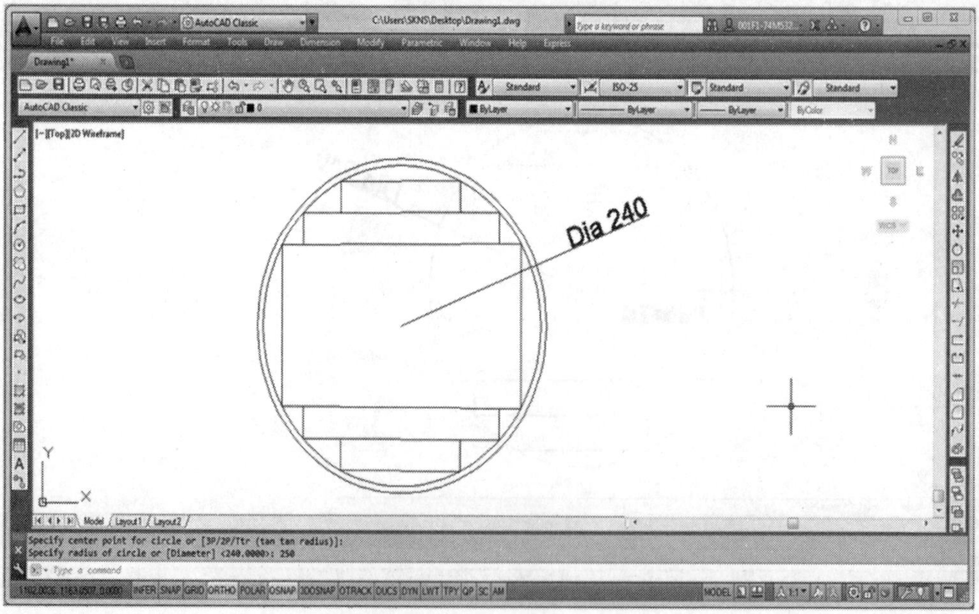

Figure 8.14(a) Drawing LV layer using circle command in AutoCAD, *courtesy:* AutoCAD®.

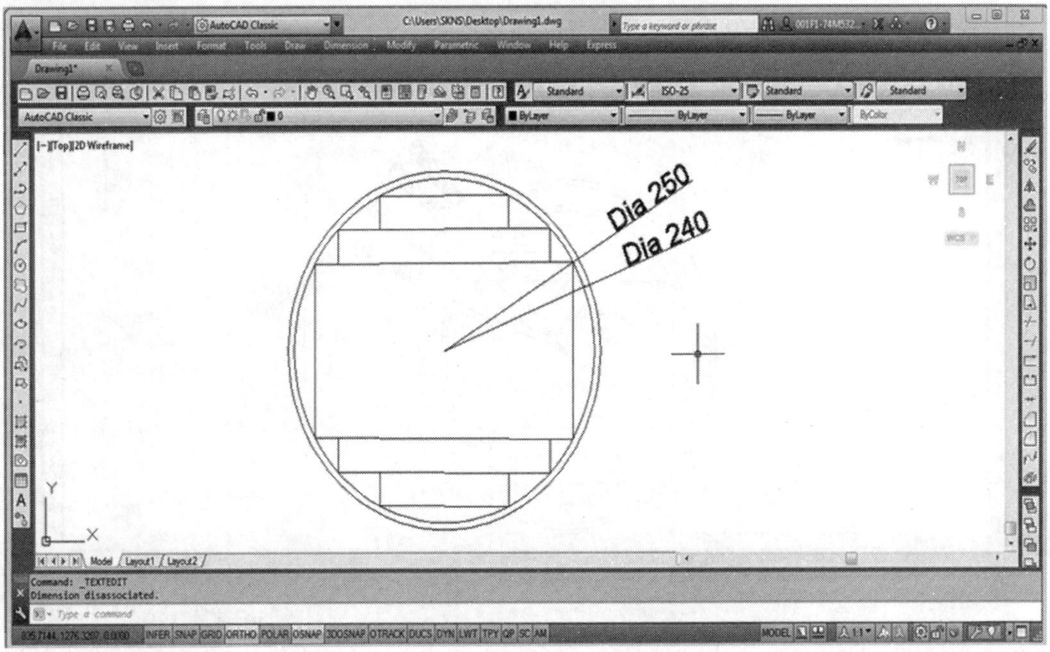

Figure 8.14(b) Drawing LV layer using circle command in AutoCAD, *courtesy:* AutoCAD®.

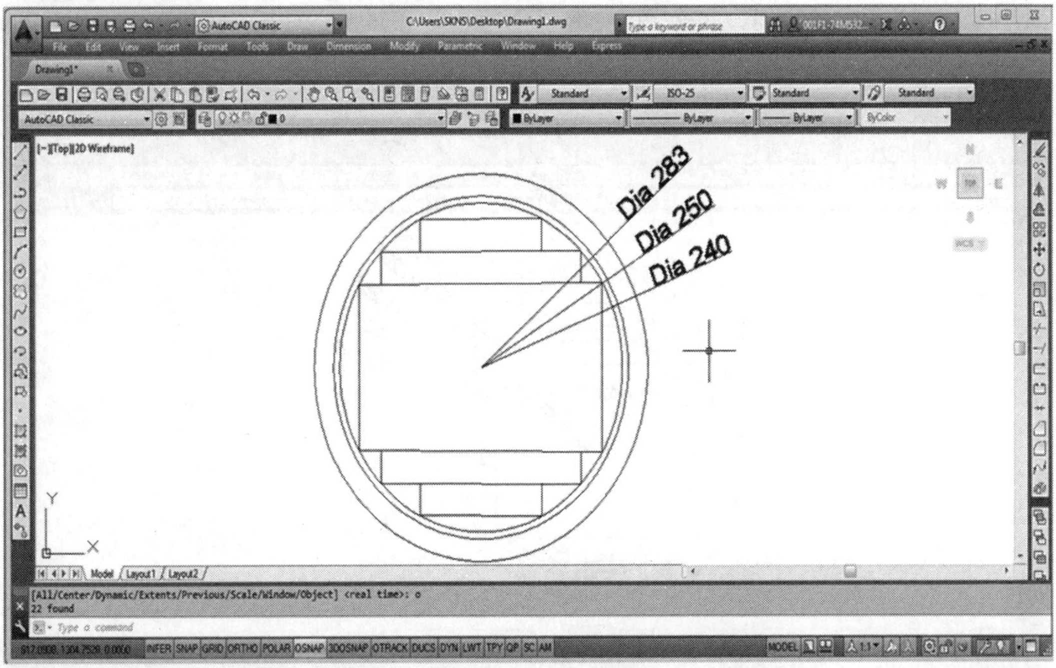

Figure 8.14(c) Drawing LV layer using circle command in AutoCAD, *courtesy:* AutoCAD®.

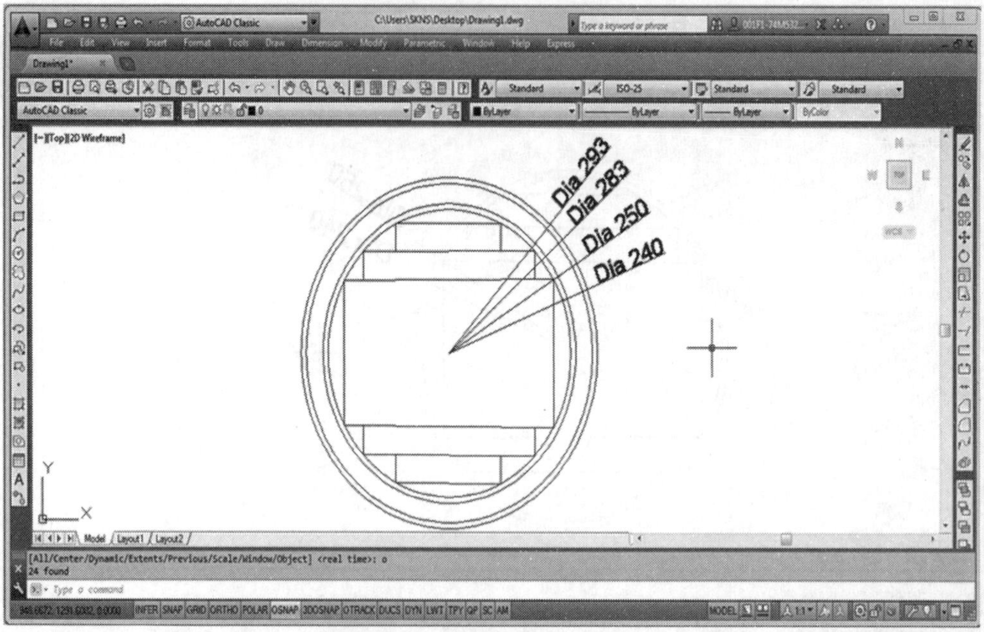

Figure 8.14(d) Drawing LV layer using circle command in AutoCAD, *courtesy:* AutoCAD®.

Step 10: Once the LV winding 1st layer and 2nd layer encircling the core is drawn completely as shown in the above figure, then draw the HV winding layer, with the diameters as stated in the problem as shown in Figure 8.14(e) and (f).

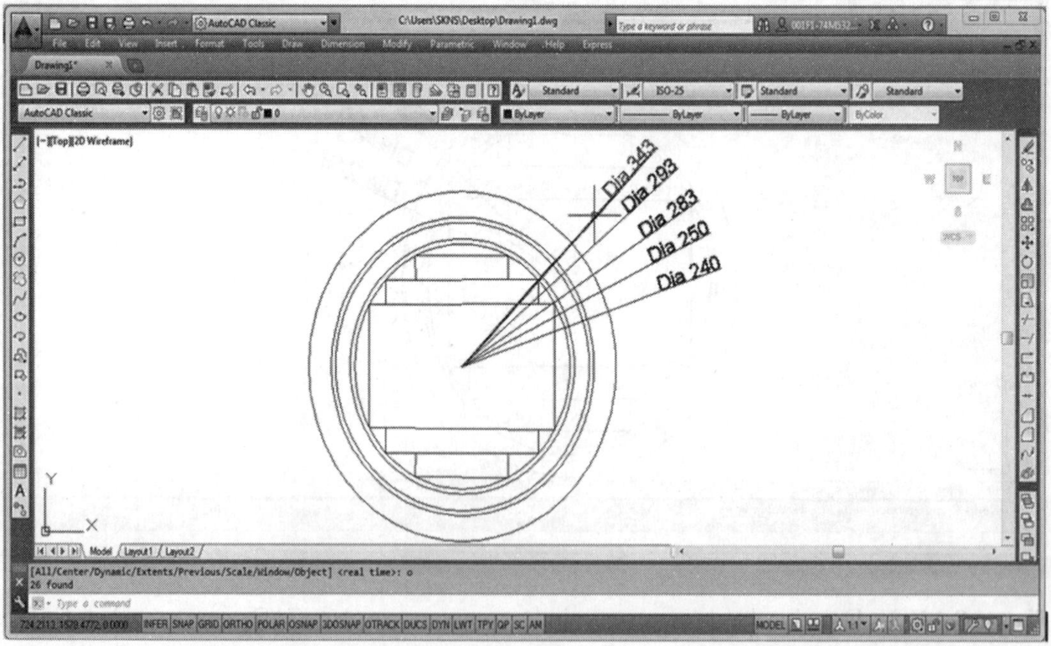

Figure 8.14(e) Drawing LV layer using circle command in AutoCAD, *courtesy:* AutoCAD®.

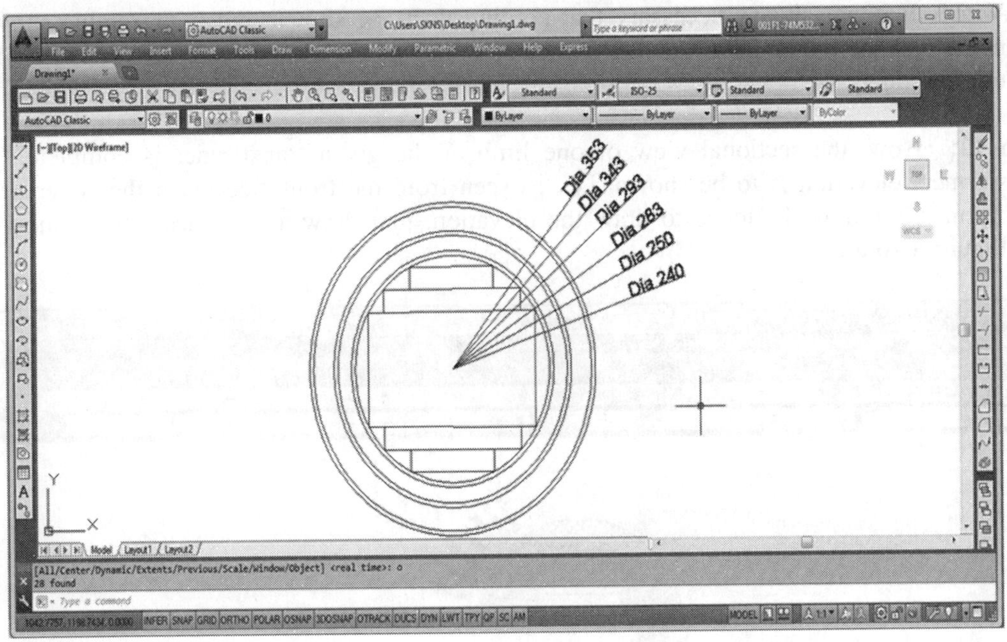

Figure 8.14(f) Drawing HV layer using circle command in AutoCAD, *courtesy:* AutoCAD®.

Step 11: Once the HV winding layer is drawn completely as shown in the above figure, then hatch both the LV and HV windings with different patterns using the hatch command as shown in the Figure 8.15 given below and also mark the ventilating or cooling ducts in between the windings as shown in Figure 8.15.

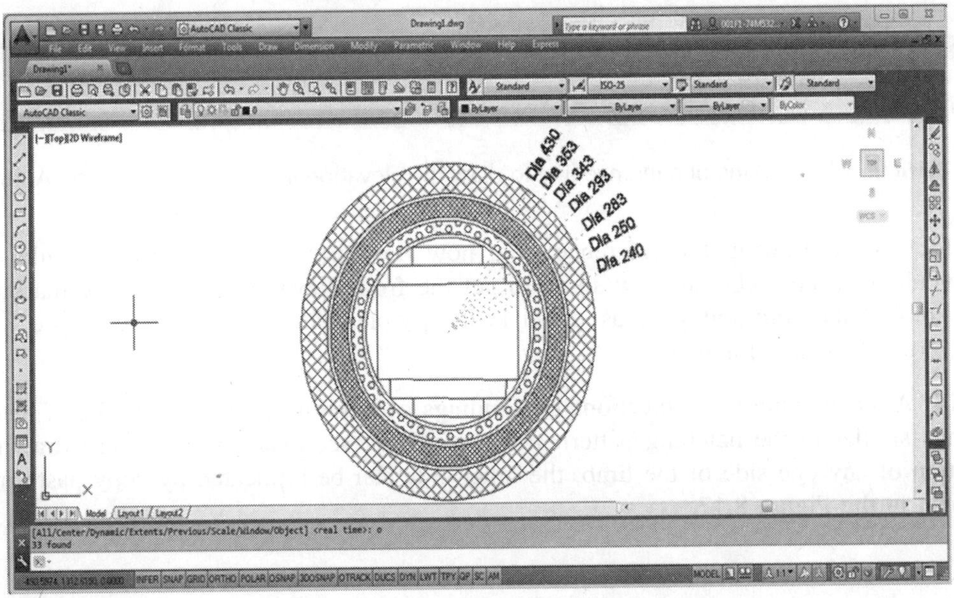

Figure 8.15 Hatching provided to windings for differentiation, *courtesy:* AutoCAD®.

****Note:*** It is not always necessary that cooling ducts be shown, but is preferable showing to ensure that the windings are cooled either by water or oil cooled methods which can flow through the ducts.

Step 12: Now, the sectional view of one limb of the given transformer is complete. This transformers elevation is to be shown, i.e., as seen from the front side when the cover of the transformer is removed. Hence to draw the elevation, first draw a reference line as shown in the Figure 8.16(a).

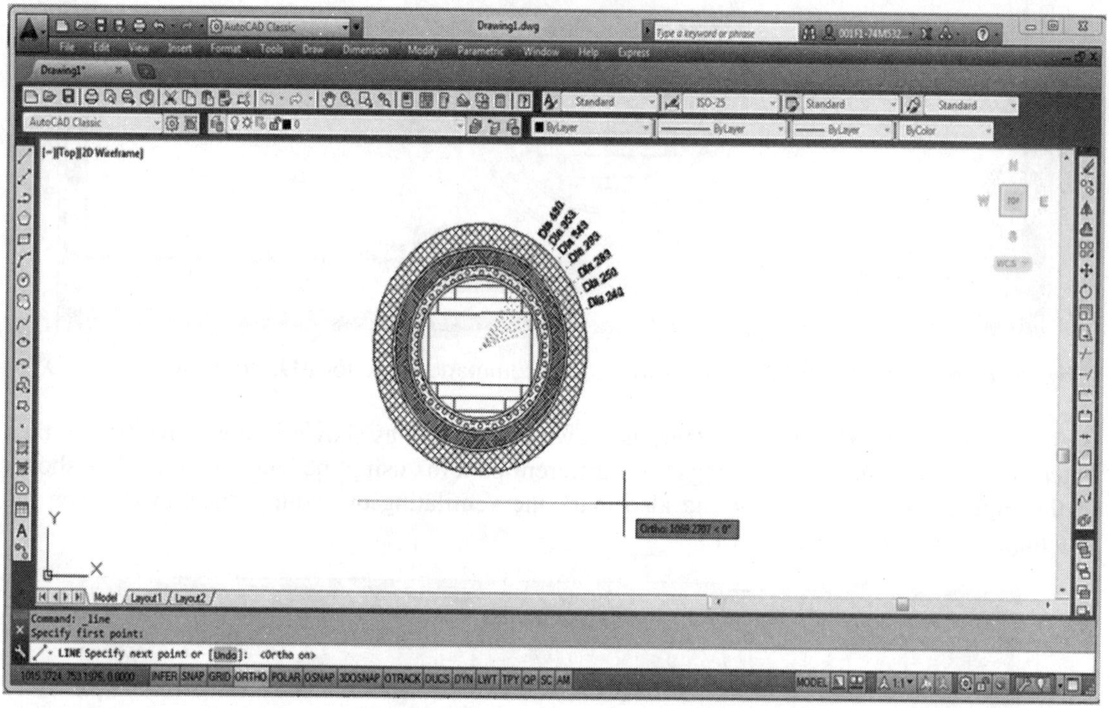

Figure 8.16(a) The marking of reference line to draw the elevation in AutoCAD, *courtesy:* AutoCAD®.

Step 13: After drawing the reference line, now drop projections or perpendiculars from each winding in the sectional view so as to get the front elevation, with clearly marking the dimensions of the core and yoke as stated in the problem and shown in the Figure 8.16(b), (c), (d), (e), (f), (g), (h) and (i).

Step 14: After drawing the projections of windings of any one of side of the limb, hatch the windings similar to the hatching pattern followed in the sectional view. By just drawing the projection of any one side of the limb, the other side can be replicated by copy paste method as shown in the Figure 8.17.

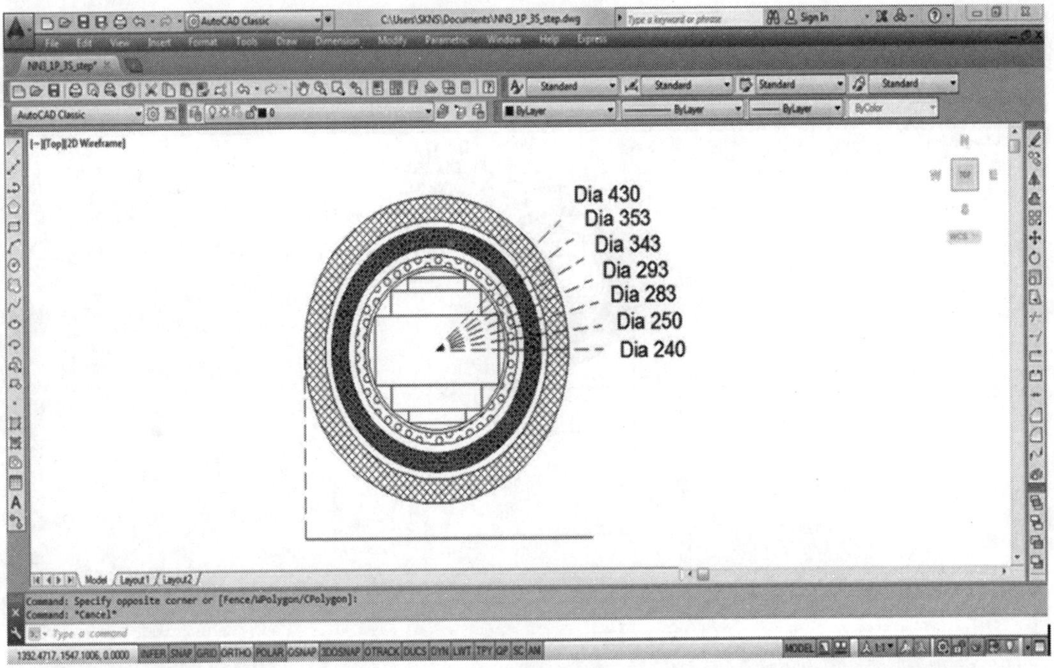

Figure 8.16(b) The marking of perpendicular line to draw the elevation of windings, *courtesy:* AutoCAD®.

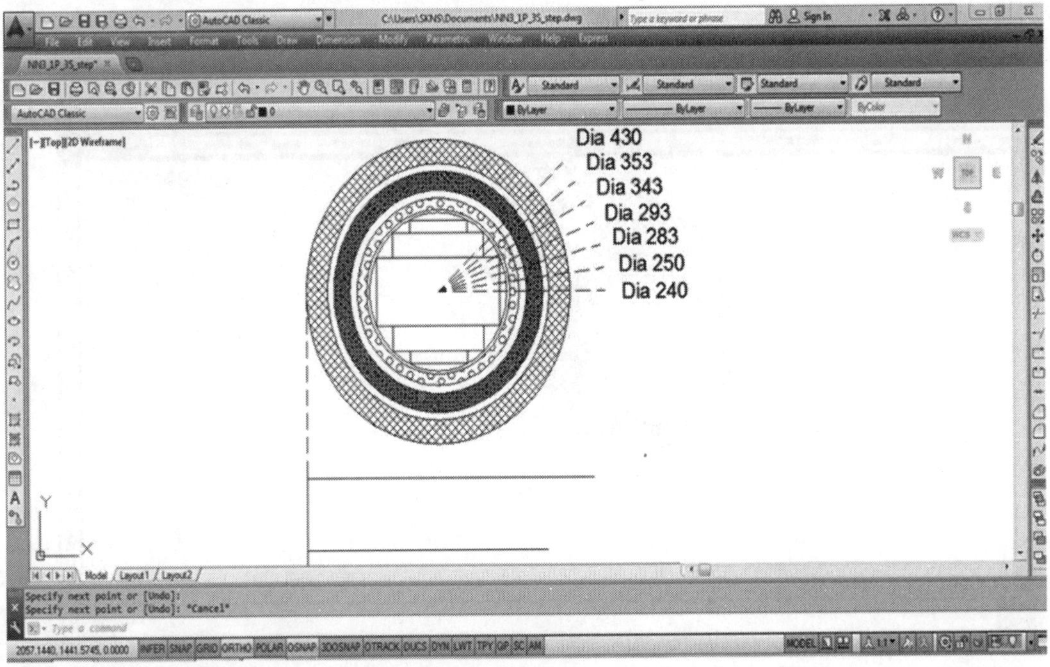

Figure 8.16(c) The marking of perpendicular line to draw the elevation of windings, *courtesy:* AutoCAD®.

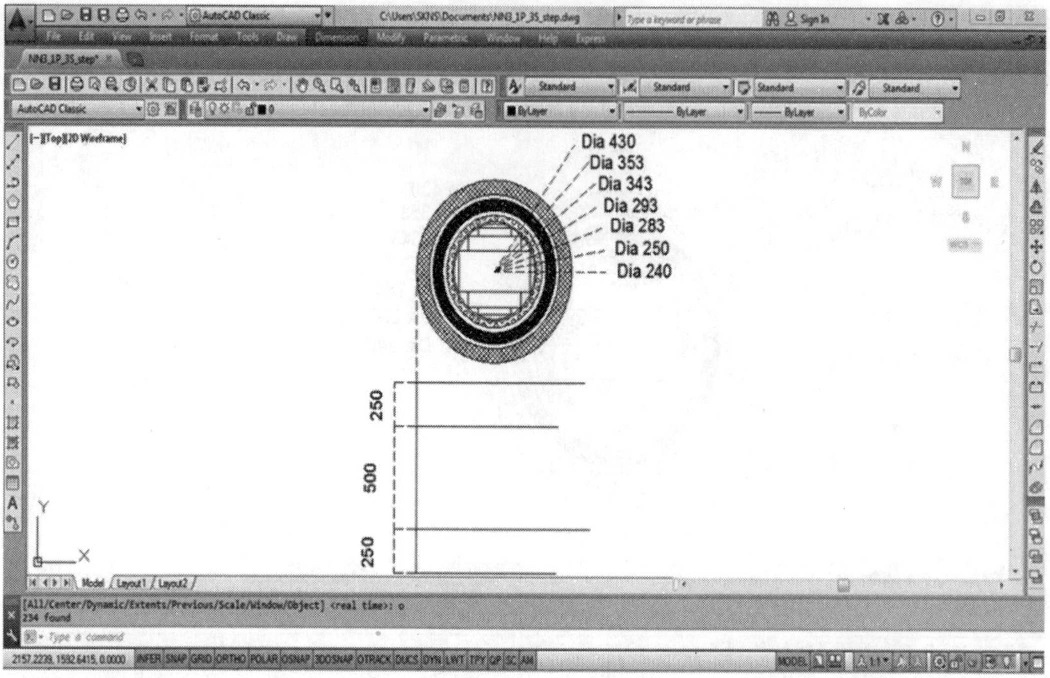

Figure 8.16(d) The marking of perpendicular line to draw the elevation of windings, *courtesy:* AutoCAD®.

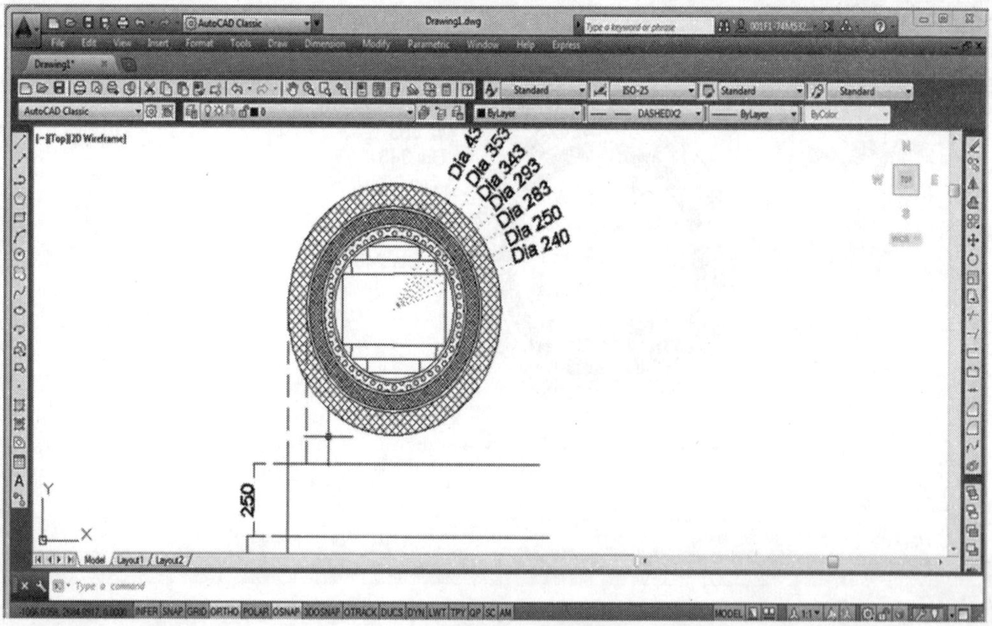

Figure 8.16(e) The marking of perpendicular line to draw the elevation of windings, *courtesy:* AutoCAD®.

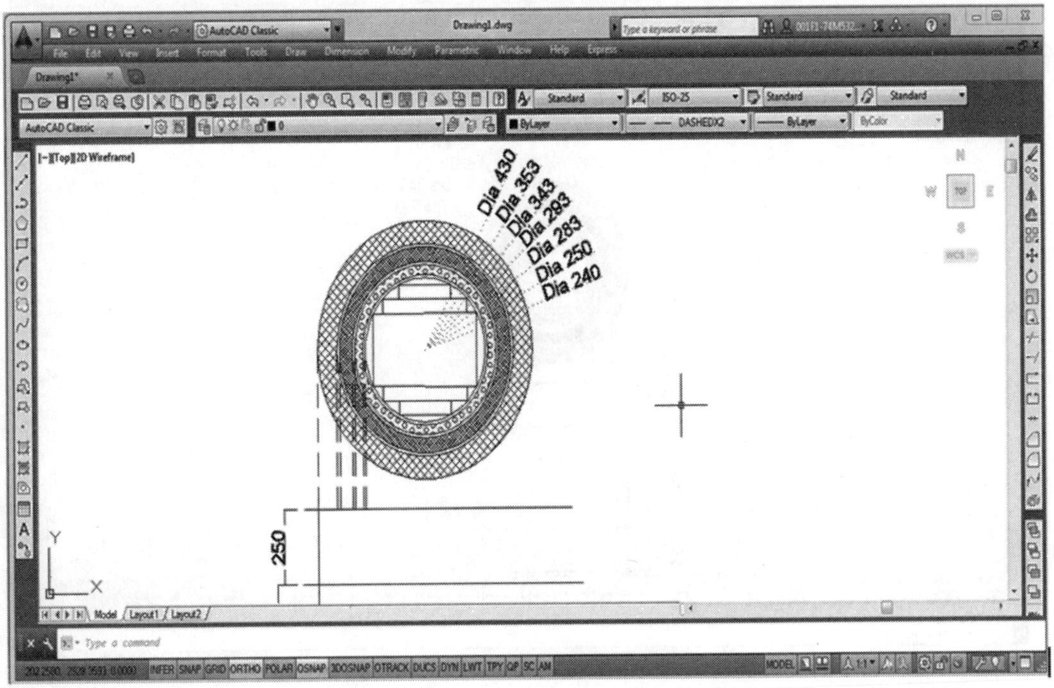

Figure 8.16(f) The marking of perpendicular line to draw the elevation of windings, *courtesy:* AutoCAD®.

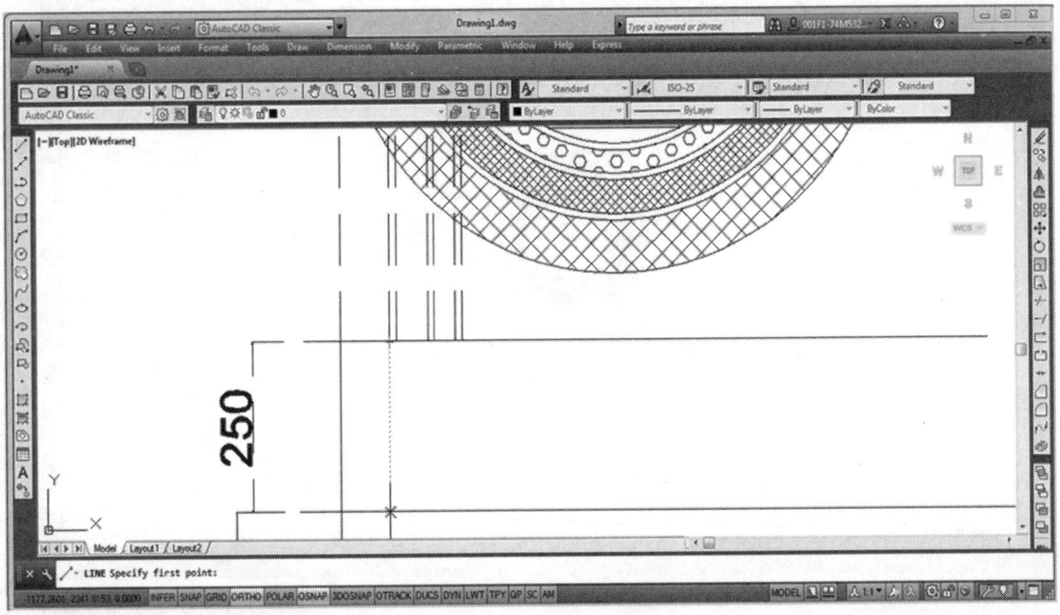

Figure 8.16(g) The marking of perpendicular line to draw the elevation of windings, *courtesy:* AutoCAD®.

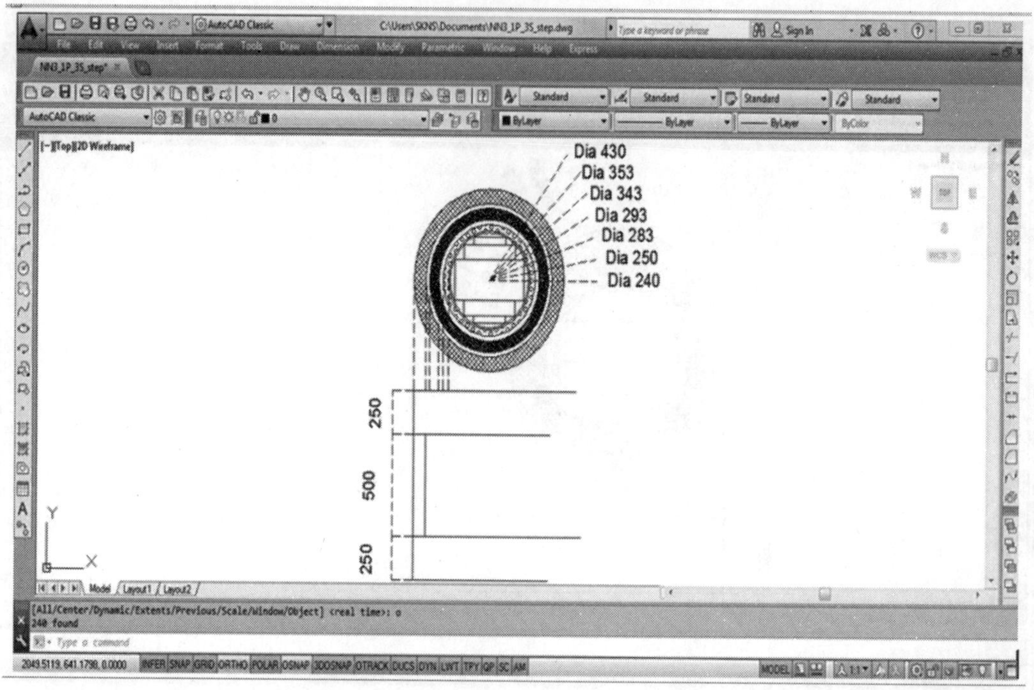

Figure 8.16(h) The marking of perpendicular line to draw the elevation of windings, *courtesy:* AutoCAD®.

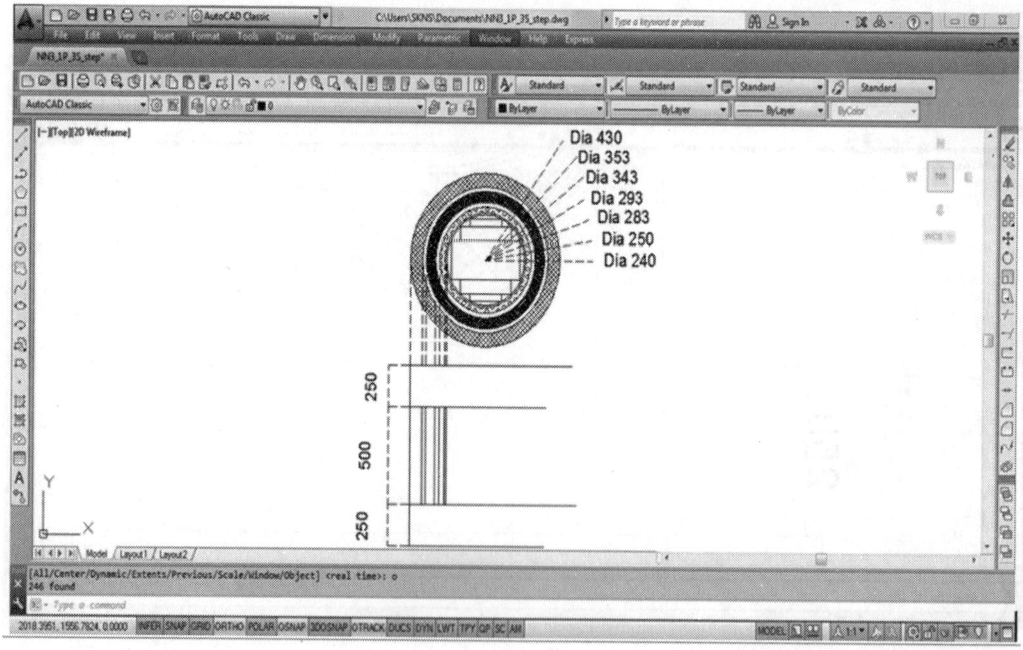

Figure 8.16(i) The marking of perpendicular line to draw the elevation of windings, *courtesy:* AutoCAD®.

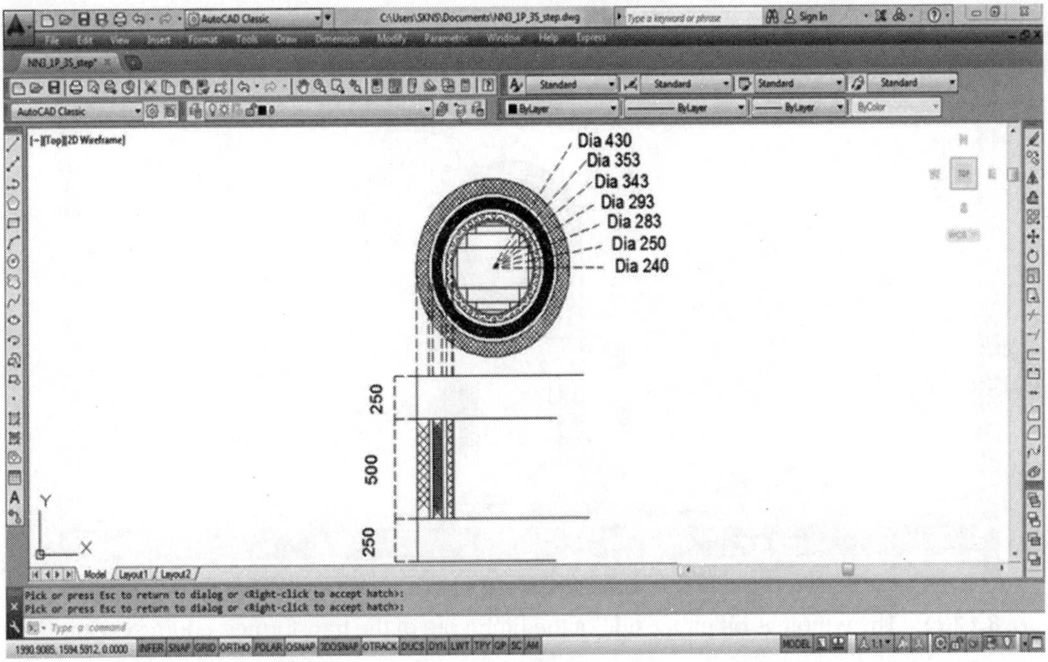

Figure 8.17(a) The hatching of windings in elevation of the transformer, *courtesy:* AutoCAD®.

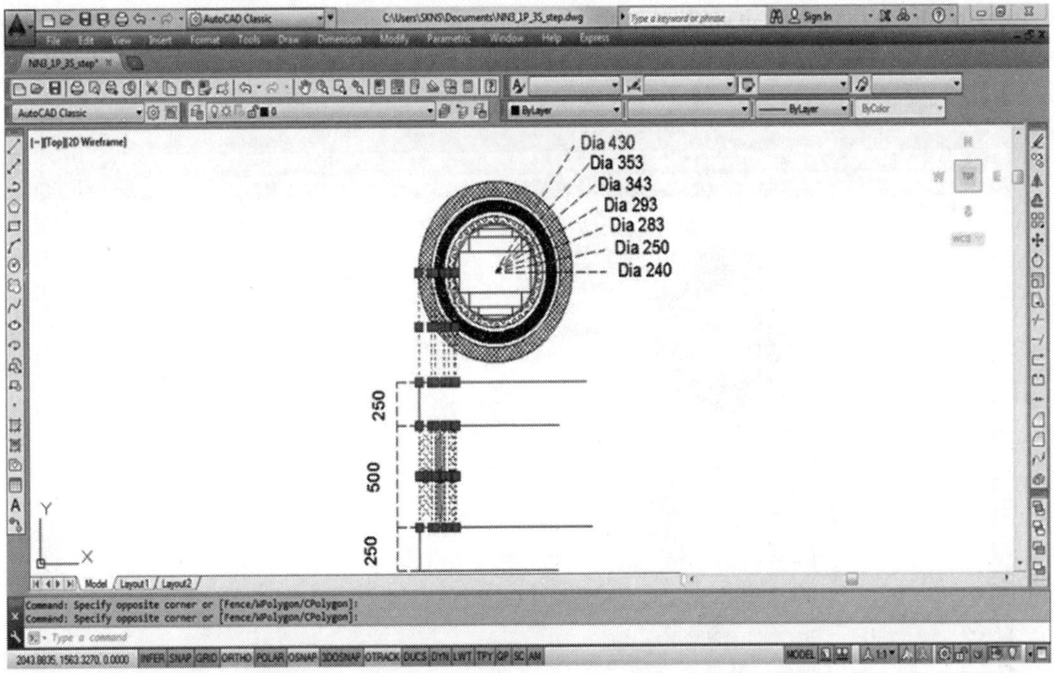

Figure 8.17(b) The copying of windings to form another side of windings on the limb, *courtesy:* AutoCAD®.

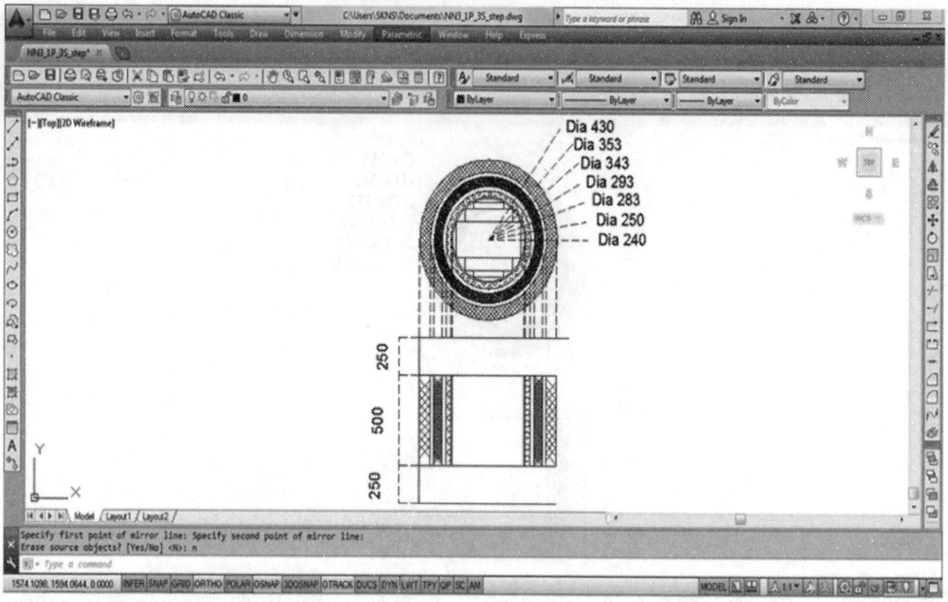

Figure 8.17(c) The windings on either side of the limb/core of the transformer, *courtesy:* AutoCAD®.

Step 15: Now, the sectional view and elevation of one limb of the given transformer is complete. Select both the sectional and elevated view and replicate it to form another limb of the transformer by copying it and pasting it exactly at the centre to centre distance of the core as shown in the Figure 8.18.

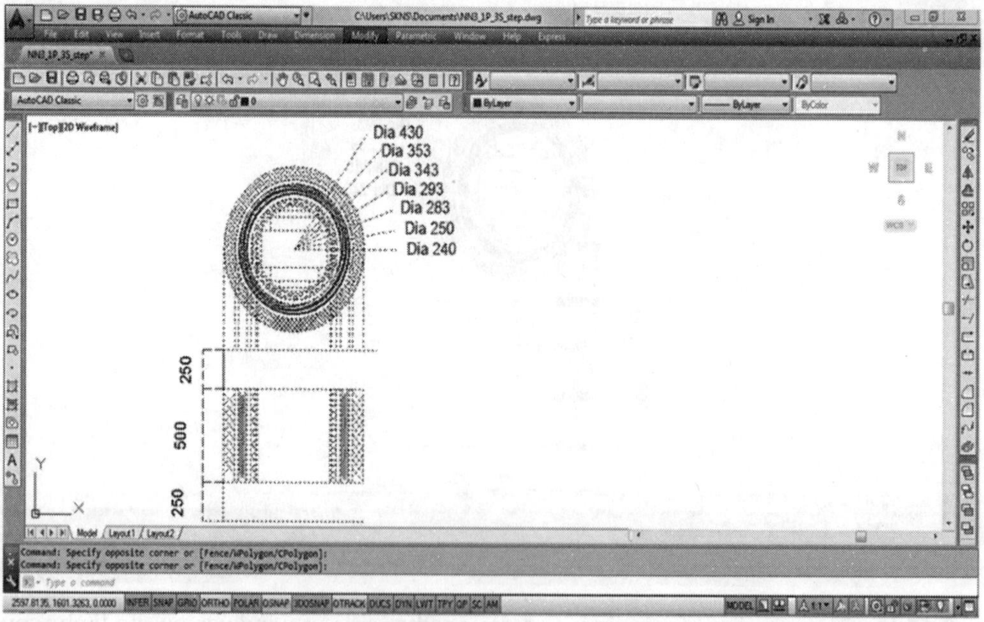

Figure 8.18(a) The copying of sectional and elevated view to show the other limb of the transformer, *courtesy:* AutoCAD®.

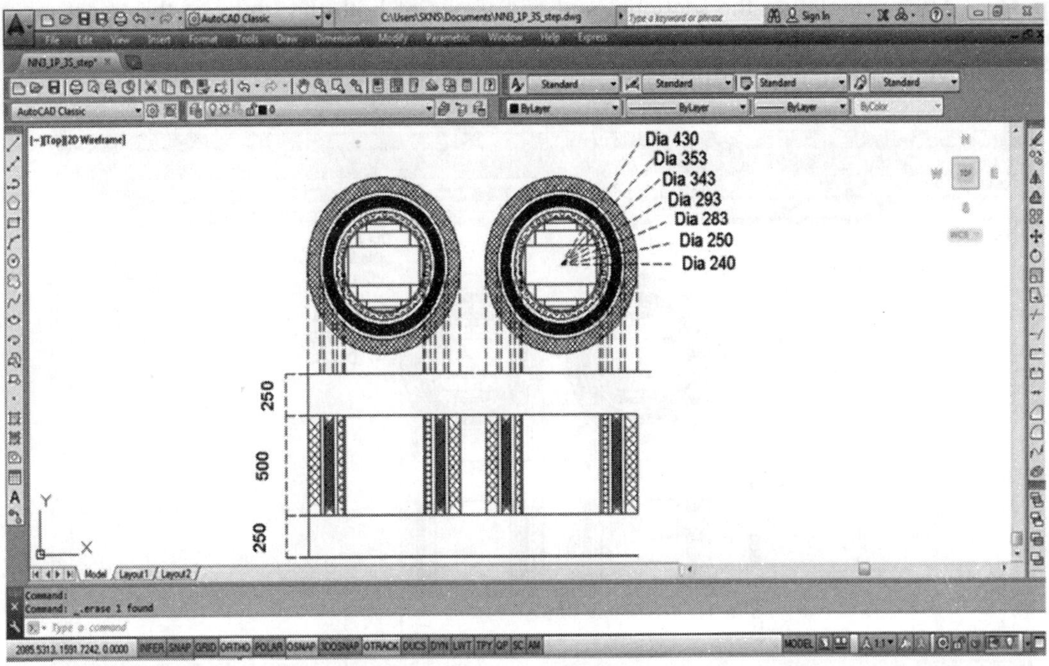

Figure 8.18(b) The sectional and elevated view of both the limbs of the transformer, *courtesy:* AutoCAD®.

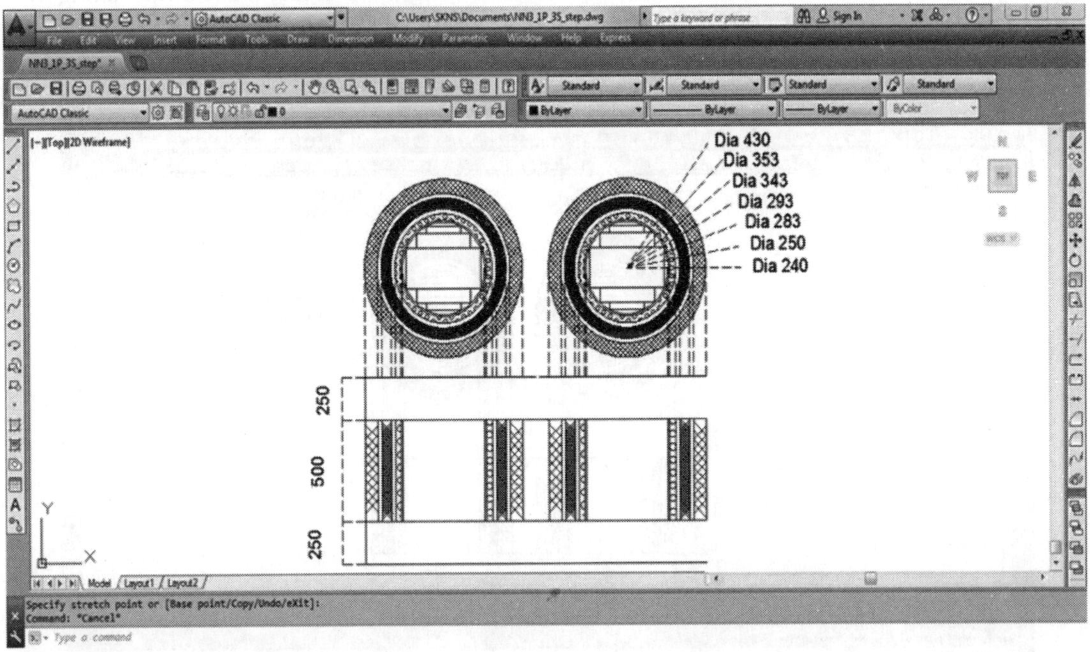

Figure 8.18(c) The sectional and elevated view of both the limbs of the transformer, *courtesy:* AutoCAD®.

Step 16: After completing the sectional and end views of both the limbs of the transformer, now provide bolts wherever necessary as illustrated in the Figure 8.19. The marking of bolts in elevated view of the transformer is shown in Figure 8.20.

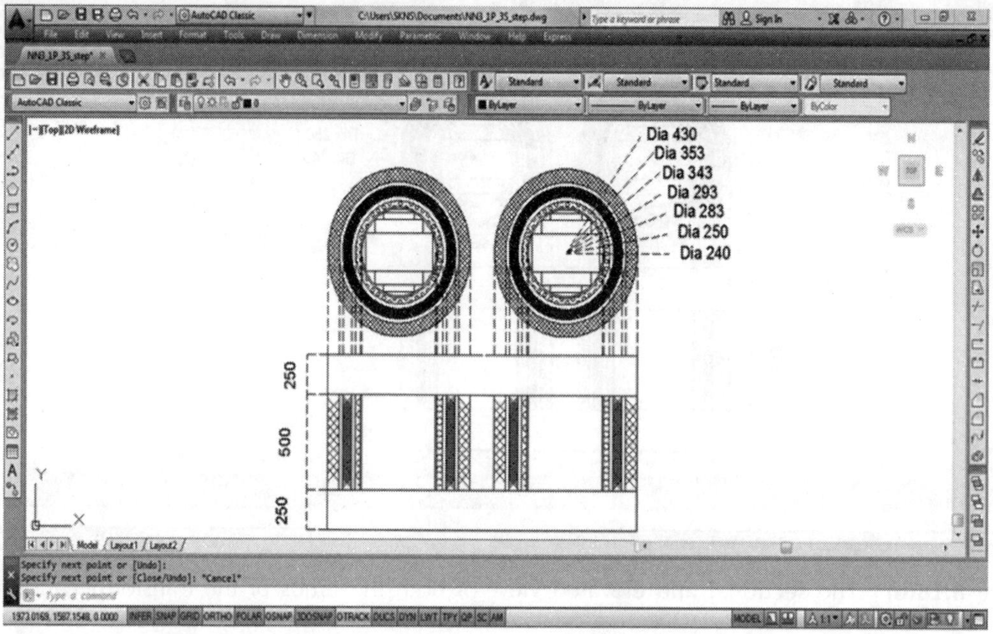

Figure 8.19 The sectional and elevated view of both the limbs of the transformer along with dimensions of core and yoke, *courtesy:* AutoCAD®.

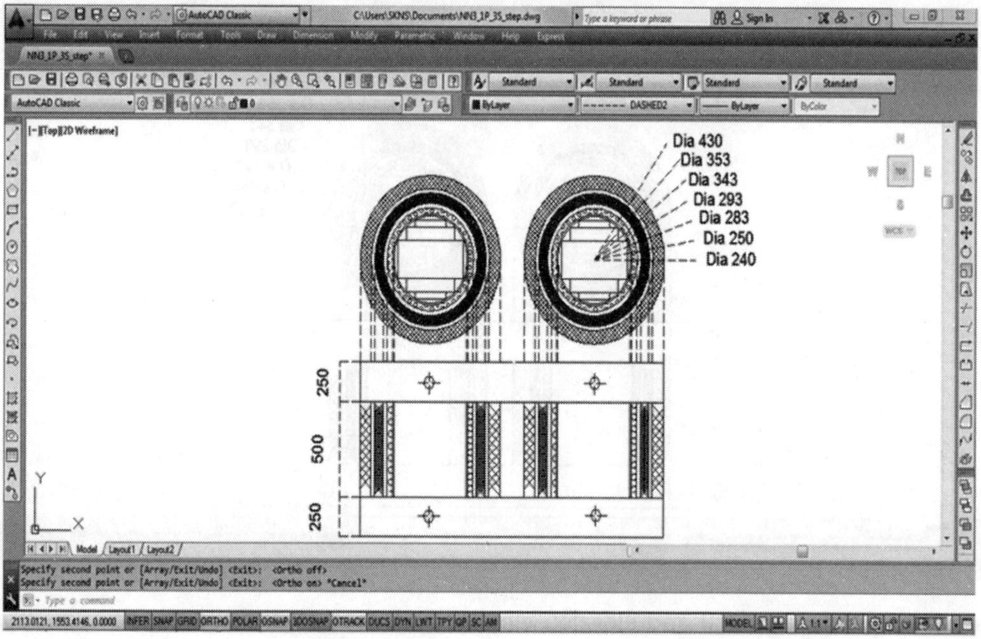

Figure 8.20(a) The marking of bolts in elevated view of the transformer, *courtesy:* AutoCAD®.

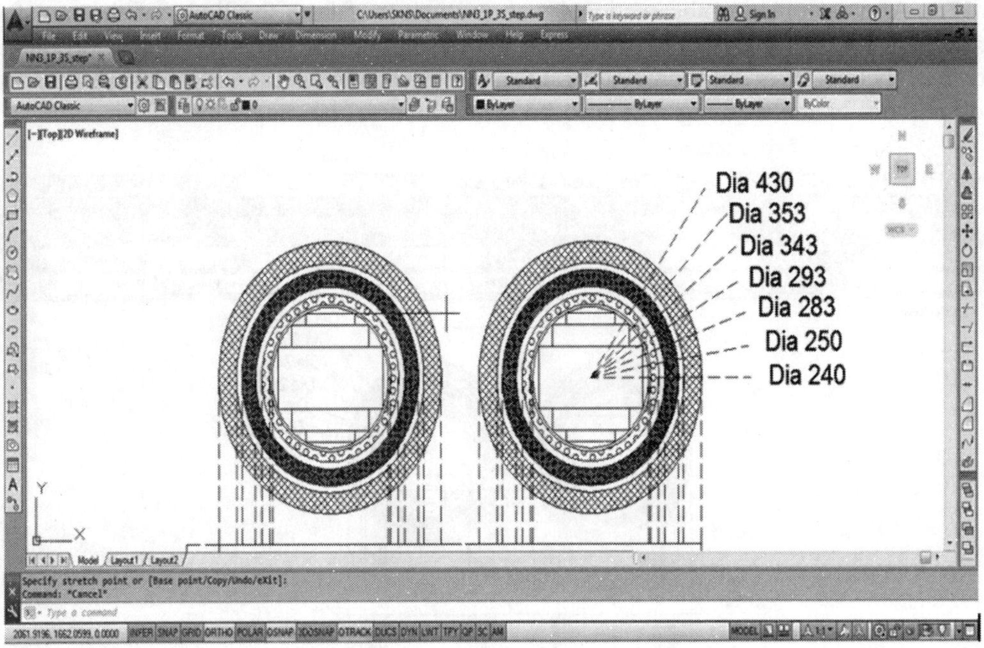

Figure 8.20(b) The marking of hexagonal bolts in elevated view of the transformer, *courtesy:* AutoCAD®.

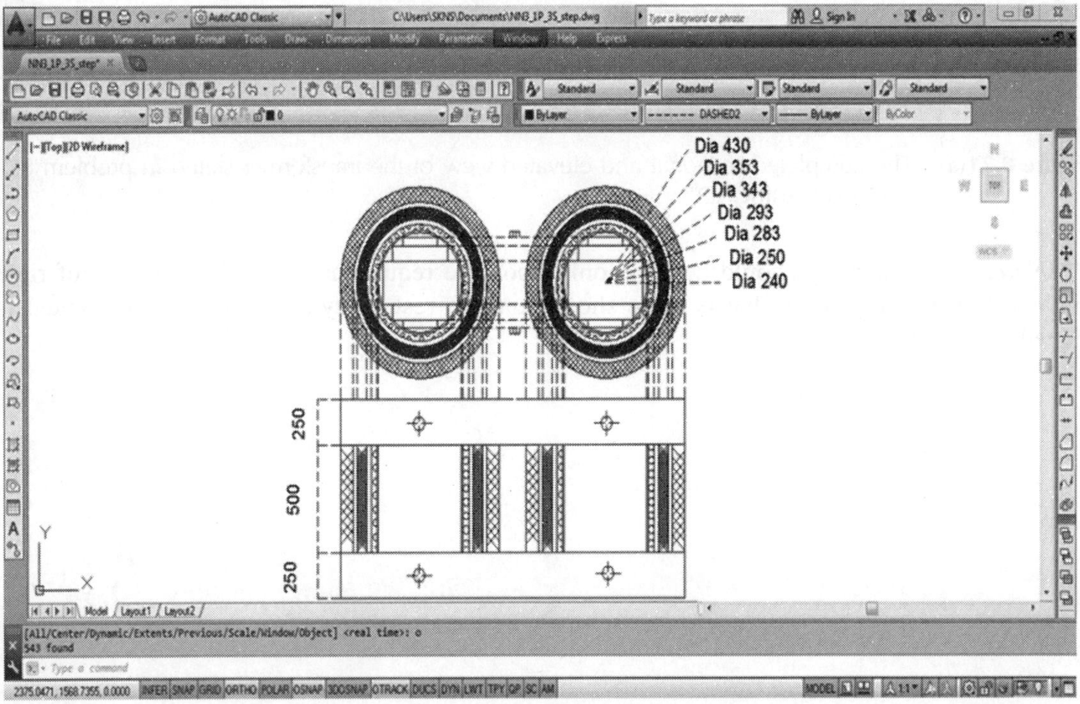

Figure 8.20(c) The marking of bolts in yoke of the transformer, *courtesy:* AutoCAD®.

Step 17: After completing the sectional and end views of both the limbs of the transformer, this results in the figure shown below which is the solution for the above stated problem. The Figure 8.21 below gives the complete transformer assembly of the single phase transformer. The description of the winding may also be stated next to the diagram.

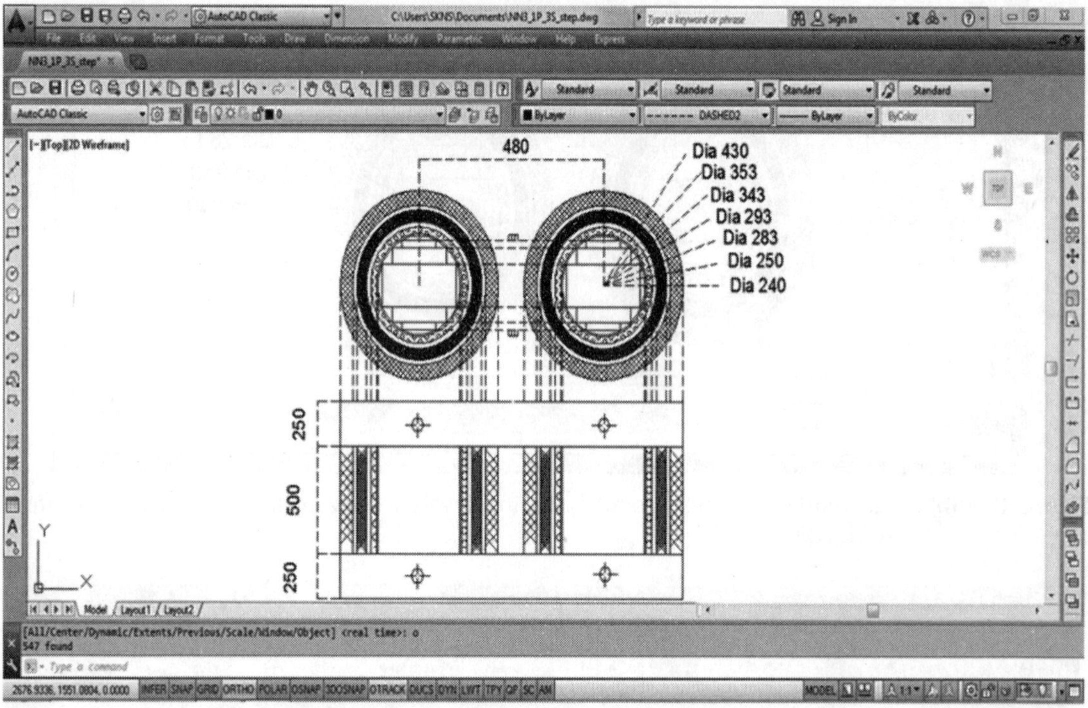

Figure 8.21(a) The completed sectional and elevated view of the transformer stated in problem 8.1, *courtesy:* AutoCAD®.

****Note:*** The hatching should be done only upon the requirement, i.e., if right half of right limb section is asked, only that is to be shown and the rest everything may be represented in dotted line format.

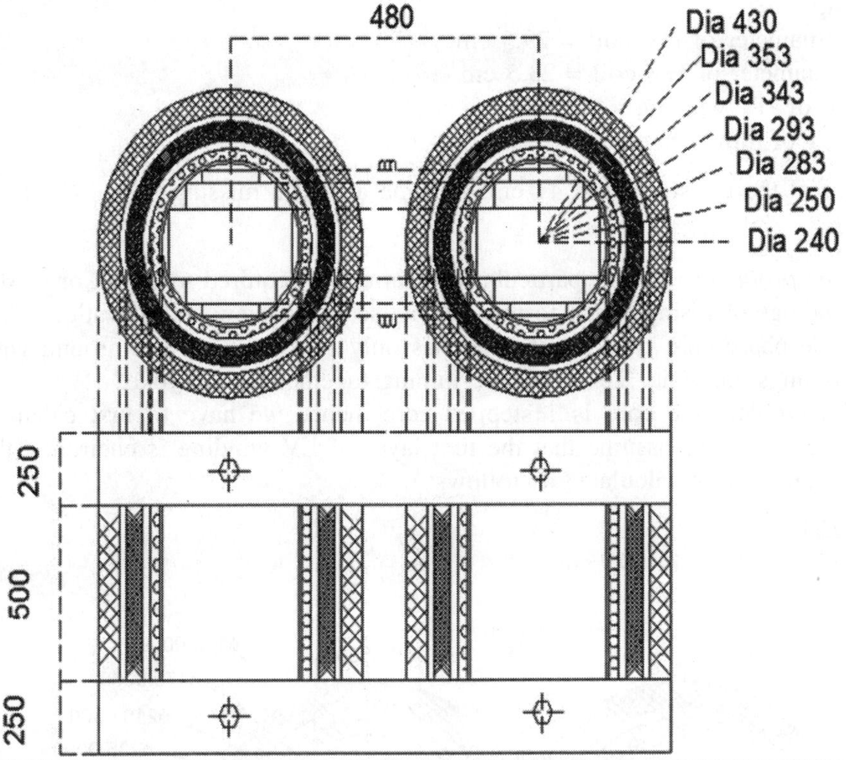

Figure 8.21(b) The completed sectional and elevated view of the transformer stated in problem 8.1.

PROBLEM 8.2: Draw the following views of a 1 phase, core type, 2 kVA, 240V/120V transformer:

- Front elevation full in section
- Plan in full section

Dimension of various parts are given below:

Core:

Cross section of the core = 1 stepped core
Diameter of circumscribing circle = 15.5 cm
Distance between adjacent core centres = 31.5 cm

Yoke:

Height of the yoke = 8 cm

LV winding:

Outer diameter of LV coil = 21 cm
Inner diameter of LV coil = 17 cm
Height of LV winding = 23 cm
Number of turns per phase = 14

HV winding:

Outer diameter of HV coil = 29.5 cm
Inner diameter of HV coil = 23.5 cm
Height of HV winding = 23 cm
Number of turns per phase = 72

Total height of the transformer is 41 cm. Assume any data missing. (VTU, June 2013)

Solution:

Analysing the problem: In this particular problem, it is required to depict or to show the LV and HV windings of a single transformer and its sectional view and elevation.

A single phase core type transformer has only two cores or legs around which the LV and HV windings are done. The cores are joining together by the yoke.

In this problem the core is 1 stepped core, hence we have to first calculate the core dimensions. Now, let us assume that the first layer of LV winding is encircling the core, the core dimensions can be calculated as follows:

$a = 0.71 \times D$
$a = 0.71 \times 155 = 110.05$ mm

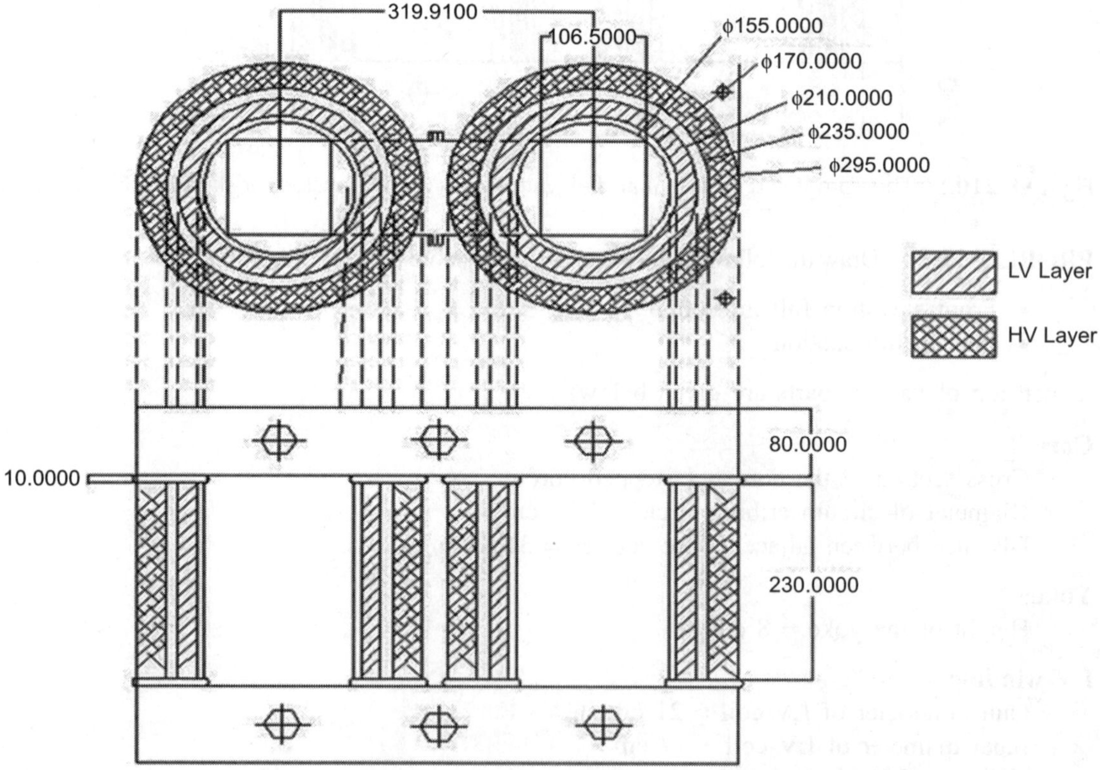

Figure 8.22 Sectional and elevated view of transformer (solution for problem 8.2).

PROBLEM 8.3: Draw the following views of a 1 phase, core type, 5 kVA, 380V/220V transformer with a frequency 50 Hz.

- Front elevation full in section
- Plan in full section

Dimension of various parts are given below:

Core:

Cross section of the core = 2 stepped core
Diameter of circumscribing circle = 14 cm
Distance between adjacent core centres = 33 cm

Yoke:

Height of the yoke = 8 cm

LV winding:

Outer diameter of LV coil = 21 cm
Inner diameter of LV coil = 17 cm
Height of LV winding = 23 cm
Number of turns per phase = 34

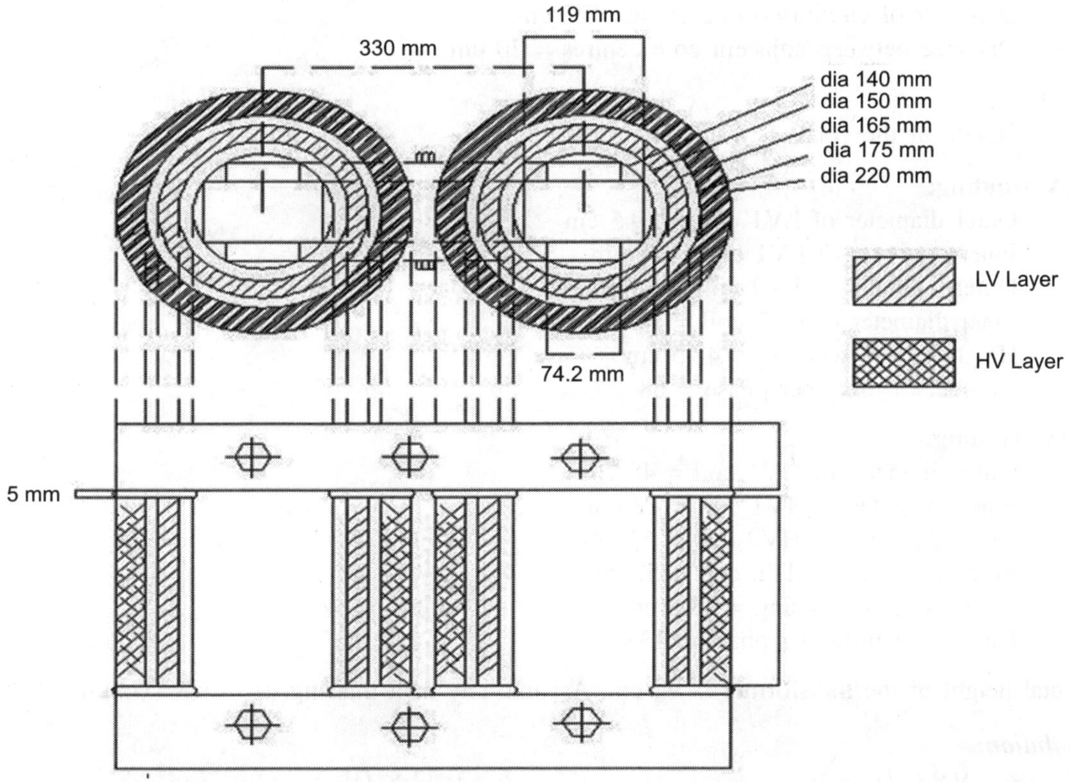

Figure 8.23 Sectional and elevated view of transformer (solution for problem 8.3).

HV winding:

Outer diameter of HV coil = 29.5 cm
Inner diameter of HV coil = 23.5 cm
Height of HV winding = 23 cm
Number of turns per phase = 80

Total height of the transformer is 41 cm. Assume any data missing. (VTU, June 2013)

Solution:

$a = 0.85 \times D$ $b = 0.53 \times D$

$a = 0.85 \times 140 = 119$ mm $b = 0.53 \times 140 = 74.2$ mm

PROBLEM 8.4: Draw the following views of a 1 phase, core type, 10 kVA, 415V/230V transformer:

- Front elevation full in section
- Plan in full section

Dimension of various parts are given below:

Core:

Cross section of the core = 3 stepped core
Diameter of circumscribing circle = 25 cm
Distance between adjacent core centres = 70 cm

Yoke:

Height of the yoke = 14 cm

LV winding:

Outer diameter of LV1 coil = 29.5 cm
Inner diameter of LV1 coil = 26 cm
Outer diameter of LV2 coil = 38 cm
Inner diameter of LV2 coil = 34 cm
Height of LV winding = 48.5 cm
Number of turns per phase = 68

HV winding:

Outer diameter of HV1 coil = 48 cm
Inner diameter of HV1 coil = 42 cm
Outer diameter of HV2 coil = 62 cm
Inner diameter of HV2 coil = 52 cm
Height of HV winding = 48.5 cm
Number of turns per phase = 138

Total height of the transformer is 90 cm. Assume any data missing. (VTU, June 2013)

Solution:

$a = 0.9 \times D$ $b = 0.42 \times D$

$a = 0.9 \times 250 = 225$ mm $b = 0.42 \times 250 = 105$ mm

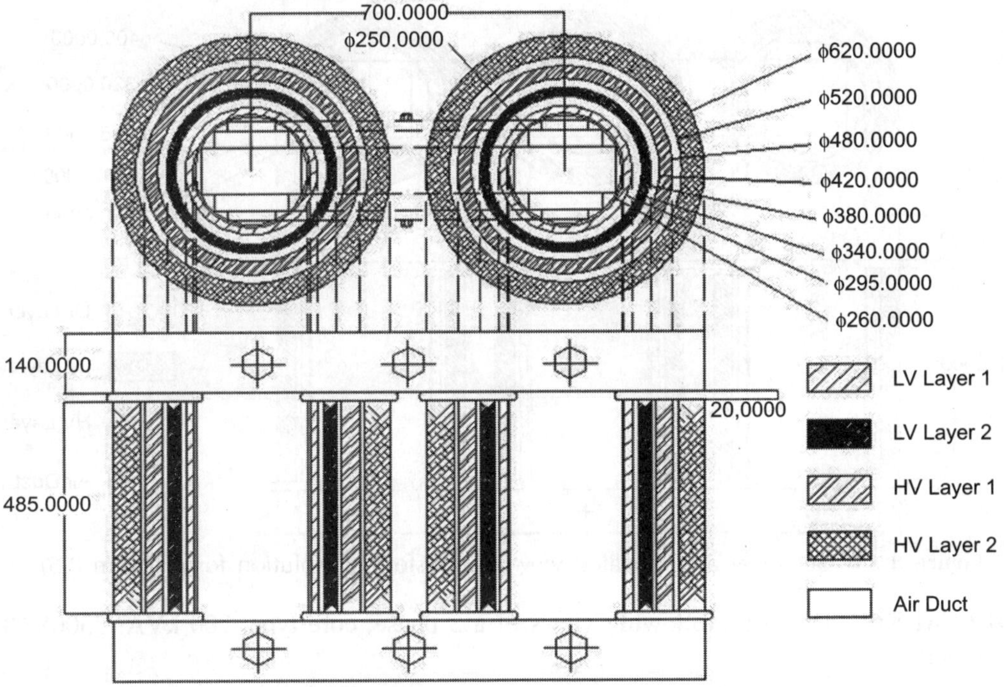

Figure 8.24 Sectional and elevated view of transformer (solution for problem 8.4).

PROBLEM 8.5: Draw the following views of a 3 phase, core type, 30 kVA, 2200V/400V transformer:

- Front elevation full in section
- Plan in full section

Dimension of various parts are given below:

Core:

Cross section of the core = 1 stepped core
Diameter of circumscribing circle = 250 mm
Distance between adjacent core centres = 465 mm

Yoke:

Height of the yoke = 200 m

HV winding:

Outer diameter of HV coil = 400 mm
Inner diameter of HV coil = 320 mm
Height of HV winding = 700 mm
Number of turns per phase = 92

Total height of the transformer is 1150 mm. Assume any data missing.

Solution:

$a = 0.71 \times D$

$a = 0.71 \times 250 = 177.5$ mm

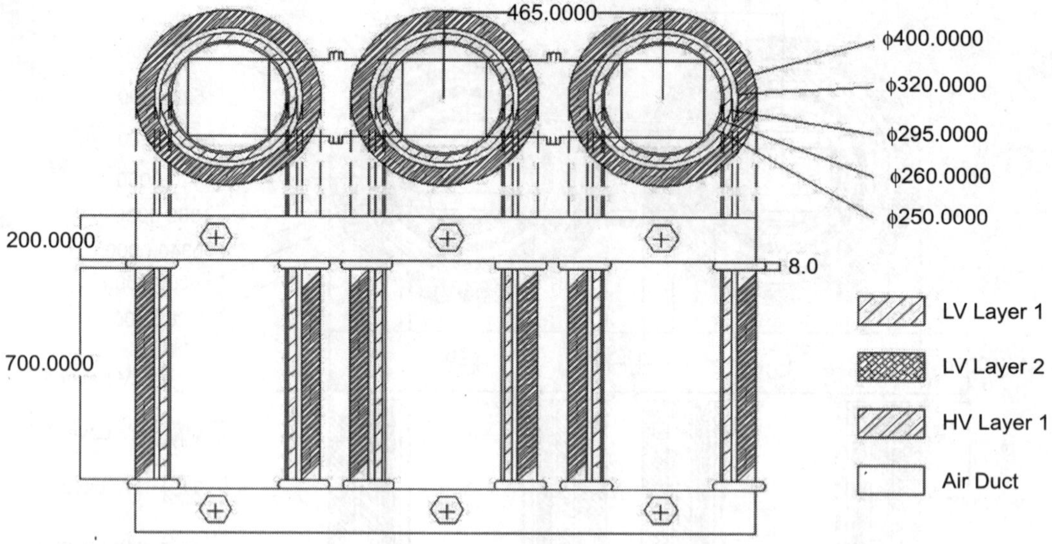

Figure 8.25 Sectional and elevated view of transformer (solution for problem 8.5).

PROBLEM 8.6: Draw the following views of a 3 phase, core type, 200 kVA, 3300V/400V transformer:

- Front elevation full in section
- Plan in full section

Dimension of various parts are given below:

Core:

Cross section of the core = 2 stepped core
Radius of circumscribing circle = 13 cm
Distance between adjacent core centres = 52 cm

Yoke:

Height of the yoke = 10 cm

LV winding:

Outer radius of LV coil = 14.75 cm
Inner radius of LV coil = 13 cm
Height of LV winding = 42.5 cm
Number of turns per phase = 61

HV winding:

Outer radius of HV1 coil = 19 cm
Inner radius of HV1 coil = 17 cm
Outer radius of HV2 coil = 24 cm
Inner radius of HV2 coil = 21 cm
Height of HV winding = 42.5 cm
Number of turns per phase = 76

Total height of the transformer is 66.5 cm. Assume any data missing.

Solution:

$a = 0.85 \times D$ $b = 0.53 \times D$

$a = 0.85 \times 130 = 110.5$ mm $b = 0.53 \times 130 = 68.9$ mm

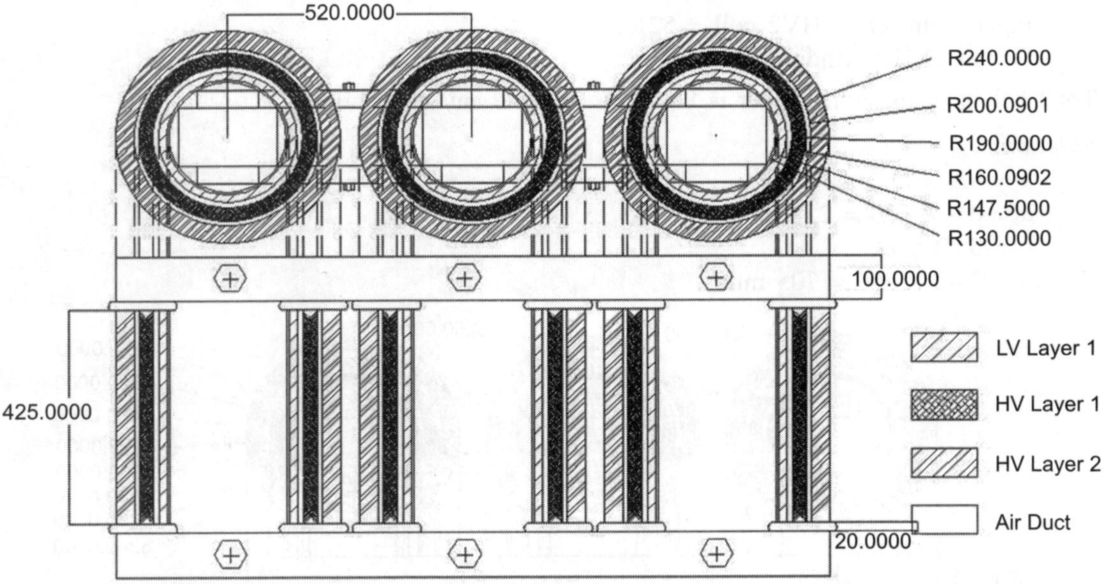

Figure 8.26 Sectional and elevated view of transformer (solution for problem 8.6).

PROBLEM 8.7: Draw the following views of a 3 phase, core type, 500 kVA, 6600V/415V transformer:

- Front elevation full in section
- Plan in full section

Dimension of various parts are given below:

Core:

Cross section of the core = 3 stepped core
Diameter of circumscribing circle = 25 cm
Distance between adjacent core centres = 70 cm

Yoke:

Height of the yoke = 14 cm

LV winding:

Outer diameter of LV1 coil = 29.5 cm
Inner diameter of LV1 coil = 26 cm
Outer diameter of LV2 coil = 38 cm
Inner diameter of LV2 coil = 34 cm
Height of LV winding = 48.5 cm

HV winding:

Outer diameter of HV1 coil = 48 cm
Inner diameter of HV1 coil = 42 cm
Outer diameter of HV2 coil = 62 cm
Inner diameter of HV2 coil = 52 cm
Height of HV winding = 48.5 cm

Total height of the transformer is 80.1 cm. Assume any data missing.

Solution:

$a = 0.9 \times D$
$a = 0.9 \times 250 = 225$ mm
$b = 0.42 \times D$
$b = 0.42 \times 250 = 105$ mm

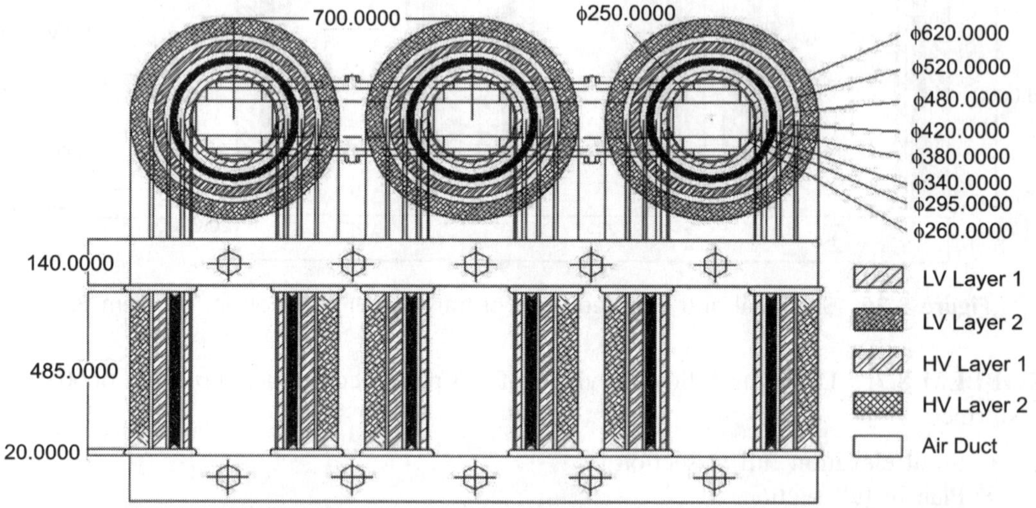

Figure 8.27 Sectional and elevated view of transformer (solution for problem 8.7).

PROBLEM 8.8: Draw to suitable scale, the half sectional elevation and plan of a 10 kVA, 50 Hz, single phase, shell type transformer with following data:

Central leg = 280 mm
Outer leg = 140 mm
Yoke = 140 mm
Window = 800 mm

HV winding:

Number of turns = 1000
Number of layers = 12
Insulation of conductors = 0.5 mm

LV winding:

Number of turns = 100
Number of layers = 2
Insulation of conductors = 0.3 mm

Insulation:

Between the layers = 0.5 mm
Between core and LV winding = 2.5 mm
Between HV and LV winding = 3 mm

Assume any missing data.

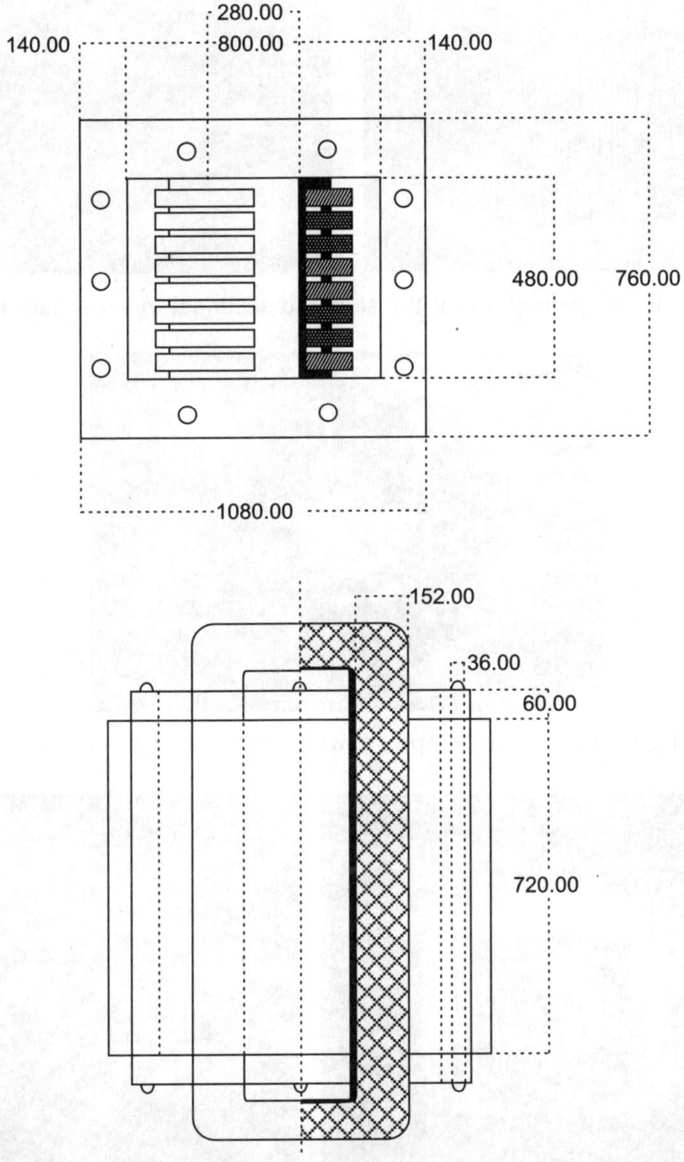

Figure 8.28 Sectional and elevated view of shell type transformer (solution for problem 8.8).

8.6 PHOTOGRAPHS

Figure 8.29 Photograph showing the side and sectional view of auto transformer.

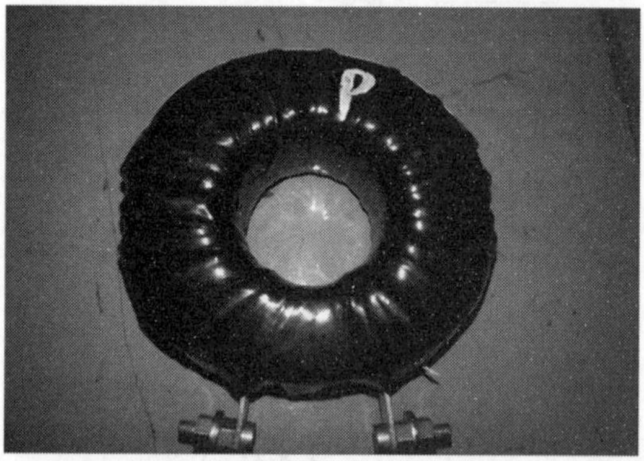

Figure 8.30 Photograph showing the current transformer.

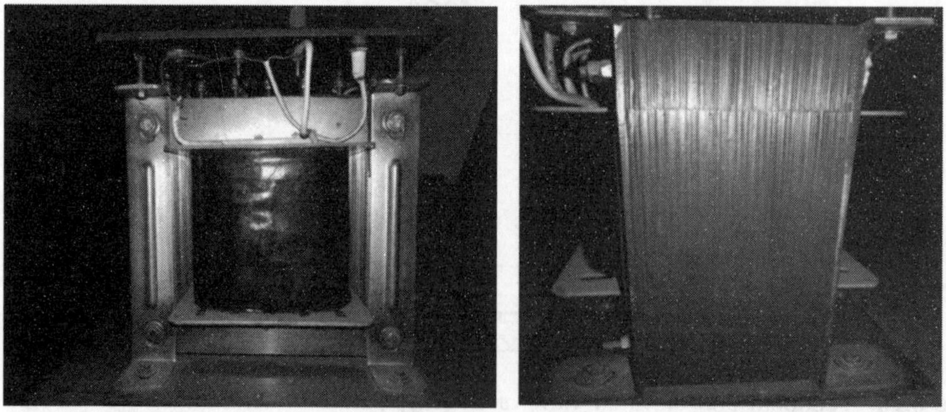

Figure 8.31(a) Front and side views of a shell type transformer.

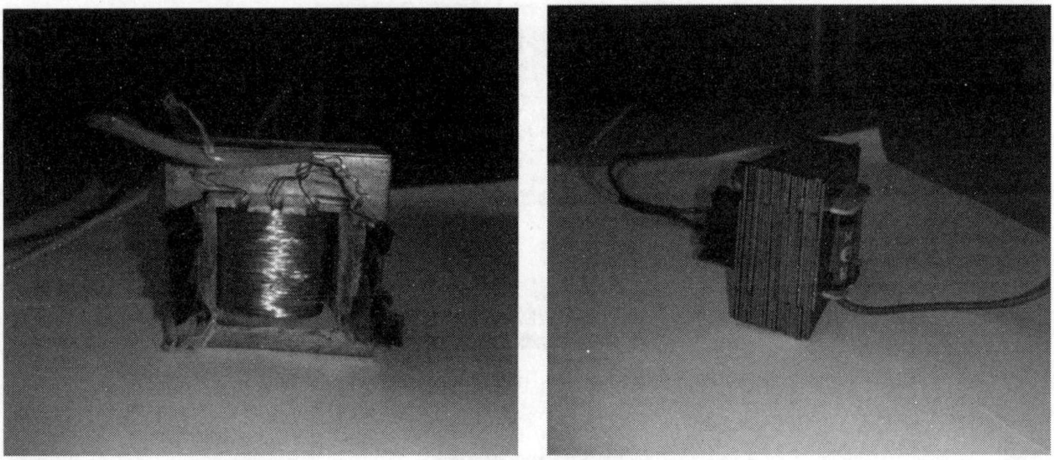

Figure 8.31(b) Front and side views of a shell type transformer showing laminated plates punched together.

Photographs of various kinds of conductors used in windings of the transformers are as follows:

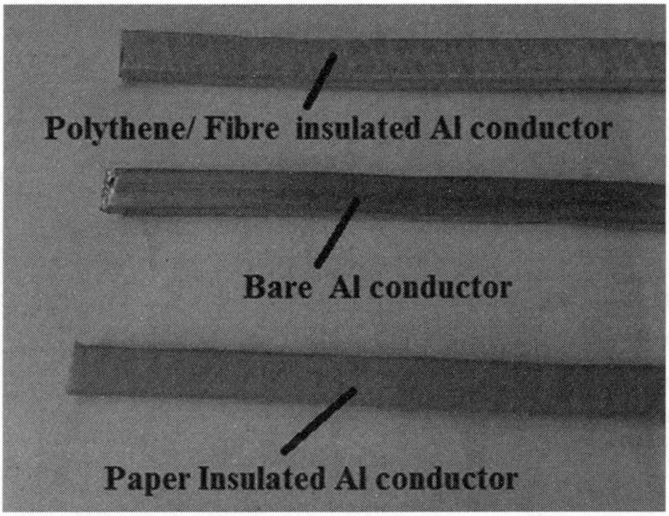

Figure 8.32(a) Conductors used in transformer winding.

Bare and insulated aluminium conductors of rectangular cross section that are presently employed in transformer windings.

Bare and insulated copper conductors of rectangular cross section and circular cross section were employed in transformer windings in the earlier days.

The dimension or thickness of the conductor depends on the rating of the transformer.

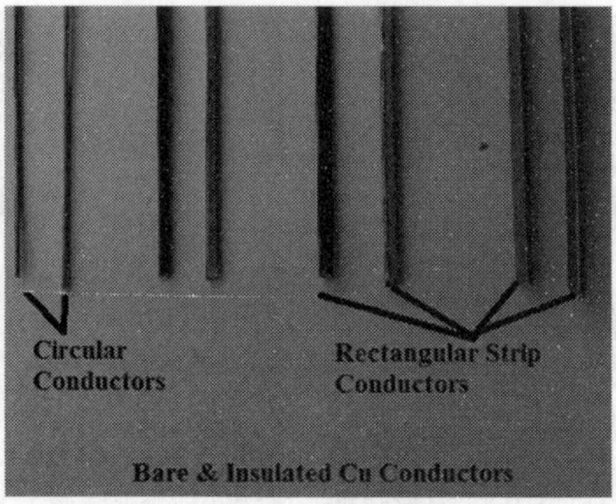

Figure 8.32(b) Conductors used in transformer winding.

EXERCISES

1. For three phase transformer, draw the half sectional plan with the following details and also show the arrangements of insulation and oil ducts positions.

   Core details:
   Three stepped core
   Diameter of the core = 120
   Width of largest stamping = 110
   Width of smallest stamping = 70

   LV winding:
   Outer diameter = 152
   Thickness = 10

   HV winding:
   Outer diameter = 200
   Thickness = 10

   Insulation:
   LV insulation = 6
   HV insulation = 6
   Oil ducts for HV = 8

   All the dimensions are in mm and show the plan for first two limbs. Assume the missing data suitably.

2. Develop the sectional plan and elevation of one limb of a single phase transformer with following details:
   (i) Two stepped core
   (ii) Circumscribing circle diameter = 11.3
   (iii) LV winding diameter = 12.5

(iv) Outer diameter of LV winding = 14
(v) Outer diameter of HV winding = 18.4
(vi) Inner diameter of HV winding = 16
(vii) Height of LV winding = 20.6
(viii) Height of HV winding = 20

All dimensions are in cm, also show the oil ducts if any. Assume the missing data suitably.

3. Draw the half sectional view of centre limb for three phase transformer with following details:

(i) Core = 3 stepped
(ii) Diameter of the circumscribing circle = 16.9
(iii) Thickness of insulation of LV winding = 0.3
(iv) Thickness of insulation of HV winding = 0.3
(v) Thickness of LV winding = 2
(vi) Thickness of HV winding = 3.6
(vii) Centre to centre distance between limbs = 11.6

All the dimensions are in cm. Assume the missing data suitably.

4. Draw sectional plan of both the limbs of a single phase distribution transformer with the dimensions given below:

(i) Core = two stepped
(ii) Cross section of core = 31.5 mm × 45.8 mm
(iii) Yoke height = 31.75 mm
(iv) Thickness of LV winding insulation = 0.5 mm
(v) Thickness of HV winding insulation = 0.7 mm
(vi) Outer diameter of HV winding = 117.8 mm
(vii) Inner diameter of HV winding = 77.8 mm

Assume missing data suitably

5. Draw the end view of the two winding transformer with the following details:

(i) Core type = 2 stepped core
(ii) Diameter of the circumscribing circle = 80 cm
(iii) Number of layers in LV winding = 3
(iv) Thickness of the LV winding each layer = 3 cm
(v) Number of layers in HV winding = 5
(vi) Thickness of the HV winding each layer = 5 cm
(vii) Insulation of LV winding = 3 cm
(viii) Insulation of HV winding = 5 cm
(ix) Insulation between each layer of LV and HV winding = 0.5 cm

Assume any missing data suitably.

6. Draw the left half section end view of the two winding transformer with the following details:

   (i) Core type = 3 stepped core
   (ii) Diameter of the circumscribing circle = 50.7 cm
   (iii) Outer diameter of LV winding = 59.5 cm
   (iv) Outer diameter of HV winding = 70.3 cm
   (v) Insulation of LV winding = 0.5 cm
   (vi) Insulation of HV winding = 0.8 cm

   Assume missing data suitably.

7. Draw the sectional plan for any two limbs and elevation for centre limb of three phase transformer with following details:

   (i) Core = 3 stepped
   (ii) Diameter of the circumscribing circle = 67.6
   (iii) Thickness of insulation of LV winding = 0.3
   (iv) Thickness of insulation of HV winding = 0.5
   (v) Thickness of LV winding = 8
   (vi) Thickness of HV winding = 15
   (vii) Centre to centre distance between limbs = 46.5
   (viii) Height of the yoke = 30

   All the dimensions are in cm. Assume the missing data suitably.

8. Draw the elevation and sectional plan (right half in section) for a given transformer details:

   (i) Three phase transformer
   (ii) Cross section area of core = 47.25 × 68.7
   (iii) Height of window = 223.9
   (iv) Width of window = 85.9
   (v) Height of the yoke = 47.6
   (vi) Number of layers in LV winding = 2
   (vii) Number of layers in HV winding = 3
   (viii) Thickness of LV winding each layer = 10
   (ix) Thickness of HV winding each layer = 15
   (x) Insulation between core and LV = 1.8
   (xi) Insulation between layers = 0.35

   All the dimensions are in mm. Assume the missing data suitably.

9. Draw the sectional plan of two limbs for three phase transformer with following details:

   (i) Core = 3 stepped
   (ii) Diameter of the circumscribing circle = 84.5
   (iii) Thickness of insulation of LV winding = 0.5
   (iv) Thickness of insulation of HV winding = 0.8
   (v) Thickness of LV winding = 10

(vi) Number of LV winding layers = 2
(vii) Insulation between each layer = 0.5
(viii) Thickness of HV winding = 18
(ix) Centre to centre distance between limbs = 58

Assume all the dimensions are in cm. Assume the missing data suitably.

10. A single phase core type transformer has the following details:

(i) Core = single step
(ii) Diameter of the core = 110
(iii) Height of the yoke = 125
(iv) Centre to centre distance between limbs = 178
(v) Outer diameter of the LV winding = 115.5
(vi) Outer diameter of HV winding = 170
(vii) Total height of the winding = 213.5

For the given data, draw the plan right of in section and elevation of right half of left limb in section. All dimensions are in mm. Assume the missing data suitably.

Appendix Print Procedure

The following procedure may be followed to take the printouts of the drawing made or convert to pdf in CAD.

Step 1: Once the drawing is completed, adjust your drawing exactly to screen size and then select the plot command available in the file option at the top left hand corner of CAD window or by ctrl+p.

This results in the plot window popping up as shown in Figure A1.

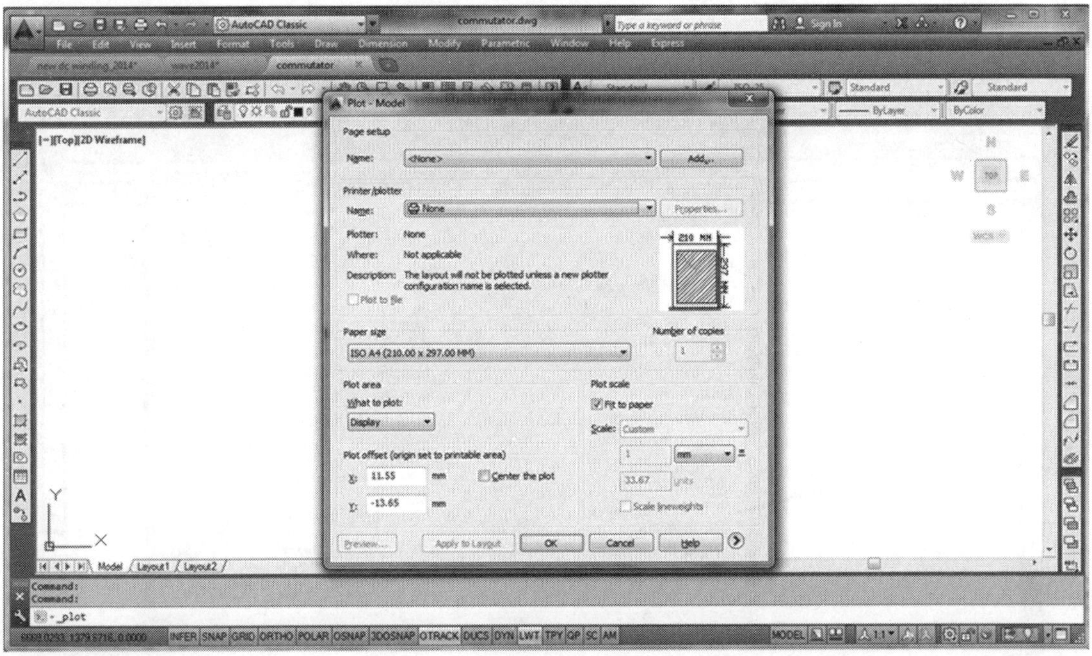

Figure A1 *Courtesy:* AutoCAD®.

Step 2: In the plot window, select the printer or pdf writer or any other depending on your requirement, select the paper size available from a wide variety of sheets, select the mode as portrait or landscape and select the centre plot as shown in the Figure A2.

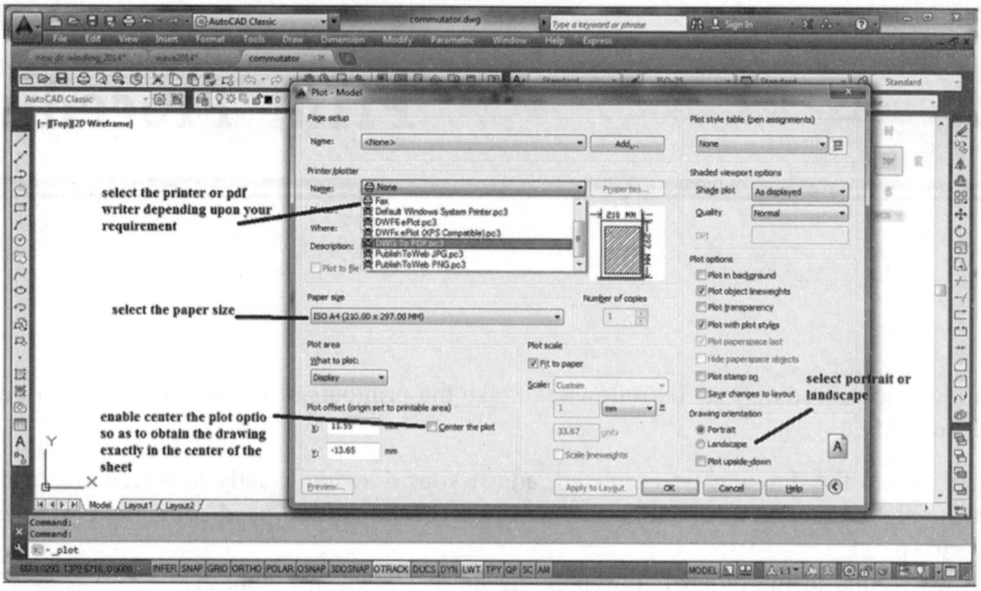

Figure A2 *Courtesy:* AutoCAD®.

Step 3: In the plot type, select the window as shown in Figure A3.

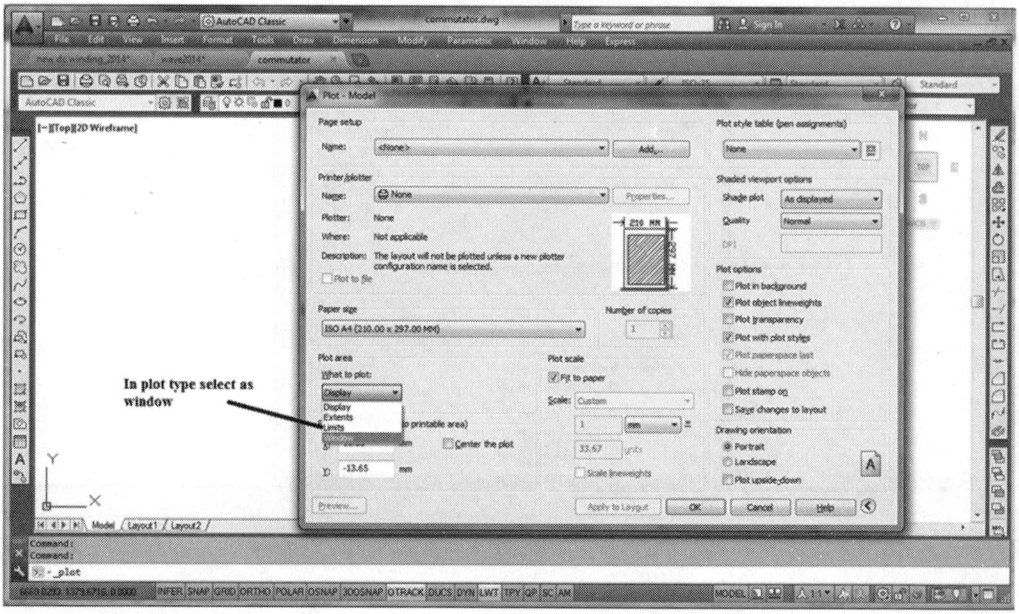

Figure A3 *Courtesy:* AutoCAD®.

Step 4: Once window is selected, the plot window vanishes and CAD window appears where you got to select the space or drawing to be printed as shown in the Figures A4 and A5.

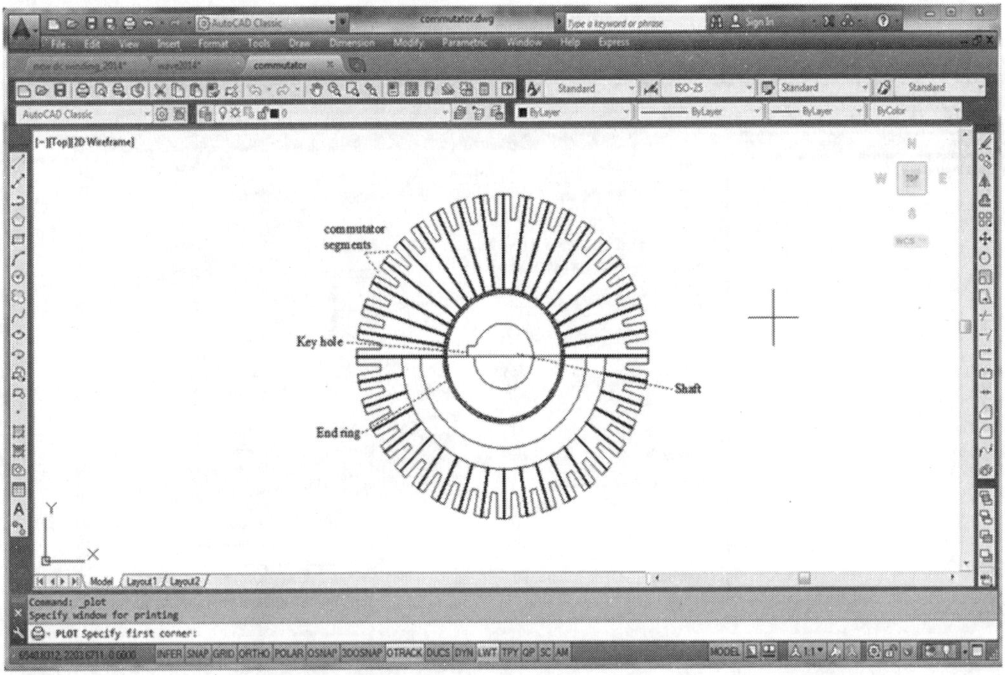

Figure A4 *Courtesy:* AutoCAD®.

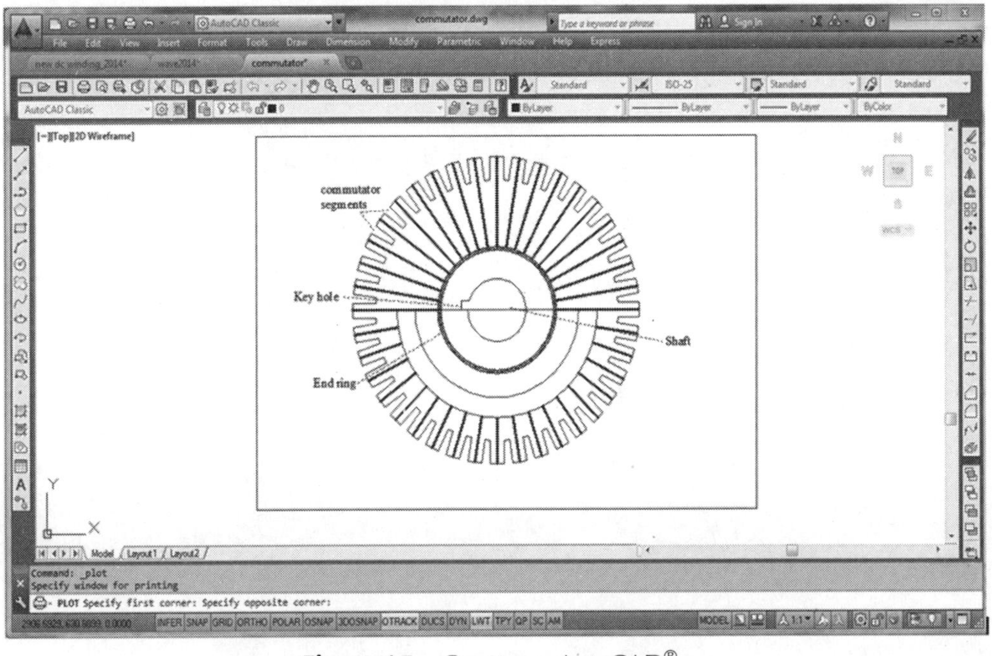

Figure A5 *Courtesy:* AutoCAD®.

Step 5: Once the drawing is selected as shown above, the plot window reappears and you can preview the drawing to be printed or directly select OK to obtain the print as shown in Figure A6.

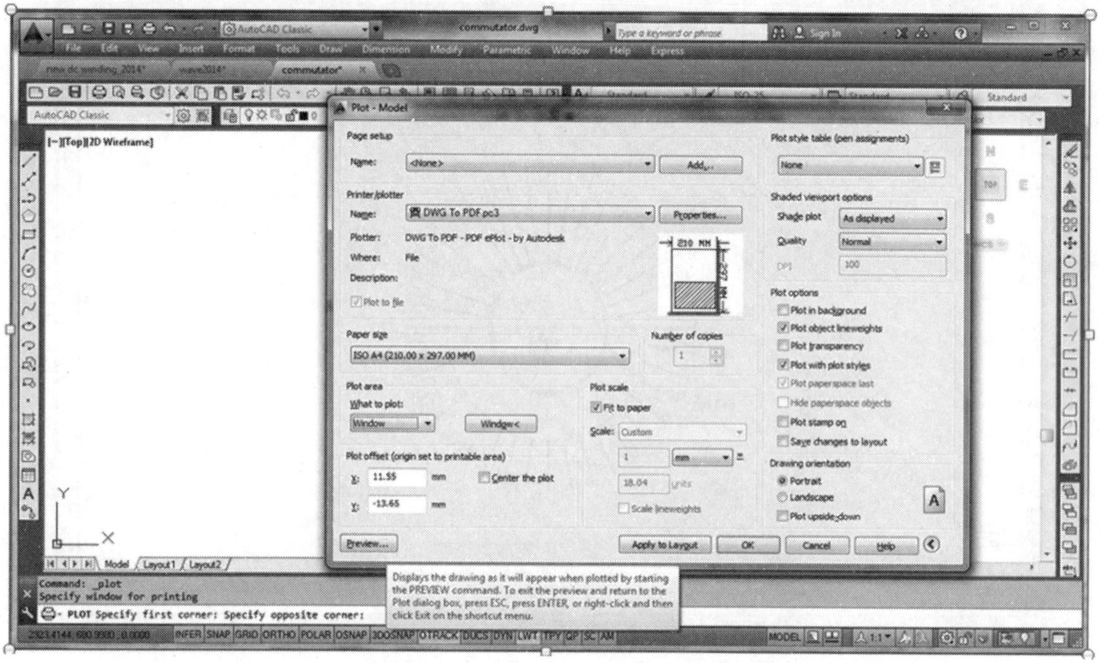

Figure A6 *Courtesy:* AutoCAD®.

Index

AC generator, 105
AC machines, 155
AC winding, 78
Arc, 3, 5, 8
Armature, 116
Armature core, 117
Armature slots, 117
Armature windings, 11
Array, 3, 7
Assembly, 169
Asynchronous machine, 157
Average pitch, 57

Back pitch Y_b, 17
Balanced winding, 80
Bifurcated winding, 80
Brushes, 56
Bus bar, 106
Bus coupler, 106

CAD, 1, 2
Carbon brushes, 117
Chamfer, 3
Circle, 3, 5
Circuits, 41
Closed type, 120
Coils, 55
Coil sides, 79
Coil span, 80, 81
Collar, 117
Commutation, 117
Commutator, 117
Commutator pitch, 57
Commutator segments, 58
Computer aided designing, 1, 2
Concentric coils, 80
Concentric winding, 80
Consumers, 105
Coordinates, 9
Copy, 3
Core, 170
Core form, 172
Core steel, 171
Coupling condenser, 105
Current, 68
Current transformer, 105

DC generators, 55
DC machines, 116
Delta star, 106
Diesel power plant, 107
Digital format, 1
Dimension, 8
Distribution substation, 103
Distribution transformer, 103, 169
Double layer winding, 41
Drum windings, 11
Dummy coil, 57
Duplex winding, 17, 43
Duplicate bus bar, 106

Earthing switch, 106
Eddy, 170
Eddy loss, 171
Electrical faults, 103
Ellipse, 3, 6
End elevation, 124
Equaliser rings, 36
Equalising connection, 36
Erase, 4
Excitation voltage, 122
Explode, 4
Extend, 4
External resistance, 158

Feeder, 106
Field coils, 117
Field winding, 13, 116
File, 59
Fillet, 3
Flange, 117
Fractional slot winding, 79
Front elevation, 124
Front pitch Y_f, 17
Full pitched winding, 79

Gradient, 4

Hatch, 4
Hatching, 66
Hexagonal nut, 117
Hydroelectric power plants, 108
Hysteresis, 170

Ideal transformer, 169
Inactive, 57
Induced emf, 40
Induction machines, 157
Insulating coating, 171
Integral slot winding, 79
Isolator, 106

LAP winding, 16
Lightning arrestor, 105
Limits, 18
Line, 2
Line with centre, 2
Lower left corner, 18, 84
Low rating transformers, 175
Low tension oil circuit breaker, 106
LV and HV windings, 172
LWT, 4

Magnetically interact, 116
Magnetic flux, 116
Master unit sub-station (MUSS), 1, 103
Mechanical balancing, 58
Mirror, 3, 7
Move, 4, 7
Multiline text, 61
Multiplex winding, 15
Mush winding, 80

Nonrenewable, 107
Nonsalient pole machine, 156
Nuclear power plant, 107

Oil circuit breaker, 106
Open type, 119
ORTHO, 4
OSNAP, 4
OTRACK, 4

Parallel paths, 17
Phase spread, 82
Phase wound rotor or slip ring rotor, 157
Plinth mounted substation, 104
Polar array, 7
Pole cores, 117
Pole mounted substation, 103
Pole pitch, 81
Pole pitch = Z/P, 17
Pole placing, 26
Pole placing technique, 26
Poles, 55
Pole shoes, 117
Polygon, 3, 6
Poly line, 3, 6

Poly-phase, 79
Potential transformer, 105
Power transformer, 169
Primary winding, 170
Progressive lap, 41
Progressive winding, 56
Projected view, 172
Projecting poles, 156

Radius and diameter, 8
Receiving station, 105
Rectangle, 4, 6
Rectangle array, 7
Rectangular core, 176
Renewable, 107
Repelling motion, 116
Resultant pitch, 57
Retrogressive lap, 46
Retrogressive wave winding, 56
Revision cloud, 3
Rotate, 3
Rotating transformers, 157
Rotor, 79
Rotor flux, 156
Rotor winding, 79

Salient pole machines, 156
Scale, 4
Sectional view, 172
Semi-enclosed or semi-open type, 120
Separately-excited, 116
Sequence diagram, 40
Series, 116
Shaft, 117
Shell form, 172
Short pitched winding, 79
Shunt, 116
Simplex lap, 17
Single layer lap, 17
Single layer winding, 14
Single line diagram, 102
Single phase, 79
Single phase transformer, 172
Slot angle, 81
Slots per pole per phase, 81
Smooth cylindrical rotor, 156
Solar power plants, 109
Solid aluminium bars, 157
Spider, 117
Spline, 3
Square, 4
Square core, 175
Squirrel cage rotor, 157
Static electrical apparatus, 169
Stator, 79
Stator winding, 79
Steel lamination, 171
Step down transformer, 106
Stepped core, 172
Step up transformer, 106
Stretch, 4
Substation, 102
Synchronous machines, 156
Synchronous motors, 156
Synchronous speed, 156

Tapping (T_g), 37
TEFC, 117
Three plane overhang, 81
Three-tier winding, 81
Top coil side, 90
Transformer, 169
Trim, 4, 7
Two layer winding, 15
Two plane overhang, 80
Two-tier winding, 80

Unbalanced winding, 80
Un-bifurcated winding, 80
Units, 18
Upper right corner, 18, 84

Wave trap, 105
Wave winding, 55
Winding, 11
Wind power plants, 109

Yoke/Frame, 117

ZOOM, 85